The Intimate Strangeness of Being

Studies in Philosophy and the
History of Philosophy

General Editor: Jude P. Dougherty

Volume 56

The Intimate Strangeness of Being

Metaphysics after Dialectic

William Desmond

The Catholic University of America Press
Washington, D.C.

Copyright © 2012

The Catholic University of America Press

All rights reserved

The paper used in this publication meets the minimum requirements

of American National Standards for Information Science—

Permanence of Paper for Printed Library Materials, ANSI Z39.48-1984.

∞

Library of Congress Cataloging-in-Publication Data

Desmond, William, 1951–

The intimate strangeness of being : metaphysics after dialectic / William Desmond.

p. cm. — (Studies in philosophy and the history of philosophy ; v. 56)

Includes bibliographical references and index.

ISBN 978-0-8132-1960-8 (cloth : alk. paper)   1. Metaphysics.   2. Philosophy,

Modern.   I. Title.

B1626.D473158 2012

110—dc23

2011039160

Lo duca e io per quel cammino ascoso
intrammo a ritornar nel chiaro mondo;
e sanza cura aver d'alcun riposo,
salimmo sù, el primo e io secondo,
tanto ch'i' vidi de le cose belle
che porta 'l ciel, per un pertugio tondo.

E quindi uscimmo a riveder le stelle.

My guide and I entered that hidden road
To make our way back up to the bright world.
We never thought of resting while we climbed.
We climbed, he first and I behind, until,
Through a small round opening ahead of us
I saw the lovely things the heavens hold.

And we came out once more to see the stars.

Dante, *Inferno,* 34.133–39

This book is dedicated to

PAUL J. BAGLEY

CYRIL J. O'REGAN

LAWRENCE S. STEPELEVICH

Three noble friends

Contents

Acknowledgments

I would like to express my thanks to David McGonagle, former director of the Catholic University of America Press, for his welcoming interest in my work, to James Kruggel for his always friendly and efficient support, to Jude Dougherty for his willingness to include this work in the series, and to Theresa Walker for her reliable shepherding of the book through the process of production. I would also like to thank Oliva Blanchette and John Manoussakis for their generous reading of my work and their role in helping to bring it to publication. I dedicate the book to Paul Bagley, Cyril O'Regan, and Lawrence Stepelevich for their companionship over many years.

Earlier versions of most of the chapters appeared elsewhere and revisions of all, some quite extensive, were made for this book. I am happy to make due and grateful acknowledgment of their previous forms: chapter 1, as the Presidential Address to the Metaphysical Society of America, in *The Review of Metaphysics* 48 (June 1995): 731–69; chapter 2 in a special jubilee edition, honoring past presidents of the Hegel Society of America, of the *Owl of Minerva* 25, no. 2 (Spring 1994): 221–34; chapter 3 in *Philosophy and Culture: Essays in Honor of Donald Phillip Verene,* ed. Glenn Alexander Magee (Charlottesville, Va.: Philosophy Documentation Center, 2002), 107–27; chapter 4, in *International Philosophical Quarterly* 45, no. 2 (June 2005): 221–41; chapter 5 in *International Philosophical Quarterly* 40, no. 1 (March 2000): 37–49; chapter 7 in *Health and Human Flourishing: Religion, Medicine, and Moral Anthropology,* ed. Carol R. Taylor and Roberto Dell'Oro (Washington, D.C.: Georgetown University Press, 2006), 53–68; chapter 8 in *Belief and Metaphysics,* ed. Peter M. Chandler and Conor Cunningham (London: SCM, 2007), 11–40; chapter 9 in *Ramify* 1 (Spring 2010), 4–26; and chapter 10 in *Philosophy Begins in Wonder,* ed. Michael Deckard and Peter Losonczi (Eugene, Or.: Wipf & Stock, 2010), 310–48.

Introduction

METAPHYSICS AFTER "METAPHYSICS"

The career of metaphysics since Kant has not been rosy. Some might wonder even if it has had a career at all. Kant sets a tone insofar as many think he is to be thanked for his demotion, even demolition, of traditional metaphysics. I have always had my doubts about this demolition, and when I went looking among earlier philosophers for the dogmatists Kant clearly sought to superannuate, it was not always easy to come up with bona fide candidates. More often than not one found thinkers whose work was marked by a symbiosis, sometimes fruitful, of skepticism and dogmatism, laced here and there (more rarely) with bold speculative daring. I mean skepticism here in this sense: the readiness to confess to hesitations about the philosophical claims one was surely entitled to make. I mean dogmatism thus: the willingness to venture some determinate philosophical affirmations, all things considered and all difficulties being reconsidered. I mean speculative daring in this sense: fidelity to a noble calling, solicited to say something about what is most ultimate for thought, all things skeptical considered, all the braggadocio of dubious dogmatism to the contrary. Kant, I concluded, was proximately much more disillusioned with the rationalism to which he himself had been committed in the earlier part of his career. To identify *simpliciter* metaphysics with such rationalism struck me as risking tarring the entire tradition of metaphysics with the brush of "dogmatism," a dubious and dangerous simplification.[1]

---

1. Immanuel Kant, *Critique of Pure Reason,* trans. and ed. Paul Guyer et al. (Cambridge: Cambridge University Press, 1989), on dogmatism and skepticism, see A ix, also B 23–24; Kant claims not to be against the "dogmatic procedure of reason" but against "dogmatism" which is dogmatic procedure "without previous criticism of its own powers" (B, xxxv). He goes on to praise "the celebrated Wolff, the greatest of all the dogmatic philosophers" in whom is to be honored the "spirit of thoroughness" still "not extinct in Germany", and without which philosophy as science is not possible, and work will be turned into play, philosophy into philodoxy (B xxxvi–xxxvii).

Of course, Kant wanted to rescue *his* version of rationalism, one centrally concerned with the power of pure *practical* reason to open us in thought to the ultimate realities about which theoretical reason can offer no warranted cognition.[2] Moreover, it has often been noted that in the generation immediately succeeding Kant metaphysics seems to have undergone a resurrection in the work of Fichte perhaps, Schelling undoubtedly, and Hegel certainly. Some now excoriate this resurrection, prefer the cautions of Kant, or call for a return to his more critical enterprise. What "metaphysics" might mean in their philosophies is not simple, however, and there are perhaps hidden equivocations here for which we need philosophical finesse. To try to put a name on some of these equivocations is part of the present work. I find significance in the fact that when Hegel, in his *Encyclopaedia of the Philosophical Sciences,* devotes his preliminary discussion to different attitudes of thought to objectivity, the first to which he pays close attention he calls "metaphysics" (the others are: empiricism and the critical philosophy, immediate knowledge, and then his own conception).[3] What he means by "metaphysics" is, in fact, the rationalism of the eighteenth century which, as I have just noted, reflected the philosophical ethos of the early Kant and against which he critically turned. Interestingly, Hegel is not at all destructive in his attitude to it. I take him to endorse the philosophical thinking of the things of reason to which traditional metaphysics, it seems, was devoted. His difficulty is the standard Kantian one: the categories we use in this rational thinking are not subject to critical reflection. I take Hegel to be seeking a rethinking of these same matters, in a post-Kantian perspective. Again interestingly, he goes out of his way to note that a philosopher like Aristotle cannot be dismissed as a "metaphysician" in the more constricted sense of this eigthteenth-century rationalism. The spirit of genuine speculative philosophy lived in the ancients. I take from this a salutary warning against too totalizing a claim that "metaphysics" has been "demolished" by the critique of Kant. Much more discrimination in needed.

2. Immanuel Kant, *Critique of Practical Reason,* trans. and ed. Mary Gregor, intro. Andrews Reath (Cambridge: Cambridge University Press, 1997).

3. G. W. F. Hegel, *Enzyklopädie der Philosophischen Wissenschaften im Grundrisse (1830),* ed. Friedhelm Nicolin and Otto Pöggeler (Hamburg: Felix Meiner Verlag, 1991); *The Encyclopaedia Logic (with the Zusätze): Part 1 of the Encyclopaedia of Philosophical Science with the Zusätze,* trans. T. F. Geraets, W. A. Suchting, and H. S. Harris (Indianapolis, Ind.: Hackett, 1991), §§26–83.

I do not offer these caveats to reinstate fully fledged Hegelianism as the saving of metaphysics. Far from it. There is much to be said in favor of the resources of dialectical thinking, and the reserves of promise for philosophy harbored in it. In a somewhat paradoxical sense, it may well be true that Hegel's efforts to "complete" metaphysics may have done more to "demolish" metaphysics than Kant's more cautious practice of critique and his more overt intent to put metaphysics in its place. I mean we may find with Hegel a new post-Kantian rationalism, a kind of new dialectical Wolffianism almost, in which the static categories of rationalism are reorganized and set in motion, all on the way to the complete system of categories of his *Science of Logic*.[4] It is an old worry, and I share it, that there is a dearth of ontological astonishment about such a system. It dangerously weakens our feel for the mystery of being that we as metaphysicians are to try to think. By mystery I mean no anti-intellectual commitment to blocking thought but rather the strange otherness of the "to be" which, also strangely, shows itself intimate to the process of thinking itself. Being is other and intimate, and our thinking about it knows something of this strangeness and intimacy. Rationalism is too callow in its lack of finesse for this. And perhaps this callowness is the justified reason for calling rationalism before the bar of critique, callowness calling also for the sophistications of speculative dialectic. But what if a different callowness, a dearth of ontological astonishment, also marks speculative dialectic? The implied consummation of metaphysics in speculative dialectic wherein is asserted a posttranscendental identity of being and thinking may well contribute more to the sickening of the metaphysical impulse. Something like this has happened after Hegel.

I mean that Hegel's confidence in reason is really an overconfidence and leads to a speculative bubble, the deflation of which we seem to have lived with in philosophy in the centuries since his demise. The overconfidence in the project of speculative reason inverts into the abjectness of a reason that lacerates itself with accusations of its own impotency. This devaluation of confidence in reason makes otherwise fairly reasonable philosophers worry about being in bad faith, should they undertake *any* attempt to think philosophically about being. Of course, the theme of the end of metaphysics is not a first for twentieth-century thought. The theme

4. G. W. F. Hegel, *Wissenschaft der Logik* (Hamburg: Felix Meiner, 1963); *Science of Logic*, trans. A. V. Miller (New York: Humanities Press, 1969).

is already seeded in Hegel and extensively developed and addressed by those coming after him. The philosophical projects of a Kierkegaard or a Marx, a Schopenhauer or a Nietzsche are in their own way responses to this theme, one setting out in search of salvation in faith, the other hyping humanity in the direction of revolutionary praxis, another again surrendering to resignation and world denial, another still again preaching for the few the hyperactivation of Dionysian poetics. These are not my concerns now. My point is that more recent discussion of the "overcoming of metaphysics" with Heidegger, or the excoriation of meaningless metaphysics with more positivistically inclined philosophy, or the deconstruction of metaphysics with Derridean thought, all seem to lie along the line of this deflation of confidence in philosophical reason that we have diversely witnessed since Kant's critique of pure reason and Hegel's reconfiguration of transcendental philosophy in terms of speculative dialectics.

I am concerned to understand something of the complex impulses at work in all of this, but I am also convinced that there is no overcoming of metaphysics as such. There are many practices of metaphysics, Platonic, Aristotelian, Thomistic, rationalistic, transcendental, realistic, and so on. To reduce this plurality to some simple univocity is far too crude. It is untrue. I fear that a secret univocalization is at work in much rhetoric about our being "postmetaphysical." I say nothing of the fact that some dismissals of totalizing thought are often themselves hugely totalizing.

The point is not just historical, but systematic in the following regard. One can live meaningfully, more or less, and one need not be a metaphysician in the explicit sense. But one cannot be a good philosopher without being more or less a metaphysician. I mean this in the sense of trying more explicitly to bring a developed habit of mindfulness to bear on what is at play in being, especially with regard to the basic presuppositions, sources, and orientations toward the "to be" that mark our being in the midst of things. To be this thing or that, to be this process or that, this or that action or undergoing, to be this or that relation, and so on—all of these are concretions in being, even if the concretion is a becoming or is as a possibility, and each participates diversely in the sourcing powers of the "to be." To be as mindful, that is, to be as human, is to live from these sources but also to strain to be lucidly attentive to them. We do not have a choice about being mindful, though how intensive and extensive that mindfulness is may follow from choices or initiatives we ourselves undertake. Being thus mindful, one does not have a choice about being an *animale metaphysicum*. The matter is not being a postmetaphysician but being a good metaphysician, under the call of truthful fidelity to the sourcing powers of the "to be."

This does not mean that metaphysics is everything, but it does mean that in all our thinking some metaphysical presuppositions about the "to be" are at play. It may well be that these are mostly unacknowledged, not only by common sense or art or science or religion, but also by "postmeta-physical" philosophy. Nevertheless, they are still at work. As a philosophical discipline metaphysics is a form of reflective thinking under fidelity to the truth of what is thus at play. It may well be true that what is being criticized or rejected in much of this talk of the "postmetaphysical" is a *certain picture of metaphysics*. It is not entirely inaccurate to say that the primary picture thus criticized is a version of Platonism, more accurately what I would call the Nietzschean cartoon version. This cartoon is drawn forth on many occasions, though it is worth noting that Nietzsche himself confessed to knowing the difference between Plato and his "Platonism." "Plato, for example, becomes a caricature in my hands": Nietzsche himself had the honor to confess this.[5] In this caricature we find the univocal fixation of metaphysical difference in terms of rigidly separated worlds: the world here and the beyond world. Metaphysics allegedly reneges on the world here in favor of the beyond world there.

I would point out that the Greek word *meta* of *meta ta physika* can be said to suggest a double meaning. *Meta* can mean both "in the midst" and "beyond." Against both the purported "Platonic" desertion of immanence and the Nietzschean assassination of transcendence, I would say that being in the between, the *metaxu,* does not enforce an "either/or" on us between "being in the midst" and being drawn "beyond." The "meta" of metaphysics is double, requiring both ontological exploration of the immanent between of finitude and metaphysical transcending to what cannot be determined in entirely finite terms. In the cartoon version of metaphysics no sooner is the "meta" intoned and we are shooting out yonder, in revenge against time and the earth. I would rather say that in true metaphysical thinking there is more of a finessed love for the in-

---

5. F. Nietzsche, *Der Wille zur Macht. Versuch einer Umwertung aller Werte* (Leipzig: Kröner, 1930), 255 (§374); *The Will to Power,* trans. W. Kaufmann and R. J. Hollingdale (New York: Random House, 1967), 202.

timate strangeness of being, a love that finds itself coming to wakefulness just in encounter with, or participation in, this being's mystery.

It is worth asking whether modern metaphysics has tended to be a form of an *entirely immanent ontology* in which there comes to be the loss of this doubleness of the "meta" and the feel for its basic significance. It is worth asking also whether various repudiations of such metaphysics themselves also continue this stress on exclusive immanence. Metaphysics is concerned with immanence certainly, and in terms of the mindful discernment of the multiple equivocities of our being native to the world. But if our sense of the "meta" of metaphysics is rigidly linked to the cartoon version of Platonism, it an easy move to accuse the philosopher of escape from reality, rather than acknowledging his or her deeper engagement with being. In my view the "meta" implies no treason to the immanence, and the wise discernment of the ontological powers of immanence, but we need not look on immanence with the univocalizing fixation of the dualistic "either/or." Wise discrimination of immanence is not incompatible with fidelity to an intimation of the "meta" in its other side, that is, in relation to the "beyond." In that regard, there is a doing of metaphysics that is well directed on immanent being, to be sure, and yet this direction may be concerned to understand the deep equivocities of our being native to the world, in which its strangeness is as much to the fore as its intimacy. This ontological strangeness may intimately put us in mind of the call of the "meta" as the "beyond" of immanence, a call coming to us in and through intimacy with immanence itself. There can be ontologies which, though claiming to offer a *logos* of *to on,* yet are so zoned on a kind of univocalization of immanence that they inevitably collapse the doubleness of the "meta," and short-change any intimation of any "beyond," or opening to transcendence as other. And what has been thus recessed in this latter respect is hived off onto the old "metaphysics" which now can only be relentlessly accused of taking us away from immanence. It is as if life were a stolen child, and what the old "metaphysics" leaves behind in its place is only a changeling. Metaphysics is not granted as offering the children of time something that time alone does not birth, something which itself births time and its children.

Such a form of ontology, tempted to absolutize a certain univocity of immanence, can take different forms, of course. I mention some. It might be defined in terms of the immanence of self-determining system, such as we find with Hegelian idealism. It might be configured in terms of the immanence of a postulatory finitism such as informs the fundamental ontology of Heidegger. It might take shape in terms of the immanence of the scientistic univocity that informs many projects of science and technology. It might take form as trying to break out of all form in the rhapsodic univocity of Dionysian immanence, whether Nietzschean or postmodern. It might develop in terms of a naturalizing pragmatism devoid of any suggestion of mystery at the heart of the intimate strangeness of given being. In a word, there are many forms of this univocity of immanence: scientistic, in the technological will to overcome all the equivocities of given being and subject creation to the homogeneity of a projected human measure; moral, through the immanence of absolute autonomy in Kantianism; calculative, in the homogeneous reckoning of hedonistic bliss or mass happiness in utilitarianism; speculative and political, in the dialectical immanence of Hegelianism and its state; dialectical and revolutionary, in the political immanence of post-Hegelian totalitarianisms, be they Marxist or fascist; antidialectical and Dionysian, in the immanent Nietzschean world that is "will to power and nothing else besides," and we ourselves also "will to power and nothing else besides."[6]

One might suggest that the distinction of ontology and metaphysics has some correspondence with the double sense of the "meta," one dealing with being immanently "in the midst," the other with a "being beyond." But it would be a mistake to think that any such distinction can undercut the inseparability between the two. Ontology, said to deal only with being as immanent, will tend to culminate in something like Hegel's system of self-determining thought, or perhaps the existential recoil back to human immanence in terms of fundamental ontology. I would say that ontology itself is unavoidably metaxological, and hence even when turned toward being "in the midst" cannot be abstracted from the intermediate space of being which also proves itself porous to what is "beyond." Metaphysics perhaps more explicitly bring us to this latter metaxological sense, insofar as it means an opening of mindfulness to transcendence as other by means of an exploration of the signs of irreducible otherness, even in immanence. This is not a matter of the system but it is a matter of systematic thought. Hegel closes systematic thinking into the system; but there is no

6. *Der Will zur Macht*, 697; *The Will to Power*, 550.

a priori necessity that thinking systematically has to take this very modern form. There are rich networks of interconnections already at work in being; but these networks do not constitute a closed or completed system to be discursively expressed by philosophy. The networks are concretized by open intermediations marked by sameness and otherness, identity and difference. I think a metaxological metaphysics must try to make intelligible sense of these concrete intermediations. Dynamic integrities of being take form as stable but open constancies; our minding of these shows the living energy of thought which opens beyond closure to what is other to thought alone; the between itself is a milieu of enabling communication in which intimacy and universality are not two opposites.

Heidegger is not entirely wrong to talk about a forgetfulness of being, even if one demurs from the epochal manner in which he makes such a claim, for this risks the above univocalizing that is putatively to be transcended. The point is more elemental than epochal. One could claim that it is our very nature to forget being, to forget our constitutive participation in the intimate strangeness of being, insofar as we turn recurrently from the intimate strangeness and try to objectify or subjectify it. We try so to determine it in pursuit of a cognitive familiarization, a familiarization that just in its mode of knowing produces an unknowing, since in truth it deprives being of its intimacy, deprives us of our intimacy with it. The development of a metaxological metaphysics in my own work can be seen as a systematic and transsystematic response to this recurrent slippage into loss of mindfulness of being. If I am not mistaken, we are witnessing today, so to say, a second forgetfulness of being, forgetfulness redoubled, and sometimes in many of those who are Heidegger's admirers. There is no doubt that many of his commentators admirably explore Heidegger's thought of being, but it is extraordinary how few today turn toward, in a more direct address, the question of being.

Again the point is more elemental than epochal. Concerning the ancient perplexities, admirably stated in their own way by Plato and Aristotle, there is nothing finally settled. This is true with regard to the premodern, the modern, or the postmodern. Nothing is settled in so-called postmetaphysical thinking. Nothing is or can be finally settled about the deepest metaphysical questions, arising from primal astonishment, and raising perplexities beyond any one determinate settlement. Such perplexities are not of any age, since they are constitutive of what we are as mindful beings, astonishingly being awoken to the intimate strangeness of being. We have to turn again and again to such perplexities, be returned to them again and again, not with fashionable mantras but with untimely mindfulness. I can see how mantras might be needed, as charms or chants that open our porosity to the intimate strangeness of being. But there are mantras that create the illusion of radicality—a quasi-radicality, since nothing ever seems to move from the spot. The well is deep, infinitely deep, but one must dip into it for the living waters. One must not perch pertly on the rim, on the safe side above, under the spell of what a previous dipper has brought up. One must risk the perhaps bottomless source—and dip again.

OUTLINING METAPHYSICS TO COME

In *Being and the Between*[7] I tried to develop a metaxological metaphysics that, cognizant of the longer tradition of philosophy, takes into account the difficulties posed for metaphysics since Kant's time, the complexities of German idealism and its aftermath, the emergence of a distrust of reason, the concomitant lack of confidence in the promise of metaphysics, as well as the many skeptical worries besetting us today in postmodernism. I wanted to do all this in a spirit that is affirmative of the promise of metaphysics. Among other things, this meant a turn again to the elemental perplexities that are not confined to any epoch of being, perplexities that are not ancient, medieval, modern, or postmodern, perplexities that emerge for mindfulness for beings like us who constitutively are metaphysical animals. From around the time of writing *Being and the Between*, I have also been composing a series of essays, some developing themes adjacent to or suggested in that work, some opening up new avenues not taken in that work. These essays are not merely supplementary, since as explorations they have a certain independence of their own. It was always my intention to gather these explorations into a volume. This is what I do in the present work. A brief overview of the whole will be helpful.

In part one, I am concerned with the status of metaphysics in light of *certain equivocities of dialectic*. Here I engage with the culmination of

7. William Desmond, *Being and the Between* (Albany: State University of New York Press, 1995).

modern dialectic in Hegelian form. As will be evident, while Kant is immensely influential on the future of metaphysics, Hegel is a Janus-figure looking back to the long tradition, claiming in modernity a certain culmination, and presaging, not always knowingly, things to come. In part two I take up some consideration of *metaphysics in the wake of dialectic*. I look at the connection of metaphysics and critique, as well as the question of whether the task of metaphysics after deconstruction is to be described as a reconstruction. My response is neither deconstruction nor reconstruction but metaxological mindfulness of the intimate strangeness of being. In part three I offer a number of more extended studies of themes in *metaphysics after dialectic*, crucial themes viewed in terms of the more metaxological option I favor and pursue. These concern the relation of metaphysics to the equivocities of the everyday; the issue of truth and truthfulness, and our patience to being; the confidence of thought in light of the companionship of religion and philosophy; divine transcendence in the light of speculative dialectic and analogy, metaxologically reconsidered; finally, a more systematic look at the diverse ways of wondering, and the importance of astonishment and perplexity, to the second degree, for metaphysics after what Vico calls the barbarism of reflection.

Let me offer a summary in advance of the different chapters. Chapter one explores the way we often identify intelligibility, indeed being at all, with determinacy. Dialectic has much to do with the question of what makes the determinate to be determinate at all. Dialectic moves beyond fixation in terms of determinate intelligibility, just in its efforts to determine the conditions making possible determinate intelligibility. My focus is on how Hegel's thought is dominantly ruled over by a logic that moves from the indeterminate to the determinate to the self-determining, and this last as the telos governing the unfolding of the process as a whole. This governing logic, I will show, has implications for the contested place of metaphysics. A certain rendition of dialectical thinking can play havoc with the openness to metaphysical thinking, the openness of metaphysical thinking itself. There is something missing in the triplex scheme of the indeterminate, determinate, self-determining. We need to recall the overdeterminate: not being as indeterminate and lacking determination, but as in excess of determination and as "too much," "more" than our self-determination. In this regard, I look at agapeic astonishment and erotic perplexity as sources of metaphysical thinking. These are overdeterminate happenings that cannot be exhausted by determinate cognition. They impel us to take issue with the deficit of understanding in much talk about the completion of metaphysics. They allow us to address Hegelian dialectic in the flawed incompleteness of its claim to completion. They also illuminate the equivocal legacy of dialectic in respect of some of Hegel's successors. The sources are never behind us. The strange yet intimate overdeterminacy of being means (as I shall indicate) that metaphysics will always continue to be reborn, beyond every claim to determinate, or self-determining completion.

Chapter two links dialectic to the idea of "thinking on the double." This allows us to explore further some of the equivocities connected with the many meanings of dialectic and its practice in the philosophical tradition. These range between the extreme of an association of dialectic with specious reasoning and the extreme of a method for dissolving specious reasoning. They include its all-but-identification in the Middle Ages with logic; Kant's linking of dialectic with the critique of transcendent illusion, when reason strays beyond its justified boundary; Hegel's dynamization of dialectic as articulating the intelligibility of processes of becoming and self-becoming; Marx's praxis-orientation application of dialectic to historical processes; and the use of negative dialectic for protodeconstructive purposes by someone like Adorno. Dialectic is also viewed with suspicion by some analytical philosophers who are wary of what is perceived to be pseudothinking (ecce Hegel as the whipping boy of the Vienna circle); and by quite a few of Hegel's continental successors who impute a totalistic imperialism to it, and by implication to the tradition of metaphysics (ecce Hegel as the whipping boy of the French Nietzscheans). Ancient senses of dialectic are connected to Socratic *maieutic,* to the description of the highest philosophical thinking in Plato's *Republic,* to the diaeretic method of the *Sophist,* as indeed also the use of certain patterns of argumentation by the ancients sophists that have a significant connection with the practices of dialectic. Hegelian dialectic, as thinking on the double, claims to overcome equivocity, yet it embodies its own form of doublethink which can be either deconstructed in the interests of exposing a secret equivocation or opened more affirmatively to the plurivocal promise of metaxological thinking. I recommend that we metaphysicians move in the latter direction.

In chapter three my concern is to present an understanding of immediacy as showing a surplus of being which cannot be adequately approached in the terms of Hegel's concept. I want to point to an overdeterminacy of being that cannot be fitted into the triad of indeterminacy, determination, and self-determination. Hegel has a rather negative view of immediacy. We find this, for instance, in his famous discussion of what he calls sense-certainty in the *Phenomenology of Spirit*,[8] or in his general approach to "feeling," say, in relation to either his philosophy of right, or his philosophy of religion. Immediacy refers to something that in itself is indeterminate, in the negative sense of being indefinite, and lacking in proper determination. By contrast, his concept makes intelligible this putatively empty indefiniteness through the developed determination(s) of thought. Conceptual thought mediates this indeterminacy of immediacy, and only when this mediation has been effected can claims be made to categorial intelligibility. In itself, and taken for itself, immediacy seems to be equated with a condition defective in intelligibility till properly conceptual thought determines its mediated intelligibility.

I would put it otherwise. There is no adequate sense of what I will call "surplus immediacy" in Hegel, that is, rich ontological givenness that precedes the determinations of conceptual thought, and that also exceeds claims to completely subject what is given to the categorial determinations of philosophy. There are a number of ways the point might be put, but I would say that there is a *passio essendi*, a passion of being, that is prior to any *conatus essendi,* the endeavor to be (or to think). This *passio essendi* is both a patience of our being and our patience to being. It has to do with surplus givenness that is presupposed by any efforts on our part to determine the intelligibility of immediate happening. Our efforts to determine conceptually the meaning of this surplus immediacy call for a fidelity to the fullness of what is communicated in this elemental givenness. If we put the dominant emphasis on the determining and self-determining power of the concept, in the way Hegel does, we risk a defection from this surplus immediacy. We risk a contraction of intelligibility to the terms of our concepts, and hence risk impoverishing not only our conceptual terms, but what is communicated in and through the surplus immediacy. The point has relevance both at the elemental level and at the more ultimate level. Vis-à-vis the first, we need a richer sense of aesthetic

8. G. W. F. Hegel, *Phänomenologie des Geistes* (Hamburg: Felix Meiner, 1952); *Phenomenology of Spirit,* trans. A. V. Miller (Oxford: Clarendon Press, 1977), chapter 1.

happening than is evident in the drift of Hegel's sense-certainty. Vis-à-vis the second, we need differently to interpret how our *passio essendi,* in encounter with this surplus immediacy, throws light on the beguiling power of art, and the religious porosity in the happening of prayer. The upshot at both the elemental and the ultimate levels is the impossibility of closing mindfulness into a self-determining thinking, at home primarily with itself alone. The porous between opens, inside and outside, downside and upside. Likewise, the self-surpassing of metaphysical thinking is not only immanently horizontal but vertically transcending.

If the explorations in part one deal with certain equivocities of dialectic, the chapters in part two deal with something of *the equivocal aftermath of dialectic,* particularly in relation to critique on the one hand, and deconstruction, on the other. Both of these are related to the practice of negative dialectic, and are carriers of an inheritance of interpreting the nature of thinking in terms of negation.

In chapter four the question is addressed as to whether there is metaphysics after critique. Of course, a lot depends on what we mean by "metaphysics" and "critique." I have suggested the point above, but the contested place of metaphysics in recent thought has much to do with the influence of philosophy understood as critique, especially after Kant. There are connections between critique and "postmetaphysical" thinking. Metaphysics, just in being critiqued, comes to be subject to a form of thought that implies its own *superiority* to metaphysics, at least in its putative claim to take into account the reflective self-consciousness that metaphysics putatively lacks. Of course, there may be something self-serving in such a self-description of critique, but let it pass. As we know, the precise sense of postmetaphysical thinking is not always easy to pin down, though we do find a generalized discontent with what is deemed, again in sometimes generalized terms, to be "metaphysical." All of this remains somewhat obscure. If we look upon part of the task of metaphysics, as I do, as asking of us fundamental reflection, more or less systematic, on the basic senses of the "to be," of what it means to be, it it hard to see how one could say that metaphysics could ever be a practice we could be "post." What happens in the position of being "post" will show itself to be informed, knowingly or unknowingly, by some basic senses of being. Some practice of metaphysics will always be with us and before us, even if some kinds of metaphysics might well be behind us, "post" in that sense. Postmetaphysical thinking will again be metaphysics. Postmetaphysical thinking will involve its own implicit orientations relative to the fundamental senses of the "to be." The question is how true our philosophical mindfulness is to these orientations. Being thus true is ingredient in the vocation of metaphysics—before or after metaphysics.

Much of what makes being intelligible and cognition possible is *recessed* in the practices of knowing and in our diverse participations in being. Metaphysics tries to give significant expression to what is so recessed. It need not claim to possess the system, though it can justifiably defend its own practice of thinking as more or less systematic in tracing the immanent connections and relations between modes of thinking and actualities. If metaphysics must try to trace these connections, this has to be done *in medias res,* from the midst of things, from the between. To philosophize from the between entails no claim to overreach the whole and include it in an absolutely comprehensive system. On this score, chapter four offers two related reflections on the question of metaphysics after critique. The first is an analysis of the project of critique since Kant, and its influence on the disputed status of metaphysics. It explores the theoretical and practical aspects of this, claiming that an understanding of *thinking as negativity,* whether in Hegelian form as determinate negation, or in more radical deconstructive forms, lies at the heart of this disputed status. Not least the relation of philosophy to religion and previous practices of metaphysics are at stake. There is more at work in critique than critique can account for through itself. In a second reflection, the arguments bearing on this "more" are explored in a more constructive spirit. On the basis of an account of the sources of metaphysical thinking beyond the resources of critique alone, the lineaments are sketched of what is needed for metaxological metaphysics after critique.

In chapter five I look at a proposal sometimes made that what we need after the deconstruction of metaphysics is a reconstruction. I argue that we are asked for more than either a deconstruction or a reconstruction. The intimate strangeness of being raises a question as to whether either deconstructive thinking or reconstructive thinking are entirely to the point. Intimate strangeness articulates something of the middle condition of our thought of being: being is strange because it has an otherness, indeed marvel, of which we are not the conceptual masters; being is intimate, for even in its strangeness we are not allowed the neutrality of an entirely disengaged thinking that surveys being from the "outside." Being gives us to be, and we are given to be, before we think about what it is to be. We are intimately within the strangeness, as much as it is about us. We are in the midst of what we try to think about, and it is intimately within what we ourselves are. Inside and outside, we are both, and in a manner that allows porous passage from the intimacy to the strangeness and the strangeness to the intimacy.

If we think only to fix the issue in terms of binary oppositions like inside-outside, reality-appearance, invisible-visible, and so on, and think there is a univocal "either/or" at stake here, we will not see the task of metaphysical thinking in relation to this intimate strangeness. Deconstruction claims that such binary thinking is characteristic of (all) traditional metaphysics, and I agree that there is something to this at one level. But there are other dimensions of consideration that do not yield simply to binary thinking—a form of thinking with the double and on the double, but not just dubious "doublethink." These other dimensions are overdeterminate and they intimate what is not to be deconstructed in metaphysics. Against deconstructive thinking, I hold that dialectical thinking already has some promise in its philosophical search beyond any such fixed binary oppositions. The point holds more true for metaxological mindfulness insofar as it embodies finesse for the overdeterminate. Our response to deconstruction, if this is true, need not be to deny its insight about binary oppositions, but there will be more, and this will not be just a balancing reconstruction, for this would be another instance of the not-quite-true binary thinking. There is something beyond construction, hence deconstruction, and also reconstruction. It is in the overdeterminate dimension of the given and the received: the intimate strangeness of being. Reconstruction can suggest that something has been leveled to the ground and rebuilt, or to be rebuilt. Reconstruction might claim to be the positive opposite to deconstruction. But the "affirmative" task is neither deconstructive nor reconstructive but asks metaxological finesse for the intimate strangeness of being. Our task is not construction, deconstruction, or reconstruction. In a way, it is no "task" at all. If it is a "task" at all, it is beyond the taskmasters of determination and self-determination. It is a thinking that does not think itself but that finds itself as porous to the intimate strangeness of being, born anew to the passion of being mindful of being in its plurivocal voicing of its ontological promise. Metaxological metaphysics seeks a philosophical way of staying true to this passion of thought.

By comparison with parts one and two, the explorations in part three have something of such a more affirmative character. They try to do some metaphysical thinking in a metaxological space *beyond* self-mediating dialectic, and its equivocal inheritances. Chapter six reflects on metaphysics and the equivocity of the everyday. Philosophers have often looked on everyday life as saturated by a dubious equivocity rather than a surplus immediacy of significance that is to be affirmed. How should philosophy appropriately respond to the equivocity of the everyday? Should we insist on pushing our own univocal precisions in a direction that would supplant these equivocities? Are there less hostile possibilities? Of course, philosophy in the twentieth century has been significantly concerned with the everyday. Vide the continental concern with the *Lebenswelt,* the analytic engagement with the ordinary and its languages. In this chapter I develop some reflections in dialogue with the recent work of Stanley Rosen whom I read as much concerned with the equivocity of the everyday. What would it mean to join him in calling ourselves "ordinary language metaphysicians"? My reflections go in more systematic directions than Rosen would go. Rosen is diffident about "system" and "theory-building." I connect this with the modern tendency to seek an "ontology" defined primarily by the self-determination of thinking, to the detriment of the interruptions of surprising otherness, many of which come from the equivocal matrix of everyday life. Hegel is perhaps the high point of this tendency to "system," offering us as metaphysics a speculative logic that is a categorial ontology. By contrast, metaxological metaphysics is less the system of categories defined by the self-circling of thought determining itself as a fundamental reflection on the basic senses of being, or "to be." There is an openness to what is beyond self-determining thought in this understanding of metaphysics, an openness more consonant with the more original experience of wonder or astonishment we find, for instance, in the Greek *thaumazein.* The ever new surprise of such astonishment keeps alive metaphysics in an age where in everyday life a flat blandness of the soul has taken widespread hold.

In chapter seven I address the themes of pluralism, truthfulness, and the patience of being. How we understand truth cannot be disconnected from how we understand ourselves, or from how we understand how we humans are to be. "How we are to be": this phrase indicates the human being as a creature with a certain *promise of being* that calls out to be realized in one way or the other. Some ways will enable fulfillment of the promise, if we are true to what we are. Some ways may betray the promise, if we are false to what we are. The intimate connection of being human and being true offers striking witness of our intimacy with the strangeness of being. The intimacy is not a merely theoretical issue but has inescapably ethical and indeed religious significance.

This discussion explores our relation to truth in light of a strong contemporary tendency to stress that there is a pluralism of truths, and that human beings are constructive of their own truth. It argues that while we might not possess absolute truth, a radical skepticism does not make sense, and there is more at issue than a pluralism of constructed truths. We are creatures of the between: we are not devoid of relation to truth, crucially evident in the exigency to be truthful that human beings know intimately. This discussion argues that there is patience to truth that is prior to our own efforts at construction. Patience to truth witnesses to our strange intimacy with being, to being's intimacy with us. This patience is not something toward which we should take a merely negative relation, such as the will to conquer it entirely through our constructivist interventions. While the active nature of human existence is not denied, there is patience to being whose elemental nature is even less to be denied. This patience is consonant with an understanding of the vulnerable finitude of the human being and its manifestation, say, in the practices of healing.

Chapter eight delves further into the ontological intimacy by reflecting on the confidence of thought and its sources. I take seriously the "co" in *con-fidence*, a "trust with." Something of a trust is confided to us in our confidence in truth, and in being true. The question also pertains to what is credit-worthy of belief, and hence the relation between belief and the confidence of thought comes up. The ancient companionship between the religious and metaphysics has been disturbed in modern thought, with consequences for both metaphysics and religion. Modern thought claims to begin anew with doubting, not with believing. If this companionship is crucial, and this companionship is newly opening in our postmodern time, then a rethinking of metaphysics is needed, as well as a renewed religious porosity in which we are attentive to the signs of the divine. My question is whether this breach of companionship in modernity is an interim:

between a premodernity where the companionship was perhaps too taken for granted; and a postmodernity when the idea of philosophy enabling itself through its own immanent resources alone has run into the ground. In the ground intimacy with the strangeness of being is quickened anew, and the immanent powers of thought recharged with fresh alertness.

We need to be alert, however, to the fact that it seems that it is just the *lack of confidence* in reason that is most notable in postmodern thought. Modern doubting seems to express a confidence in autonomous reason, but as I see it, there is an overconfidence whose inflation reverses into a deflation, and not only subjection but abjection follows supreme projection. The confidence of modern reason, if coupled with critique, can mutate into a lack of confidence in reason. Again I think of Kant and what he offers to succeeding generations of antimetaphysicians. There can be a strange combination of overconfidence in reason and lack of confidence that is disastrous for any metaphysics that would be true to the in-between character of human thinking. Too little confidence, and there is no metaphysical daring; too much, and we betray our in-between condition, and generate philosophy that is no philosophy. Loss of ontological intimacy brings estrangement from being, not the sense of being the confidant of the strange mystery of being. We then no longer feel we share in the enigmatic confidences of things. The issue of confidence directs us to the roots of all thinking, and its trust in being true: our being true in the trust that there is truth to be known, or that will make itself known to us. Here the metaxological way addresses a primal trust in the intelligibility of what is. The old companionship with the religious is relevant, not just vis-à-vis this or that determinate belief, but in terms of the endowing source of original trust. Confident philosophy has no rancor to religion. A companion is a confidant, one from whom one receives confidences, one to whom one is willing to trust confidences. This companionship of philosophy and religion is worthy of renewal in the confiding spirit of metaxological giving and receiving.

Chapter nine continues on a similar line in reflecting on analogy, dialectic, and divine transcendence, and asking what kind of dialogue might be conceivable between St. Thomas and Hegel. Of course, analogy and dialectic could be said to be almost coextensive with the entire tradition of philosophy from its inception in Greek thought. Both bear on the nature of intelligible discourse and indeed the intelligibility of being itself and our mindfulness of it. As suggested before, dialectic is also associated with diverse practices of philosophy. For its part, analogy is bound up with the senses of being in classical metaphysics, as well as how we might intelligibly speak about the divine. Since around the time of Hegel, *affirmations of divine transcendence* have often been attacked in terms of a variety of philosophies of immanence. The roots of this are in Kant again, but the transcendence thus attacked is defined in very dualistic terms: immanence *versus* transcendence, time *versus* eternity, and so on. Such dualistic conceptions, sometimes imputed to the entire Western tradition of metaphysics ("Platonism") and theology (Christianity as "Platonism for the people") are not nuanced enough. There is a fury to Nietzsche's attack on all "beyonds" as draining value off life, and his fury is the echo of many echoes of many other such attacks on the "beyond" since Hegel. But once again the cartoon version of Platonism comes home to roost in a simplistic "either/ or" between here and beyond, as the "meta" loses its rich doubleness. Alas, we now seem to live in a time of "Nietzscheanism for the masses," where just the eclipse of the "beyond" of the "meta" makes the many take themselves to be their own little gods of self-satisfied immanence. The intimate strangeness of being as metaxological is both "in the midst" and "beyond," intimating a communication of divine overdeterminacy beyond determination and self-determination: finitude porous to infinity, immanence to transcendence, immanent transcendence to transcendence as other.

I am interested in whether the notion of analogy has still resources enabling us to challenge the rejection of transcendence by such philosophies of immanence. I take Hegel's dialectic to be antagonistic to dualistic thought, but his philosophy of speculative dialectic lies on the same plane as these philosophies of immanence. As exemplary of modern dialectic, he claims to be the measure of every form of dualism, with results that culminate in an entirely immanent philosophy. Aquinas wants to balance sameness and otherness, likeness and unlike, yet he is hugely insistent that with regard to divine difference the dissimilitude always exceeds the similitude. How analogy and speculative dialectic enable us or disable us in relation to divine transcendence has significance beyond Hegel for our contemporary philosophical and theological (indeed atheological) options. A metaxological reconsideration of analogy does not have to be a retrospective glance at a tradition judged exhausted. It may harbor promise for a renewed thinking of the thought of divine difference, after both Hegel and the deconstruction of Hegelian totality.

In the concluding chapter ten, I return to the differences between astonishment, perplexity, and curiosity but now dwell on them more intensively than I did in the opening chapter. I suggest that wonder is not a univocal concept but a happening making us porous to the intimate strangeness of being. Importantly, as a happening it is plurivocal. For reasons I will explain, I believe that it is important to distinguish the three different modalities of wonder as astonishment, perplexity, and curiosity. While they are internally related to each other, a different stress is to be found in each. Lacking appreciation of these different stresses, we risk holding that all wonder is nothing other than the curiosity that turns all of being and beings into objects of determinate cognition. Setting out thus on the fatal path of the death of wonder, losing finesse for the intimate strangeness, we become the assassins of metaphysics—and all in the name of determinate cognition. What Vico calls the barbarism of reflection (*barbarie della riflessione*) is this death of wonder that takes itself for the life of thought.

We need to rethink astonishment, perplexities, and curiosity more intensively with respect to the porosity of our being which is constitutively at the origin of our being metaphysical creatures. The barbarism of reflection is a paradoxical outcome of the development of knowledge. This barbarism eventuates from the surfeit of a certain kind of determinative knowing when we betray piety and trample on all traces of ontological reverence. Thankfully, wonder as astonishment, is beyond deconstruction and reconstruction—and beyond such trampling. In the return of astonishment at the end, there is something of a Vichian *corso e recorso* in this book. Is there a festive wonder associated with metaxological metaphysics, after the barbarism of reflection runs its course? As long as philosophy, indeed mindful life persists, one has to say yes to wonder. It is not that we can have some "project" for reviving our capacity for wonder. It is not that first we have a capacity for wonder but rather that we are first capacitated by wonder. We cannot determine this capacitation through ourselves alone. All our thinking comes to itself out of a given porosity of being that endows us with the promise of mindfulness. Coming home to this porosity, we are mindful again of the intimate strangeness of being, and hear again, after long sojourn in the equivocities of dialectic, the living call of metaphysics.

Part 1

Metaphysics and the Equivocities
of Dialectic

1 ∽ Being, Determination, and Dialectic

On the Sources of Metaphysical Thinking

HEGEL AND THE COMPLETION OF METAPHYSICS

Dialectic is tied to the entire range of ways of thinking about being that we find in the tradition of metaphysics.[1] I will return to that range in diverse ways throughout this work, but now I am concerned with the connection of dialectic and metaphysics. Metaphysics, of course, often now meets with outright rejection, as purportedly dealing with what lies beyond our ken, or as a conceptual projection onto an illusory transcendence of our own powers and impotences, or as the cunning conceit of an intellectual will to power. The intimacy of connection between dialectic and the thinking of being also defines part of the problematic situation of so-called postmetaphysical philosophy. It has been a recurrent catch-cry for some time that we are now to think beyond all that, beyond dialectic, beyond metaphysics, beyond being. None of these more recent claims is immune from question. I want to consider this contested place of metaphysics, and the complex, indeed ambiguous, role dialectical thinking has played in defining that place.

Often we attribute the sources of this contested place to Hume, and in a more qualified way to Kant. By contrast, Hegel is frequently presented as embodying a postcritical resurgence of metaphysics, a recrudescence of what seemed to have been safely stowed in its grave. True, one finds interpretations in which Hegel as metaphysician is subordinated to Hegel the true heir of the Kantian project. Nevertheless, Hegel's continuity with the prior tradition is so massively evident, and not least in his respect for the Greeks, especially Aristotle, that this interpretation has much to do with

---

1. A version of these reflections was given as the Presidential Address at the annual meeting of the Metaphysical Society of America, held at Loyola College in Baltimore, Maryland, March 11, 1995.

the commentators' own embarrassments with metaphysics. Even granting that, yet Hegel has been a contributor, sometimes witting, sometimes not, to the contested place of metaphysics.

The view that Hegel represents a kind of summation of major strands in the Western tradition is not without *some* truth. This being so, if we wish to follow in his footsteps, we must strive for as comprehensive and nuanced an understanding of the possibilities of the philosophical tradition as he had. This is extraordinarily difficult. One might say that it is something of Hegel's *stature* that has made things more difficult for metaphysics rather than easier. To be a philosopher of such stature is not only to release essential possibilities of thinking, it is to cast a shadow over descendent thinkers under which they must struggle for light. Excess of light can illuminate but it can also blind.

If Hegel offers a kind of summation of the essential possibilities in the metaphysical tradition, more accurately, the modern rationalist tradition, there can seem something unsurpassable about him. And yet just the alleged consummation leaves us strangely disquieted and hungry. The completion attributed to Hegel shows forth starkly that something was missing in the quest, perhaps from the outset. If any such completion suggests the full richness of metaphysics, yet the richness seems also to show (in Marx's phrase) the poverty of philosophy. If we are to "surpass" the alleged end of metaphysics, we must do so beyond the alleged poverty of philosophy. It goes without saying that such language about "the end of metaphysics" is not only the fashionable rhetoric of post-Heideggerian thought. It names a task that a plethora of thinkers set themselves in Hegel's wake: Marx, for instance, in his will to realize, complete, and surpass philosophy in revolutionary praxis; Kierkegaard in his desire to be "postphilosophical" in religious faith; Nietzsche in his eros to be a "philosopher of the future," celebrating the aesthetic theodicy of Dionysus. As much as, indeed more than, the more positivistic or scientistic heirs of Kant or Hume, the continental heirs of completed idealism have been the "surpassers of metaphysics," be they rhapsodic descendants of Nietzsche or deconstructive heirs of Heidegger.

I do not invoke this throng of "postmetaphysical" overcomers of "metaphysics" to enlist in their company. I think that much of the contestation of metaphysics is bound up with crucial ambiguities in dialectical thinking. I will explain what I mean in due course. But in advance I want to reject the view that Hegel embodies the culmination of the tradition of metaphysics. I say this not because I want to surpass metaphysics, in whatever direction, be it to praxis or rhapsody or poesy or scientism or grammatology. I say it because Hegelian dialectic represents a very powerful interpretation of thinking, yet one that hides nuances, nuances that, if resurrected for rethinking, shed a different light on metaphysical thinking, and the possibilities of its contemporary renewal.

The claim that Hegel represents the culmination of metaphysics has had disastrous consequences, not quite because Hegel was a disaster, but because the reiteration of this claim has stood in the way of rethinking metaphysics. It is like a mesmerizing fetish whose bewitching spell we cannot break. Why are we in its spell? Perhaps because of Hegel's stature, and the great difficulty of thinking philosophically at a level comparable to Hegel's. We cannot surpass Hegel because Hegel surpasses us, and the seemingly comprehensive system freezes us, or exhausts us, instead of freeing us. It need not be so. Nor need one's strategy be just the predatory exploitation of this one aspect of Hegel's system to call that other aspect into account, as if we could beat one bone of Hegel's head with another bone taken from the dismembered body. We cannot confine ourselves to Hegel and his legacy. We must return to the sources of metaphysical thinking.

I cite four reasons why we need to do this: first, to have self-knowledge of what we are doing, and thus to understand the lack of understanding in much talk about the completion of metaphysics; second, better to understand Hegelian dialectic in the flawed incompleteness of its claim to completion; third, to search out clearer direction from the equivocal legacy of dialectic in respect of some of Hegel's successors; fourth, to see how and why metaphysics will always continue to be reborn, beyond every claim to determinate completion, since the sources are never simply behind us. In the considerations to follow I will be primarily focused on the *sources* of metaphysical thinking, and will offer only a mediated glimpse of *what* one thinks when thinking thus.

ORIGINAL WONDER

The beginning of mindfulness is in an original wonder before the givenness of being. Such wonder is often recognized but its significance is not always plumbed. Being is given to us; we are given to be, and to be as mindful; we do not first produce being, or make it be as for us; originally it is given as an excess of otherness which arouses our astonishment that it is at all. There is something childlike and virgin about this. I do not say childish. A child looks into the night sky and sees the silver orb of the moon. He or she may merely point, or exclaim: Look, the moon! The point is not definite indexical reference but an elemental acknowledgment of the being there of that beautiful being.

None of this is determinately known as such. It is lived, with a mindfulness that may be more or less rudimentary, more or less articulate. As has often been pointed out, children tend to ask the "big questions." They are not normally chastised for this; sometimes they are indulged. There are philosophers who will chastise the child in themselves for the seeming indulgence. There are philosophers who believe that if this virgin openness is lost completely then metaphysics has truly reached its dead end. The metaphysician keeps alive this elemental astonishment, and it is never dead even in the most articulated and developed of his categorial thoughts.

Why do we sometimes chastise the child, or more mellowly, indulge him or her? Because we have this inveterate tendency to think that to be is to be intelligible, and that to be intelligible is to be determinate. But—and this is the rub—the original astonishment is not determinate in that way at all. We tend to believe that we must make definite every indefiniteness, made determinate all indeterminacies. Only thus, we hold, do we come to the proper knowing of being. Moreover, this movement from the indefinite to the definite is often seen as a progressive conquering of the indeterminate, and hence a progressive process of leaving behind the original astonishment. Astonishment may be a beginning but it is one that is left behind as knowing fulfills its own destiny of completely determinate cognition.

Something of this is implied, for example, in Aristotle's discussion of *thaumazein* (*Metaphysics* 982b11ff.). Wonder may be the beginning of philosophy, but the end of the question is the dispelling of wonder in as determinate as possible a knowing of matters. This is why he uses geometry as an example of knowing (*Metaphysics* 983a13ff.). There is a solution that leaves behind the indefiniteness of the initial wonder, and that offers a definitely articulated answer. It is not that wonder is deepened in the end, it is dispelled. Significant for our purposes here is the fact that Hegel cites Aristotle's opening observation, and while he does not see the end in geometrical cognition, for this, after all, is not true self-determining know-ing, nevertheless, he does hold that the attainment of true knowing is the overcoming of wonder. Thus Hegel connects wonder with intuition and indeterminate certainty, but "philosophical thought, however, has to raise itself above the standpoint of wonder." Intuition and wonder are only "the beginning of knowledge."[2] Not incidentally, we find a similar fate of the dispelling of wonder when Hegel reflects on the destiny of art.[3]

By contrast, one has the sense that Platonic wonder in *Theaetetus* (155d3–4) is not to be simply dispelled in the end but deepened. I know it was said that over the gates of the Academy the admonition stood: Let none who has not studied geometry enter here! But this directive does not say that geometry is all we will study, once having entered, or that it epito-mizes the highest kind of knowing. Indeed if we take geometry as a figure for completely determinate cognition, it is not incidental that it reappears as an honorific goal throughout the tradition of philosophy. We see it in Descartes, Spinoza, Kant, and Husserl, to mention some. What Pascal calls *l'esprit de géométrie* stands for a way of knowing deeply beloved by philoso-phy. But as Pascal knew otherwise, there may be needed other modes of mindfulness, captured under the name of *l'esprit de finesse*. There may be indeterminacies or overdeterminacies about the ontological situation that demand metaphysical finesse that does not conquer astonishment or per-plexity but deepens and disquiets thinking even more radically.

What are some instances of such overdeterminacies? The question of being is one such: why being at all, why not nothing? The question of nothing is another. The question of the very givenness of being at all calls forth an indeterminate perplexity before an overdeterminacy that resists complete conceptual determination. So is the question of the meaning of freedom, as posing an enigma beyond complete determination. Our con-frontations with, say, the suffering of the tragic, with the enigma of death, with the monstrousness of evil, offer occasions of the resistant indetermi-nacies, if not hints of the overdeterminacies, in the ontological situation. One could make similar claims about philosophy's constant concern with the being of truth, of the good, of the beautiful. Likewise, the question of the ground of intelligibility falls in the same family of perplexities: Can we

2. *Encyclopaedia*, §449, *Zusätz*.
3. On this, see my *Art, Origins, Otherness: Between Art and Philosophy* (Albany: State Uni-versity of New York Press, 2003), chapter 3.

give sufficient reason for the principle of sufficient reason? Is there a surd to intelligibility—that the intelligible is intelligible at all—a surd that is not just absurd?

Such questions put thinking on trial. They provoke determinate thinking, but they issue in perplexities that do not yield a univocal answer; indeed, they resist being conclusively formulated as univocal problems. A constitutive ambiguity persists, a constitutive openness remains, beyond our efforts at determination. Since such questions concern the being or the good or the intelligibility of the determinate, they come to articulation from beyond the determinate. We may not be able univocally to answer such perplexities, but we cannot negate them. They continue to be reborn. Though we cannot master or dissolve them completely, we must return to them again and again, and with thinking informed by mindfulness of what comes to be at the edge of determination.

The point is not to undermine or deconstruct the importance of definite cognition of the determinacies of beings or processes. Rather, philosophical mindfulness is not simply a progressive conquering of an initial indefiniteness by a more and more complete determination or definite cognition. There is something about the beginning that is not only in excess of objectification and determination at the outset, but that remains in excess at the end, even after our most strenuous efforts at determination.

ASTONISHMENT, PERPLEXITY, CURIOSITY

I think we need to distinguish between original astonishment, perplexity, and the curiosity that leads on to definite cognition. Astonishment is closest to the original wonder. I use the term "astonishment" because contemporary usage of the word *wonder* easily slides into the sentimental. We are struck into astonishment. We do not think our way into astonishment; we are overcome by astonishment. There is a certain shock or bite of otherness in astonishment. There is also a certain receptivity, indeed patience. The givenness of being is offered for our beholding. We are patient to its giving insofar as we do not produce it, or bring it toward ourselves only for it just to be cognitively possessed by us. There is always an excess in astonishment. Something is both given to mindfulness, and yet is in excess of what mindfulness can grasp clearly and distinctly in that given. Astonishment is aroused when there is, so to say, a "too-muchness" about the givenness of something that both overcomes us and fascinates us. Moreover, this astonishing, although not at first within our control, and though resistant to exhaustive illumination in clear and distinct concepts, is not a mere vague indefiniteness. If we were to say that it is indeterminate, it would have to be called indeterminate in a positive and affirmative sense. This is why I prefer to speak of an *overdetermination:* such a sense of the indeterminate/overdeterminate is not antithetical to determination. Rather it exceeds every determination we will later attempt, exceeds complete encapsulation in a definite and exhaustive definition. This affirmative overdetermination of the beginning is crucial to granting the surplus sources of all thinking, and will be very important in understanding the equivocities of dialectic below, and indeed the reason why there is no end of metaphysical thinking.

Perplexity, by contrast, is a movement of mindfulness that arises subsequently to the first astonishment. The very excess of what is first given rouses thought and questioning on our behalf. Something excessive is given, and we would fain interpret its meaning. Perplexity arises when mind becomes troubled about the meaning of the original astonishment and what is given to thought in it. There is something indeterminate about perplexity, but there is also a more concerted movement to overcome the indeterminate. The very troubling of thought here seeks its own overcoming in a peace of mind that is no longer troubled or perplexed. Thus we find the beginnings of the movement toward determinate cognition, but in such a fashion, so to say, that the aura of the beginning still wraps itself around mindfulness. Perplexity is not patience to the otherness of being in quite the same way as is the original astonishment. In its troubled mindfulness there works a vector of self-transcendence that would go toward this otherness of being, and if possible overcome its own perplexity. Thus perplexity is often felt as a lack of definite cognition, driving out beyond itself to overcome that lack.

From this drive there arises the movement of mind toward determinate cognition. That is, perplexity becomes *curiosity* when the indefiniteness of perplexity is focused more specifically on particular beings and processes. Perplexity may have an indefiniteness about it, in that one might be perplexed and not know quite what one is perplexed about. But curiosity is more clearly definite; one is curious about this, that, or the other. Curiosity is not vague, though it may be itchy, that is, greedily extend itself to everything coming within its purview. It is with curiosity that definite questions arise about particular beings and processes, definite questions that seek determinate answers. Yet like perplexity, the movement of curiosity is out of an initial sense of lack: I lack the definite knowing of this, that, or the other; nevertheless, I take the definite steps to acquire proper determinate knowing; and the goal is just such determinate cognition as brings to an end the thrust of curiosity, and overcomes the initial lack of knowledge that drives the seeking.

Overall, then, there is something excessive and overdetermined about the astonishing beginning; then there is a troubled indeterminacy and sense of lack, in the perplexity of mind that is subsequently precipitated; finally, there is a drive to definiteness and determination in curiosity that seeks to overcome any survival of troubled indefiniteness and lack, such as we find in perplexity.

Why is it important to distinguish these three? Because in the main we have tended to think of the process of mindfulness, whether philosophical or scientific, in terms of the third possibility, and in such a fashion that certain fertile resources in the first two are easily distorted. I think the first two are not reducible to the third. But because we often put primary stress on the third, we have a predilection for modes of cognition like mathematical knowing or objective science as seeming most fully to live up to the inner exigency of the desire to know. These modes of cognition seem to epitomize the ideal of knowing that is as completely determinate as possible, wherein all indeterminacy and indefiniteness seem to be progressively conquered. *L'esprit de géométrie* is tempted to make redundant the *l'esprit de finesse,* and to do so with a clean epistemological conscience. After all, is not this redundancy just the inevitable end of proper progress to epistemic enlightenment? Who could possibly want to sing the praises of the indeterminate? In response, I ask allowance to offer another way to describe the differences between astonishment and perplexity, with implications for curiosity and determinate cognition. I use the classical language of eros and agape. Astonishment is agapeic, perplexity is erotic. When determinate cognition, begotten of curiosity, forgets or denies its origin in these parents, it becomes an ungrateful child, at times begetting some unsweet issue of its own. It becomes the wasp that stings, not the bee that gives us honey.[4]

4. I borrow the apt image from St. Bonaventure: "the curious man lacks devotion. There are many such persons, devoid of praise and devotion, though they may have all the splendors of knowledge. They make wasps' nests that have no honeycombs, whereas the bees make

What I mean in calling astonishment "agapeic" is that it arises from a surplus or excess out of which an affirmative movement of mind as self-transcending emerges. The beginning is already full, overfull, and out of this overfull beginning a movement of self-transcending toward the other arises. It is to the excessive richness of the origin that I want to call attention. Moreover, the arising movement of self-transcending is not simply for purposes of a return to the self. I do not go out from myself toward the other to appropriate the other and through the other to return to myself. I go toward the other because the other is for itself and always irreducible to what it is for me. It is its being for itself that is affirmed, celebrated in this movement of going beyond self. It is the stunning beauty of *the moon* that the child's exclamation celebrates, not the child's own feelings. This agapeic relation to the other as other must be kept in mind by metaphysical thinking, especially since other possibilities can come to distort its promise, as indeed does a certain rendition of dialectic.

By contrast, I call perplexity "erotic" because it arises out of a troubled sense of lack and desire: as ignorant, one lacks definite knowledge of the other that is given to mindfulness in astonishment; and yet one desires to overcome that lack of ignorance. The beginning of perplexity is this indigence of knowing, out of which indigence there is a movement of self-transcending toward the other. I also call this movement erotic because, while the other sought can be acknowledged as other, and must be so in some sense, the seeking is qualified by the aim of alleviating perplexity's own troubled mindfulness. In this regard, it is tempted to turn the self-transcending into a search that finally is for the sake of returning the self to its own epistemic peace or satisfaction with itself. Then I go toward the other out of my own lack, I tend to the other not primarily to attend to the other, but as perhaps requiting my own lack. I am tempted to possess the

honey"; see *Sermons on the Six Days of Creation*, I, 8, cited in *The Journey of the Mind to God*, trans. P. Boehner, O.F.M., edited with an introduction and notes by Stephen F. Brown ((Indianapolis, Ind.: Hackett, 1993), 44. By contrast, I am put in mind also of Rilke when he says: "We are the bees of the invisible. We ceaselessly gather the honey of the visible to store it in the great golden hive of the Invisible"; see R. M. Rilke, *The Poet's Guide to Life: The Wisdom of Rilke*, ed. and trans. Ulrich Baer (New York: Modern Library, 2005), 23. Obviously, unlike St. Bonaventure, Rilke wants to distance himself from the Christian sense of things (22) and claim his concern for the earth. In what is a fairly typical post-Hegelian fashion, the "innering" of his honey making points "not into the beyond whose shadow darkens the earth but into a whole, into *the whole*" (22). Rilke's *"metaxu"* is a "meta" in the midst, not a between that also is an opening of creation to the "meta" of the "beyond."

other to enable my own achieved self-possession. Then there eventuates a return to self through the other; the movement of minding turns into a complex self-mediation that passes toward and through the other on the way back to itself; and now, at the end, we no longer live in the initial lack of perplexity but think we have fulfilled the eros of knowing in attaining its own fuller self-knowledge. The lack of the beginning seems to be overcome in the end that returns to the beginning in a more consummated self-knowing.

Note that if our major philosophical emphasis falls here, the other is no longer for itself, but is a medium in which I become for myself. Then the drive of self-transcendence puts primary stress on the self rather than on the transcendence. By contrast, when we remember agapeic astonishment properly, there is also self-transcendence, but the transcending is *more* than the self and, in a way, the self is more than itself, in genuinely exceeding itself toward the other, without definitive enclosure of the other, or self-knowledge closed on itself.

Curiosity, it seems to me, issues more proximately from erotic perplexity than agapeic astonishment. It is driven by a lack of knowledge, and this it wants to overcome through cognitive possession of the other it first lacks. Curiosity seeks its own alleviation in the mitigation of its ignorance of what is other to itself. In contradistinction to perplexity proper, it exhibits greater insistence on the determinacies of knowing. The eros of perplexity has an openness to its self-transcending; it can be willing to let its deeper exigencies be troubled by questions that perhaps exceeds its present, even future, determination. There may be perplexities about life, about death, forever beyond complete determination. And yet the eros of perplexity is not brought to a standstill by this always unavoidable failure of determinate cognition. Its very failure may augur something other that is positive, and may incite a new restlessness of self-transcending thinking. The ultimate failure of completely determinate cognition may energize mind in another dimension to determinate curiosity. The eros is infinitely restless.

Let me offer this illustration. One can read Kant as a thinker marked by this restless perplexity, even though he was also marked by an insistent desire for as much determinacy in cognition as possible. When he speaks about the exigence of asking metaphysical questions as ineradicable, even despite his claim to tame the pretensions of theoretical knowing, he recognized something that resisted reduction to complete determination. And in its own way, his system is developed with the view to liberating a self-transcending, at least in thinking, beyond the validated cognitions of theoretical science, a noncognitive approach to what lies at the boundary, or beyond the boundary of scientific cognition. I think, however, that Kant had a bit of a bad conscience about this restless perplexity, since as both restless and perplexed it did not quite fit into the system. Something of its energy generates the system, and generates the movement from one *Critique* to the next, but it is not a determinate element within the system, and indeed outlives the system in all its scholastic categorial determination.

For curiosity is definite, hence limited. Of course, curiosity is potentially unlimited in a quantitative sense, in passing from this concern to that other concern, and so on ad infinitum. This infinity is merely the unending, hence limitless, distention of limited mindfulness over limited matters. Curiosity's proper focus is on a limited matter to hand over which it anticipates an epistemic ascendancy. It would grasp it, come to grips with it. It is limited also in that it is always inclined to turn away from what it cannot thus finally cognitively possess. To Kant's honor, he did not turn away. With lesser thinkers, what cannot be made cognitively determinate will be dismissed as an intractable equivocity against which we must methodologically quarantine ourselves. Metaphysical problems will be dismissed as pseudoproblems in a quasi-positivistic fashion. Or they will be suspected as signs of sickness, a pathology whose roots we must extirpate. Of course, just such signs of discomfort may be the symptoms of real health, insofar as the erotic restlessness of thinking cannot be entirely stifled or consumed by determinate curiosity and its answers. Perhaps the absolutization of determinate curiosity is the real infection: in stifling the restless eros of mind while seeming to epitomize its most hardheaded expression, it generates its own pathology, a pathology that preens itself as being the nonpareil of epistemic robustness.

DIALECTIC AND DETERMINATION

What has all this to do with dialectic? What has it to do with metaphysical thinking in the wake of German idealism? I will comment now on the first question, then in the next section turn to the second.

With respect to the first question I must confine myself to the relation of dialectic and determination. One might make the case that throughout the philosophical tradition we find a very strong adherence to the view that to be is to be intelligible, and that to be intelligible is to be determinate. The intelligibility of being, the being of being at all, is unthinkable apart from determinacy. This view is also connected with a predilection for the univocity of being. To be is to be a determinate this somewhat *(tode ti)*. A being is itself and nothing but itself. To be is to be something, to be self-identical and one. Likewise, in answer to how we know beings and their intelligibility, and in line with this emphasis on the determinate, we think of knowing as a determinate answer to a specific curiosity that leaves behind the indeterminacy of both astonishment and perplexity.

The problem here is not just the negative view of astonishment and perplexity. It is the risk of losing sight of *another* perplexity about the determinate itself. Suppose beings are intelligible as determinately there, is this determination itself immune from our further astonishment and perplexity? How comes the determinate to be determinate? How comes it to be at all? Such questions are not about another determination, but about the coming to determination of something. Is the process of coming to determination just another determination? I think one has to say no, since then the product of a process would be indistinguishable from the process itself, and then any exclusive emphasis on the determinate would itself become questionable once again. Beings are determinate but they are determinate because they come to be determinate. They are the issue of a coming to be that is not a determination but a determining. How then do we think of the determining? Our answer cannot be just another univocal solution to a specific curiosity.

The issue is further complicated in that there are difficulties in completely fixating beings with absolute univocal determinacy. A spade is a spade, we say. So we uphold the univocal sense of determinate being. But we also say there are spades and there are spades. And then we imply ambiguity and indeed a more equivocal sense of being that resists specification in entirely univocal terms. There are differences as well as identities, othernesses as well as samenesses, determinings that resist complete determination, comings and goings that exceed this or that object, which has appeared in the process of coming and going. Things are themselves, but they also are differentiating, and other to any simple fixation. They exhibit nuances that demand *l'esprit de finesse*, as well as determinations that can be fixed and formulated by *l'esprit de géométrie*. These differences and nuances and othernesses speak to the modes of mindfulness that find form out of astonishment and perplexity.

I suggest that dialectical thinking emerges at some such juncture between indetermination and determination. It arises when there are recalcitrances to univocal determination, and when definite curiosity about a straightforward problem does not quite do justice to what is at play in the situation in question. For instance, Socratic dialectic is a way of dealing with differences, not only of propositions, but of living interlocutors. Their differences, even their hostilities, demand a way beyond sheer difference, demand a reasonable mediation of conflicts, wherein the forthcoming of a more complex determination of a question will be elicited. While Aristotle's view of dialectic is different to Plato's, his view is revealing concerning the above question of determining. For him dialectic deals with the scrutiny of premises that are generally accepted, or of premises that are probable, or generally accepted as persuasive. It has a function in intellectual training, even though it is not a method of demonstrative knowledge that offers valid deductions from true and self-evident premises. For Aristotle, dialectic also has value for arguing with others in terms of their presuppositions and premises. Further it helps us—and this is the important point now—in our approach to the first principles of demonstrative science, principles that are not themselves demonstrated or demonstrable. The ultimate principles of sciences cannot be approached within the terms of the determinate science itself, since these principles are prior to and presupposed by the determinate science. These principles are to be approached through the discussion of the generally held opinions—to do this is a proper function of dialectic.

If dialectic has this last function, crucial consequences follow. Dialectic, we may say, opens up the matter of the intelligible beyond determinate, demonstrative intelligibility. Aristotle says that dialectic offers "a process of criticism wherein lies the way [path] to the principles of all inquiries."[5] This is an extraordinarily important statement. In effect, it is an acknowledgment of the other to determinate intelligibility without which demonstration could never be demonstrative. Demonstration is made possible by ultimate principles that are not themselves univocally demonstrable. The drift to ordered determinacy is so strong in Aristotle that he

5. Aristotle, *Topics* 101b3–4.

does not seize here on something coming into the open that exceeds all determinate systematization, and that hence demands quite another sense of dialectic that eludes fixation in any determinate logic.

Hegel, I think, grasped the importance of the opening hinted at in Aristotle's point, namely, that there is a *determination process* more ultimate than determinate intelligibilities. The dynamization of self-transcending thinking has to be understood differently to think this process articulately. The systematic determinations of formal logic will not do justice to the process as other to fixed determination. A different logic will be required, a "dialectical logic."

Hegel confessed to being aided here by the Kantian sense of the antinomies. Kant himself says that ancient dialectic was always the logic of illusion *(Logik des Scheins).*[6] In fact, he misrepresents the variety of views of the ancients by all but reducing dialectic to its sophistical exploitation. Dialectic now is used by Kant in an almost opposite sense, namely, in the critique of dialectical illusion. Transcendental dialectic deals with the illusions that inevitably arise when, by means of pure understanding, we try to pass beyond the limits of experience. And yet transcendental illusions, it seems, are somehow unavoidable, never to be completely dispelled. There is something inherent in metaphysical thought that inevitably comes to such an impasse.

Here I see Kant equivocating with respect to what I call the *second* indeterminate perplexity, one that arises *beyond* determinate cognition. This metaphysical perplexity might be called illusory, if by this we mean its transgression of the determinate univocities of validated science. But this is to accept determinate univocity as the standard of what is ultimately valid. And despite the quarantine imposed by Kant's transcendental dialectic, metaphysical mindfulness, by the inherent movement of its own self-transcending, finds itself still and always perplexed by what lies at the limit of determinate univocity. Kant tends to see only an equivocity, or an antinomy there; he vacillates between univocity and equivocity, very often with a bad conscience, as I suggested before, for he could not snap free of the idolatry of the univocal determinacy. And yet he also had a metaphysical bad conscience from the other side, because as a philosopher he knew intimately the self-transcending of mind that inevitably served to carry him beyond ("meta"). Kant was tortured by being between two forms of

6. Kant, *Critique of Pure Reason,* A61, B85–86.

bad conscience: a bad conscience concerning scientific univocity and a bad conscience concerning a stifled metaphysical mindfulness. Of course, what one stifles can often perversely express itself in strange *incognitos* or secret disguises. Kept under wraps it outs itself in warped guise.

I think one can see the vacillation as potentially positive. It may make us think more intensively of the play of indeterminacy and determination, beyond univocity and equivocity. And in all fairness to Kant, he did seek something more positive here, though in terms of practical reason rather than theoretical reason. Kant's antinomies made possible for Hegel this movement into another conceptual space, and in relation to the opening suggested by Aristotle with respect to dialectic as a path to the principles of all inquiries. Dialectic, as Hegel understood it, is not mired in an oscillation between univocity and equivocity such as Kant displays, but shows a dynamism of thinking at work, even in this vacillating oscillation between indeterminacy and determination. This dynamic of dialectic is made possible by another side of Kant that also takes us to the edge of determinate univocal intelligibility, though here from the side of the self, and not, as in Aristotle, from the side of being. This is Kant's sense of the transcendental subject, understood in terms of *the self as process of synthesizing* that is prior to all determinate analyses and syntheses. This opens up the dynamism of thinking as determining activity within minding itself. In other words, the deduction of the transcendental unity of apperception is beyond a merely formal logical deduction, for it is a regressing movement toward what *exceeds* determinate form. This is said to be the source of the formal and the determinate, the source indeed of the formal intelligibility of the categories and their unification with the manifold of sense that for Kant goes into the constitution of ordered, that is, intelligible, experience of the world. Dialectic, as Hegel saw, must be newly redefined relative to this transcendental self.

Hegel expands the notion of dialectic immeasurably beyond transcendental subjectivity, yet the latter makes possible the transformation of dialectic and its comprehensive renewal. Hegel offers no static formalization of thesis, antithesis, synthesis (now recognized by scholars to be attributed to Fichte, more properly speaking). The passing of opposites into opposites is more nuanced. Nor is contradiction to be denied; it rather assumes an *enhanced role* as a way to truth. All of being will be said to be dialectical: nature, history, God. Hegel will claim to articulate the logical necessity in all this. He will offer dialectic as articulating the logic of the whole, the *logos* of the whole. The subjectification of being by transcendental idealism will be expanded beyond subjectivism. An interplay between self and other will be granted, and a recognition of the interplay of indeterminacy and determination. This interplay will be subjected to dialectical self-mediation. Thus there persists the heritage of the univocity of thought thinking itself, and of the privileging of the self in post-Cartesian, and especially post-Kantian, transcendentalism. Moreover, Hegel will continue to be an Aristotelian in that determinacy still wins out, though in the form of self-determination. He will forget the transcendence that Plato fought tirelessly to preserve and affirm.

We might summarize Hegel's account of the interplay of indeterminacy and determination in the following terms. What Hegel does is renew the self-transcending thinking of what I am calling "erotic perplexity." I say erotic perplexity rather than agapeic astonishment because Hegel's sense of the beginning is always that of a lack that must be progressively overcome by a further process of development. The beginning is an indefinite lack that must be determined in a process of determining, in order to be itself fully, and to manifest properly the intelligibility that initially is merely rudimentary. He recognizes a process of determining that we must grant in order to make determinacy intelligible, but his sense of intelligibility is still tied to the determinate. Philosophical thinking is driven by an erotic perplexity that progressively overcomes its initial indefiniteness and puts in its place greater and greater conceptual determination.

Moreover, the process is for Hegel ultimately one of *self-determination,* and here again the erotic movement of transcendence is evident. The process that originates in the indefinite beginning is itself to be made intelligibly determinate, but it is the process that *makes itself* thus intelligible. In other words, intelligibility is inherent in the self-unfolding of the process; indeed it is the self-mediation of the process. What is other is not denied, but rather otherness and differences are seen as moments through which the process of self-mediating knowing comes to be itself. Beings come to be themselves by becoming other to themselves, and what they become as other is not absolutely other to themselves, but is just themselves again in more properly articulated form. The movement is from the indefinite, to the determinate, to the self-determining, and then from there we move all the way on to the absolute self-determination of the absolute whole.

When I say that Hegel sees a movement from the indefinite to the determinate to the self-determining, I am simplifying slightly for purposes of highlight. A more nuanced view would run thus: from the indefinite to the determinate, to what I will call *exclusive self-determination*; then from exclusive self-determination to mutual determination; and then from mutual determination to what I will call *inclusive self-determining*. By "*exclusive* self-determination," I mean a self-determination in which the self is set against, or sets itself against, the other: it determines itself over against the other as an opposite. But by the nature of the case, this exclusive self-determination cannot be the final word, for the other is necessary to its self-determination; the self is as much determined by the other as the other is by the self; hence the move to mutual determination. By "*inclusive* self-determining," I mean the claim that the doubleness of self and other in what looks likes mutual determination is held by Hegel to reveal that both self and other are included in a more embracing process of dialectical self-determining. It suggests a dialectical inclusion of self and other in a more comprehensive self-determining process. Only the absolute whole is inclusively self-determining in the fullest sense. The absolute whole *is* inclusive self-determining.

This might be illustrated, for instance, in the theological articulation of Hegel's position. God must other Himself in finite creation, not to allow finite creation to be as irreducibly other to Himself, but because without God's own self-othering, God Himself as beginning is all but nothing. The creation is God's self-othering and hence not other, but the ontological mediating detour in God's dialectical self-mediation with Himself. This is the erotic absolute that is love disporting with itself, as Hegel puts it in the preface to the *Phenomenology,* and that later reappears at the end of his *Encyclopaedia,* when in a kind of lover's echo, he consummates the system by reiterating Aristotle's *noēsis noēsis noēseōs,* thought thinking itself.[7] It is not that Hegel ends with a complete table of univocal determinations; rather he ends with a complete self-determining that dynamically renews itself in beginning once again. Nevertheless, in the self-returning circuit of

---

7. *Phänomenologie des Geistes,* 20; *Phenomenology of Spirit,* §19; *Enzyklopädie der Philosophischen Wissenschaften im Grundrisse (1830),* ed., Friedhelm Nicolin and Otto Pöggeler (Hamburg: Felix Meiner Verlag, 1991); *Hegel's Philosophy of Mind: Being Part Three of the Encyclopaedia of the Philosophical Sciences,* trans. W. Wallace (Oxford: Oxford University Press, 1971), §577. The passage Hegel cites after this paragraph is from *Metaphysics* 1072b18–31.

the concept, there is the implication of a complete categorial determination, albeit in Hegel's own dialectical sense. This emphasis on dialectical self-determining is deeply continuous with the modern ideal of autonomy, though in this case the other or *to heteron* is not denied, but serves the fuller self-activation of an inclusive process of self-determination whose freedom, in the end, is identical with rational necessity.

Notice that in this account what I have called agapeic astonishment does not play the part it should. There is a dearth of such astonishment, and at best it is quickly transmuted into erotic perplexity, which is driven forward to categorial determination by a will (or *Trieb*) that is not unlike the restlessness of curiosity that wants to know definitely, to the utmost possible. The sense of plenitude of the beginning, the sense of the over-determined that also shadows the entire process of determination and self-determining, the surplus that remains even when we have attained an end of determinacy, all these play no part in the process. Were they to play a part, we would have to acknowledge an excess to being-other at the beginning that is never completely conquered by our conceptual mediations—not in the beginning, not in the between, not in the end. We would have to acknowledge a patience to the process that does not fit with the ideal of absolute self-determination. We would have to rethink the place that otherness plays in every process of determining, and hence in the very definition of intelligibility.

More, perhaps even intelligibility itself, might have to be seen as the daylight side that turns the face of lucidity toward us of what, otherwise and nocturnally, so to say, is reserved in a deeper enigma. The very lucidity of determinate intelligibility may not itself be lucidly intelligible in terms of determinate intelligibility. This very lucidity is perplexing and mysterious in a way that astonishes thinking into a different metaphysical mindfulness. We may have to rethink the claim that the telos of coming to be is that of complete autonomous self-determination. There may be a heteronomy, a patience, to the truth that is on the other side of all such autonomous determination. All of these possibilities are occluded just by the seeming success of the Hegelian venture. That very success is the death of what gives life to the success. For erotic perplexity and its dialectical completion could not be at all, were not the self-transcending of perplexity first precipitated out of the original agape of astonishment. The Hegelian success is made possible by failure to live with, and by covering over, the overdetermined surplus given by the beginning. Just that original agape is then made unintelligible by what originates from it. And the closure is not just the closure of erotic perplexity, but the closure of erotic perplexity to its own more original source.

METAPHYSICS IN THE WAKE OF HEGEL

What has the above to do with metaphysical thinking in the wake of German idealism, and relative to the equivocal legacy of Hegelian dialectic? I will make four main points in the four following sections: first, in relation to the continued place of determinate intelligibility; second, in relation to categorial reason and its perplexity about itself; third, in relation to what as other to reason resists the idealistic model of dialectically self-mediating thought; fourth, in relation to the so-called end of metaphysics.

First, one development of metaphysics after Hegel relates to a renewed emphasis on determinate intelligibility, only now understood in the light of the modern *mathēsis* of nature and the effort to define beings in terms as univocally mathematical as possible. This is *one* legacy of scientific enlightenment which can take a scientistic form. I say "scientistic," not "scientific," since we are talking about metaphysics, hence not science in itself, but a philosophical interpretation of science. Scientism is one such interpretation which is moved by the faith that all the basic problems will yield to scientific solution. Those that do not so yield are redefined as not essential, having more to do with the psychology of humans, or the incompletely eradicated toxins of past obscurantisms. Even if science is not now entirely comprehensive, science *will* be comprehensive.

We have here a *project* for the complete embrace of all basic questions by science or its methods. This project proposes a radical development of specific curiosity and its quest of determinate solutions to determinate problems. Anything that cannot be thus formulated will have to be excised, or consigned to subjective psychology, or otherwise rendered epistemically innocuous. Not surprisingly, most of what traditionally counted as metaphysical questions must here be consigned to oblivion, or the junk heap of history, or to the safe keeping of harmless, intellectual antiquarians. I see here a mind-numbing contraction of both astonishment and perplexity to definite curiosity and its specifiable problems. Positivism, in a number of guises, represents such a contraction of metaphysical thinking. Of course, on reflection one sees that this attitude is informed by metaphysical assumptions that are not correlated with curiosity in the definite sense it erects into its ideal of determinate intelligibility. This development does not lead to the end of metaphysics but to the death of metaphysics—at least for those who are mind-numbed.

Interestingly enough, Heidegger's view is in strange collusion with this "positivist" view. Heidegger sees metaphysics completing its destiny by its being overtaken by cybernetics. In my nomenclature cybernetics is a very effective form of the univocalization of being, and the confinement of mind to determinable questions. How strangely Comtean Heidegger is![8] How inversely Comtean Heidegger also is! We look at historical unfolding and we see the same, though the last judgment is not the same. Religion (the gods) is displaced by metaphysics, only in turn to be displaced by positive science. Of course, Comte and Heidegger have a different view of the beginning as well as the end. Maybe the historicist progressivism (not to be identified with "progress") is what might be found questionable in both. Heidegger erects this end in cybernetics into the destiny of metaphysics, indeed the destiny of the West as under the sway of reason. But it is not the destiny of metaphysics, nor of the West. It is one possible interpretation, albeit powerfully influential in modernity, which shortchanges the meaning of astonishment and perplexity, and the sense of the

---

8. I am proposing an understanding of metaphysical thinking that cannot be fitted into any *progressivist* or indeed *regressivist* model of mind. The former models are pervasive in modernity. Comte's triadic unfolding of theology, metaphysics, and positive science is only one example. I do not think of religion and metaphysics as fumbling ancestors of positive science, necessary relative to the childhood and adolescence of the race, but now thankfully outgrown. We are all sons of Comte in that we blanch at the accusation of *regression*. We find such blanching even in opposed thinkers like Marx and Nietzsche. Even critics of modern Enlightenment have not entirely escaped the progressivist model. Such progressivism only makes sense if mind's unfolding and deepening is determined by a telos of univocally determined cognition. Not surprisingly, Comte has a very negative view of astonishment. See *Introduction to Positive Philosophy*, edited, with introduction and revised translation, by Frederick Ferre (Indianapolis, Ind.: Hackett, 1988), 38–39, and my discussion in *Being and the Between*, 38–40. Descartes's view is similarly reductionistic. In *The Passions of the Soul*, part 2, section 73, in *The Philosophical Writings of Descartes*, ed. J. Cottingham et al. (Cambridge: Cambridge University Press, 1985), 1.354, Descartes says, and entirely in terms of the mechanics of movement of the "animal spirits": "Astonishment is an excess of wonder and it can never be other than bad." One is not surprised by Descartes's, so to say, almost "neurophysiology" of surprise and his association of the good use of wonder with overcoming ignorance and acquiring knowledge: "after acquiring such knowledge we must attempt to free ourselves from this inclination [to wonder] as much as possible" (sect. 76, 355).

overdetermined surplus of being going with them, and shoehorns them all over an epochal unfolding into the one mold of scientific curiosity. Astonishment and perplexity are more deeply implicated in the destiny of metaphysics, if destiny it has. But this is a destiny that does not have any historical telos in quite the determinable sense that positivism and Heidegger seem to suggest. I know there is some strain of lament in Heidegger's account of this destiny, since the completion is also a loss. Acquiescence in this interpretation, in positivist or Heideggerian mode, does not help us adequately to recover the promise of agapeic mind and perplexed thinking. And recovery is needed not least because too many of us still remain, so to say, Comteans in the closet.[9]

I should add that the above scientistic line of development goes hand in hand with an objectifying approach to things, and hence to a devaluation of being. Things are just there, neutrally there, homogeneous through and through. There is no charge of inherent value, such as would make us jubilate before the being there of beings, or celebrate the marvel of their being given. The agape of being has become the indifference of being, all

9. I find Heidegger less ambiguous in his 1929 inaugural lecture "What Is Metaphysics?" (see *Pathmarks*, ed. W. McNeill [Cambridge: Cambridge University Press, 1998], 82–96) than in "The End of Philosophy and the Task of Thinking," where metaphysics is forthrightly said to complete itself in the different sciences dealing with the different beings and in cybernetics. Thus metaphysics shares in the same forgetfulness of the opening of truth and becomes immersed in the things given in the opening, preparing the way for the ascendency of the sciences seeking completely determinate cognition. See Martin Heidegger, "Das Ende der Philosophie und die Aufgabe des Denkens," in *Zur Sache des Denkens* (Tübingen, Germany: Max Niemeyer Verlag, 1969), 61–80; English translation, Joan Stambaugh, "The End of Philosophy and the Task of Thinking," in *On Time and Being* (New York: Harper & Row, 1972), 55–73. What if agapeic astonishment and the second indeterminate perplexity are in another dimension to determinate cognition? Then they are beyond science at the beginning, and remain so at the end. Where Heidegger gives a privilege to *Angst*, I see his thought as more nurtured by erotic perplexity than by agapeic astonishment. Not surprisingly, nothingness is given more attention than being as overdetermined plenitude. (The latter is not what later will be called the "metaphysics of presence," which can be viewed, in my nomenclature, in light of an excessive univocalizing of determinate being.) The kind of thinking issuing from Heidegger's anguished encounter with nothing is somewhat different to what below I speak of as posthumous mind and born-again thinking. His sense of metaphysics in *Einführung in die Metaphysik* (Tübingen, Germany: Niemeyer Verlag, 1957), *Introduction to Metaphysics*, trans. R. Manheim (New Haven, Conn.: Yale University Press, 1987), has a strongly agonistic, polemical character. His later thinking, I sense, is closer to agapeic astonishment, though how one gets from *polemos* to *Gallassenheit* raises serious questions for me. On Heidegger's historicist totalizing, also on *theōria*, see *Beyond Hegel and Dialectic: Speculation, Cult, and Comedy* (Albany: State University of New York Press, 1992), 43–55. On Heidegger, *polemos*, agapeic astonishment, and the between, see *Art, Origins, Otherness*, chapter 7.

the more to make it easier for our calculative exploitation. The prevalence of this interpretation creates a kind of a priori attitude antithetical to fostering the modes of mindfulness that go with metaphysical astonishment and perplexity. I cannot argue the point fully here, but if we generalize this objectifying devaluation, I cannot see how we can avoid ending in nihilism.

REASON'S PERPLEXITY ABOUT ITSELF

My second point concerns categorial reason. Instead of an interpretation of the determinacies of science, I now consider a philosophical interpretation of reason itself. This too is a development of perplexity, but this time with regard to the status of reason itself. The thrust of modernity, on the whole, takes shape in a turn to self; but this proves impossible to complete short of the *self-critique of reason itself.* Let scientific reason claim cognitive mastery of the world of nature, there comes a juncture when *reason becomes perplexing to itself,* troubled by its own status.

Ironically, this self-perplexity of reason arises in the train of reason's self-apotheosis by the idealisms of self-thinking thinking. Hegelian system seems the consummation of reason, the complete categorial self-determination of erotic perplexity; but this consummation makes idealistic perplexity perplexed about itself, makes it wonder if its own perplexity puts roots down into something more original and darker than reason itself. There is something infinitely restless revealed in perplexity; but in the present instance certain potential equivocities in reason itself rear their heads. Most extremely, reason does not appear to be completely transparent to itself, despite the claims made to this effect by the idealists. Quite to the contrary, its self-transparency seems to be borrowed from a darker source that allows the lucidity but that is not itself thus lucid. In effect, perplexity turns into suspicion about the high claim made on behalf of idealistic reason. Thought thinking itself is shaken by the suspicion that it has given short shrift to what is other to thought thinking itself. The other to thought thinking itself calls for thought, an other kind of thought to idealistic thinking.

There is the further complexity too, stemming from the fact that perplexity proceeds by negating its present position and moving on restlessly. Perplexity signals a form of negative self-transcendence. This is just what Hegel puts to work in his logical exploitation of the link between negation and determination. Thus, self-determination works by negation of what is other to self, and the incorporation of this other into the embrace of a fuller self-definition. And, in fact, the line of development I am now examining is driven by the lack or negativity in erotic perplexity, but it has turned *against* the affirmative consummation claimed by idealistic thought thinking itself. For it is just out of its own sense of lack and negativity that transcending reason here has grown suspicious of itself. There arises a proclivity to skepticism whose energy is carried precisely by thought's power to debunk the limitations of every determinate position. I cannot state some needed qualifications, but perplexity here becomes a negative dialectic, in the sense of a negating dialectic. For it turns the same power that drives Hegel to his consummation against just that consummation and Hegel's own affirmative self-completion of dialectical thinking.

I am put in mind of some uses of dialectic by Marxists, especially the negative dialectics of the Frankfurt school. I think of Nietzsche and some deconstructive strategies. Nothing determinate can stand as final before the erotic drive of perplexity; every univocity of determinate curiosity and its solution seems to generate a further equivocation, driving mind on restlessly, without cease or peace. Perplexity grown thus skeptical and suspicious can issue in the torment of metaphysical mindfulness. But as with the scientistic development, there is a deficiency of astonishment needful to balance the lack of erotic perplexity. There is insufficient mindfulness of the overdetermined agape that is the original giving of being and that even in torment is still given. Were its givenness acknowledged, at least one might be given pause, perhaps even made to stop in one's tracks, and reconsider whether the teleology of minding is rightfully understood in terms of just the self-transcending drive of erotic perplexity.

In that pause the hermeneutics of suspicion would have to balanced by a hermeneutics of generosity. Without the generosity of being that is intimated in astonishment, the spirit of suspicion easily turns into a vengeance against the inflated claims for false autonomy we fear contaminating the idealistic self-apotheosis of thought thinking itself. Reason tears apart this, *its own idol,* but it is caught up in such a tailspin of negativity that it can no longer see itself as reason. For, after all, it is reason itself tearing reason to pieces. And perhaps this tearing is perversely with the intention of somehow finding a way back to the astonishing thereness of being. But the splendor of the latter is not best prepared for by this torture. There can be no regaining of contact with the sources of metaphysical thinking until that self-laceration rediscovers the origin of perplexity in astonishment, and the deeper source of its own lack in the overdetermined agape of being. At best this tortured way augurs a breakdown of false closures, but there is not always an adequate hint of, indeed patience to, a breakthrough beyond the breakdown.

DIALECTIC AND THE OTHER OF REASON

My third point is continuous with the second. It concerns the other of reason that cannot be accommodated to the model of dialectical self-mediation and idealistic thought thinking itself. Again the work of erotic perplexity is crucial here, coupled with an atrophy of astonishment. What I mean is that perplexity becomes darker and darker as its eros seems less and less fulfilled, and the more it loses rapport with its own origin in the agape of being. I stress that *both* astonishment and perplexity suggest that not all of being can be included in a complete categorial self-mediation and self-determination. But what remains thus not included is susceptible to a number of different interpretations. I cite some important post-Hegelian instances.[10]

We can think of Marx's invocation of praxis as a turning to something other to self-thinking thinking. We need a different thinking and praxis of

10. Since I am focusing on the equivocal legacy of Hegelian dialectic, I must confine myself to cases more directly relevant to that legacy. Obviously, there are significant voices in post-Hegelian philosophy whose importance is undeniable, but these too might be viewed in light of the terms I propose. I suspect that much of post-Enlightenment philosophy of the analytical sort either attempts to consummate the univocal sense of being, or comes to discover significant equivocities, revealed especially through that consummation. By contrast, as I shall indicate, a lot of post-Hegelian philosophy of the continental sort explores, sometimes revels in, significant equivocities following the claimed completion of idealistic dialectic. By contrast again, one might say that the classical American pragmatism of thinkers like Charles Sanders Peirce and William James is a distinctive mixture of astonishment and curiosity—astonishment before being, curiosity before beings and processes—and this mixture without the old European slide of perplexity into skepticism and nihilism. Traces of that slide are present in thinkers, like Richard Rorty, who claim allegiance to pragmatism, and yet who are marked by the infertile perplexity of the latecomer. One does not find the slide in thinkers like Paul Weiss and Robert Neville, whose thought remains in touch with an originating astonishment, without this necessarily being thematized.

philosophy to deal with this other, all purportedly beyond the comprehensiveness of Hegelian dialectic. The complexities of this view of praxis are not now the issue. Despite its claim to be other to Hegel's self-determining thinking, the view embodies its own logic of determination. So too it is not immune from infatuation with a productivist mentality, and the calculative technicism that is one pragmatic offshoot of curiosity and the urge to determination. Determination still means self-determination, though now concretized by our pragmatic determination of the otherness of material nature, by our imposition on the matter of nature and society of the supposed necessity of the communist ideal. The restless eros driving philosophy is transmuted into the revolutionary impatience that would impose its dream on the present, determine it in the image of the dreamt utopia, and thus determine the indeterminate. In this revolutionary, praxis-dominated determination, metaphysical astonishment and perplexity, once again, are given short shrift. Another kind of closet Comtean rebaptizes sociology (Comte's child, after all) as "scientific" socialism. Metaphysical astonishment and perplexity are especially given short shrift insofar as the scientifically enlightened revolutionary thinks just like the scientistic technicist that metaphysics and the religious are phases of the infantile mind, lost in the "mystification" that prevents our more robust, socialist determination of reality as *for us.*

Two other citations are perhaps more important, namely, Schopenhauer and Nietzsche. They represent developments of the idealistic completion that issue in its subversion. "The world is my representation": thus Schopenhauer in the opening pages of his magnum opus. Nor did Nietzsche ever escape the activist idealism of a kind of Kantian constructivism: no facts only interpretations; what is real is not given as real; what is real is real for me, is indeed my reality, the reality that I as strong interpreter, as ascendant will to power, impose on the so-called given. The philosopher of the future creates values, legislates to reality, he does not find being. That said, in both Schopenhauer and Nietzsche there is an other to self-thinking thinking.

Recall Aristotle's description of dialectic: dialectic offers "a process of criticism wherein lies the way [path] to the principles of all inquiries." Hegel thinks dialectically in order to articulate what he believes is the determining source of determination, and names it *Geist* or the Idea. I think Schopenhauer and Nietzsche can be seen to follow a similar path toward the determining source of determinate intelligibilities. But they will not name it *Geist* or Idea. Schopenhauer will call this determining source Will, Nietzsche will to power, or mythologically Dionysus. The notion that there is something unprecedented about Hegel's successors is overstated. They are doing what metaphysicians have always done, and not always with the great self-consciousness they have claimed for themselves: thinking the ultimate origin or sources of intelligibility. Still there is a crucial difference here. I mean that, perplexity having given way to a darker skepticism in the aftermath of Kant and Hegel, this origin or those sources of intelligibility are not themselves seen in the mode of light, or of intelligibility itself. Quite the opposite: the source of intelligibility is said to be itself unintelligible. The determinacies of univocal intelligibility and its definite grasp of things give way to the indeterminacies of darker origins and to equivocities of being, ever elusive to complete grasping. The other of thought thinking itself cannot be thought again: it is other as Will or will to power.

Consider Schopenhauer's discussion of the principle of sufficient reason. This principle, in one of its forms, claims that to every event there is a determinate or determinable cause or reason. Our specified curiosity can be answered in terms of such determinate reasons or causes. But there is another, different kind of question or perplexity: What of the principle itself? What grounds this principle? Contrary to the idealistic response which, in the end, will claim that it is self-justifying, that reason justifies itself, Schopenhauer's approach finally implies that the principle has no ultimate rational justification, because the ultimate source is not in itself reasonable at all. It is a dark origin forever on the other side of sufficient reason. Indeed, if there is to be any salvation from the darkness of being it must be by means of escape from this dark other, whether through philosophical or aesthetic contemplation or religious release. Notice in all of this that Schopenhauer's way of thinking is moved by a basic metaphorics of eros. His descriptions of Will clearly show this: all willing begins in lack and suffering; willing is originally a dark, insatiable striving, endless, futile. He could not be more blunt: the genitals, he exclaims, are the real *focus* of the Will![11]

11. Arthur Schopenhauer, *The World as Will and Representation*, trans. E. F. J. Payne (New York: Dover Books, 1966), 1.330 (§60): "Real focus" translates *Brennpunkt* but this also might be very literalistically translated as "burning point"—the genitals as the point of the will's

Like Hegelian *Geist,* Schopenhauerian Will objectifies itself in rational forms, which he identifies with the Platonic Ideas. But in itself, and unlike *Geist,* Will is not rational. Moreover, as expressed in human eros, it seeks its own eternal fulfillment of which it is eternally frustrated. Indeed this insatiable restlessness is an *eros turannos* (tyrannical eros), not an *eros ouranios* (heavenly eros). To my mind Schopenhauer's description of the origin is not informed by metaphysical astonishment, and an affirming sense of the surplus of being in its givenness. There is a kind of disgust and recoil at the ultimate givenness. (One is put in mind of Sartre's nausea before *l'être en-soi.*) Perplexity has turned into a kind of revulsion before the absurdity of being at its putatively most basic origin. Not surprisingly, our final response to its futility must be to escape it, or to extirpate it at the root. As Schopenhauer reiterates: better not to be at all, or if in being, better to be quit of it quickly.[12] Perplexity before the darkness of the original source of being turns into a nihilism, a nihilism to be overcome through negation of that same darkness of being.

Nietzsche may differ in many ways from Schopenhauer, but his perplexity was shaped by similar concerns. There is the exploration of the other to reason. There is the image, indeed caricature, of metaphysics as only concerned with the bright face reason turns toward us. We find perplexity, first turned skeptical, then turned radically suspicious, manifested in the desire to unmask all the (dis)guises of reason and find nothing behind or beyond, except will to power. There is the deconstruction of deter-

---

burning. "The genitals are the real focus of will [*sind die Genitalien der eigentliche Brennpunkt des Willens*] and are therefore the opposite pole to the brain, the representative of knowledge. . . . The genitals are the life-preserving principle assuring to time endless life. In this capacity they were worshipped by the Greeks as the phallus and by the Hindus as the lingam, which are therefore the symbol of the affirmation of the will." See also §20, where he says: "Therefore the parts of the body must correspond completely to the chief demands and desires by which the will manifests itself; they must be the visible expression of these desires. Teeth, gullet, and intestinal canal are objectified hunger; the genitals are objectified sexual impulse. . . ."

12. This is a statement of which Nietzsche also makes play in *The Birth of Tragedy* (section 3), in *Basic Writings of Nietzsche,* trans. Walter Kaufmann (New York: Modern Library, 1992), 42, reminding us that it expresses the wisdom of Silenus, companion of Dionysus. It is not insignificant that the older Nietzsche changed the subtitle of this book to *Hellenism and Pessimism* from *The Birth of Tragedy Out of the Spirit of Music.* The stress is on the darkness of being rather than its music. It is true that Nietzsche thinks tragedy can allow us to grant the vision of darkness and be also protective against its destructive danger. How it can be *both* remains dark, I believe. The darkness is more primordial and more ultimate. Our aesthetic protection is between two darknesses, both the same, and as the same they invade the protection and all is dark then.

minate intelligibilities and ideals as merely human constructs, all soaked in the mire of man's equivocity. More positively, we find a claim to release a more fulfilling determining power beyond these human determinacies. It is creative artistry that supposedly serves as salvation from the rigidities (for Nietzsche "taming") of determination (for Nietzsche "domestication" of the eros of animal energies). The tragic artist is he who brings us closer to the sources of being by bringing us to the determining process beyond all determination.

Nietzsche replaces the thinking of the metaphysician with the aesthetic celebration of the artist. Yet Nietzsche himself wanted an artistic metaphysics, not only vis-à-vis its human fabricator, but also vis-à-vis how we are to interpret being as other to the human being. Thus: "World—a work of art giving birth to itself."[13] The ultimate determining power, will to power, most fully expressed in art, is on the other side of reason, thought thinking itself, on the other side of the principle of sufficient reason. The end of idealistic metaphysics is the beginning of a new artistic metaphysics.

Will to power for Nietzsche, like Will for Schopenhauer, is beyond the principle of sufficient reason. It is something other to determinate intelligibility; indeed the creative indeterminacy (Nietzsche's "chaos") of will to power is what makes determinate intelligibility possible. In Nietzsche we find astonishment, perplexity, and curiosity, as well as a subtle play of determination and indetermination. We come across a strong emphasis on the equivocal as opposed to the univocal, and a kind of dialectical virtuosity in which opposites are transmuted into their opposites, and back again, and all of this without recourse to a Hegelian *Aufhebung*. Determinate curiosity is not enough, nor its problem-solving techniques. Nietzsche clearly saw the nihilism resulting from this technicism and scientism. Artistic metaphysics was his rejoinder to metaphysical perplexity, and it is in art that the agape of being is celebrated, if anywhere at all.

More so than Schopenhauer, Nietzsche saw that there was an affirmative excess out of which creative origination emerged. And this notwithstanding the fact that he was well aware that the origin of much human self-transcending lies in suffering. He knew this intimately in his own suffering and thinking. He was no stranger to the eros of self-transcending mindfulness and willing. Man is a being that must be surpassed, Zara-

---

13. *Der Wille zur Macht*, 533; *The Will to Power*, 419.

thustra chants. Yet I find him equivocal on the agape of being, insofar as this is assimilated to a certain erotics of becoming, agonistically inflected. The affirmative excess that sources origination is understood by him as being for purposes of self-affirmation. I do not object to self-affirming, but ask about its being sourced in a love of being that is not to be confined just to self-affirming. There is in Nietzsche no radical self-transcending that is released for the other as other. Creation comes perilously close to being a matter of just *stamping oneself on the flux,* and with the view to finding one's self there again.

While we can find an equivocal mixture of agapeic astonishment and erotic perplexity in Nietzsche, there is a side of his thought that remained an heir of a kind of Kantian constructivist idealism: the real is the real for me; and not as what is given but as what I make of the given. And even though Nietzsche (like Schopenhauer) so develops idealism that he dissolves idealism—for not only is the real a construct, so also is the "self"—he still remains captive to thinking in terms of an agonistic form of erotic self-transcending. As Nietzsche himself declaims: Become what you are! Indeed Zarathustra is made to sing: "What returns, what finally comes home to me, is my own self." Indeed he asks: "For me—how could there be any 'outside-me' [*Ausser-mir*]?" "There is no outside! [*Es giebt kein Ausser!*]"[14] A paradigm of *self-creation* runs through the entire enterprise. Indeed, the world is a work of art giving birth to *itself.* This sounds suspiciously like an aesthetic transposition of the old *causa sui,* a notion normally the butt of intemperate abuse by Nietzsche. I find that some descriptions of the will to power sound like Dionysian reformulations of Hegel's descriptions of the eternally self-mediating Idea. Will to power is an erotic absolute. Nietzsche cannot get clear to a more affirmative view of the agape of being, and with this its givenness as other to us and for itself, and not just simply for us. Nor does he see how we are for it, and not just for ourselves through its being as other. Perhaps the closest he comes to it is in the notion of *amor fati,* but this is hard to square with his accentuated will to self-apotheosis. *Amor fati* asks a release of selving to an ultimate other to self. The radical release of agapeic transcendence is not really understood by Nietzsche.[15]

14. Friedrich Nietzsche, *Werke: Kritische Gesamtausgabe,* ed. G. Colli and M. Montinari (Berlin: De Gruyter, 1967–1984), VI, 1, 268; *Thus Spoke Zarathustra,* trans. R. J. Hollingdale (Harmondsworth, U.K.: Penguin Books, 1961), 234.

15. See *Art, Origins, Otherness,* chapter 6, on Nietzsche's Dionysian origin.

Other figures than the above, such as Kierkegaard, or Heidegger, or Adorno, or Derrida, might have been adduced relative to the other of dialectical self-thinking thinking. All display some tendency to claim to think beyond metaphysics, for they tend, in one way or the other, to closely identify metaphysics with the Hegelian consummation, and believe themselves, and in some sense rightly, to be thinking a possibility that exceeds idealistic metaphysics. If they are right about the latter, it is questionable to identify idealistic metaphysics with the essential promise of metaphysical thinking. In the main, we often find a rebirth of erotic perplexity beyond the univocal determinacy of scientific and commonsense intelligibilities. We find traces of agapeic astonishment also, but since philosophy is often assimilated to the determinate intelligibilities of science, or perhaps to the self-determining intelligibilities of Hegelian idealism (as if Hegel filled up all the space for philosophy), it is not always granted that *philosophy* too reveals its own promise as a mode of agapeic astonishment. Traces of the latter may be found in religion, or in art, or in ardor for the coming utopian perfection, or in some undefined ecstasy of existence or the body or language or whatever. But to the extent that the promise of agapeic astonishment is denied to philosophy, the full range of thinking is not released. Without that further release, philosophical perplexity can fall away into an orgy of debunking before which nothing is finally allowed to stand. We do not come to the end of metaphysics; we *will* to end metaphysics. In the space left vacant by the whirl of negating, some opportunity may be offered for another seed of astonishment to sprout, be it aesthetic, religious, or ethical. But this is still a failure to exhibit agapeic mind toward metaphysics itself.

THE DEATH OF PERPLEXITY AND THE END OF METAPHYSICS

My fourth point concerns once more the so-called end of metaphysics. Perhaps what is called the end of metaphysics is the death of one kind of erotic perplexity, one that has defined itself in terms of an epistemic will to power that subordinates the otherness of being to the categorial determination of the human knower. But this is not the only possible development of erotic perplexity, nor coincident with the promise of metaphysics.

There is no end of metaphysics precisely because the sources of metaphysical thinking are in a beginning that always exceeds complete objectification. Moreover, the modes of mindfulness that go with the overdermined beginning also exceed complete determination. When Heidegger calls for a new beginning beyond the so-called end of metaphysics, he may be right about the need for something other to calculative thinking, and so beyond the determinacies of curiosity, but this other thinking is not just back there before Plato and Socrates did their "bad" work, nor yet before us yonder, in the coming mission of being. The sources are always here now. Agapeic astonishment and perplexity cannot be thought of as before and after a temporal span, since they are promises ingredient in all spans, and hence permeate the middle, as much as the extremes of the middle. The excess is as much in the middle as at the extremes, and it is this overdetermined middle we must think.

In other words, I am not talking about a move from the overdetermined to the indefinite to the determinate to the self-determined. I am talking of the overdetermined that is there always with all of these particular possibilities. At any point there can be a resurgence of agapeic astonishment, at any point there can be a resurrection of erotic perplexity. There is a second indeterminate perplexity that exceeds all the hard-won gains of determinate science, and that is not itself an instance of a new curiosity that will be answered for in terms of a further determinate solution. It is in another dimension, even while it permeates all the dimensions of the determinate. This second indeterminate perplexity that is not exhausted by determinate cognition drives the restless self-transcendence of philosophical thinking.

Is this all that drives philosophical thinking? I do not think so, though in some cases it may seem to be all that is available to a particular thinker. What I mean is that, finally, erotic perplexity is lacking just in its lack. It does not always comprehend the significance of its lack. The very restlessness it expresses is itself grounded in a prior more affirmative energy of being that cannot be expressed in merely lacking terms. The self-transcendence of erotic perplexity could not be the self-surpassing it is, but for transcendence that is more than self and lack. Lack becomes restless just because in lack there is an affirmative original energy driving lack out beyond itself. This more original source is, from the start, beyond lack. It is agapeic in the sense of being given out of an affirmative surplus. Lack does not exceed itself; rather the self exceeds itself as lack because already it is the promise of more than lack. Without adequate understanding of this, erotic self-surpassing can become a negating self-transcendence that finally comes to nothing. Indeed, it may be consumed by what it takes as nothing, not only the nothingness of things other to itself, but by its own nothingness. But all of this is to not grant the agape of being, and its promise, that is first granted.

In a word, we need the resurrection of astonishment. Of course, this is a poor way to put the point. For you cannot just say: we need astonishment, and then go out and find it, as if we could whistle and have it come. Calling it forth at will, this is just what we cannot do. We cannot will astonishment. It is a given. It is a gift. There is required preparation, waiting, purified willingness, opening, tireless thinking. There is a willingness beyond will to power. Self-transformation is called for but this cannot be a process of self-mediation only. Something from beyond self must be allowed to give itself, if it will give itself at all. This is all the more difficult in our time when the general spiritual ethos is pervasively pragmatic and oriented to instrumental problem solving. We give our concern to things about which we can do something, where we seem able to will it and bring them under some control. Since astonishment is in another dimension, we have to place ourselves, or be placed, in that different dimension, beyond all will to power.

METAPHYSICS, PLURIVOCITY, METAXOLOGY

If there can be an activation of a second perplexity beyond determinate cognition, and a resurrection of astonishment, do we then simply return to the purely indefinite about which, in the end, we must be mute? Must we then give up on philosophy? Would not this silence make metaphysics an autism of mind? Must we yield the field to poetic celebration, or the self-apotheosis of an *Übermensch,* or to religious decision or discipline, or to revolutionary praxis that would pour its flames upon the hated past, or to a *Denken* that cannot be quite specific about itself except that it will be different, verily it must be different? Are we too just singing that song, whether of hope or sorry delusion, who is to say: Somewhere over the rainbow . . . ? Can one be more forthcoming and constructive? Do these reflections culminate in the assertion of a something beyond and other, an "I know not what," as undefined as the proverbial *Ding an sich,* into whose empty space might be poured the most sublime thought, but also the most wicked?

These questions are questions for the full doing of metaphysics in light of the excess of being and the modes of mindfulness proper to this excess.

Let me not be misunderstood. My point is not the rejection of determinate intelligibility or of significant gains with dialectical ways of approaching the determining of intelligibilities. I do not want to jettison the determinate to proclaim the glorious anarchy of the indefinite that just in its emptiness can be filled in any way one wills. Rather the meaning of the determinate has to be interpreted, as well as the meaning of determining, self-determination, and the surplus of the overdetermined. What we need are appropriately rich resources of thought whereby the plurality of possible intelligibilities and unintelligibilities will make sense. Just as one must grant the lesson of those who insist on determinate articulation, one can learn the lesson from dialectic to be always on guard against an unnecessary "either/or." One might learn this lesson, not because we seek one all-inclusive totality wherein the different possibilities are to be enclosed, but because the very excess of being as overdetermined is itself plurivocal. The plurivocity of being calls for a plurivocal metaphysics.

We need not say this as camp followers of the latest post-Heideggerian, poststructuralist glorification of plurality, a glorification glorying in its hyperbolic antithesis to the alleged monistic metaphysics of traditional philosophy. We can say it in homage to Aristotle and his famous saying: *to on legetai pollachōs* (*Metaphysics* 1003b5). There are legitimate questions being asked in recent thought, but Aristotle's saying suggests some traditional recognition of the plurivocity of being, and not with the view to gainsaying the importance of determinate intelligibility. We can even see Hegelian metaphysics as peculiarly plurivocal. For there are many voices within the Hegelian system, as a quick perusal of the *Phenomenology of Spirit* makes clear. True, these voices, whether charmed or pressured by the hypnotic voice of dialectical logic, all transmute into variations of the same voice: they are the different voices, some more, some less complete, of the one seeking its own dialectical self-mediation in the others that are the one itself again in its own otherness. With Hegelian dialectic the plurivocity is *within* the system, but in such a manner that the many are finally subordinated to the one: the many are the self-diversification and self-return of the one. There is an interplay of one and many here, just as there is in any philosophy, including self-styled postphilosophical philosophies that pride themselves on being beyond metaphysics. There is no being beyond metaphysics in the sense intended, for the very effort to be beyond inevitably invokes its own dilemmas of the one and the many, unity and difference, community and pluralism, and hence is not beyond.

Elsewhere I have tried to say what I mean by a plurivocal metaphysics. Since my focus has been on the sources of metaphysical thinking, I offer a brief review of one or two important points, if only to address the charge of autism. I suggest a fourfold way to rethink the perplexities of metaphysics. This fourfold way is not at all indefinite but complexly defined by the univocal, the equivocal, the dialectical, and the metaxological understandings of being.[16]

Our understanding of what it means to be comes to definition in a complex interplay between indetermination and determination, transcendence and immanence, otherness and sameness, difference and identity. Very broadly and first, the *univocal* sense of being stresses the notion of sameness, or unity, indeed sometimes immediate sameness, of mind and being. Correlative to the univocal sense of being is the search for determinate solutions to determinate problems, impelled by specific curiosity. Second, the *equivocal* sense accentuates diversity, the unmediated difference of being and mind, sometimes to the point of setting them into oppositional otherness. Perplexity in its restless encounter with troubling ambiguities can be correlated with this sense of the equivocal. Third, the *dialectical* sense emphasizes the mediation of the different, the reintegration of the diverse, the mediated conjunction of mind and being. Its mediation, at least in modern philosophy, is primarily self-mediation, hence the side of the same tends to be privileged in this conjunction. Above we have seen how this leads to a strong stress on self-determination. Fourth, the *metaxological* sense gives a *logos* of the *metaxu,* the between. It puts stress on the mediated community of mind and being, but not in terms of the self-mediation of the same. It calls attention to a pluralized mediation, beyond closed self-mediation from the side of the same, and hospitable to the mediation of the other, or transcendent, out of its own otherness. It puts the emphasis on an intermediation, not a self-mediation, however dialectically qualified. Moreover, the *inter* is shaped

16. See especially *Being and the Between;* also *Perplexity and Ultimacy: Metaphysical Thoughts from the Middle* (Albany: State University of New York Press, 1995). Also *Desire, Dialectic and Otherness: An Essay on Origins* (New Haven, Conn.: Yale University Press, 1987), and *Philosophy and Its Others: Ways of Being and Mind* (Albany: State University of New York Press, 1990). The opening chapter of *Being and the Between* focuses, like the present discussion, on the nature of metaphysical thinking, but subsequent chapters give more and more comprehensive articulation of the four senses of being, both in themselves and in relation to the metaphysical themes of origin, creation, things, intelligibilities, selves, communities, being true, and being good. Relative to these considerations, what I say in the present chapter is just a beginning.

plurally by different mediations of mind and being, same and other, mediations not subsumable into one total self-mediation. This brings it closer to an opening of dialectic to certain ancient practices of philosophy, for instance, Socratic-Platonic dialogue. The metaxological sense keeps open the spaces of otherness in the between, nor does it domesticate the ruptures that shake the complacencies of our mediations of being. Moreover, it tries to deal with the limitations of dialectical determination, especially so with respect to the excess of the overdetermined givenness of being.

There is an immediacy to the metaxological, in the sense that it is at work before we articulate it reflectively in our categories. There is an immediacy to metaxological intermediacy. It is shown in what we might call the preobjective community of mindfulness and being that is inarticulately given in the original astonishment. It is at work in the univocal, the equivocal, the dialectical, but not known explicitly as such, and when stated exclusively in their terms it is distorted, because truncated. The metaxological is the truth of the univocal, the equivocal, the dialectical. When we try to articulate it, we are trying to find the right words for what is given in the overdeterminacy of the original astonishment. The other three senses help to articulate the truth of the metaxological, but we risk error when they are absolutized and claimed to cover the entire milieu of being. Our sense of metaphysical thinking must try to be true to the being of the between. Nor must it falsely claim to have the categories that finally determine what itself is not exhausted by any determination.

Does this fourfold mean we conceive of metaphysics simply as a science of categories? There is a categorial side to this fourfold, but this side does not exhaust the matter. While we require systematic categorial thinking, we also require a thinking of being, open to perplexities at the edge of systematic categorial determination. They trouble the self-confidence of systematic categorial thinking, and call for a different ruminative mindfulness. Metaphysics must find room for the thought of such limit perplexities, as well as the originating sources of astonishment that, in the first instance, precedes yet precipitates determinate mindfulness through which we become provisionally at home with the more familiar world. The fourfold offers an interlocking set of articulations of transcendence—both the transcending of mind, and the transcendence of being—and without the closure of either to ultimate transcendence.

What I call metaxological metaphysics offers itself as an unfolding interpretation, both systematic and ruminative, of the many sides of the plenitude of the happening of being, as manifest to mindfulness in the between. It is all but impossible for us to be absolutely true to the plenitude of this happening. Failure of some sort is inevitable. But this impossible truthfulness is asked of us, even if inevitable failure brings us back to the truth of our finitude. This failure may itself become another success of sorts, if it renews metaphysical astonishment before the enigma of being that was, and is, and always will be too much for us, in excess of our best efforts at conceptualization.[17]

METAPHYSICS AND THE OVERDETERMINATE

Again one can press the question: If the excess of the overdetermined is so important, will not every effort to think metaphysically always fall short of determinate scientific intelligibility? My answer is: it is not that metaphysics falls short of determinate intelligibility, but that determinate intelligibility is itself not the ultimate horizon on intelligibility; hence in the measure that metaphysics extends mindfulness to the ultimate sources of intelligibility, its thinking is at the edge of, if not beyond, the border of determinate intelligibilities. Without denying a systematic and "scientific" side to its concern with determinate intelligibilities, there is a side that is necessarily nonsystematic and other than scientific.

Is this to give up knowledge for faith, like Kant? Not quite: knowing for Kant is scientific, and faith is moral faith. But there are modes of mindfulness that are not scientific, and that yet are forms of knowing in their search to understand the meaning of these ultimate horizons and sources. And yet they are not just concerned with a moral faith, but with the meaning of being, and in a sense not reducible to scientific objectification. At this boundary the affiliation of metaphysical thinking with art and religion becomes more evident. So also does our dismay that in modernity so much of supposedly legitimated thinking has been confined to its scientific or instrumental modes. Art and religion are speakers of transcendence, and to their voices the philosopher must listen.

Does not this invocation of art and religion bring us back, perhaps

17. Consider Plato, for instance, as always returning to beginnings, and beginning again and again. Thinking may reach through dialectic a limit of determination, but failure of definition does not occasion misology, but asks for a further beginning of thinking.

unexpectedly, to Hegel and the dialectical determination of being? For, of course, Hegel places art and religion together with philosophy at the level of absolute spirit. I take this to suggest, rightly, that these three are in a different dimension to the finite sciences and the instrumental deliverances of the analytical *Verstand*. Does Hegel loom here at the end, as he has loomed for so many before us, in the end endlessly forgiving of our prodigal straying, extending to us a rehabilitation within the reabsorbing embrace of his totality?

One must decline this embrace. Why? Because Hegel conceives of the relation of these three in terms of dialetical self-determination; and so philosophy's attentiveness to these its others is focused on what they offer philosophy for dialectical determination. What I mean is that, for Hegel, art, while said to be absolute in content, is subordinate to philosophy in terms of form; for the form retains the externality associated with sensuous manifestation, and hence, for Hegel, just because of this residue of otherness, it resists the completion of dialectic, as he views this, namely, as complete self-mediating, self-determining thinking. Likewise religion, while said to be absolute in content, is less than ultimate in terms of form, which again is burdened with a beyond or transcendence that is not completely incorporated into autonomous self-determining thought. Only philosophy fulfills the destiny of the dialectical determination of being that is the self-determination of conceptual thinking itself. And so, as I said before, the plurality of these three is finally subordinated to the self-mediation of one, namely, philosophy as the pure thought that thinks itself, even while thinking its others. Art and religion finally cede to the sovereign autonomy of philosophy.

This is not what I intend. I agree that art and religion are not to be determined in terms of scientific objectification, and here they reveal their affinity to philosophy, each as in this other dimension of being. But I think there is an open intermediation between them, not a dialectical mediation which finally turns into a dialectical self-mediation of philosophy. This implies that just what Hegel takes to be a deficiency of art and religion actually reveals their fertile challenge to philosophy, and not the challenge Hegel sees, namely, as to how we must incorporate their otherness into the philosophical concept. Rather, just their otherness serves as a reminder that a sense of transcendence might be manifest that is not at all reducible to the self-determination of dialectical thinking.

Consider how we find something inexhaustible about the great work of art, and this is not entirely determinable by any finite analysis. We are shown the manifestness of just that overdetermined sense of excess, spoken of previously. Consider how religion can bring home to us the mystery of the divine in such a fashion as to make it impossible to think of the divine as the Hegelian concept dialectically disporting with itself. Philosophical attentiveness in the mode of metaxological intermediation cannot be intent on extracting some core of inclusive self-mediation it claims to find in these others, thence to jump to the conclusion that the essence of all three is dialectical self-determination, which *mirabile dictu* only philosophy truly instantiates and understands.

There can be in each an opening to transcendence that surpasses self-transcendence, for it is the transcendence of the other that is coming to manifestness, and coming to manifestness in a manner that also brings home to us that we are not the masters of that manifestation; for even in its manifestness, there remains an enigma and a reserve of hiddenness. Transcendence in being manifest is not deprived of its transcendence, a fact brought home to us as soon as we do make claim to have mastered determinately what elusively appears before us. On the contrary, a certain patience, indeed humility, is asked of us in face of such unmastered manifestation. Art and religion stand as irreducible others to philosophy that as others challenge, provoke, and rouse it from its propensity to brilliant but somnolent cleverness. The excess of overdetermined manifestation proves to be ever drawing of thought, ever daring of it to extend to the extremes, ever renewing of it when it wearies, redoubling it beyond self-determination and all its putative completions. It strikes us into astonishment again, disturbing the complacency of our conceptualizations with a perplexity that may be deepened but never will be totally dissolved.

In sum, while Hegel understood the affiliation of art, religion, and philosophy, his advocacy of the dialectical *Aufhebung* of the first two into philosophy proves unacceptably ambiguous. The signs of transcendence for him are finally but dialectical passageways on the necessitated path to absolute conceptual immanence. Moreover, insofar as the arresting enigma of beauty and God's transcendent mystery are subordinated to the determinate cognition of Hegel's logic, the resurrection of agapeic astonishment is blocked. What I find in Hegel is rather a will to fulfill the eros of perplexity in a complete self-determining *logos*—Hegel's own science of logic. Yet Hegel is inescapably ambiguous, even despite himself.[18] Something of the energy of transcendence in art and religion continues to live on in his philosophy, and so the latter continues to pay witness, sometimes even despite its overriding tendency to conceptual self-determination, to the second indeterminate perplexity. This is never completely determined, despite all explicit claims to the contrary. Officially Hegel may make this claim, but the pathos and profundity of his best thought rises from this other perplexity that his categories never quite succeed in subjugating.

Art, religion, and philosophy need not be metaphysically autistic: they can be attempted articulations of transcendence, and not either just of human self-transcendence. I am suggesting that each may signal a rebirth of mindfulness *beyond* determinate science. In mindfulness of art and religion as articulations of transcendence as other, the metaphysician must be, as it were, a *born-again thinker,* born again in this other dimension of perplexity.[19] Of course, any mention today of transcendence as other will arouse anxiety that we *backslide* to dark theology or some culturally disenfranchised practice. We will be irritated, not to say alarmed, with transcendence as other, as a threat to our prized autonomy, won so dearly in the teeth of the oppositions of wily obscurantism. We have set up our abode in the crystal palaces of determinate knowing, and the suggestion of an other dimension to thinking cannot but prove dismaying. We are happy in our forgetfulness of our first birth to being in astonished mindfulness. And we resist been reawakened from the sleep of determinate knowing. The dreamless contentments of determinate knowing are enough for us, and we spurn the suggestion of a further birth. The mindfulness that is *posthumous* to determinate science will make no sense. It will look like a ghost, a wandering shade from an extinct past. It really should not still live on at all, we might believe, and yet there it appears, walking abroad uneasily. Of course, it may not be a dead ghost at all but the living spirit that, even though deathless, must be perennially reborn.

In speaking of another dimension, I do not mean that agapeic aston-

18. See chapter two, "Thinking on the Double: The Equivocities of Dialectic."

19. Is something of this hinted at, for instance, in Socrates' nescience? Though he says he knew nothing, surely this is artful? Socrates knew a multitude of determinate things. Is not the nescience in another dimension, beyond that kind of determinate knowing? Surely his quest of the good cannot be reduced just to determinate cognition?

ishment and the second indeterminate perplexity about transcendence as other desert our middle condition. We might say they are *meta* in the double Greek sense of "above" and "within": beyond determinacy and yet at work in the midst of it. To do justice to both determinate being in the middle and transcendence at the limit, a plurality of ways of saying are needed. There is no one way or specific method by which the rebirth of agapeic astonishment is given to the philosopher. There is something beyond mastery about it. Yet it has been given and humans have struggled to name it and say what it might mean. Here religion and art can be not only two articulations and carriers of its promise, but reminders of what is easily overlooked.[20] They can keep its promise alive in the sleep of quotidian familiarity. They attend to the better angels of thinking. This is why they can aid thinking beyond determinate science, in the second dimension of perplexity, beyond the geometry of the intellect, and beyond the dialectical determination of being.

Despite our protections and resistances, agapeic astonishment will still strike home. It may come from anywhere, and from nowhere, from any direction, or no particular direction, to anyone, for any or no reason, at any time, or it may come and seem to suspend time. It does not have to arrange an appointment before it arrives disturbingly at our door. It gives its gift, and no preconditions are extracted for its offer. Its gift is what makes each of us to be as primally metaphysical. Again there is no question of turning our backs on determinate cognition. The very gift solicits our perplexity that seeks to make sense of this astonishment, the meaning of being as thus appearing, as well as the plurality of possible responses in the middle of being. Included among these responses is the specific curiosity that extends minding to the intricate particularities and ordered regularities found in determinate beings and processes.

We are impelled to think the extremes, but we cannot overlook the middle we must traverse to think the extremes. So far as metaphysics must explore the determinate formations of mind and being, it must respect the determinate cognitions of science and common sense. So far as it extends itself to the extremities, it reveals its affiliation with other modes of naming transcendence as other that are beyond reduction to any deter-

---

20. The point could be amplified, and I have made some remarks in a number of other places, for instance, in *Beyond Hegel and Dialectic*, chapter 2.

minate cognition, such as religion and art. Transcendence without determinacy deserts the finite middle; determinacy without transcendence domesticates the extremes. As this first desertion dissipates into an empty indefiniteness, this second domestication dulls us to the marvel of the determinate itself. As a thinker of the between, the metaphysician must be mindful of both determinacy and transcendence. He must make articulate to thought the ways of their metaxological togetherness. He cannot do this without memorial mindfulness of the originating sources of metaphysical thinking. But there is no dialectic to determine completely the refreshing of these sources. This freshness, arising always young from the unthinkable oldness of original being in its intimate strangeness, is what keeps dialectic itself renewed.

2 ∽ Thinking on the Double
The Equivocities of Dialectic

DIALECTIC AS PLURIVOCAL

Dialectic has a plurality of meanings which in some respects define the repertoire of possible ways of thinking offered to us by the philosophical tradition. These meanings range from dialectic's identification with specious reasoning to a method for dissolving specious reasoning. They include its all but identification with logic, as in the Middle Ages, and Kant's view of dialectic in relation to the critique of illusion, when reason strays into contradiction in treating of transcendental objects. They include the Hegelian notion of dialectic as articulating the process of development in being and in mind. Hegel's successors, Marx notably, apply dialectic to historical process, as does Hegel himself. Dialectic is viewed with suspicion, both by analytic philosophers who often identify it with specious reasoning, pseudo-thinking, and by many of Hegel's continental successors who are critical of its imputed totalistic imperialism, an imperialism also imputed to the entire tradition of metaphysics. There are other senses of dialectic connected to Socratic *maieutic,* to the description of the highest philosophical thinking in Plato's *Republic,* and to the diaeretic method of the *Sophist.*

I will be concerned with what I call the equivocities of dialectic in Hegel and his successors. Variations on such equivocity are not absent prior to Hegel, as I shall also indicate. But such equivocities have so significantly influenced philosophy after Hegel that one can say without exaggeration that contemporary philosophy is defined by such a pervasive context of equivocity. The point is evident with respect to continental philosophy. Variations of negative dialectic, even when not named as such, or renamed in other terms, define many modes of thinking, deconstruction not excluded.[1]

1. One might see the sophists in antiquity as making use of a kind of negative dialectic. They offered a dialectical *technē* in the services of any point of view, making the weaker appear

The current pervasive influence of Nietzsche is of paradigmatic importance here. Nietzsche was a philosopher of the equivocal, and indeed an equivocal philosopher. His writings are, as the subtitle of *Zarathustra* says, for everyone and for no one, *für Alle und Keinen*. One might say that equivocal philosophizing allows everything and allows nothing.

It is just such an indefinite ambiguity of "openness," allowing nothing and everything, that is so exasperating to more analytically inclined philosophers. What irritates and frustrates them is precisely equivocal indeterminacy in whose place they seek to put, wherever possible, the most univocal determinacy conceivable. Of course, it is a mistake to think that nonanalytic philosophy is exhausted in terms of an equivocal indeterminacy. For one thing, an interpretation of Hegel is possible, as I will try to show, that does not fit into these alternatives of merely univocal determinacy and equivocal indeterminacy. I will not deny certain equivocations in Hegel's dialectic, but our response to these need not be either exultation in sheerly equivocal indeterminacy or reduction to univocal determinacy. There is possible what I call a plurivocal philosophizing that is mindfully attentive to the many voices of being itself. Philosophy might have to be plurivocal because being is plurivocal. As thinkers we may need to give due acknowledgment to a multiplicity of voices to deal with the indeterminacy of being, now understood not as equivocal indefiniteness, but as overdetermined surplus that always surpasses our every effort to encapsulate it completely in determinate concepts.

Analytic philosophy, though it might will, or hope, to displace every equivocation with a univocal concept, is itself not immune from the return of the equivocal. Recent considerations, whether from within analytic philosophy as from outside, suggest the need for a greater pluralism in modes of philosophical speech. For instance, the question of founda-

---

stronger, the stronger weaker. Thus dialectic can become an instrument that might be directed to contradictory ends. Such a double possibility cautions us about the degeneration of dialectical thinking into a will to power to dominate the other or the opponent. This is a charge sometimes laid against all dialectic in contemporary continental philosophy, but the charge is too coarsely put. Dialectic was always understood in its own potential for equivocal employment. Thus Plato (when he speaks of *eristic*) and Aristotle (in *De Sophisticis Elenchis*) took pains to dissociate a free dialectical mind from dialectic in the services of will to power. This gives us pause when Nietzscheans tell us that all dialectic is only another form of the will to power, masking itself as pure and free of power. Of course, the great perplexity evoked by this double possibility concerns the seeming *self-opposition* of reason itself, and how dialectic might help us find a way through and beyond this self-opposition.

tionalism is just again the question of pluralism, the question whether the rejection of a univocal foundation leads one to a relativism that is impossibly equivocal. The best responses have tried to transcend these alternatives. While the question of plurivocal philosophizing is more pressingly put in continental philosophy, it cannot be deferred in other practices of philosophy also.

THINKING ON THE DOUBLE

"Thinking on the double" is a colloquialism whose significance is relevant to our purpose. A person who can "think on the double" is one who "can think on his feet," as we also say colloquially. The quickness, the alacrity, the very vivacity of thinking in act is here implied. One thinks on the double when one is confronted with a perplexity that might not have been anticipated according to a preordained scheme. One extemporizes, one improvises. One does so in mindful attention to the living perplexity that is before one. All one's powers are channeled acutely into mindful response to the matter at issue. Thinking shows itself as a living dynamism which, in the concentration of its attentive mindfulness, stands open to the living issue before it.

In important respects dialectical thinking might be said to be a thinking on the double. For its appeal comes just from its claim to be a dynamic mindfulness of the matter that is unfolding before us. It claims not to superimpose a system of categories on that unfolding matter, but to unfold in a kind of extemporizing conversation with that matter. This is especially evident when the dialogical dimension of dialectic is kept to the fore. The "*dia*" of *dialogue* and *dialectic* are signs that something is in play that cannot be stated in monological terms. To think on the double demands a dynamic mindfulness of an *other* that solicits one's response. It cannot be the monologue of thinking alone with itself, or thought thinking itself. That relation to the other will be in question below when I ask whether Hegelian dialectic displays a marked tendency to reduce the *dia* or "double" to the monologue of thought thinking itself, a monologue albeit said to encompass the whole. The question I will put is whether this *dia* has to be kept open in a more robust pluralistic way than Hegelian dialectic allows.

But there is another relevant sense of "double," one immediately recognizable to students of modern philosophy. I refer to doubleness interpreted in the light of "dualism." As we all know, modern philosophy has unfolded in terms of a set of dualisms, frequently identified with Cartesianism, though actually pervasive in the entire worldview of modernity. Modern philosophy not only unfolds these dualisms, even to the point of their final nihilistic implications; it also fights against them, seeking either to overcome or mitigate their consequences. Postmodern thinking seeks to arrive at a mode of thinking on the other side of such dualisms, though it has to pass through them, deconstructing them on the way. Hegel is "postmodern" here in an extended sense, insofar as all of his thinking is determined by the rejection of the double of dualism. Dualism for him is no solution, but simply the problem to which dialectical thinking responds and thus surpasses.

Obviously, there are crucial difference between Hegelian and other postmodernisms. The major one is that Hegel will surpass the double of dualism in the direction of a more encompassing unity that embraces both sides of the opposition. Other postmodernisms, in the main, refuse such a unity, but surpass dualism in the direction of an equivocal pluralism which is either supremely suspicious of, or outrightly hostile to, any claim for integral unity or wholeness.

Hegelian dialectic responds to dualism as a problem to be overcome. But such dualisms are themselves formulated under the sign of univocity: in Cartesian terms, thinking substance is thinking and nothing but thinking; extended substance is nothing but extended substance; the two are so determined in their own terms that no relation to the other seems possible. But this determination of dualism turns out to be equivocal, in defining the two in terms of their unmediated difference. More, this definition is doubly equivocal, since it presupposes some ability to speak of the two together. To assert that there is an unmediated difference between mind and matter is already in some sense to think together the two in their difference.

Unmediated difference cannot have the last word. Hegel will claim that these equivocities of difference have to be mediated, and that dialectical thinking does just that. It thinks on the double, thinks dynamically about the perplexing matter, which now itself shows itself to be a developing matter, not a univocally fixated stasis. In thinking on the double it sees that in the end you really cannot think one without the other, or vice versa. The thinking of the two together is more true to the matter than the fixed assertion of their unmediated difference. Classically the language here will be: the identity of opposites, indeed Hegel's famous definition of the absolute as the identity of identity and nonidentity *(der Identität der Identität und Nichtidentität).*[2] Dialectic offers a mediation of the equivocities of doubleness, equivocities themselves generated by a misleading will to fix the terms of difference into univocally congealed realities.

I note that this mediation is in terms of the togetherness of the terms of the double, togetherness interpreted as dialectical identity in difference. I beg excuse for the Hegelian jargon, but the essential point is that for Hegel dialectic will mediate a more encompassing unity that holds the two together. The two will not be only an equivocal pluralism; really the two will be two moments of the one encompassing process of absolute self-mediation. The double is the penultimate moment of the encompassing unity. Thinking on the double means thinking beyond the double to this encompassing unity, and thinking the double as not really an irreducible plurality at all. Plurality is subordinated to unity.

I take issue with this from the metaxological point of view. Briefly: While the univocal sense stresses the notion of oneness or unity, indeed sometimes immediate sameness, the equivocal sense accentuates the more-than-one, the unmediated difference of being and mind, sometimes to the point of opposition or dualism. The dialectical sense emphasizes the mediation of the different, the reintegration of the more-than-one in a mediation that is primarily self-determining, such that the inclusive one is privileged and plurality embraced by totality. The metaxological sense gives a *logos* of the *metaxu,* emphasizing the intermediated community of mind and being. Granting the more-than-one, it is marked by redoubled intermediation, beyond closed self-mediation from the side of the same, and hospitable to the mediation of the other, out of its own otherness. It keeps open the pluralized spaces of otherness in the between, and does not entirely smooth over the jagged breaches of discontinuity we sometimes come against there. In sum: univocity speaks in one voice, equivocity in a doubled voice, dialectic in a doubling of voices, for the *dia* refers us to a doubling of *logoi* in *dia-legein.* This doubling can tend toward the self-doubling of the one voice, but we need not close off the possibility that there is a doubling and redoubling of a plurality of voices, not reducible to one

2. *Hegel's Science of Logic,* 74; *Wissenschaft der Logik* (1832), 60.

single overriding voice. Hegelian dialectic tends to the first, while the metaxological not only lets open but requires the second. It is thus closer to the practice of dialectic we find in Socratic-Platonic dialogue. Because we see the *dia* as a promise of plurality, there is not simply one essential form of dialectic. The dialectical sense has to be itself *pluralized*.

HEGELIAN DIALECTIC AND DOUBLES

Here we may throw some light on certain equivocal doubles still at work in Hegel's dialectic, though overtly the claim is made to overcome their equivocity. For it is striking that no sooner was the ink dry on Hegel's *co-incidentia oppositorum* than the opposites began to pull *against* and *away from* each other. The magnificent synthesis of the system decomposed into a set of striking opposites. These opposites define much of the context of contemporary philosophy. Strangely enough, they also define the disputed terrain of the interpretation of Hegel himself. Hegel himself, it seems, turns out to be an embodiment of equivocity. I would not quite quote against Hegel the epithet of Nietzsche—that Hegel is a thinker *für Alle und Keinen*. But it is not inapposite, since in certain hands the dialectic can alternative-ly debunk everything, and just as easily canonize everything. In the first case, nothing is sacred, in the second, everything is, including the malig-nant horrors of world history. And both these extremes have been charged against Hegelian dialectic—or indeed celebrated in its name.

The equivocal double lived on in the Hegelian synthesis, and awaited its return. It emerged both in the decomposition of the Hegelian unity, and in the dialectical battle to interpret the equivocities of the Hegelian system. Those equivocities might be summarized in terms of four basic oppositions.[3]

The *first* doublet is: on the one hand, Hegel has been accused of "pan-logism," and, on the other hand, of being the progenitor of "irrational-ism" in his successors. One views Hegel as marked by an excess of logic, the other by an excess of illogic, masquerading as logic. The *second* dou-blet bears on the relation of philosophy to one of its most significant oth-ers, namely, religion: on the one hand, Hegel is excessively religious, to

3. See my editor's introduction to *Hegel and His Critics: Philosophy in the Aftermath of Hegel* (Albany: State University of New York Press, 1989) where I elaborate a little more fully on these four oppositions.

the point of "mystifying" the processes of reality; on the other hand, he is an insidious "atheist," equivocally masking his godlessness in a categorial system that seems to sing a hymn to God. Once the mask is taken off or penetrated, Hegel is seen to be the opposite of what he seems to be. What is this but the essence of equivocity?

The *third* doublet concerns the opposition, as we might put it, between foundationalism and deconstructionism. Hegel is seen, on the one hand, as supremely a foundationalist, insofar as all of being and thought seem to be reducible to one absolute principle, named the Idea or *Geist,* or simply the absolute. On the other hand, Hegel is said to be an essentially historicist thinker who deconstructs the metaphysical appeal to eternal foundations. Hegel as foundationalist is the philosopher of absolute identity, Hegel as historicist/deconstructionist is the first philosopher of difference, as the high priest of deconstruction, Derrida himself, put it. Hegel is Hegel, but he is also other than Hegel. Hegel is the first post-Hegelian philosopher.

A *fourth* doublet concerns the relation of dialectical philosophy to science and art. I mean the opposition of scientism and aestheticism that still defines much of contemporary culture. In the first case, Hegel is accused of being an enemy of science, for criticizing empirical and mathematical science, siding with Goethe against Newton, and for resorting to a priori reasoning in his philosophy of nature. Hegelian "science" is only metaphoric imagination. In the second case, he is accused of lacking metaphoric imagination, of not being sensitive enough to art, proclaiming its end, of making excessive claims for his science of philosophy as putatively subordinating art and religion to its own absolute comprehension. He seems to be either too scientific or not scientific enough, too metaphorical or not metaphorical enough. He is too much of one or the other, or too little, or perhaps even not one or the other. What strange figure is this? Is he not but a figure of the equivocal?

Given these four doubles, the suspicion arises that there is deep equivocity in the Hegelian system, which reasserts itself when concerted pressure is put on Hegel's claim to have subsumed the double into a more encompassing unity. Indeed, it seems we now live in the return of the equivocal, facing perhaps its *vengeance* against overinflated claims made on behalf of idealistic reason. We seem to have been living in the return of the equivocal since the time of Hegel himself.

DOUBLESPEAK AND SOCRATIC IRONY

Let us think on the double again in relation to dialectic. As is well known, *dialectic* is derived from *dialegein. Legein* is related to *logos,* and "to speak"; *dia* can mean "through," as when we speak of something being diaphanous, and it has a relation to the word for "two" (see the English *dyad*). One might translate *dialectic* as "speaking through" or "doublespeak." Today this latter word has pejorative connotations, but the connotations are not just historically adventitious, indeed they have a more far-reaching implication. Dialectic is a speaking with or through another. There is a relation to the other ingrained in its meaning. Of course, this relation can itself be double: that is, the relation to the other can be truthful or dissimulating; indeed it may contain the possibility of *both* at one and the same time. The term "dialogue" also carries related connotations; the doubling of *logos* in dialogue itself contains the above possibility of "doublespeak," and this despite the generally honorific aura that enshrouds the word *dialogue* in our time.

Every form of dialectic has its own potential for "doublespeak." Why? Because if there is speaking to or through the other, the possibilities of doubleness, in the sense of *duplicity,* are always ingrained in the situation. The "doublespeak" of dialectic is its own harboring of equivocity, understood now as a duplicitous communication, a communication that is other than it seems to be. This equivocal possibility of dialectic has always been suspected, rightly or wrongly, by many hostile critics of Hegel. But it is signaled more generally in the ambiguous evaluation of dialectic in the philosophical tradition. This, as I said, shows its meaning to range from the highest way of being mindful to the most sophistical form of specious reasoning.

Dialectic speaks to and through an other, but this speaking is double and potentially equivocal. I want to illustrate this briefly by two references. First consider Zeno's mode of thinking, Zeno whom Aristotle named as the originator of dialectic, a baptism with which Hegel concurs. Zeno thinks through the position of the other, in this case, the proponents of the thesis of the many. He takes their view, and by unfolding its logical implications, leads it to what ostensibly is an absurd conclusion. Thinking through the other, Zeno claims to reveal the absurdity of the opposing other's position. Henceforth, the field is made open for the opposite of the opposing other's view to come into its own; in the present instance, this is the Parmenidean thesis of the One.

We see the affinity of this way of thinking to the reductio ad absurdum, as well as to some strategies of negative and deconstructive dialectic. The equivocity of the *other* is said to be revealed immanently on the terms of the other; our dialectical reduction to absurdity of the other's speech allows us the thought opposite to the other's, namely, the thesis of the One. In Zeno the deconstruction of the "doublespeak" of the pluralists is taken to reverse into an affirmation of the metaphysical univocity of the Parmenidean One.

Quite patently, deconstructive thinking does not accept the latter conclusion. It rather wants to continue to live with the equivocity, live with it differently, without reduction to univocal unity. We might say it wants to live more "knowingly" with "doublespeak." It will practice "doublespeak" differently. It will equivocate in terms of its own living with equivocation, even as it claims to show the "doublespeak" of all other claims to univocity. How exactly the deconstructionist lives with the "doublespeak" of the equivocal remains equivocal, so far as I can make out.

My second example offers a different way of living with the double of equivocity. I mean Socratic dialectic. This shares much with Zeno's strategy, but it is not just a logicist reduction of the equivocity of the other to the univocity of the One. The "doublespeak" of the other as a *living singular interlocutor* is as much at issue, as are the more general propositions that he utters. Socrates too speaks to an other, and speaks through the other. He too develops the view of the other in terms of a logic that is putatively immanent in the view of the other. The insufficiency of the other is revealed when that view is shown to be infected with equivocity, shown to speak doubly. The view of the other is said to speak itself in more senses than one, all of which are putatively impossible to utter together. The surface of univocity disguises a subsurface babble of equivocity. Dialectic brings the babble to the surface.

That is, the "doublespeak" is not coherent with itself, and its putative intent to communicate truthfully; it communicates duplicitously, and so, if univocal truth is our ideal, it is in the untruth. But again it is not just the *proposition* of the other that is thus exposed in its equivocity. It is the speaker as other, as a singular self, who is being as much tested as his propositions. The other does not truly know himself, and hence speaks doubly, even when he seems to speak with singular self-coherence.

I said that there is a way of *living with* equivocity here. How so?

Socrates never conclusively succeeds in offering the absolutely univocal definition he says he seeks. More often than not he ends in an *aporia*. An impasse confronts dialogue; perhaps two ways open, and it is not univocally clear which of the two one is the choose; in the *aporia* the double reappears, equivocity returns. Consider, for example, the end of the *Euthyphro* where Euthyphro and Socrates simply go their own different ways. They remain double and other right at the end. As we say colloquially, and in more senses than one, "they split." Nevertheless, the equivocity that returns is a different equivocity from that with which we started. It can be more consciously known as such, even when it is never completely dispelled. This is why we can dwell in it differently, more mindfully. The return of the equivocal also means that in a sense dialogue will never be completed. There is no absolute univocity that will completely overcome the possible duplicity of "doublespeak," or that will conceptually exhaust the secret promise of philosophical dialogue.

There is another element of living differently with and in the equivocal which signals both the affinity and divergence of the deconstructive and Socratic-Platonic way. I mean the famous Socratic irony. Deconstructive thinking is quite akin to the spirit of a certain irony.[4] Irony is very interesting as an example of thinking on the double. All living irony has to have some of the energy of extemporization and improvisation that I said is characteristic of thinking on the double. Otherwise it is merely wooden and flat. The genuinely ironical always wears the stamp of surprise or the unexpected. The ironical mind has to be immensely attentive to the nuances of a conversation; and the response has to be marked by finesse more nuanced than the occasion that generates the irony. Ironical thinking always, so to speak, thinks on its feet. On its nimble feet it can also now and then dance, even leap. Perhaps this is part of what it means to philosophize in the agora.

While Socratic irony thinks through and with the other, it is not simply a celebration of the equivocal. It is not an equivocal living in the equivocal. Rather the irony is that there is something self-subverting about the sheerly equivocal; it speaks as if it were the truth, but speaks doubly and hence potentially duplicitously; but just the discordance of its overt claim

4. I discuss this in more detail (also with reference to Hegel and romantic irony) in *Beyond Hegel and Dialectic,* chapters 5 and 6; see also my *Art and the Absolute: A Study of Hegel's Aesthetics* (Albany: State University of New York Press, 1986), chapters 5 and 6.

and its covert truth shows that its truth is not really as truthful as it presents itself to be; its discordance shows its truth to be untruthful. It is double, but it does not really think on the double; it lives the double duplicitously. Moreover, because this truth is itself only equivocally manifest, it may not be manifest to everyone, and the duplicity may still appear as truth to many. It all depends on who is mindful of the equivocal. To echo Nietzsche a third time: Its truth may be for no one or for everyone. Or for someone else again.

I take Socrates' irony to suggest that he at least has in some measure seen through the equivocation, even though he cannot say this overtly or univocally, on pain of ceasing to be an ironical thinker. Socrates *must remain masked,* that is, equivocal, if he is to remain properly in conversation with the equivocal other, with the speaking of the other as equivocal. This makes the interpretation of his speech extraordinarily difficult. There are multiple ironies here, indeed equivocations on equivocations that tax our mindfulness to the utmost. The Socratic therapy for the "doublespeak" of the equivocal remains in some respects more enigmatic than the studied ambiguities of deconstructive thinking. More may be hidden there than even deconstruction could ever reach.

There is irony in the services of the hidden truth; there is irony in the services of the equivocal reduplication of the equivocal. The first seeks a truthful mediation of the equivocal in service of truth; the second mirrors in its own equivocity the equivocity it has claimed to unmask. There is no true reference to truth as other in the second, whereas the power of irony of the first is just its revelation of truth as always other to our complete mastery. The ineradicable reference to the truth of the other, and of the otherness of truth to our complete mastery, remains in play. But just that reference calls into question, again and again, the "doublespeak" of every and any form of equivocation, including what we might call the "noble equivocation" of Socratic irony and dialectic.

These are among some of the reasons for considering both Plato and Socrates to be plurivocal philosophers. The task of philosophical mindfulness is to interpret the equivocity of human knowing, speech, and doing, and indeed of being itself. Sometimes it is appropriate to interpret the equivocity in terms of its failure to reach a more univocal clarity. But this is not always so, and not the only requirement. There are voices of philosophical mindfulness that are not exhausted by univocity and equivocity. Sometimes the equivocity has to be mediated in terms other than univocal. There may even be ambiguities that, while being interpreted, are never entirely dissolved, ambiguities to which we must return again and again, once more to try to mediate mindfully. Sometimes there are univocities that must be debunked and deconstructed. The post-Heideggerian critique of the so-called metaphysics of presence, "logocentrism," rightly reminds us of this task. It errs in thinking that this univocity is the essence of the tradition. It itself totalizes the tradition as univocity, which it then totalistically debunks for totalistic thinking—a rather equivocal service, it would seem.

I have dwelt a bit with Plato and Socrates to suggest that the tradition of philosophy reveals a more plurivocal promise. Plato in particular is often identified with the fake univocity of "metaphysics of presence." But this identification is itself fake, insofar as Plato was a plurivocal philosopher. He says everything and nothing; he does not speak univocally in his own voice, and yet his own voice is sounded in the voices of the others who are his dramatis personae. Nor can we always identify his voice unequivocally with Socrates' voice, apart altogether from the equivocity of the latter voice. With a fourth bow to Nietzsche: Plato writes dialogues for everyone and for no one. We may think of the Platonic dialogue as itself a philosophical image of mindfulness that seeks to show the passage of truthfulness in the work of the equivocal.

Plato, like Nietzsche, was a philosopher of the equivocal, but he was not an equivocal philosopher quite as Nietzsche was. He dwelt in and with the equivocal differently. Dialectic is one mode of mindfulness that already tries to think beyond an oscillation back and forth between univocity and equivocity, while facing both of these fair and square. And as I said, even then there may be a recognition of ambiguities whose potential for "doublespeak" can never be completely extirpated. What I call "metaxological mindfulness" is another such a mode of mindfulness. Plato and Socrates themselves practice an open dialectical thinking of the equivocal that answers to metaxological thinking and its plurivocal thinking on the double.

I offer a final remark on deconstructive thinking. Deconstruction has made the claim that "metaphysics" is determined by a set of binary oppositions, doubles, like essence/existence, universal/particular, reality/appearance, and being/becoming. To deconstruct "metaphysics" is to think on the doubles. Moreover, it is to show a hierarchy of privilege in the doubles: very concisely, "one" is put on top of the "other." The "one" dominates the "other," and our task is to expose the subordinating order of doubling, and moreover to suggest that there is no reason to put the "one" over the "other." We might just as easily put the "other" over the "one." It might be "one" or the "other"; whether it is "one" or the "other" is perhaps "undecideable." Derrida will even speak of a "double gesture" toward "metaphysics." This thinking on the double, while implying that it launches itself toward a new, unprecedented thinking, seems to arrive back at a very old skepticism which we might express in the words of Sextus Empiricus: To every *logos* an equal and opposite *logos* can be opposed.[5] It might be "one" or the "other," and we cannot decide between the two. As we say colloquially: there are two sides to every question. This is commonsense's deconstruction of a too fixed univocity. Common sense also speaks of "having your cake and eating it too." This too is a kind of "double gesture"—a gesture very sound common sense most often takes to be an *evasive* equivocity.

But what if the deconstructionist thinking on the double is not the only one? What if metaphysics always was more than such a rendition of the double? What if metaphysics *always* was a thinking on the double, perhaps always the possibility of a plurivocal thinking? There would be no deconstruction of metaphysics, if the promise of plurivocity were always there, as I think it was, as can be rendered by a plurivocal interpretation of Plato as a metaxological, rather than a univocal, thinker. It may mean that far from a deconstruction of metaphysics, we need its *resurrection* in which the old, ever new fundamental perplexities are rethought again, beyond reductive univocity, evasive equivocity, and totalizing dialectic. This would be metaxological metaphysics. The elemental ontological perplexities will not go away. Indeed they contribute to the matrix out of which perhaps emerges something of the archaic notion of "*philosophia perennis.*" This will be dismissed as hopelessly old-fashioned. But the dismissal may soon find itself out of fashion, as thinkers tire of leapfrogging "metaphysics" into an "I know not what"—not into plurivocity, or communivocity, but into ever shifting Babel.

---

5. One is reminded of the doubling of propositions in the ancient *dissoi logoi;* of the medieval *sic et non* such as we find with Abelard; or of Pascal's method of *pro* and *con;* or indeed of Nietzsche's praise of his own virtuosity relative to "the reversal of perspectives."

THINKING BEYOND THE EQUIVOCAL DOUBLE

We turn again to Hegelian dialectic, now as a thinking on the double that claims to go beyond the equivocal double. Hegelian dialectic, as already indicated, can be seen as a thinking on the double, viewed as a dualistic opposition that has to be transcended. It is transcended, Hegel's claim is, for the two sides of the double are themselves self-subverting and self-surpassing. No one side can be so fixed in its isolation from the other. Rather each is defined relative to the other; thus the fixity of univocal identity gives way to a process of identity passing into its opposite or other. The equivocal emerges in the passage of identity, surpassing itself toward what is opposite. And this is a double passage, since the self-subversion and self-surpassing occurs from both sides. In echo of Zeno we might say: The one becomes itself through the other.

If Hegelian thinking on the double shows Hegel to be a philosopher of the equivocal, unlike Nietzsche, he would resent any hint of being an equivocal philosopher. Why? Not because he dwells in the equivocity simply; not because he is a Socrates/Plato who plurivocally dwells in the equivocity; but because he holds that thought, even as entering into the equivocal double, can also surpass this, and mediate its possible duplicity in an entirely conceptual way. In one sense he is like Plato, who did think that philosophy could mediate the equivocal doubleness. But there is a difference in their understanding of the mediation. This is now important.

The equivocal double can be thought through. Through to what? In Hegel the double is not ultimate, though it may be penultimate. What is ultimate is the exigency Hegel claims is intrinsic to thinking, even on the double; that is, that thought be as true to *itself* as possible, that it be self-coherent. This is not to deny a certain qualified openness of thinking to what is other to thinking, but for Hegel this other of thought is penultimate to the proper self-coherence of thought at home with itself. As he puts it in the *Encyclopaedia*: "For thinking means that, in the other, one meets with oneself."[6] Thinking on the double is thinking on thinking itself, even in thinking on the other. The double, between thinking and its other, is not final. The double is a mediating detour by which thinking comes to itself again, through the other.

6. Hegel, *Encyclopaedia*, §159.

In other words, the double, as thought upon, is mediated, but the form of Hegel's dialectical mediation drives toward a more inclusive self-mediation of thought. Even when Hegel acknowledges a plurality at play, his general logical strategy is to say that each of the plural partners at play, in interplay, are characterized by this power of thought to mediate with itself through its own other. So what holds the plurality together is just that each exemplifies thought's dialectical self-mediation in and through its own other. Each member of the plurality becomes itself a manifestation of, or prepares the way for, the more ultimate and encompassing process of dialectical mediation. This telos is at play from the beginning, and the play itself extends all the way to the end of absolute process, the absolute self-mediating totality. In fact, the end is just the express self-mediation of the beginning which is the implicit whole. Hegelian dialectic serves the articulation of the implicit whole. While there is a passage into doubleness and opposition, there is no staying with the equivocal as duplicitous. As mediated, it constitutes itself as a moment on the way to the absolute self-mediating totality. Thinking on the double must yield to a self-sublation double thinking into the one. In seeming to count to three, Hegel does not get beyond one, in the end, since the double is the self-doubling of the one, and the one as first is also the one as last, and hence we have not counted beyond one. Nothing counts but the one, the one counting itself as double on the way to counting itself as absolute one. So it is not entirely surprising that the final amen of the *Encyclopaedia of the Philosophical Sciences* is an encore that, in singing the Hegelian absolute, literally redoubles Aristotle's metaphysical hymn to the highest, namely, *noēsis noēsis noēseōs,* thought thinking thought.

This kind of thinking on the double is resisted by a host of Hegel's successors. Whether they remain devotees of equivocal doubleness, or something else, is a large question, too large for this space here. I think many responses to Hegelian dialectic are equivocal. In many cases, Hegel's conclusion is found repulsive, but the logic leading to it is not adequately comprehended, and as a result Hegel often has something of the measure of his detractors, and for no other reason than that he too is a philosopher of the equivocal. The same point could be made for Plato, with all due qualifications.

It is not enough to reject Hegel in a form that in the end is equivocal. Or rather we have to think on the double differently; and this also means making a response to it which seeks to do justice to the dialectical thinking of the double. In the long run, the strategies that celebrate equivocity with proper discrimination only evade the task of thinking the meaning of the possible duplicity of equivocity. I say the duplicity of equivocity. I do not deny that there is a fertile power to the equivocal, a doubleness that is not merely duplicitous. Put otherwise, the *promise of plurivocity* may be just that which in regard to the equivocal is most *engendering* for philosophy. An other thinking may be needed, to acknowledge the equivocal, as well as to think beyond its possible duplicity, a thinking beyond in both a dialectical and a metaxological sense.

In fact, this suggests another implication of those equivocities relative to Hegelian dialectic that I pointed out earlier. What I mean is this. Despite the evident heterogeneity and pluralism *within* the Hegelian whole, the whole proclivity of his thinking still exhibits a "monistic" emphasis. This is the traditional perception of Hegel, but traditional or not, it is essentially accurate. Hegel, adapting Derrida's phrase, is only the first philosopher of difference in a very equivocal sense.[7] For this equivocal sense would also hold true for many of the "monists" in the tradition of philosophy prior to him. So it is not very illuminating to call him the first philosopher of difference. Every genuine philosopher is a philosopher of difference. If you like, every genuine philosopher "thinks on the double." The differences between philosophers are in how they understand difference, not in the fact that every philosopher worth his salt is concerned with the problem of difference.[8]

"Thinking on the double" does not mean that thinking itself always ends up double. Sometimes it does end up a double-think in the bad duplicitous sense. Sometimes it ends up in a quite different double thinking, not at all equivocally duplicitous. In the terms I defend, metaxological thinking always exhibits a double exigency: to be as self-coherent as possible, as self-mediating, but yet also to be as open as possible to what

7. Jacques Derrida, *Of Grammatology,* trans. G. Spivak (Baltimore: Johns Hopkins University Press, 1974), 26.

8. It is not that we must necessarily eschew thinking about the absolute one. But I do question an absolute one, relative to which all finite others are mere moments to be incorporated back into what I called an absorbing god (in *Desire, Dialectic and Otherness,* chapter 1). Paradoxically, the one would have to be thought plurivocally and not monistically; the one would have to be a one that actually grounds real, irreducible plurality. In *Being and the Between,* chapter 6, "Origin," I try to give an account of such a one.

as other transcends thought. Thought must think itself, but it also must think what is other to itself. Any monologue of thought thinking itself, no matter how comprehensive of otherness it claims to be, runs the risk of not doing justice to this double exigency of thought: thought thinking itself, and thinking what is other to itself, what may indeed be always in excess of thought thinking itself.

I detect one of Hegel's most fateful equivocations in relation to the possible plurivocity of dialectic itself. Remember again the *dia* of *dialectic:* this *dia* might be seen as the harbinger of genuinely plurivocal thinking; but in Hegel's hands, it is the prelude to the return of thought to itself, to thought thinking itself in the other. Here the other is no ontologically robust other, in the end, since it finally comes down to thought itself in its otherness; hence the double is prelude to a dialectically inclusive one. Ironically, Hegel's own equivocation on equivocation is the prelude to the reinstatement of a *new univocity.* We might call this the dialectical speculative univocity, in contradistinction to the analytical univocity that Hegel, along with deconstructionists, excoriates for its abstraction of identity. Nevertheless, there is a return of speculative univocity in the end, and in a manner that compromises the potential plurivocity of a more open style of dialectical thinking.

THINKING BETWEEN THREE: ART, RELIGION, PHILOSOPHY

If what I have said might be deemed too abstract, let me conclude with an illustration in terms of what I always think is a test case, namely, Hegel's understanding of the relation of art, religion, and philosophy—a theme I touched on at the end of the last chapter. This is a triad rather than a dyad, but the relation of any two pairs, and of the first two to philosophy itself, can be shown to illuminate the point at issue with the Hegelian way of thinking on the double.

Suppose in this triad we suggest that we have a *community of others,* each with its own identity, but with an identity that defines it in co-implication with others. Suppose we say that to think what is ultimate (Hegel calls it the absolute, but we do not have to agree with Hegel's understanding of the ultimate), we need all three. We need these three voices to bespeak being as itself in excess of univocal determination. We need art, religion, and philosophy, each understood as its own voice, but a voice that can speak in community with the voices of the others, in order to be true to the inexhaustibility of being, and the otherness to our finite categories of what is ultimate.

In one respect Hegel would not disagree. Yet he would say that while each has its claim to absoluteness, the correct logical way to apprehend their relation is in terms of a progressive *Aufhebung* of art into religion, and finally of both into philosophy. This *Aufhebung* claims that what is essential in art and religion is not merely negated, but is preserved in the process of thought's surpassing of them. Philosophy conceptually preserves the essence of what is worthy to be preserved. Notice that the telos of this dialectical relativity is oriented to the end of philosophical self-understanding, self-knowing. Both art and religion are unsatisfactory because each has an inadequate relation to an otherness still not overcome, in the case of art, the sensuous otherness of the medium of expression, in the case of religion, the representational otherness that tends to define the divine as a *Jenseits,* a transcendence set in dualistic opposition to immanence.

Notice there is a thinking on the double here, but the double is superseded in the final form of philosophical self-knowing, where thinking is absolutely adequate to *itself,* all otherness having being dialectically superseded and appropriated. It is at the end that the Hegelian hymn to the dialectically self-mediating One is sung: thought thinking itself. The equivocities of Hegelian dialectic yield to the speculative univocity of the absolute One at home with itself. And I do not forget the plurality that is *in* the system; but that is not at the height, the acme, of the truest thought, the thought of the absolute. Hegel is a speculative-dialectical Spinozist.

Metaxological philosophy thinks otherwise on the double and the relativities than does Hegelian dialectic. It seeks to be a plurivocal philosophizing. There is a community between art, religion, and philosophy, but the meaning of that community cannot be exhaustively rendered in the language of a dialectically self-mediating whole. The differences of the voices in interplay remain, indeed they are absolutely necessary as *other to each other* for their community at all to be a community. Plurivocal philosophizing must listen to the voices of these others, and not simply reformulate their voices in terms of its own more familiar voice. Or rather its own voice must be willing to revoice itself under the impact of hearing the voices of these others. And this revoicing of the other must strive to be as true to the otherness of the other voices as is possible.

The plurivocal philosopher does not stand on the top of the pyramid majestically surveying the others beneath him, satisfied in his own self-completion, as if he had, as we say "eaten all the cream" of the others. Quite the contrary, the voice of such philosophizing takes shape in the middle: between itself and art, between itself and religion. It always thinks in, inhabits, this between. In this between it tries to think on the double by remaining true to the double exigency of thought: thought must think itself, and thought must think what is other to thought, even when that exceeds its present determinate thought forms. It is because of the second exigency of the double that there is no closure to the self-transcending movement of thinking. There are voices for thought that are in excess of thought at home with itself.

Plurivocal philosophizing relates to that otherness differently. It does not reduce the double to univocity; it does not merely celebrate the equivocal, though it does acknowledge that one must dwell deeply with the equivocal, if one is to glean from it its elusive truth; nor does it dialectically sublate the double into the one self-mediating totality. It seeks to think on the double beyond reductive univocity, duplicitous equivocity, self-sublating dialectic. Where univocity fixes falsely, it releases; where equivocity dissipates dubiously, it recovers; where dialectic falsely recovers, it exceeds, releasing thinking anew for what is other to self-thinking. It learns from univocity the need to be as appropriately determinate as possible; it learns from equivocity the unavoidability of certain recalcitrant indeterminacies; it learns from dialectic the need to mediate the indefinites, and indeed to self-mediate. But it exceeds all, in opening to the overdetermined otherness of being as beyond our thought.

Art and religion offer us two voices of that transcendence. Plurivocal philosophy listens to their voices. Like Hegel, it rethinks identity and difference, sameness and otherness. Unlike Hegel, and like many of his critics, it gives a stronger emphasis to difference and otherness than Hegel does. Like Hegel, and unlike some of these critics, it acknowledges the inescapability of some mediation. But unlike Hegel, it denies that the mediation of the Hegelian dialectic exhausts the promise of mediation. There is a more open dialectic; and the form of self-mediation does not exhaust mediation. There is an *intermediation* between philosophy and its others that is not reduced to the self-mediation of philosophy with itself. Once again, the meaning of the *inter,* the between, the *metaxu* is what is in question. In this intermediation, and its rethinking of identity and difference, we need systematic philosophy. But system is not intended as a closed set of formal categories. System is open, open indeed to the nonsystematic that lies at its limit, or that nests in the forgotten origins of its own categories.

It is especially relative to the latter that the voices of art and religion should be heard. For they remind us that the plurivocal thinking of philosophy is not self-produced, *à la* idealist or transcendentalist. It has its origin in what is other to its own categories. Its own voice is in debt to the voices of others, which too often it forgets ungratefully or hides shamefully. The hermeneutics of suspicion has to be transcended, for it sometimes strikes one as informed by shame before an other it would expose and indict. It proclaims itself as open to the other, but when a putatively dubious other comes within the range of its evil eye, the good of that other is doomed to debunking. Criticism of the other has to be formed and reformed out of a hermeneutics of generosity. The other is not always either the duplicitous other, or the dualistic other. It may be the other without whose voice I myself would have no voice. Plurivocity can be a communivocity, just as philosophical mindfulness can be agapeic. Philosophizing, even in the utmost of its troubled perplexity, can still be an act of gratitude.

3 ∽ Surplus Immediacy, Metaphysical Thinking, and the Defect(ion) of Hegel's Concept

SURPLUS IMMEDIACY AND THE MATRIX OF THOUGHT

We come across the notion of the "imaginative universal" *(universale fantastico)* in Vico, and initially one might think that it has only a minor importance for metaphysical thinking. After all, it bears more on *mythos* rather than on *logos,* on imagination rather than reason, on pictures rather than concepts, on intuitive immediacy rather than discursive mediation. Yet there is more to be said for it than this alone. One might ask if it has significance for the very matrix of metaphysical thinking; ask if and how this imaginative mother of thought is inherited in the practices of her children, her offspring metaphysics included. Some offspring repudiate their progenitor, some maintain fidelity to, indeed love for, their engendering origin. Here I want to reflect on this engendering origin as more in the nature of a given happening than a constructed result, a happening that asks of us a mindfulness steeped in its own proper fidelity to being as given to be. This being given to be comes to utterance in the imaginative universal before it does in the rational concept. Has metaphysical thinking, as first philosophy, have anything to do with such first utterances? Must metaphysical thinking be referred back to a more original birth in an imaginative mother to whom there is to be a family fidelity, a *pietas* of reflection, more elemental than rational conceptualization and more outliving than conceptual systematization?

For Vico our humanity is emergent from more feral conditions and is first enveloped by what he calls the "barbarism of the senses" *(la barbarie del senso).* We become properly human with the thunderbolt of Jove which lights up the sky and shows the difference of earth and heaven. In this first emergence Jove is named in terms of the "imaginative universal."[1] Imaginative universals are thus bound up with original sacred differentiation and the first naming of humans, and while this is mythological rather than conceptual, it is decisive for us in constituting the kinds of beings we are. Moreover, the first humans were poets and the first poets were theological. Prose comes later, as also do the intelligible universals of more reflective and rational thought. What is the relation of these intelligible universals to the imaginative? What is the relation of thought to the given happening of being as sensuous, as aesthetic? It is just a supersession of its immediacy, its replacement with univocal concepts or theories, or its dialectical *Aufhebung* with speculative universals?

Clearly the Hegelian response moves in this latter direction. Though this supersession is not intended as just a mere negation, yet the "setup" governing Hegelian thought is such that sensuous immediacy as such must be superseded, must be more universally mediated. There is no maternal piety in Hegel's practice of metaphysics. I recall a very good question posed by Cassirer about Hegel's beginning of the *Phenomenology*: Why did he not begin with myth as closer to the more original matrix of imaginative articulation and understanding? Myth, in the above Vichian sense, might be said to be far more intimate with the origin than the epistemic gestalt of "sense-certainty" with which Hegel begins his quest for absolute knowing.[2] One has the suspicion that his beginning is already an

1. Giambattista Vico, *The New Science of Giambattista Vico,* abridged translation of the third edition (1744), by Thomas Goddard Bergin and Max Harold Fisch (Ithaca, N.Y.: Cornell University Press, 1970), §§377–84.

2. Donald Verene in his recent *Hegel's Absolute: An Introduction to Reading the "Phenomenology of Spirit"* (Albany: State University of New York Press, 2007), 42–43, reminds us of this point. The present reflections are composed with respect for and gratitude to Verene who helped open my eyes to Vico's inspiring work and the importance of the imaginative universal. I well remember, while doing doctoral work, being a member of a small group of Vico's admirers who would meet, almost as a secret sect, and with Donald Verene as our guide, to study and enjoy the *Scienza Nuova.* Vico, I found, was the kind of thinker, perhaps like Plato, who becomes a companion and inspirer, even while not necessarily being for one an "object" of scholarly research. Verene has also awakened us to the philosophical importance of images in Hegel, and especially his *Phenomenology.* See his *Hegel's Recollection: A Study of Images in the Phenomenology of Spirit* (Albany: State University of New York Press, 1985). He offers us a more winged Hegel than the usual commentary. This is a "Hegel" to whom, I think, Hegel himself came to *play false.* As Verene remarks: "There is nothing like Vico's 'poetic wisdom' *(sapienza poetica)* in Hegel" (*Hegel's Absolute,* 43). Vico not only gives our imagination wings, as Joyce said, but also had more wings than Hegel, whose version of speculative reason betrays what I would call the intimate strangeness of being. A properly winged philosophical imagination knows this intimacy and this strangeness. Reading Vico one feels that something beyond the circle of thought thinking itself is always on the verge of breaking through, whether from

epistemological "setup" oriented to the telos of the *Phenomenology*—absolute knowing as that form of self-consciousness or spirit where knowing no longer needs to go beyond itself. Hegel's beginning is *already belated*, in being "set up" in light of a version of the intelligible universal that will make no ultimate reference to anything beyond its conceptual mediation. The overdeterminacy, the "too-muchness," of the beginning counts more as an indeterminacy to be made more conceptually determinate and self-determining rather than an astonishingly rich matrix in which all thought germinates, which endows all thought, and which no thought of ours can exhaust.

Hegel is a philosopher of the intelligible universal, and while one might not quarrel with that per se, one does ask about his version of the intelligible universal, and whether he has a subtle enough feel for what might be entailed by a metaphysics of the imaginative universal. If my reflections here have a more Vichian than Hegelian stamp, they concern whether Hegel's concept, hence his whole practice of philosophical thinking, shows a defection from what the happening of immediacy shows or communicates. My question will be: Is there a fullness to the givenness of immediacy which asks more of philosophy than Hegel's concept can give, something more intimated in its own way, for instance, in Vico's imaginative universal? Is there, so to say, a maternal surplus to the immediacy of givenness that allows and asks for a plurivocal articulation? Does this surplus immediacy perhaps testify to *the intimate universal,* in which the imaginative and the intelligible universals both participate, an intimate universal of which a metaxological mindfulness is asked of us.

My concern is not the exegesis of Hegel but an exploration of how metaphysical thinking might relate to its nurturing matrix, and this at two extremes: at the elemental extreme, where being as given shows itself as aesthetic happening; at the more articulated extreme, where our sense for being at all, and our own participation in the happening of being, finds expression in the rich significance of works of art and the enigmatic communications of being religious. Relevantly, Vico's philosophy of myth has illuminating implications for both these extremes: at our beginning, the elemental sensuousness, at the other end, the poetic intermedium of our lives, exterior and interior, and our religious reverence for the superior.

---

sources more deeply immanent in the human soul itself, or from powers or happenings that exceed the capacity of any determinate or determining concept.

Relative to the elemental level, first I will offer a brief interpretation and criticism of the Hegelian approach to immediacy. Hegel has a rather negative view of immediacy as in itself a mere indeterminacy. Conceptual thought mediates this indeterminacy of immediacy, and only when this mediation has been effected can claims be made to categorial intelligibility. In itself, and taken for itself, immediacy seems to be equated with a defective condition. I would put it otherwise, and this will be my second concern. There is no adequate sense in Hegel of what I have called "surplus immediacy"—a sense of rich givenness that precedes the determinations of conceptual thought, and that also exceeds claims to completely subject what is given to the categorial determinations of philosophy. Surplus immediacy is overdetermined. Moreover, there is such an ontological surplus not only in the dimension of the exterior but also of the superior—as true religious reverence teaches us.

These points are general, but I will develop them with some more definite reference, both at the elemental and the more ultimate level. With respect to the first, I will say something about sense immediacy, preferring as I do to speak in terms of aesthetic happening, and relating this to the general orientation revealed by Hegel's conceptual approach in the *Phenomenology*. If there is a significant sense of surplus immediacy, with relation to what I will call the *passio essendi*, "the passion of being," we will not be able to endorse the strategy of Hegel. While not defective in asking for determinate thought, this strategy does defect from the ontological fullness of aesthetic happening and the full requirement of thinking, in light of the surplus of immediacy.

With respect to the second, the more ultimate level, I will remark on art and religion, the two other domains which, along with philosophy, Hegel significantly assigns to the realm of what he calls "absolute spirit." My aim will be to suggest that something is given and at work that exceeds the terms of Hegel's philosophical assignment. *Relative to art:* The immediacy of art evidences something of this surplus immediacy, indeed otherness that still cannot be determined in terms of a thinking that would be absolutely self-determining. *Relative to being religious:* while many important issues arise here, especially in connection with religious otherness and transcendence, I will offer some words about what might be communicated in terms of a crucial instance of religious surplus immediacy: the happening of prayer.

GIVEN HAPPENING AND THINKING

One might say that immediacy has been taken to present something like the following general problem for philosophy: when we are, we seem simply to exist or experience; when we think, a "distance" or difference is introduced that moves us away from existing or experiencing, simply as being or undergone. That distancing or difference can be taken as expressing the difficulty. We seem forced into an "either/or" that is insurmountable. We exist, and we participate in a happening of being that is prior to and other to thought. We think, and we have immediately lost touch with this happening qua happening, immediately deserted immediacy by resort to mediating thought. It seems we must chose one or the other: either the happening of being and its immediacy, or the truth of thought and its mediation.

It would be simple-minded to grant that this "either/or" is, or can be, the last word. It cannot be from the standpoint of the happening, since it is this itself, and our perplexity about it, that moves us "away" from it into thought. It cannot be the last word from the side of thinking, since thinking may well be the desire for the articulated truth of the happening of immediacy itself. Either immediacy or thought? Plump for immediacy, do we have to sacrifice mindfulness? Chose thought, has mind destined itself to abstraction and emptiness? It is fair to say, I think, that most philosophers have refused that choice, though again most have refused it in the name of thought, and the best in the name of a thinking that is not simple-minded, but that in a variety of registers tries to seek the truth of the happening of immediacy, seek even the truth in the immediacy itself.

I agree it is simple-minded to insist on an "either/or" here. Yet, there is not any *one* simple relation between the happening of immediacy and the truth of thought. There are a number of possible relations. Indeed, depending on the kind of immediacy that is happening, the form of that relation will be different, as well as the kind of being truthful that is called forth by the happening. I say this because we are tempted to think of some *one big problem* of immediacy and thought. In fact, there are important and indispensable plurivocities to both the happening and the thinking, and the relations between the two, some of which are subtle and need discerning discriminations.

Of course, one of the classical places for discussion of the issue bears on *sense experience,* as if that were paradigmatic for the happening of immediacy. Thus, for instance, the empiricist doctrine of impressions—they strike us with vivacity and power, and lie outside the power of our complete voluntary deliberations. This "being beyond us," in striking us with an intrusive, even overwhelming, impressiveness, is often taken as close to what is paradigmatic for the happening of immediacy. Notice too how "ideas" are described by empiricists like Locke and Hume: mere *pale* images or copies of impressions, as if they were the *defective* versions of the immediacy. I am not endorsing that form of empiricism, though it does give voice to an important sense of contrast. I think this form of empiricism may well turn out to focus on one of the more crude forms of the happenings of immediacy, which is not to discount immense subtlety in aesthetic immediacy, as I will suggest. But there may be other happenings of immediacy that are simply not attended to, if we focus all our attentions, or our primary ones, on the sensuous, and in the terms that certain kinds of empiricism dictate.

The most important point, I think, is to negotiate the "either/or" without softening the demands made by the terms in contrast, and not by either an abdication of thought to the happening of immediacy, or an infidelity to that immediacy by abstract or dictatorial thought. This applies both to aesthetic being and mediating reflection. And it may turn out that it is a question of something that is prior to, that takes precedent to this "either/or"—something more original and preceding, something more ultimate and exceeding.

AESTHETIC HAPPENING AND HEGEL

You might rightly ask: Does not Hegel already provide us with the successful negotiation of philosophy beyond this "either/or"? Does not his version of speculative dialectic not only reject the "either/or," but offer the affirmative resolution in a sublating "both/and"? We need not choose because thought attains the truth of immediacy; thought is the mediated truth of the happening of immediacy, without which the happening itself is just happening and not truth at all: a mere lacking "that it is," or empty being.

I grant something like the desideratum of Hegel to do justice to both, but deny that his understanding of immediacy, and also his articulation of the character of thought, do the justice that is asked of us. Let us now look a little more closely at the Hegelian approach to immediacy. As I said, Hegel has a rather negative view of immediacy. We find this, for instance, in his discussion of what he calls "sense-certainty" in the *Phenomenology of Spirit*, or in his general approach to "feeling," say, in relation to either his philosophy of right, or his philosophy of religion. On the whole, immediacy refers to something that in itself is indeterminate, in the negative sense of being indefinite, and lacking in proper determination. By contrast, it is by reference to his view of the concept that this putatively empty indefiniteness is to be made intelligible through the determinations of thought. Conceptual thought mediates this indeterminacy of immediacy, and only when this mediation has been effected can claims be made to categorial intelligibility. In itself, and taken for itself, immediacy seems to be equated with a defective condition—defective of intelligibility, hence poverty-stricken for philosophy, until properly conceptual thought determines its mediated intelligibility.

Consider what he says about the "this-here-now" in the *Phenomenology*. Hegel presents the self-understanding of self-certainty as claiming to be the richest gestalt of consciousness. Hegel claims to show it is the most indigent. Among his ways of indicating the point concerns the need to *bespeak the richness*, to articulate the plenitude. To speak of the richness is already always to mediate the immediacy, and in terms beyond the immediacy, that is in terms of mediating universals. The richness of articulation is elsewhere than sense-certainty itself understands. And, of course, Hegel does grant there is *more* in sense-certainty; there is more than pure being.[3] But what is this "more"? It turns out to be the mediating universal, something more than can be accommodated on the terms of sense-certainty themselves. It is not the surplus immediacy that I mean.

Take Hegel's example, an example far more full of rich ambiguity than Hegel realizes: "Now is night." Then (Hegel says) I write this down. But by tomorrow noon, it is no longer night, and now the truth written down is stale. The truth of night has wilted in the noonday light. Hegel's point is that the "now" as *this* "now" cannot be fixed; its truth escapes that kind of fixation; and surely this is true. I would say you cannot *univocalize* the "now," precisely because "now" is as process, always ever ongoing, and as othering beyond "itself." Immediacy is this always ever ongoingness

---

3. G.W.F. Hegel, *Phänomenologie des Geistes*, 80; *Phenomenology of Spirit*, 59 (§92).

as othering beyond self. It reveals the universal impermanence, as I have spoken of it in *Being and the Between*.[4] There is something here excessive to fixed determination. You cannot univocalize and hence reduce it to a determinate identity. But the meaning of this excess, and this elusiveness to univocal fixation, is what is at stake.

Clearly by naming it as such, I do get some fix on it. Hence the issue is not the fixed against what is not fixed at all. It is rather what it is about the process as process that allows a certain determinability, and yet exceeds all determination. The question of immediacy, vis-à-vis Hegel, concerns where we situate the nub of the issue, and hence the kind of analysis or thinking that is consequently forthcoming. It is very clear what Hegel wants to communicate by telling us that the truth of night becomes stale in the noon. It is that "this-here-now" cannot be named as such, just insofar as it is a "mere" immediacy (how many questions are hidden or avoided by that little word "mere"). We need mediation to say anything at all about what is given in the immediate. Hence the drift of Hegel's account which, as it turns out, is also in search of what remains the same in the ongoingness. Not this "now," or that "now," but the "now" as such, the universal "now."

There is some overlap here between Hegel's approach and Kant's transcendental aesthetic: just as in the latter, we bring the a priori forms of space and time to the sensuous manifold, so in the former, the universal appears to be emergent in the flux of sensuousness; it is the universal "now," for Hegel, that really appears with mediating thought, itself embodied in the language that talks about the "this-here-now." There is a long way to go in Hegel, and he will want to say that this mediation is not merely subjective, since it concerns the mediation of the object as much as the subject. But in both instances of object and subject, it will be a process of determination that takes the shape of a more inclusive self-mediation, or self-determination. Determinability will reveal itself as *self*-determination; and here again we witness the complex continuation of the transcendental turn to a "higher subjectivity" that includes the more normal, determinate subject and object. This ultimate inclusive power will be, in the end, the self-determination of thought itself. This indeed is what the *concept* is for Hegel, and impossible to understand without some reference to the self-positing of the transcendental ego or self.

4. W. Desmond, *Being and the Between*, chapter 7.

Hegel will justify the noninterference of this inclusive power by claiming that the "now" undergoes its own process: night passes into day. Not so clear, as some commentators have pointed out, is the "this-here"; for *we* have to turn around, for the process to move further; the tree (Hegel's example)[5] does not quite so overtly turn itself around, though a generous sense of self-moving could be applied to this too. One thinks of the way a heliotropic plant or flower *turns itself* toward the sun. Perhaps this is more compatible with the metaphysics of a Plato whose heliocentrism of the Sun-Good is more truly Copernican than Kant's turn to the transcendental subject. Where is the Sun in modern subject-turned thought? The "house" of Hegel's example is no heliotropic plant, and does not turn itself thus.[6] Here we have space, but "space" also evidences the emergence of a more universal concept or categorial determination: the universal "space." This reveals the thrust of Hegel's way of dealing with the immediacy: it is nothing in and for itself until the process of mediation, ultimately a self-mediation, articulating the universal form of thought, articulates for us what is there. Immediacy qua immediacy must always be downgraded to a "mere" beginning, albeit necessary in its own way, but not sufficient, and in fact, absolutely insufficient. The absolute insufficiency of the immediate is its poverty. There is always, and primarily, a *teleological* thrust to Hegel's interpretation. It is not *archeological* relative to the givenness of a rich beginning. The end is the fullness, the beginning the indigence. How you can get fullness in the end, if the beginning is thus indigent, is not explained. The dialectic is always driving away from the maternal source.

SURPLUS IMMEDIACY AND NOCTURNAL HAPPENING

I would put it otherwise to Hegel, and this is my second concern. There is no adequate sense of "surplus immediacy" in Hegel—a sense of rich givenness that precedes the determinations of conceptual thought, and that also exceeds claims to completely subject what is given to the categorial determinations of philosophy. There are a number of ways the point might be put, but I would say that there is a *passio essendi*, a "passion of being," that is prior to any *conatus essendi*, the endeavor to be (or to think), on our part. This *passio essendi,* this patience *of* being, or patience *to* being,

---

5. *Phänomenologie des Geistes,* 82; *Phenomenology of Spirit,* 60 (§98).
6. *Phänomenologie des Geistes,* 82; *Phenomenology of Spirit,* 61 (§98).

has to do with surplus givenness that is presupposed by any efforts on our part to determine the intelligibility of immediate happening. Our efforts to determine conceptually the meaning of this surplus immediacy call for a fidelity to the fullness of what is communicated in this elemental givenness. If we put the dominant emphasis on the determining power of the concept, in the way Hegel does, we risk a conceptual defection from this surplus immediacy. In the name of categorially determining its intelligibility, we risk a contraction of intelligibility to the terms of our concepts, and hence risk impoverishing, not only our conceptual terms but what is communicated in and through the surplus immediacy. My point is not to deny the necessity of concepts, it is to question whether Hegel's concept as self-determining thought can be the last word, or indeed the first. It is the subordination and overriding of the otherness of the surplus immediacy that I question. Hegel speaks of thought as overreaching its other, so making it *its own other*, and hence not irreducibly other. This cannot be the appropriate way to put it, if there is this surplus to immediacy. A different thinking is also needed.

How advance the point? Look at the whole happening of *night* otherwise. "Now is night." Do not obey Hegel, do not write down: now is night. Sleep in the night, dream in the night, look at the sky in the night, marvel at the moon in the night. Write it down, as Hegel commands us, and one senses something hurried and anxious about this writing it down, lest darkness covers one, lest something less fixed passes beyond one, lest too the night overwhelms one. Let it overwhelm one. Let Hegel bridle. This is not the night in which all cows are black. We cannot let him move so quickly from the dark to the shadowless noon, when, to Hegel at least anyway, the truths of night appear false ("stale"—is this not Hegel's beloved putdown, namely, calling something he does not like "insipid"?). But what other can happen in the night? Love can happen in the night. Different loves, some erotic in a more normal sense, some perhaps philosophically erotic, or perhaps loves that communicate a longing for truth beyond diurnal demonstration, a longing that might make the truths of day blanch. Woo in the night, and while waiting, call to mind Mnemosyne, mother of the Muses.[7] Now is night: sing it, do not write it down. Or if you must

7. This mother is very important in Vico too. Memory would require another study, memory being an essential mode of mindfulness in the between, involved in intricate affiliations with imagination, mimesis, eros, and mania. See my *Art, Origins, Otherness*, chapter 1.

write it down, do not write it in words that die in being written. Write it, say, in the dark illuminating utterance of the poetic word.

"Now is night." I think of Zarathustra's *Nachtlied*.[8] Not to glorify Nietzsche, or Zarathustra; but just such a phrase, or one close to it, is a refrain in this immensely poignant song: "Night is come." It comes; meaning perhaps, night has closed around us, while we might not have noticed it, but coming on and closing around us, saturating us, dark falling around us, on us, as we go about the day, night releases something in us. What does it release? And what kind of release? And what has the word of the poet to do with the release? What has the release of the song to do with what is set free? Much. And night has much light, paradoxically, to throw on the meaning of the immediacy.

This is one of my points, soberly put: there are modes of articulation that in one sense are quite determinate, but the manner of the determination is such as to retain a fidelity to the surplus immediacy that is given. The poetic bespeaking can be one such mode of articulation: light on one side, dark on the other, and the dark is there on this side too of the light; determinate yet overdeterminate, itself a likening to the determinate overdeterminacy of the happening of surplus immediacy itself. Such a bespeaking can be more faithful to an original, in the sense of originating, beginning: a bespeaking of the surplus.

I would say that what Hegel discusses as sense-certainty is not really the beginning. It is already a "setup," a gestalt, in a manner mediated by his philosophical presuppositions. I would say that there is a more primordial happening of immediacy relative to the advent of mindfulness, and the opening of relation between us and the givenness of aesthetic happening. As I did earlier, I call it agapeic astonishment,[9] which is not quite marked by the complex set of determinations of Hegel's gestalt of sense-certainty. It opens or finds itself opened to what is overdetermined rather than indeterminate; to what is not absent of determinations but saturated with determinacy, but this is not to be understood as a kind of set of univocal determinations, predicates, properties, or whatever. It is closer to an equivocal matrix promiscuous with interminglings, rather than any neutral space where a "this-here-now" offers itself for univocal consideration,

---

8. *Das Nachtlied*, in *Werke*, 6.1, 132ff.; *Zarathustra*, 129–30.
9. See also *Being and the Between*, chapter 1.

either as a particular or a universal. It is an ethos of suggestion and pre-sentiment prior to that, an ethos of the plurivocal communication of the otherness of being: an intimate strangeness. Agapeic astonishment opens to the happening of aesthetic givenness in process, yes, but also *there* with the striking plurivocal otherness whose truth we will come to seek in per-plexed thought. Aesthetic happening shows itself as a plurivocal otherness communicated to and in astonished mindfulness. Both the showing and the mindfulness each testify to a plenitude rather than to an indigence; and each is saturated with a richness of possibility that is not mere possi-bility, for it is a richness of promise open to articulation on the side of the happening and the side of the mindfulness.

Hegel entirely neglects agapeic astonishment, fails in fidelity to the opening of mindfulness prior to determinate objectification and subjecti-fication, reduces the richness of the beginning to a lacking indeterminacy which then is addressed in terms of an eros of perplexity that determines intelligibility in the other-being. In all of this thinking "subjectivity" lat-er becomes, through many self-mutations, *Geist,* which *finds itself again,* that is, its *own* determinations of intelligibility. Hegel is amnesiac about the more primal *passio essendi* and driven by the cognitive distension of an overriding *conatus essendi.* The self-determining process reflects an eros of a determinative will to know that mediates its own initial indi-gence, namely, ignorance, through its cognitive relation to other-being, that elevates itself above its given indigence through the intelligibilities posited by an immanent process of self-determining thought. The satu-rated happening of immediacy is assimilated to this self-determining pro-cess of self-mediated thought. Every immediacy ends up by being medi-ated thus by Hegelian thought.

Again, while there are important differences, there are here impor-tant overlaps between Hegel and Kant's sense of the sensuous manifold. This manifold may "be," but its being there qua being is nothing intel-ligible without the categories—it is a mere thereness, nowness, happen-ing without intelligibility: bare indigent being. Thus Kant and existence: mere position, being posited—and this "position" referring to a relativity to the knower that is the more ultimate determining, positing power. In Hegel, there is a more total assimilation of intuition to concept: there is no qualitative difference, there is no otherness irreducible, of sensuous and conceptual. Kant has some right on his side, insofar as one can see him as intending to guard some important *differences,* even if with resources that seem to undercut the intention. In that both Kant and Hegel are transcendental philosophers, Hegel is probably the more consistent on *those* terms. These terms can be said to lead to the devaluation of the surplus immediacy in its given otherness. I dispute those terms.

This devaluation is at the opposite evacuated extreme to the happening of agapeic astonishment. The meaning of agapeic astonishment, and its bearing on surplus immediacy, is not confined to some thin epistemological thesis. The mindfulness at stake can be concretized in different registers, one of which is intimately connected to art. This has significance for the philosophical understanding of immediacy, as I shall shortly indicate, but now I want to conclude these present remarks with a very important consideration.

Hegel often reduces immediacy to mere "fact," something that is a problem for him to be raised to the level of self-positing necessity (see, e.g., his treatment of Jacobi). He misses here one of the deepest senses of immediacy that is almost always taken for granted: *the givenness of creation.* What is, as being granted, creation, is taken for granted. Nevertheless, what is taken for granted is, in its being granted. There is a primal *passio essendi,* or ontological patience of being in the given receiving of being at all. This signals an "It is" entirely different from Hegel's mere fact or indigent being. This deepest ontological immediacy is not the spontaneous happening of this or that, or the living participating in this or that experience, undergoing, or whatever, of life. It is a more primal ontological immediacy: that things are at all: in being and not nothing. This is an ultimate immediacy in that, without it nothing finite, or nothing within finitude, could mediate its being there at all. For this *being there at all* is presupposed by all such mediations; and indeed all such mediations are made possible by it as the primal immediacy of being given to be. Before it there is agapeic astonishment before there is determinate or self-determining cognition. Yet also this primal immediacy enables all subsequent self-mediations and intermediations in the happening of the finite between or *metaxu.* "Creation" is an immediate ontological intermediation that brings being to be, enabling the finite between to be, and possibilizing its plurivocal promise. This immediate intermediation of "creation" is a surplus happening presupposed by all intermediations *within the metaxu* of the finite given world.

ART AND SURPLUS IMMEDIACY

The above elemental points have application all the way to more "ultimate" levels, and now, in this light, I want to consider Hegel's attitude to the surplus immediacy, as we find it in art and religion. What is at stake is not only a different account of "givenness" in art and religion, but also a different sense of philosophical thought and system bearing on what the idealistic interpretation overlooks or underplays. The richness of surplus immediacy counters the inflated claims made for knowing as completely autonomous and self-determining, and asks a metaphysics closer to what I call the metaxological approach rather than to Hegel's (and indeed to others in the post-Kantian line, even when they deconstruct idealism). Reflection on art and religion indicates something of the saturated richness of "immediacy."

The point with respect to *art*: Importantly, art is given an absolute status by Hegel, but it is just its immediacy that finally creates a defect for him in terms of the absolute requirement of thinking. The immediacy of art evidences a not-yet-overcome otherness that still burdens thinking that would for him be absolutely self-determining—conceptual thinking that here, I would say, defects from the *passio essendi,* and absolutizes its own *conatus essendi,* as pure self-thinking thought. Great art, I would argue, is truer in its sensuous witness to the *passio essendi,* and what is enigmatically communicated in the surplus immediacy. The great artwork is an articulated concretion of surplus immediacy, that communicates something of its significance in excess of complete conceptual determination. (Kant had perhaps a better intuition of this in his "aesthetic idea.")

The point I suggested above in relation to *night* might be seen to draw our attentions to the articulating powers of art. Not incidentally I cited a song, or poem. That the *Nachtlied* is by Nietzsche/Zarathustra is not now to the point, though it is worth granting that Nietzsche had finesse for the aesthetics of happening, and appreciation for the articulating powers of the poet by contrast with the abstractions of the rationalist philosopher. Remember the "either/or" I mentioned at the outset. Here philosophers have had a predilection for the concept or category as *the* most proper way to articulate the happening of immediacy, and justified as such often because it putatively can *account for itself.* This often means a depreciation of other modes of articulation, such as poetry or art generally. We tend to forget that there are other modes of *articulation*—they are not "mere" happenings of immediacy. They essay to speak, hence sing, something of the happening, and also its significance. Song sings significance, significance that remains in tune with the happening qua participation in the *passio essendi.*

The choice is not between a certain form of philosophy as *the* articulated significance and the inarticulate. Poetry was called by Eliot a "raid on the inarticulate" (in "East Coker," *Four Quartets*). Not quite: it is not just a *raid,* since this implies a kind of rustling, or robbery, or attack. We are not thieves. The movement of poetry is not just an opening onto the inarticulate, since the happening of immediacy *already* is *not* mute—it speaks, it sings itself. The poem is a responding song that sings to co-respond to the first song of the happening. (One thinks of Michelangelo and how he heard the figures in the rock calling.) Its point is not just an articulation that accounts for itself. It is not just *itself* that is in question; it is the happening, and the happening as calling into question such modes of articulation that make the *self-accounting* into the most important. (Socrates imputes that task to the poets in the *Apology* [22b–c], but in doing so he hides the point at issue here.) If this is so, then the determination of the philosophical task purely in terms of thought's ability to account fully for itself is also in question.

Do not misunderstand: I am not arguing against efforts to account for oneself. I am suggesting that such an accounting could never just be a pure self-accounting, since it draws on sources of articulation that could not be described in the language of autonomous knowing, or self-determining thought. I am saying also that there is a fidelity to the happening from which we defect if we are so exclusively focused on self-accounting that we forget the primal *passio.* There are forms of art that enact this fidelity, and that remain modes of articulation; and, interestingly, modes of articulation that, while determinate, resonate in themselves with what exceeds determinability. This resonance of excess is not necessarily a defective equivocity that with better univocal thought would be entirely dispelled. Such an attitude is false, in the name of truth; untrue in thinking that to be true is a matter of univocally dispelling all ambiguity of immediate happening.

Thus comes *night* again. Night may be a benighted condition from which we must be freed, as those prisoners in the cave of Plato are to be released toward truth. But night may also be the mysterious matrix in which the most intimate ontological perplexities emerge. The truths of day may be false to that night, not because the night is false, but because day saturates us with a light that strangely topples us into a different fall into darkness. Excess of light produces darkness. It is the day that can then be dark, not night. Remember too that justice demands that the philosopher who has had a glimpse of the light of the Sun must *go back down* into the cave where he must see the shapes of things by the aid of *night vision.*

Excesses of the intimate—this is what spontaneously draws us to the immediate; to happening that addresses us directly at a level that can circumvent the police guards of categorial correctness. A song does that by articulating this rapport with the *passio essendi.* It hence has a relatively involuntary aspect. It does not ask permission to arouse us; it comes over us; we hear a music, and we are transported. Kant hated this, as when he speaks of the power of music on analogy with the perfumed handkerchief of the dandy: its odor is diffused throughout the room and we are overtaken by it, though we have given it no express rational permission to affect us at all. As if Kant were saying: What a cheek music has to affect us so! For Kant it violates our rational autonomy, indeed our predilection to determinate *logos,* since the meaning of the music is not thus determinable in words.[10] Though again, revealingly, the piece of music can have singular thereness of presence. The true song sings a word that no other word can substitute. The true incantation is a singular incarnation. Is the singular happening of being like as a song of songs? What would a singing philosophy be? A mindfulness not just of thought thinking but of thought singing its other? Vico knew the primal roots of articulation in song. What does that mean for philosophy? I find no help from Hegel.

I insist again: my point is not at all to counterpose art and philosophy and indict the defections of the latter in terms of the fidelities of the former. It is not "Newton versus Homer" (as Kant suggests), or "Homer versus Plato" (as Nietzsche does). Rather perhaps the issue is something exceeding both art and philosophy, considered as supposedly distinct activities. It has to do with the intimate sources of the *passio essendi* that flowers in all forms of human articulation; that subtends the difference of

10. See Immanuel Kant, *Critique of the Power of Judgment,* ed. Paul Guyer, trans. Eric Matthews (Cambridge: Cambridge University Press, 2000), §53.

art and philosophy; that exceeds both in terms of the intimate overdeterminacy of the happening of being; that has to do with the excess of the primal givenness of being that no human articulation could possibly exceed; that has to do with the deeper source of original creativity in which both art and philosophy participate without exhausting. It has also much to do with the ethos of thought itself: the culture, the *cultus* in which thought is offered form. If this *cultus* and ethos, this culture, is porous to the communication of art, it may well be that philosophical articulation will carry the resonances of these significant others. In a culture that emphasizes a scientific or technical univocalizing, the way philosophy understands itself may be deficient of these enabling or possibilizing porosities.

You might think my view is very postmodern in relation to art. In one sense, yes: there is an important porosity of art and philosophy. In another sense, no. Postmodern art, one fears, is sometimes devoid of the spiritual seriousness we find in the great art of the past. (One thinks of recent winners or anticipated winners of the Turner Prize: elephant dung paintings, an empty room in which the lights go on and off; for some reason, a disheveled bed and soiled underwear, well regarded by some critics, did not win.) Postmodern philosophy can sometimes mirror postmodern art in its studied banality. I think of Andy Warhol, and then of Richard Rorty as the Andy Warhol of our philosophical culture. Was Andy superior in not taking himself with the seriousness Rorty does, all appearances of irony notwithstanding? One looks intently at the blank face of Andy and one is never sure if the blink of an eyelid has passed one by, like half a shadow in the night. One looks for the wink of an eye in Rorty but does not see it, especially when in his later writing he assumed the role of secular preacher of a chirpy pragmatism, blithely free, in a mysterious innocence, of the darker shadows of nihilism. The old-time preacher at least believed there was some ground in truth to his homily. Without ground why should we listen to Rorty's edifying discourses, much less believe his sermons? I recall an image I used elsewhere, one that came to me in an idle moment of musing on his homilies: the traveling performing hypnotist we knew in our youth.[11] We went happily to the hypnotist, eager to see him work his spell and dreading to be put under it ourselves. At the end of the show, he would enchant some, and admonish them to care for

11. *Art, Origins, Otherness*, 280.

their companion leprechauns for the duration of the night. For now it was night. After the show, it was glorious fun to watch the spell-bound people entice their leprechauns down from trees. This happened in the night of enchantment, and the morning after they would wake again to day. There would be nothing "stale" about the night. Instead we had a good laugh at the nonsense of it all. Perhaps the good laugh, benign in its absurdity, was the point of it all. In the irony of Rorty I do not find enough of the festive laughter of the enchanted night.

Far from endorsing a certain kind of postmodern banality—the deflated defection that mirrors in reverse the inflated defection of Hegel's conceptual overstepping—I would argue for a secret intimacy of great art with sources of origination that bring it more truly into communication with being religious. Vico knew something of this, and I mean it in a more Vichian than Hegelian sense. There does seem a kind of doppelgänger of Hegel here, who binds art, religion, and philosophy together. While the appearance is not entirely untrue, it is not entirely true either. Hegel is quite right to treat art and religion with the same seriousness of ultimacy he treats philosophy. But because of the defection of his concept from the overdeterminacy of the happening of immediacy, there is a "carry-on" effect in how the character of art and religion is conceived, as well as their relation to his conception of the philosophical concept. All are teleologically bound toward the completion of absolutely self-determining thinking. This latter is what his concept is, in fact. But this is from the outset systematically to miss what is at issue in the porosity of art and philosophy to the *passio essendi*.

BEING RELIGIOUS AND SURPLUS IMMEDIACY

In conclusion I want to say a few things on this, with our sights on being religious more so than being aesthetic. Elsewhere I have said a few things about the so-called end of art and being religious.[12] An analogous point pertains to religion as to art, though here even more radically we meet resistance to the categorial determination of immediacy in terms of self-determining thinking. Here surplus immediacy suggests something that exceeds our determination and self-determination, and with a deep bearing on a much stronger sense of the otherness of the human and the divine

---

12. *Art, Origins, Otherness*, chapter 8, for instance.

than Hegel allows, or can allow. While there are many relevant points here, such as this otherness and transcendence, I will offer a few words about what might be communicated in terms of a crucial instance of religious surplus immediacy: the happening of prayer. If there were no immediacy to prayer as a happening, it is hard to know if any sense could finally be made of being religious. Yet this happening as immediate need not be a defect of being but the communication of the surplus overdeterminacy of the divine. We may be graced amazingly with a "too-muchness," an exceeding, hyperbolic immediacy.

Hegel is not guilty of any simplistic conceptualization of being religious—quite to the contrary. But the complexity of his conceptual appropriation of religion is entirely equivocal. I see it as embodying a dialectical equivocity rather than the superior speculative dialectical resolution of equivocity. I mean a dialectic that hides or evades the equivocity rather than addressing it honestly. But I do not deny Hegel's acknowledgment of some immediacies related to being religious, and I will mention the most important.

Very relevantly in the present context is when Hegel speaks (e.g., in the *Encyclopedia Logic*, §§61–78) of faith itself in relation to *immediate knowledge*. This concerns Hegel's debate with Jacobi about immediate knowledge of the absolute or "God" (if the absolute is God, something to be questioned).[13] Interestingly also, immediate knowledge is the third attitude of thought to objectivity after metaphysics (first attitude) and empiricism and the critical philosophy (second attitude). Immediate knowing is granted by Hegel, but Hegel's "yes" now, often turns out to look more like a "no" later, when fuller dialectical speculative qualifications are brought into play. The granting of immediate knowing is immediately followed by its critique, just as immediate. Immediate knowing entrenches dualisms between the human and the divine, hence cutting off the relation of the

---

13. Jacobi attacked rationalism (and Spinozistic pantheism) as leading finally to nihilism. Either God or nothing—the choice. Immediate knowing is identified with *faith*. What is here called "faith" is not the set of determinate doctrines of the Church, but an immediate knowing of the unconditioned. Hegel discusses issues like intellectual intuition, the unity of mediation and immediacy, and criticizes Jacobi for an *exclusive* "either/or" between immediacy and mediation. See above my opening remarks about such kinds of "either/or." Very interestingly, Hegel says that the entire second part of his *Logic*, the book two on essence, "deals with the essential self-positing unity of immediacy and mediation" (*Encylopaedia Logic*, §65). Notice the revealing phrase "self-positing unity." I engage with, and take my distance from, Hegel's "God" in *Hegel's God: A Counterfeit Double?* (Aldershot, U.K.: Ashgate Press, 2003).

two that it ostensibly affirms. Hegel will claim to affirm the "immediate" relation differently in a fully mediating, self-mediating form: God known by the concept, and God as the Concept.

I do not want to speak for Jacobi but I would say that the immediacy of being religious pertains again to the *passio essendi* in which we awaken to a primal porosity between ourselves and the divine beyond us, even in the most intimate immanence of our own being for ourselves. This is not something we create, but is a given opening and communication in virtue of which all our self-transcending is possibilized. It is a porosity preceding the more normal determinate doublet of "passivity" and "activity," and also exceeding that doublet and more determinate forms of passivity and activity. If it is such an opening, it is also precedent to and exceeding of every finite form of determinate openness. It is not a mere indefinite openness, but an overdeterminate opening that makes possible the determinate forms of finite openness. Because, as communicated in being religious, it is a porosity *between* the human and the divine, it can never be accounted for in terms of any determinative thinking, nor of any form of self-determining, be this attributed to the human or to the divine (as Hegel, in fact, does).

There is further the matter of *feeling*, where we sense ourselves to be in the region of this porosity. Religious feeling is granted as important by Hegel. But once granted, again it is seen as a "mere" immediacy which must be also dialectically negated and mediated; feeling does not carry the cognitive certification, justification, and validation that can only come from rational knowing, and in the form of self-determining reason. Hegel's "yes" to the immediacy of feeling is so qualified by the dialectical speculative considerations that flow from self-determining reason that we wonder what, *at the end*, the "yes" can amount to. It is a provisional "yes," yes, but a "yes" that looks more like a "no" when we come to the end, when the tolerance of the provisional must yield to the self-certainty of absolute self-knowing

Similar considerations apply to the "*heart*." The same pattern of thinking is exhibited by Hegel. The heart is a seed, he suggests, and this is not a bad metaphor if we remember the fullness compacted in the seed. But as is Hegel's way, it is not this compacted fullness he stresses. In his hands, this "seed" is all but nothing, outside of its teleologically driven development. But not forgetting the porosity of being religious, suppose what is there is a surplus immediacy—perhaps suggested when Pascal says the heart has reasons of which reason knows nothing. Perhaps a mindful finesse might come to some understanding of this surplus reason. Suppose the heart is a *reserve*. And the kind of reserve it is, is not fully described in the metaphor of the seed: a reserve out of which extraordinary expression comes, but one that remains reserved no matter what determinate expression of itself is forthcoming. The heart is an intimacy of being that even when communicating itself remains in the reserve of intimate(d) surplus. The heart reaches into the root of the *passio essendi* more intimately than the diurnal cognitions of reason. The heart is night, now is night in the heart, though the heart is not just dark.

Is night a religious-poetic name for the primal porosity? Of this, do we not have some intimation when the heart is released? Prayer: porosity flooded by the intimacy of the divine? We speak of living with a free heart. Can the self-transcending of the free heart be fully determined in the language of Hegelian reason? No. The heart is a reserve in the idiocy of being, but on the heights in that intimacy. The religious heart is put on the line—it is as a *being put on the line*—between itself and the divine. It is daimonic: between the monstrous and divine, though it is not the divine. Something of this is known in night. Something of transcendence is known in the intimacy of immanence, and transcendence as other to immanence communicated in the endowment of immanence itself.

Hegel's version of mediation inverts this into an immanence of transcendence in which there is no true transcendence. It often requires a certain feel for nuance to be able to detect this with Hegel. Hegelian immanence mimics transcendence, and often to the point of being a *parodia sacra*, perhaps even without knowing that it is so. As an example of this, I cite a very revealing account of cultus from his *Lectures on the Philosophy of Religion* of 1827:

In the cultus, on the contrary, God is on one side, I am on the other, and the determination is *the including, within my own self, of myself with God,* the knowing of myself within God and of God within me. The cultus involves giving oneself this supreme, absolute enjoyment. There is feeling within it; I take part in it with my particular, subjective personality, knowing myself as this individual included in and with God, knowing myself within the truth (and I have my truth only in God), i.e., joining myself as myself in God together with myself.[14]

14. G. W. F. Hegel, *Lectures on the Philosophy of Religion: One Volume Edition, The Lectures of 1827,* ed. Peter Hodgson (Berkeley and Los Angeles: University of California Press, 1988), 191.

This is a dense statement, for it condenses something essential about Hegel's views. Notice how Hegel speaks of "giving oneself" the supreme, absolute enjoyment. Can we give ourselves this absolute enjoyment, or is there a more ultimate "being given"? Notice how, even when I find myself in God, the inclusion of my being within God is *within my being with myself.* Not only "giving oneself," and "knowing myself," but note the concluding *hyperbole of immanence to self* "joining myself as myself in God together with myself"—the "self" of "myself" that gives itself all this is surely an extraordinary self. It seems more extraordinary than any God "on one side," not least because this self gives itself, within its own immanence, the absolute relation between itself and the absolute (God). It articulates a complex relation of the self with itself in which it finds God in its own relation to itself, a relation that seems entirely immanent. Not marked by any transcendence beyond itself, immanent self-transcendence enfolds in itself ultimate transcendence. *Instead of the surplus immediacy of the givenness of prayer, we have the necessity of an absolute self-mediation, inclusive even of "God," and to which there is nothing more surplus.*

What Hegel speaks of as cultus *completely reverses* what the giving of a surplus immediacy might mean, as pointing to what is beyond all self-mediation, beyond all our self-determination. The relation implied by him is not agapeic, as a gratuitous communication of the generous God; it is not erotic as released to the beloved as more than my self-mediation; it is autoerotic in coming back to itself through the other that is itself. And we look closely to see any line of difference between our self-elevation to God and God's communication from God's own being as other to us. (Indeed we look and have to squint to see what seems to be for Hegel God's own strange self-elevation in and through us.) We cannot see any more the asymmetry of the hyperbolic God, and the "more" of our being gifted from beyond ourself. And this point about asymmetry applies whether we are dealing with eros or agape.

In Hegel's version of prayer, eros is not a *passio essendi,* perhaps not a *conatus essendi,* but it is an *auto essendi.* By contrast, the surplus immediacy of the happening of prayer makes it more like night. Suppose it happens that a secret generosity is communicated in the night, as those who pray have often said. (There is a strengthening in the night of Gethsemane garden: passion of being—becoming nothing—extremity of porosity in suffering—secret strengthening.) Generosity is an intermediation with the other but a mediation that enacts the happening of the surplus immediacy of free giving: giving for nothing—nothing beyond the good of the giving.

If there were no immediacy to prayer as a happening, it is hard to know if any sense could finally be made of being religious. Yet this happening as immediate need not be a defect of being—it may be a form of the surplus immediacy in which the *passio essendi* of the mortal creature is awakened to the porosity between itself and the divine, an awakening that exceeds the power of the creature's own self-determination. As a surplus immediacy and a porosity, this may not be an autism of being *(auto essendi)*, but rather a communication of the ultimate: the communication may be within the intimacy of the finite being, but it is not closed into that intimacy; it rather solicits a communication, religious and ethical, beyond all determinate closure.

This might seem to desert the ground of philosophical thinking, but I would suggest that reflection on surplus immediacy here rather deepens the sense of what it means to think philosophically. Instead of the defect(ion) of the Hegelian concept, we may need, so to say, a different *poverty of philosophy* to remain mindfully true to the happening of being religious.

Paradoxically, the surplus of the happening asks for a poverty that, even despite itself, is rich beyond itself. It is more awakened to the porosity in the intimacy of its being, waked to the reception of what of ultimacy is given to it from beyond itself.

Part 2

Metaphysics in the Wake of Dialectic

4 ⟀ Is There Metaphysics after Critique?

Is there metaphysics after critique? Much depends, of course, on what we mean by "metaphysics" and "critique."[1] It is evident, I think, that the contested place of metaphysics in recent thought has much to do with the influence of philosophy understood as critique, especially after Kant. It is also evident that critique is related to the modern practice of dialectic. Further, it is evident that critique is connected with what is called postmetaphysical thinking. It is not always entirely clear what is meant by "postmetaphysical thinking," but if we look upon metaphysics as asking from us a certain fundamental reflection, more or less systematic, on the basic senses of the "to be," or of what it means to be, metaphysics will never be a practice we can put behind us. It will always be with us and before us, in that postmetaphysical thinking will involve its own implicit orientations relative to these fundamental senses of the "to be." The real question concerns how true philosophical mindfulness is to these orientations, orientations more often recessed than expressed in the various practices of knowledge and life itself. Nor does the philosophical need to be systematic in one's thoughts entail that one claims to possess *the* system. Rather, there are immanent connections and relations between modes of thinking and actualities, and metaphysics can try to trace these systematic connections. We can do this from the midst of things, from "the between," and not by claiming to overreach the whole and include it in an absolutely comprehensive system.

To philosophize from the between, and about the between, makes its own demands on us. One of its demands is that we not deracinate philosophy from the intimate strangeness of being, and persuade ourselves that the resulting abstractions constitute the system of intelligibilities that

1. A version of these reflections was given as keynote address to the Graduate Student Philosophy Conference on the theme "Metaphysics and Critique," at Fordham University, March 5–6, 2004, at the invitation of Dr. David Zinn and Professor James Marsh.

exhausts the overdeterminacy of being. While critique often presents its task as the relativizing, indeed dismantling, of the claims to absoluteness of such systems, one wonders if it is itself a form of deracinated thinking that lost, or turned from, ontological intimacy with the overdeterminacy of being. One might say that while rejecting "system," it lives off the same negativity of thinking that fuels dialectic. Dialectic, unbridled of "system," releases the energy of thinking as negation, now suspicious of any systematic goal and ignorant of the origin of any more affirming thought in the intimate strangeness of being. In the following, then, I will offer some remarks under these two main headings: first, relative to the ethos of critique in modernity; second, relative to a more affirmative sense of metaphysics after critique.

ON THE ETHOS OF MODERN CRITIQUE: FROM SKEPTICISM TO NEGATION

Kantian Critique

What do we mean by "critique"? At the outset it helps to distinguish between a more theoretical and a practical sense of critique. These two senses are intimately bound together, of course, but we can get our bearings by first distinguishing them. Perhaps the practical sense is more familiar to us: critique seems tied up with the questioning, perhaps the unmasking, of dominant forms of living, of modes of social organization, of systems by means of which economic, cultural, and political life is ordered. This practical sense of critique usually marks thinkers on the "left," though one might wonder what a right-wing practice of critique might look like. The general point is that the practice of philosophy has bearing—crucially practical, even if in some mostly mediated way—on exposing to the light of reason and ethical accountability forms of life that hide their "sins," their dissimulated deficiencies, omissions, and repressions.

Such a practical critique is not itself void of deeply embedded presuppositions of a more theoretical nature, and we will come to these. But turning now to the theoretical sense of critique, we can best talk about it by reference to one of its great exponents: Kant. *The Critique of Pure Reason* is enacted by a reason that would be critical about itself and its own theoretical pretensions. This theoretical critique is obviously not separable from practical concerns, most evidently in Kant's enterprise, at the heart of which lies the desire to make sense of our moral being, both in its autonomy and in its sense of unconditional obligation. Both the theoretical and the practical senses of critique are also joined together by a belief that a certain earlier practice of metaphysics, most proximately the rationalism of the eighteenth century, has reached an end, and that henceforth the practice of philosophy must be different. Critique in both senses is bound up with the *self-questioning* of philosophy as metaphysics, and the question of the future identity or role for philosophy. Hence the question we pose: Is there metaphysics after critique?

We have heard much in recent decades about the "end of metaphysics," "the overcoming of metaphysics," most vociferously from those influenced first by Heidegger, and later in a somewhat altered register by deconstructive thinkers. This theme goes back to the end of the eighteenth century, of course, and it should be associated first of all with Kant. Kant is famous for his critique of the pretensions of metaphysics. This means, in fact, the pretension of the rationalist philosopher to transcend the boundaries of experience and purely on the basis of a priori reason make claims of necessary and universal truth. Kant situated himself in relation to dogmatism and skepticism, but clearly it is the dogmatic rationalists he has primarily in his sights in his critique of metaphysics.

Once, Kant says, metaphysics, the queen of the sciences, ruled despotically, through the dogmatists; but her empire, bearing traces of the ancient barbarism, has fallen into decay, and through inner war *(durch innere Kriege)* has given way to anarchy, and the skeptic, a "species of nomad," despising all settled life, breaks up civil society. Of these nomads, for Kant fortunately, there are few.[2] His project is an attack on the conceptual idols of the rationalist metaphysicians. But while he seems to eschew skepticism, is not his critical mode of thought itself a formation of skepticism? Will these roots in skepticism have a longer life than Kant himself anticipated, since he thought he was always silencing the grumblings of the skeptics in the new form of philosophy he envisaged to replace traditional metaphysics? Do thinkers succeeding Kant enter so much into the mode of critique that a vagrant dynamic of skepticism is unloosed whose negating energy has still not run its course into our time?

The enterprise of critique must also be strongly associated with Kant,

---

2. *Critique of Pure Reason*, A ix.

given that his *Critique of Pure Reason* is alleged to be a *watershed* in the fortunes of metaphysics, ominous with significance for its possible future. Many take Kant to be a turning point in the history of philosophy, a turning of revolutionary character. I confess to hesitations about the way this claim is pressed, sometimes with transcendental, sometimes with posttranscendental condescension toward "metaphysics" (we must begin to use the scare quotes) and the tradition of philosophy prior to Kant.[3] There are many aspects to what I mean, but one might venture that Kantian philosophy is less revolutionary as reflecting a long process of development in modernity, a process that reaches closer to the height of its arc with Kant. I mean the belief in, nay, the project of, reason as entirely self-determining, and with this the practice of philosophical thinking as one of absolutely autonomous reason. The so-called Copernican revolution signals something that is closer to the end of this longer process rather than some aboriginal new beginning. Copernicus offered us a heliocentric vision, but one must ask again: Where is the Sun in modern philosophy turned to the "subject"? Where is the Sun in Kant?

One need not deny that Kant impels something further into motion here that has had fateful consequences for metaphysics since then. *Prior* to the Kantian culmination, half-hid in its metaphysical hinterlands, are the following: an alternation in our inhabitation of the ethos of being, in which there is a changed relation to otherness, be it the other-being of nature, or of God; a massive objectification of nature, coupled with a huge subjectification of human existence; a stripping off of other-being of the qualitative signs of givenness that communicated of transcendence as other to premodern man. *After* it, we find a certain intensification of an innerness that, on the one hand, seems to betoken a truer way to the ultimate and the divine but that, on the other hand, too often simply led to will to power, to the tyrannical soul rather than the noble *Übermensch*. And the *end of it all*—this is to anticipate—less the summum bonum, as the emptiness of life itself as a brief bewitched sparkle of nothingness.

Kant comes at a point where the objectified mechanism of Newtoni-

3. We find this not only in the idealistic line of succession from Kant, but also in the anti-idealist line, anti-Hegelian line. Thus Schopenhauer: Kant's "complete overthrow of the scholastic philosophy" is his third greatest merit; *The World as Will and Representation*, 1.422. "Speculative theology and the rational psychology connected with it received from him their death blow"; ibid., 423.

anism is reaching perfection, a perfection that would spell the loss of humanity were it to be taken as the last word. Absolute perfection here would be absolute defection from the moral being of the human. But the modern turn to the subject is itself inherently ambiguous, and, instead of the moralism of earnest duty, it can also lead to the desolation of nihilism, anticipated by some, wrongly, as the promise of a truer freedom. Kant's efforts to think freedom in a moral sense are essays to recuperate a sense of inherent worth in a world otherwise void of such value. The objectification of all other-being makes given creation into a kind of valueless whole; and only with respect to the human being as moral and an end in itself can some sense of the worthiness of life, the worth of being at all, be reaffirmed.

Whether Kant is successful or not in all this is another question—I do not think he is, or can be (my reasons for saying this are to be found in *Ethics and the Between*). Nevertheless, metaphysics is recovered by him in a moral sense, as we see from the title of his famous book: *Groundwork of a Metaphysics of Morals*. Of course, the opening to metaphysics in a moral register is already prepared in the *Critique of Pure Reason*. All this is connected with a wider sense of critique. Kant himself said: *our age* is especially the age of critique, and to it everything must submit; and even though religion may seek exemption, through its sanctity, just as lawgiving may also seek exemption, through its majesty, both religion and law thereby rather may well awaken a *just suspicion* toward them.[4] Everything in our time, Kant intones, and not without a touch of ominousness, must pass the bar of critique.

This is not a merely theoretical matter but is bound up with claims of our moral, perhaps political, maturity. We have come of age, it will be said, and we show this, *must* show this, by not accepting anything as given. There is a moral imperative at work in what critique exacts of us. We (must) question our fathers and forefathers. We (must) question those who claim to rule us, the categories claiming authority over us, the leaders claiming to represent our will, the religions claiming to offer us salvation, and so on. Here we encounter the enterprise of practical critique to match what looks like the more theoretical one above: a certain *task* or *project* that in principle can be, must be, extended to the whole.

If the project is to be extended to the "whole," it must inevitably have some implicit assumptions or anticipations of what that whole is, or must

---

4. *Critique of Pure Reason*, xii

be. Or if it claims to have none, then one must ask about what having a *project* entails. Does it not suggest something about our power as potentially projective over a range of beings, or over being(s) as a whole? Then again our relation to the "whole" is still at stake. Does not, must not, metaphysics in some fundamental sense come back in here again? That is not always recognized as such. This is, in part, because the rhetoric of critique directed against *already given systems* of metaphysics seems to have been effective, and so we think *metaphysics as such* is behind us irrevocably. In part, and perhaps more importantly, it is because the underlying impetus of the whole project is, in fact, more practical than theoretical. It looks not to speculative outcomes but to ethical and political "advances." This is perhaps why, when we hear the word "critique" today, inevitably we think less of Kant and more of the work of those engaged in ethical, social, and political critique, for instance, members of the Frankfurt school. How are "advances" determined? Often by exposing the putatively unjustified assumptions and claims made on behalf of particular systems of morality and politics: they are said to rest on the de facto possession and exercise of power rather than being fully accountable for themselves. But is this not true of all *projects*? The fully self-determining, the fully free, is said to be self-accountable. Can the project of full self-accountability account fully for *itself*? We would have to ask: What is the implicit *relation to what is other* in all of this? Is the longer life of a wayward skepticism (mentioned at the outset) still uneasy and restless in all of this? What more would this uneasy restlessness portend— for critique, for all projects, for metaphysics after critique?

Critique, Suspicion, Skepticism

When we associate critique with such an ethical-political form, Hamlet's worry tends to descend on us: Something is rotten in the state of Denmark. The established situation, the ancient regime, the given conditions of life—about these something is not right, and the malaise must be rooted out. If I am not mistaken, skepticism here can easily takes the form of *suspicion,* and it is not fortuitous that some virtuosi of certain kinds of critique have also been called the masters of suspicion, masters more or less also dismissive of traditional metaphysics: Marx, Nietzsche, Freud. But if suspicion extends to the whole, as it may well do, if there is implicit in the project of critique an extension to all of being, what does this portend for how we live? Does a potentially totalizing suspicion, even if it avers suspicion of all "totalizing" thinking, run the risk of tearing up thinking by its roots? Instead of attaining the goal of a higher self-accounting morality, in fact, does it not lead to the *utter demoralization* of human life, and the evaporation of those spiritual ideals, themselves the more original sources of the truthfulness demanded by honest critique?

One might talk here about an inheritance from Kant that is ambiguous between construction and destruction. The old metaphysics is "demolished," but what is put in its place? In Kant perhaps something like a metaphysics of morals, but after Kant? Kant was extremely confident that he had brought the project pretty much to its proper completion.[5] His successors speak the language of more idealistic apprentices, eager for more radical employment in a project as yet unfinished. There is uncompromising critical work to be more fully accomplished, they say. Are there not residual elements of the "given" in Kant: the "fact of reason," soon to be mocked; the givenness of the categories from the traditional logic; and so on? These apprentices to the new self-determination query further: Must a more accomplished critique *accept nothing as given*? Or if anything is given, must we not refuse to accept it as such, at least until it has passed the ordeal of critique? Does not this mean it is to be accepted only when it has been reconstructed *after* critique? For the immediately succeeding generation after Kant, including Fichte, Schelling, and Hegel, this project certainly was the urgent desideratum. All the categories must be deduced or produced from one principle, and so the whole must be properly accounted for in terms of one absolute or whole.

My point now is not to offer a survey of post-Kantian developments but to highlight how in the project of critique the stress comes to fall on thinking as negation. Among major successors of Kant, Hegel is perhaps most notable when he describes his *Phenomenology of Spirit* as a "self-accomplishing skepticism *(sich vollbringende Skeptizismus)."*[6] In accomplishing itself, skepticism overcomes skepticism, gives up its vagrancy, and comes home to itself in absolute knowing. Here knowing no longer feels the need to go beyond itself; it is finally at home with itself, having absolved itself from all alienating otherness, for all otherness proves finally to be its own otherness. It even surpasses the *desire* for wisdom we

---

5. See *Critique of Pure Reason,* A, xiii, xx.
6. *Phänomenologie des Geistes,* 67; *Phenomenology of Spirit,* 49.

find in previous philosophy and becomes, Hegel claims, the possession of actual science, *Wissensschaft*. Previous philosophy was always *between* ignorance and wisdom, hence was marked as intermediate. Now there is no such between, since everything is between knowing and itself, in the circle of its own self-determination. In Hegel, after the old metaphysics, and the new critique, we are offered the new speculative philosophy which in posttranscendental form offers the totality of categories, each allegedly justified beyond critique, because each and all have been radically critiqued by dialectic.

I want to stress how with Hegel the notion of thinking as a negativity becomes central, even in successors who "critique" Hegel himself. Thus Hegel: thinking in relation to the other entails a determinate negation that proves to be self-relating: the subject as thinking is hence defined as "self-relating negativity." After Hegel, such a definition tends to play some central role in many practices of critique. Even if there is a determinate negation of the other (considered questionable), this is ordained to a more articulate and self-accounting self-relativity—even if the "self" here might be the social whole, or *Geist*, as the true subject of history, or even the absolute itself qua subject. The idea of philosophy as the critique of presuppositions plays a role here. Hegel is again the *nec plus ultra*: we need not deny the initial givenness of presuppositions, but by means of critique we can transform any such givenness into something that has been ratified by rational thought, and hence it is no longer "presupposed." Immanent in the Kantian-Hegelian line is the worry that without the critique of our categories, we risk dependence on unacknowledged *heteronomies*. Only after critique are they to be accepted as free of, purified of, hidden presuppositions. Critique means "overcoming" the givenness, and only then can a speculative system finally be beyond critique.

(I need legs to walk from A to B; this is a given presupposition; but if I critique this presupposition, has the fact that I need legs to walk somehow been elevated to a higher presuppositionless level? I negate my given legs, but then I negate the negation, and *presto I have presuppositionless legs.* They are now legs that can account for themselves, self-responsible legs that did not take for granted their ability to walk. Now I have an enlightened permission, a legitimate right, to walk with them. Previously I was not walking in a properly legitimated way, but merely by virtue of a given fact of nature. What difference does all this make? Does it make a lame leg faster, or do away with the need for legs? Does critique make a stupid mind any the more intelligent? Postmetaphysical legs—are they capable of walking with more grace, to say nothing of dancing?)

Not many now accept Hegel's claim about speculative science but rather will insist on our constitutive entanglement in presuppositions. Nevertheless, the task of critique will not necessarily be given up, even if we do away with Hegel's speculative telos. With the loss of faith in this end, of course, the question does emerge as to what justifies the whole enterprise of critique. And what end, if any, can it now, does it now, serve? You might say critique is ad hoc, relative to problems appearing in medias res. Very well, but what makes critique different from just thinking about things? Does not reflection in the midst of things, by an inherent exigency, itself lead to metaphysical thought? Perhaps to something like what I call a metaxological metaphysics? I come back to this in the second part of my reflections

What of Hegel's distinction between dialectic as negative reason and speculative reason as positive?[7] There is something to this. Hegel does see something more than just negative dialectic. But the form of the "positive" raises serious issues. I see here a kind of "sublationary infinitism" which does not do justice to our middle being as finite. We are offered a self-relating, inclusive holism instead of a metaxological intermediacy. That certainly is true of the form in which Hegel held philosophy must be expressed: at its truest, philosophy must be absolutely self-determining thought. This is the *saltus* by which negative dialectic jumps over its own shadow and converts the negative into the positive. The positive might be understood as the "*pure* self-recognition in absolute otherness"[8] but it is the pure *self*-recognition that gets the laurels: the absolute otherness is *its own*, it is absolved from otherness. This is not true to the intermediacy of human thinking, and the kind of metaphysics that should go with our metaxological nature.

Post-Hegelian Critique and Human Emancipation

After the repudiation of the Hegelian speculative totality, often an ethical and political agenda continues to be invoked: critique is for purposes of human emancipation. But what is this? "Freedom" is the bewitching word

7. G.W.F. Hegel, *Encyclopaedia*, §§79–82.
8. *Phänomenologie des Geistes*, 24, *Phenomenology of Spirit*, 14

of modernity. It is on everyone's lips, including those of the tyrant. But what does it mean? And there are many kinds of freedom. One of them is the freedom of thought to negate. Hegel himself seems to hold that the most elemental freedom resides in the power of the thinking subject to withdraw into itself from external determination. This is elementally indeterminate to be sure, and must be made more fully determinate and self-determining in social and political institutions, but it is basic for him. Despite the fact that few accept Hegel's speculative system as the true successor to critique, the turn against rationalist metaphysics affects many thinkers, and the energy of skepticism takes hold again, but with further twists and turns in its waywardness. Hegel, it will be claimed, offers a speculative, hence theoretical, reconciliation, beyond Kantian critique and the old metaphysics, but he has short-circuited the completion of critique. Hegel's speculative reconciliation with the modern state reneges on critique as a political project; he reverts to a "false positivism or a merely *apparent* critique," as Marx puts it.[9] Critique must again take up its weapons, but now more and more radicalized in the direction of a political project to be accomplished.

Hence the left-Hegelians, and especially Marx come into their own. Hegel is taken to exhaust *all* the possibilities of theoretical reason, so we must turn to something other, if there is to be a future for philosophy—a role other to its traditional theoretical one. Hence the battle cry: till now philosophers have only interpreted the world, now the point is to change it. This is the most famous of Marx's theses on Feuerbach, a student of Hegel, another rebel son. The young Marx took note of how the Athenians, threatened with the ruin of their city, turned to an element other than the land, to the sea. We must go beyond even critique and take to another "element": revolution.[10] Metaphysics is accomplished: fulfilled and

9. Karl Marx, *Frühe Schriften, Werke,* vol. 1, ed. Hans-Joachim Lieber and Peter Furth (Darmstadt, Germany: Wissenschaftliche Buchgesellschaft, 1971), 654; *Early Writings,* trans. and ed. T. B. Bottomore (New York: McGraw Hill, 1963), 210. This is from "Critique of Hegel's Dialectic and General Philosophy." Also: "There can be no longer any question about Hegel's compromise with religion, the state etc., for this falsehood is the falsehood of his whole argument" [Von einer Akkommodation Hegels gegen Religion, Staat etc. kann also keine Rede mehr sein, da diese Lüge die Lüge seines Prinzips ist]; *Werke,* vol. 1, 655; *Early Writings,* 210.

10. See the letter to Arnold Ruge, September 1843: "[F]or we do not dogmatically anticipate a new world, but will find it through the criticism of the old. Up to now philosophers had the solution of all riddles lying in their lecterns, and the ignorant world of the present had but to gape in order that the roasted dove of Absolute Knowledge fly directly into its mouth.

dead. A new "project" of communism calls us on. And it would be too mild to say that skepticism, and the search for hope, inform the new turn taken by this "project" and its social critique. For critique inciting itself to revolutionary praxis can turn violently impatient with the given as such, which is said to be the alienated condition of the human being. To utter any "yes" to what is, would be (I almost said metaphysical) treason.

I draw attention to this earlier episode of the so-called end of metaphysics and its relation to critique because there are some significant echoes in debates in the twentieth century. Terms may vary but there is a somewhat shared dynamic. This is certainly true so far as this dynamic is moved deep down by the negativity of a certain skepticism toward traditional metaphysics. Deconstruction puts one in mind of a naughty cousin of critique, French and flighty, not Germanic and earnest, but still a family relation, make what one will of the recent turn to hyperbolically earnest ethics—and even religion—without religion.

The connection of religion and metaphysics seems to be at issue in the analogies between the earlier and more recent debates. Recall, for instance, Comte's law of the three states of humankind in history: first theology, then metaphysics, at the last positive science. Interestingly for Comte, metaphysics is merely intermediate: as abstract, he refers to it as the chronic transitional *malady* of the West. Metaphysics is an intermission bounded by a more original polytheism, superior to monotheism, and more fertile, and by a postmetaphysical age when positivism will renew, at a level of higher completeness, the impulses of polytheism and fetishism. What is prior to monotheistic theology and metaphysics will have a renewed significance for postmetaphysical humanity.

A kind of acoustical illusion might make one believe that it is Heidegger or one of his relatives speaking here, but it is not. For not all will agree

---

Philosophy has made itself worldly, and the most striking proof of this is that the philosophical consciousness has not only externally, but internally as well, been pulled into the torment of the worldly struggle. If then it is not our concern to construct the future and to establish eternal answers, then it is all the more certain what we must now bring to fruition, I mean *the unrestrained criticism of everything established* [die rücksichtslose Kritik alles Bestehenden], unrestrained not only in not fearing its own results, but even less of a conflict with whatever powers may be." See *The Young Hegelians,* ed. Lawrence S. Stepelevich (Cambridge: Cambridge University Press, 1983), 307–8. Stepelevich's translation of the italicized phrase modifies its sometime rendering as "the ruthless criticism of everything existing," and by this "reading renders Marx a bit less ferocious and a bit more clinical" (ibid., 306). Larry Stepelevich is a gentleman, but all things considered, however, I'm afraid the ferocity in Marx is undeniable.

with Comte's positive evaluation of the positive third, even while granting it as a kind of historical fatality. Heidegger issues a call for another thinking in his version of Comte's positive age, namely, our consummate cybernetic epoch. The connection of monotheistic theology and metaphysics in ontotheology is not absent in Heidegger's diagnosis of the chronic malady of the West. Heidegger worried about the poverty of the end of "metaphysics" in its denoument in cybernetic, calculative thinking. One might even speak of a metaphysical emptiness of the end of metaphysics, though Heidegger seems somewhat disingenuous in his relation to "metaphysics." In earlier reflections, he seemed more willing to see something other in "metaphysics," prior to his later somewhat totalizing teleology of the completion of metaphysics in cybernetics.[11]

Heidegger is a complex case, of course, but more generally, it is the intimacy of metaphysics and religion (sometimes theology) that tends not to be to the taste of many practitioners of post-Hegelian critique. The Enlightenment self-image of the philosopher has many afterlives, even in thinkers who take pride in themselves as critics of Enlightenment. As religion is a conspiracy of priestcraft, metaphysics is a ruse of the conceptual mandarins: veils are drawn over our eyes, concealing a truer encounter with history or the event of being. In the left-Hegelian line, the veils are dressings of a more naked power. Hence for Marx: "The critique of religion is the presupposition of all critique" *(die Kritik der religion is die Vorausetzung aller Kritik)*.[12] Religion insinuates consent to the given, but God and the gods are the alien powers that are the alienations of our power. Critique softens up the fixity of the illusion—it seeks to take the power back—and if successful, man will be (a) god. We say: do not accept the given—we accept only what we give to ourselves. If we must grant a given, we grant it only under the terms that allow us to give it to ourselves. Liberation becomes our release from all constraining forms of otherness. These constraining forms are secretly driven by will to power, it will be claimed in demystification. But is the drive of critique for release from constraining otherness, and most evidently in its drive for revolution, also not driven by will to power?

11. Martin Heidegger, "Das Ende der Philosophie und die Aufgabe des Denkens," in *Zur Sache des Denkens*, 61–80; English translation by Joan Stambaugh, "The End of Philosophy and the Task of Thinking," in *On Time and Being* (New York: Harper & Row, 1972), 55–73.

12. *Werke*,1.488; *Early Writings*, 43. This is the opening sentence of "Contribution to the Critique of Hegel's Philosophy of Right."

The ruling ideas of an epoch are the ideas of the ruling powers, to paraphrase Marx. But if we change the ruling powers, and hence the ruling ideas, do we change the constant rule that it is still power that rules, nothing more, nothing less?

> Hurrah for revolution and more cannon-shot!
> A beggar on horseback lashes a beggar on foot.
> Hurrah for revolution and cannon come again!
> The beggars have changed places, but the lash goes on.[13]

Skepticism, Negation, Terror

Let me round off this first reflection with a word on skepticism, negation, and terror. Skepticism is ambiguous: it is at the least two-faced. *A first face:* Skepticism can be seen in the light of a *justified refusal* of what is not to be affirmed, be it cognitive claims, or ethical forms, or political systems. But the "no" of justified refusal grows out of the presentiment that there is a norm or ideal that is short-changed or betrayed. The justified refusal is in the name of a justice refused or violated, and hence it is implicitly an affirmation of that justice. Maybe we cannot always say explicitly what that ideal of justice is, but it can be operative as a presentiment or promise of a truer condition, even expressed in terms of the restlessness and guilt and uncertainty we feel in the face of a dubious claim. The "no" of genuine skepticism is the overt expression of something more deeply recessed—something not just a matter of negation.

A second face: there is an energy in negating, and this can be intoxicating, and its vagrancy can turn into the demolition of all homes. Think of the child discovering the word "no"—once this word is let loose, the child loves to say "no," "no," "no." Implicit in it is the feel of its own freedom—it is not determined by an other; there is a space that can be peopled with forms conjured by the intoxicating energy of negation itself. I do not deny that the "no" may be a sign of the genuineness of freedom—but this "no" can easily become a freedom in the void and can turn to destruction for the sake of destruction.

Bakunin (in)famously announced: "The urge to destroy is a creative urge." Nietzsche said: "What is falling should be pushed." Think of the lan-

---

13. W. B. Yeats, "The Great Day," in *The Poems*, ed. Daniel Albright (London: Everyman, 1990), 358.

guage of weaponry in Marx: "Just as philosophy finds its *material* weapons in the proletariat, so the proletariat finds its *intellectual* weapons [*geistigen Waffen*] in philosophy."[14] One of Marx's revolutionary sons, Mao, is well known for his claim that "power grows out of the barrel of a gun," and these weapons are not just *geistigen Waffen*. Paraphrasing a favorite saying of Lenin, Mao liked to say: "The unity of opposites is temporary; antagonistic struggle is absolute." War is king, first and last.[15]

Some of those who want to resurrect Marx see the first face—justified refusal—and seriously underplay the second face. But much of the élan of the revolutionary spirit comes from the charge of negation. In my view, retaining fidelity to the ideal requires something from beyond critique. But if you have executed religion, from where is it to come?

It is unfortunately the case that often the revolutionary can come to be defined by his or her negations. Perhaps he or she is initially energized by ethical and political ideals, but the spirit of suspicion, first turned against the "system," or indeed "bourgeois morality," then turned against the informers and the secret police, then finally is directed against the enemy within, the traitor, or the suspected traitor. But this leads to a *generalized spirit of suspicion,* and then no one is entirely safe from assassination. This is even more so the case once power is assumed or taken over by the successful revolutionary. From critique to assassination the steps to be taken are sometimes, alas, few and short. Is there a critique that does not end in murder? Where find the resources to prevent that? Has it something to do with metaphysics—metaphysics after critique? And a new ethical and religious porosity?

The case is perhaps analogous to the way that some claims to autonomy, when not properly qualified, can quickly mutate into tyranny. For *auto-nomos* is the law of the same, but the absolute same must be a one, an absolute *auto* that either includes all others, or liquidates others that challenge, or are suspected of challenging, the hegemony of this one.[16]

---

14. *Werke,* 1.504; *Early Writings,* 59.

15. See Philip Short, *Mao: A Life* (London: Hodder & Stoughton,1999), on power out of the barrel of a gun, 203, 368; on antagonistic struggle as absolute, 459.

16. See Herbert Marcuse's "Great Refusal" (a term borrowed from A. N. Whitehead in connection with the aesthetic) in *Eros and Civilization: A Philosophical Inquiry into Freud* (New York: Vintage Books, 1962; Routledge, 1997), 136. See also *One Dimensional Man* (Boston: Beacon Press, 1964), 63, where, in the context of the conquest of the unhappy consciousness, he says: "Whether ritualized or not, art contains the rationality of negation. In its advanced

From thinking as negation, to the critique of critique, we come to the "terrorism of theory." This was language Bruno Bauer used toward the middle of the nineteenth century, but it is not entirely dissimilar to the kind of language tempting some forms of cultural critique not too long ago.

Notice how critique has reverted to a kind of relation to theory, and its own practice embodies theoretical presuppositions, but at the heart of them one worries about a suspicion, if not a hatred, of the other as other, even when the rhetoric shows a saturation with talk of "the other." One worries about the "terrorism of theory" in two senses: the terrorizing *by* theory which, alas, then becomes the terrorizing *of* theory. Terrorizing *by* theory, as the dissident intellectuals call into question the status quo. Terrorizing *of* theory, as the dissident intellectuals are put against the wall and shot by their erstwhile comrades in arms.

FINESSING CRITIQUE, FINESSING METAPHYSICS

Discerning beyond Negativity

In this second part of my reflections I turn to the question of metaphysics after critique, but in a sense more affirmative of a future for metaphysics. First, we need to remind ourselves about the ethos of modernity in which the culture of critique is fostered. We dwell in being as the milieu of givenness, a givenness not devoid of promise, the promise of our self-realization, yes, but surely not only that. We configure, reconfigure, the given milieu of being, and build a second ethos in the first ethos, a second ethos reflecting what we consider to be intelligible and true, what we deem good and of value, what we divine of ultimate importance. We can-

---

positions it is the Great Refusal—the protest against that which is." Marcuse sees negation in terms of a liberation, but what prevents a great refusal from becoming a generalized spirit of suspicion extending to everything or everyone, such as we find under tyranny, and the totalitarianisms of the left? Critique can be a form of intellectual vigilance, but how avoid this vigilance becoming a hyperbolic suspicion, not only of what was and what is but even of what may be, and thence from descending into death to the other? We find this generalized spirit of suspicion, extending in every direction, for instance, in *Macbeth*; on this, see my "Sticky Evil: *Macbeth* and the Karma of the Equivocal," in *God, Literature and Process Thought*, ed. Darren Middleton (Aldershot, U.K.: Ashgate Press, 2002), 133–55. Of course, there are different kinds of great refusal, some out of lack of courage, rather than excess of daring. One is put in mind of Dante who "saw the shade of the one who through cowardice made the great refusal [*il gran rifiuto*]"; *Inferno*, canto 3, lines 59–60. Who was that one? Many commentators identify him with Pope St. Celestine V who abdicated the papacy after three and a half months.

not but do this, in the measure that we try to make ourselves at home in given being, and try to take the measure of its givenness. This in no way means we cease to be porous to the ontological mystery of being. In this our reconfiguration we can bring some aspects of the promise of being, or ontological potencies, to the fore, while at the same time sending into recess other aspects of this promise, or ontological potencies.

If I am not mistaken, the (second) ethos of being in modernity is predominantly a reconfiguration of given creation which is now stripped of the signs of ontological worth, of tokens of the good of the "to be," with a concomitant development of the human being thinking of itself as the original of value. Knowing itself, the human being will be also critical of itself, to be sure. But must its critique, thus understood, be anchored on some more basic understanding of being? Must not metaphysics in some fundamental sense always be in play and indeed prove to be most relevant when it is most declared to be redundant?

Critique as the kind of "negative dialectic" described previously is inseparable from certain metaphysical presuppositions about the nature of the "to be" which seep into its characteristic practices. The declaration of the "end of metaphysics" is itself informed by such metaphysical presuppositions that are not allowed to come out of their deep recess. Would not this be one of the tasks of metaphysics, before and after critique: to enable some genuine mindfulness of these ultimate presuppositions about the significance of the "to be," and especially the good of the "to be," both in human and nonhuman senses? Perhaps in the tradition of philosophy, this task was not always as well performed as it could be. I think that rationalistic metaphysics is not entirely free of blame here, and indeed idealistic speculation. But we are metaphysical animals before we are philosophical metaphysicians. And the charge of the latter is a mindful fidelity to what the former means, and indeed its promise, not in a merely abstract way, but in its significance for a way of life, and hence its mediated effects on ethical and political life.

We could begin this rethinking by recalling that the word *critique* comes from *krinein,* variously translatable as "to judge," "to discriminate"—and if this translation has too strong a charge of power or dictation, one might say "to discern": to be able to tell the difference, to tell of significance differences. One might read *krinein* not as an imperative to construct an unsurpassable theoretical system but as soliciting us to the practice of a certain mindfulness. (Parmenides enjoins us in fragment 7: *krinai de logoi.*) I would say: at issue is not the geometrical rationalism of many practices of metaphysics but rather the mindfulness of a certain finesse: metaphysical finesse for the nuances of differences—a finesse, of course, inseparable from the ability to identify, to say that something is something, and what that something is. To discern differences might seem a matter of negation, but it is not, since both identification and difference are forms of affirmation. Thus without affirmation, no difference; without a certain "yes," no negation; and negation that tries to free itself from this "yes" easily degenerates into the spirit of a generalized nihilation or suspicion.

My suggestion: there is a finesse of *krinein* more basic than critique as determinate negation or its relatives. Geometrical, rationalistic metaphysics forgets or loses touches with this finesse of *krinein*, as much as does the negating critique that has turned against the rationalistic metaphysics which it identifies too indiscriminately with metaphysics as such. The keeping alive of this finesse has immense bearing on how we inhabit the ethos of being, and how we hold ourselves open to the basic sense(s) of worthiness, ontological as well as ethical and political. Such a finesse helps keep open a primordial porosity to being (and to the good of being) that lies at the root of all (genuine) self-transcending—be it in practices of philosophy or in practices of critique. This is to be rooted in a kind of ontological love of the given, rather than a suspicion, or hatred.

From where does the "yes" come? Here is an approach. I have spoken about the origins of metaphysics in an astonishment that is prior to both perplexity and curiosity.[17] Wonder is the pathos of the philosopher, it is said in Plato's *Theaetetus* (155d).[18] Modern philosophy begins in doubt,

17. See *Being and the Between,* chapter 1; also chapter 1 of the current work; for further remarks, see the chapter to follow, and more fully chapter 10.

18. *Thaumazein* is the *pathos* of the philosopher, and *archē* of all philosophizing: as our patience to being, pathos suggests what I call our porosity of being, our porosity to being. As mentioned in a previous discussion, Aristotle talks about the desire to know, and says metaphysics and myth are not unlike in that both are linked to a kind of marveling (*Metaphysics* 982b11ff.); but later in the *Metaphysics,* it is to geometry that he appeals to indicate what it means to give an answer to the original wonder (*Metaphysics* 983a13ff.). Geometry offers a determinate answer to a determinate problem, at which point the originating wonder is dissolved. Geometry, in fact, does not express originating wonder, but rather determinate curiosity. If we are unable to discern the difference of these two, it may reflect loss of the more primal pathos. There is no dissolving of the originating wonder, only its deepening. It dissolves when

and the difference of doubt and wonder reflects a different sense of the ethos of being, reflected also in the drift toward system and critique in modernity. Wonder is prior to system and beyond system. It enables system but is not a part of the system. It opens to an engendering origin. Wonder is closer to the generous mother, one of whose prodigal and wayward offspring is doubt. Doubt can become so wayward that it ceases to know it has a mother.

Differently put, astonishment has the bite of an otherness, given before all our self-determining thinking: it opens a mindfulness that we do not self-produce. Astonishment is a precipitation of mindfulness before something admirable, or loveable, or marvelous, communicated from an otherness that has the priority in speaking to the porosity of our being. It comes to us, comes over us, and we open up in response. We do not first go toward something, but find ourselves going out of ourselves because something has made its way, often in startling communication, into the very depths or roots of our being, beyond our self-determination. We are struck into astonishment.

Thus later, too, we find that thought *strikes* us. We do not think; we are startled into thinking, as an access of light or understanding, or fresh astonishment or perplexity, comes to flare up in us. We cannot "project" ourselves into such startlement. If we think we can, we are already feigning it, faking it. The best thought always surprises, and less by its own self as thinking as by what is being given to selving for thought. Thought is a being overcome by what is thought-worthy, a being struck into mindfulness: the thought-worthy comes over us first, and we are called beyond ourselves. And, of course, *that at all* we are called into this porosity in thinking can itself become an occasion of astonishment.

This astonishment is overdeterminate, or has the promise of the over-determinate in it. Not merely indefinite, there is a certain "too muchness" to it: it exceeds every determinate thought. It is not just an empty indeterminacy to be made determinate through a process of negation. It is indeed true that *perplexity* follows astonishment, in that the "too muchness," being given calls forth our thinking about what it might mean at all. The thinking in perplexity is sometimes troubled by its own inability to

---

we go to sleep—when we take for granted the being granted of the happening of being. When we are awake we are in the porosity of being, given into the porosity as ourselves ontologically porous beings. I return to these issues in part 3, especially chapter 10.

be the measure of what gives itself as worthy for thought. In perplexity we move away from the primal astonishment and the beginning of our own determining thinking emerges. For we try to put the question now, more and more; and the more we seem to find an answer to our perplexity, then the less the "too muchness" seems to exceed the measure of our thinking. We allay the trouble of thinking by both determining our thinking, and by seeking determinate answers, and thinking we have the determinate measure of all being as other.

Now *curiosity* comes to the fore: determinate questions seeking determinate answers. Often the primal wonder is associated with curiosity, but this is not correct. Curiosity makes determinate the original opening of minding: it contracts the porosity of minding to this or that; hence the sense of the excessiveness of the givenness is replaced by a sense of determinate measure relative to this or that. We can easily think we are the masters both of our thinking and of the content or objects of our thought. For with curiosity we are more and more placed in the realm of determinacies, and our search for knowing progressively seems to be the measure of all determinate processes in being, as well as specific problems and curiosities we formulate ourselves. Curiosity is indispensable, and yet its contentment with its own forms of determinate cognition can lead to forgetfulness of the more original opening of minding, and the cramping of the more elemental porosity of our being.

Where locate *critique* now? See critique in relation to what might be termed *the sleep of curiosity*. That is, a new perplexity arises to stir up the dubiously allayed curiosity, a potentially suspicious perplexity about the fixities that have come to seem congealed by (self-)satisfied curiosity in the midst of things. The sleep of curiosity happens paradoxically in its untroubled wakefulness. This middle ceases to be perplexing when curiosity is allayed, and then we take the granted for granted. Givenness is accepted but there is no sense of marvel, or mystery: these are recessed by the ascendancy of a sense of mere thereness and matter-of-fact givenness. Here we can see critique as a form of *disturbing perplexity*, alerting us to the fact that such matter-of-fact givenness is not the last word.

And, of course, this is right. Nevertheless, our allayed taking for granted of being as given is not the last word because there is something *prior* to it, and something that always *exceeds* it. This is true both of the fixations in which curiosity rests, and of the fuller promise of the "too muchness" that is sent into recess when the granted is simply taken for granted. Critique essays to wake us from this sleep of taking things for granted wherein, in a way, we are "dead to the world." But waking us from this, to what does critique wake us? To the ability of thought to critique? To certain ethical and political ideals that are recommended as more worthy? Then again the question comes back: What is the meaning of the worthy and the most worthy? What if our thinking has been irremediably marked by perplexity for the strangeness of being at all? And what if thinking understands itself too much in terms of the negative energy of its own skeptical form?

These questions again return us to the meaning of the good of the "to be"; return us as well to the meaning of the good that is "to be." "The good that is to be": this formulation captures both something already given, and something toward which we can also move more fully. One might say: what is given as too much is full of a promise of more again. The "to be" is promising, and its promise is the fullness of the good, of being good and its truer realization, truer in the sense of its more faithful realization. Critique must not become so obsessed with the negation, even destruction, of the falsely fixed, or taken for granted, that it loses sight of this further awakening beyond the unfixing (task) of critique itself.

Awakening beyond Critique

This further awakening is connected with the promise of a metaphysics after critique. The granted must be taken as granted, not for granted. This is to call again on, or be called again by, the recessed astonishment. And it is from there that the "yes" comes that is not the "no" of either doubt, or critique, or deconstruction. We cannot command this "yes." We have to recover some of our own porosity. In a way, we have to become wooers rather than commanders. We have to become lovers again.

This is consonant with the original understanding of philosophy as a form of love. It is a friendship of wisdom, a friendship that in some traditions is also inseparable from eros. What does critique love? Think of eros in the myth of Diotima in terms of its double parentage in *poros* and *penia*. You might say critique would speak on behalf of the poor, the penurious—and this is part of its mystique on "the left," I suppose. What of its own *penia*: What poverty of spirit informs it? Is negative dialectic such a poverty? But then what about *poros*? "Resource" is one translation, but also we find reference to something a little less negative, in that *poros* refers to a way, a way across. An *aporia* of perplexity is an impasse across which thinking cannot find a way: it cannot move in the middle, and is paralyzed. *Poros* opens up a way when we seem paralyzed by the perplexity of an insurmountable *aporia*. A way is opened by *poros* become porous.

Suppose we can connect the *poros* of eros with the idea of porosity: the porosity of love to the other and its communication. For out of this porosity, closely related to *penia*, might come a "yes." In such porosity the "yes" comes, as much from the other beyond us, as from the self in waiting. This is the porosity of wooing. And if there comes a "no," the "no" is not the most primal. The resource of *poros* is in a porosity whose affirmative promise is inseparable from a poverty: in both the porosity and the poverty, a "yes" to the good of the "to be" comes to be communicated. The poverty of this porosity is, in a sense, our "being as nothing." I am as nothing, holding myself open to the communication of the intimate strangeness of being, its otherness beyond my determination and self-determination. The nothing I am or have become is not the power of determinate negation. It points to a "being as nothing" that is more primal than the power of determinate negation. And again paradoxically, this "being as nothing" is also more primally affirmative, as the porous between through which is communicated to us a "yes" from beyond ourselves. We ourselves affirm because we have been affirmed.[19]

It seems to me that if there is a metaphysics after critique it will be only attained by nourishing its thinking on a renewed accession to astonishment understood thus: astonishment prior to ontological perplexity, of which one might claim critical thinking is but one child. Critique can present itself as the mature adult, but, in fact, it is a child. It is a child that is less orphaned than one liable to wander off and think its hard questions are truly original in serving only the interests of self-determining thought and humanity. In truth, these questions are derivative. In a way, openness to the gift of astonishment asks of the thinker that he or she become again as a child. For the resurrected astonishment, the renewal of the elemental "yes," cannot be brought about through philosophical thought trying to determine the matter through itself alone. For this latter ideal

<hr />

19. See my "Religion and the Poverty of Philosophy," in *Is There a Sabbath for Thought? Between Religion and Philosophy* (New York: Fordham University Press, 2005), chapter 3.

of philosophical thinking has already reconfigured, even clogged, our elemental porosity to the communication of irreducible otherness. I mention a point to which I return again, namely, that art and religion are the great helpmates of philosophy in assisting it to the renewal of this astonishment. These offer us the gifts of appreciation, admiration, marveling, reverence. In becoming porous to these significant others, philosophy can also exceed the circle of self-determining thinking, and become a thought that thinks what is other to itself, thought that perhaps even can sing what is other. It can become a love of wisdom in the between.

I appreciate that some will claim that it is platitudinous to refer to astonishment. Nevertheless, there is something here excessive to critique: a ready porosity and "yes" to the givenness of being, and givenness as good. The good of the "to be" is an admirable happening. Think this, and it is not that critique has no role, but its negative definition must be qualified severely. The "no" is derivative from a "yes," a "yes" that is found to be violated or betrayed in many forms of life, or in different human practices. Genuine critique, as justified refusal, or justifying refusal, is always in the name of the good, but what is this good? We cannot separate metaphysics and ethics. We can be given an entirely new energy for thinking. To think in the name of the good has also a political as well as a metaphysical dimension to it. One wonders whether if without granting the latter, the former will inevitably turn out to be either too thin or mutilated.

Nihilism Again

One might relate these reflections in particular to the experience of nihilism in modernity. In my view there are deficient forms of critique that contribute to this nihilism by their mockery or even hatred of the "yes"—as if the latter were a dishonest sanctification of an unjust status quo, a form of collaboration in evil rather than the memory of a communication of worth that shows us the shabbiness of the many human betrayals of the good. The "yes" makes the occurrence of evil all the more disturbing—and awakens a kind of hyperbolic vigilance, more extreme than even the worried thought of critique.[20]

Consider the following argument relative to the valuelessness of being

---

20. See "The Sleep of Finitude: On the Unease of Philosophy and Religion," in *Is There a Sabbath for Thought?* chapter 1.

we find in nihilism. The ethos of much of modern critique shares in this sense of valuelessness, in response to which humans are to be the saviors of a more intrinsic worth. But if the whole is valueless, or void of inherent value, if there is no inherent good of the "to be," then we humans cannot sustain the claim to being alone ends in self, as Kant alleged, or alone the origin of value, such as Nietzsche exclaims.[21] We can claim to create value in the valueless whole, and so seem to save it from the indifferent insipidity of mere thereness, but what happens when we remember that we are also parts of this valueless whole? We also partake of the same valuelessness of the valueless whole—from the standpoint of the whole—hence our claim to be the source of value looks like special pleading or making of ourselves a self-serving exception. If we are honest about this, and if it is true that the whole is valueless, and we awaken to our ultimate participation in its valuelessness, we cannot continue to take ourselves with full seriousness as putative originators or creators of value. If the whole is valueless, if there is no (other) good to the "to be," then our every project of moral earnestness, or even defiant will to power that claims to legislate to the whole, must collapse under the truth of its own honesty. These projects too come to nothing. Every project of moral earnestness, every project of forceful will to power, is itself a manifestation of the truth of the valueless whole: every such project is itself ultimately valueless.

In truth, on this view, we ourselves instantiate the valuelessness of the valueless whole. Nietzsche squints at this: one eye honestly on the worthless abyss, the other eye on the consoling illusions or lies of art. "We need art lest we perish of the truth"—the "as if" truths of art, that is, aesthetic fictions, save us from *the* truth which is the dark origin of Dionysian chaos. Contrariwise, honesty might dictate that we confront our "being as nothing," grant our *penia* differently, namely, by a new acknowledgment of our being as given to be, of our being a *passio essendi* before our being a *conatus essendi*. In this patience of being there might be something like a "return to zero" that looks like nihilism but in fact it allows the return of the question of the good of the "to be," beyond nihilism. It is in a return to the patience of being that a more original sense of the good of the "to

21. Friedrich Nietzsche, *The Gay Science*, §301 "Nature is always worthless—but one has at some time given, donated worth to it, and *we* were those givers and donators! [die Natur ist immer wertlos: sondern dem hat man einen Wert einmal gegeben, geschenkt, und *wir* waren diese Gebenden und Schenkenden!]."

be" can be communicated, prior to the projects of our endeavor to be, and nurturing them with energies of being that are truer to life itself and the good of its "to be."

At the origin and at the furthest horizon of all our "projects," there is an ontological sense of the good of the "to be," within which even our efforts to enact, even construct, values participate. Always in the middle, we are participations and participants in this other sense of the good of the "to be" which is not first the product of our self-determining reason or will. The latter presuppose it, and if we fail in the finessed recognition of what this asks of us, our will becomes will to power spinning ultimately empty constructions in the void. Granting this other sense of the good of the "to be" is not a matter of thinking as negation or philosophy as critique. Something other is required—another kind of thinking. And maybe more than thinking is also required—things like singing, like praying, for instance.

To develop a thinking that would address this sense of valuelessness, as well as the good of the "to be," would be a great task for metaphysics after critique. It would not only be an addressing of one of the extreme forms of critique: skepticism of given truth and intelligibility to the extremity of nihilism. One of the amazing things about nihilism is that it makes the light strangely perplexing in a new way. Were nihilism the ultimate truth, we would expect no light, and yet light there is. *Nihilism strangely makes the light itself strange.* We see the "truth" of nihilism in a light that nihilism, were it true, would render untrue, not to say, impossible. What is that light? Is it something in which we are, in the more primal ethos of being, which we do not bring to be, but rather *simply are what we are* as a participation in it? Does the resurrection of astonishment awaken metaphysical thinking to this old and ever young light?

This matter has nothing to do with the old chestnut charge of "quietism." Quite the opposite, it is most concretely urgent relative to the sources, the resources, out of which genuine ethical and political critique might emerge. What is suggested here has a bearing not only on theoretical critique but also on ethical and political critique. Without some fundamental sense of the good of the "to be," all our critique finally is out of nothing and toward nothing, and, like all our "projects" in this perspective, finally comes to nothing.

One of the hindrances here is *impatience in philosophy:* unwillingness to take the longer view, the look at more than foreground things, the willingness to acknowledge complexities that militate against easy practical solutions. For impatience leads to us imposing our categories on situations that require more distance, greater amplitude of mindfulness. One of the attractions of critique consists in its promise of a more activist intervention. Nevertheless, there are disastrous interventions, as well as creative and constructive interventions. And again finesse is needed to tell the difference between the two, to tell what is the most fitting here and now. Sometimes the urgency of situations dictates an intervention even when our vision of things is partial or blurred—we have no choice. A crisis can be a situation in which a certain urgency of ultimacy can be manifested. But precipitancy is not always the right direction of this urgency. At other times waiting for the right angle on the situation to crystallize is the wiser course of action. This means a finesse for the moment of *kairos*, or the best approximation thereto.

Granted, I am primarily here talking about reorienting thinking in a way that takes critique into account, and indeed the philosophies of nihilism, indeed the philosophies of finitude that are pervasive in the centuries since the so-called end of metaphysics. The orientation of thinking is crucial, for if one is turned in a sterile direction everything that follows from this will only increase the sterility. *Crisis* has everything to do with a point of turning, of discerning and choosing between different ways. All philosophizing is in crisis in that sense and asks itself: What is the best way to choose? One might venture: *Turnings in thought are all important.* Turnings are not methods and not systems of thought; though particular turnings may well produce different methods and different systems. The *periagōgē* of the soul was the old Platonic way to speak of this turning (*Republic* 518d). Conversion is another way, as is revolution. Periagōgē is a revolution in the right direction, as is true conversion. We have been turning and turning in the widening gyre and the falcon cannot hear the falconer (Yeats, "The Second Coming").[22] We need to listen differently and turn differently. Turnings offer directions, but you have to follow the direction of the way opened. And I do think a different systematic orientation can come from this.

22. *The Poems.*

Promise beyond Promissory Notes

That said, I do not want to issue manifestos about metaphysics or merely promissory notes drawn on blank possibility. Thinking through the issues involved in this turning asks for the development of what I call a metaxological metaphysics. This seeks to give a logos of the *metaxu,* the between that is not captured either by the sublationary infinitism of Hegelianism and idealism or by the postulatory finitism of postidealistic philosophy of Nietzsche and his successors. Neither a sublationary infinitism nor a postulatory finitism, a different philosophy of the between is needed that thinks differently of finitude and infinity, and the boundary between them: between determinacy and overdeterminacy; between definite cognition and wonder at the mystery of being. To philosophize in the between is not to sublate the finite into the infinite, nor to insist on finitude and nothing but finitude, but to become mindful of both the poverty and the plenitude of finitude. It is to come to know the between as also a porous boundary between finitude and what exceeds it, the between where the overdeterminate power of being is communicated in the determinacies of finite happening.

To conclude, perhaps I can say a few words about what a metaxological metaphysics after critique might look like. *Being and the Between* might perhaps be seen as trying to retrieve the question of being from the Heideggerian monopoly. This work is systematic without the system, in Hegel's sense: it entails open systematic thinking, which also marks boundaries where systems become porous to what exceeds system. The *metaxu* first is to be seen as a happening: the milieu or ethos of being within which we find ourselves. A metaxological metaphysics bears on our efforts to offer a *logos* of the *metaxu:* this concerns the mode(s) of articulation of the happening of the *metaxu.* In this latter task, the univocal, equivocal, and dialectical ways of being and mind are each taken to be ways of trying to articulate the *metaxu.* Each of these three exhibits characteristic emphases, characteristic underemphases: something is expressed, something recessed. A metaxological metaphysics tries to take the next step with a more faithful articulation of the *metaxu,* in terms of the deepest definitions of sameness and otherness, identity and difference, and the forms of relation and interplay between self and other, and so on. It works through the determinacies and self-determinations of being toward the overdeterminacy. It offers a philosophy of intermediacy and intermediations, beyond univocal determinacies, equivocal indeterminacies, speculative self-mediations; also beyond the critical deconstruction of univocal determinacies and speculative self-mediations, though it too comes to the testing perplexities concerning what lies at the boundary of all our intermediations. Apropos of the discussion above, it offers a reading of Hegel dissident to those who think he completes metaphysics, and hence dissident to the practitioners of critique or negative dialectic or deconstruction, as their proposed alternatives to the putative Hegelian completion.

Ethics and the Between, one might say, seeks to retrieve the question of being good from a current Levinasian monopoly on ethics. In premodern metaphysics there was an intimacy between being and good which was lost, or betrayed, or distorted in post-Cartesian philosophy. One cannot charge the entire tradition of Western thought of ontology as a philosophy of power. *Ethics and the Between* tries to address not an ethics of the other simply, though the stress on the community of agapeic service, indeed the ethical porosity to the other in a *compassio essendi,* is not at all unsympathetic to some Levinasian emphases. Primarily it addresses the good of the "to be" in its extensive sweep and intensive depths. The power of Levinas comes from his obsessiveness of focus on the other; but the world, the ethical world is wider. All human promise is implicated, and more again: the givenness of creation and the secret love of God.

A metaphysics of the good of the "to be" would require a *step back* out of ethical and political systems. It might be as something analogous in ethics to Heidegger's claim to take a step back out of metaphysics. What would its point be? To recover some sense of the overdeterminate ethos of the "to be" as good, and more determinately the diverse sources of value, be these ontological or ethical or political. I call these sources the potencies of the ethical, and they are plural. But they take shape in an ethos that we do not ourselves first produce: we first participate in the between as the charged ethos of being, in which our ethical potencies are plurivocally articulated. I name these diverse potencies the idiotic, the aesthetic, the dianoetic, the transcendental, the eudaimonistic, the transcending, and the transcendent. On the basis of an exploration of ethos, the potencies and ways of being ethical, the nature of ethical selving and ethical communities can be illuminated. The issue is first not Nietzsche *versus* Kant, or either of these *versus* Christianity or Platonism, and so on. As asking the "ethical step back," it is the exploration of the ethos of the ethical between, and these potencies of the ethical, relative to which we can throw new light on different ethical systems. One system emphasizes this potency, for instance, Kant the transcendental potency. Another way emphasizes the transcending potency, Nietzsche, for instance. Religious systems emphasize both the transcending potency of the human and the transcendent good. The exploration in *Ethics and the Between* of ethical communities, with social-political consequences, is crucial for our theme: different formations of community will tend to stress the idiotic, the aesthetic, the erotic, the agapeic. But the crucial point would be to develop ways of being mindful that allow the discernment of differences, their sources and resources, with respect to ethical and political systems, not to homogenize them.[23] An understanding of these sources and endowments throws light on what is the more and the less worthy to be affirmed as good, and the most worthy, the transcendent Good.

A third volume of such a metaxological metaphysics after critique is *God and the Between.*[24] This parts ways with the Heideggerian identification of "metaphysics" with "ontotheology," and tries to deliver on the promise of a metaxological metaphysics to renew fruitfully the philosophical exploration of God. It addresses modern atheism, not least in its connection with the devaluation of being, and the apotheosis of human autonomy. It offers a way beyond godlessness by means of a plurivocal approach in which the univocal, equivocal, dialectical, and metaxological senses of being open up, though sometimes occluding also, our ways to God. In light of the fourfold sense of being, it offers an account of the different understandings of God, culminating with an essay in philosophical theology about the being of God understood in light of a speculative metaxology. Since it is especially important that the relation of religion and metaphysics needs new thinking for a metaphysics after critique, I will close with some words on this topic, for it bears on the secret sources out of which all metaphysical thinking comes.

23. See also my "Neither Servility nor Sovereignty: Between Metaphysics and Politics," in *Theology and the Political*, ed. C. Davis, J. Milbank, and S. Žižek (Durham, N.C.: Duke University Press, 2005), 153–82.

24. *God and the Between* (Oxford: Blackwell, 2008); see also *Hegel's God: A Counterfeit Double?* and *Is There a Sabbath for Thought?*

Recall again the previously mentioned Comtean secular teleology of human history: religion/theology, metaphysics, positive science. I find myself sympathetic to those who are critical of the metaphysical smugness of secular reason. Such a secular teleology does not get it right in relation to astonishment and perplexity, the deeper sources of genuine metaphysics, and indeed the intimate companionship of artistic appreciation and religious celebration. Metaphysics after critique asks for a different porosity of philosophy to its significant others, art certainly, but especially religion. We need an ensuing dialogue between philosophy and its others that is not just oriented to positive science, or autonomous self-determining thinking. And oriented not just to critique or deconstruction either, except insofar as both of these help prepare the way for the new porosity of philosophy. In themselves they are not that porosity, and one can live and think this porosity without having anything to do with critique or deconstruction.

Earlier I coupled *krinein* with discernment and discrimination and crisis. Now perhaps one might say we need more than anything else something like *religious finesse,* somehow seeping into the heart of philosophical thought—or at the least the latter becoming again more porous to the former. Of course, there are forms of religious vehemence in which violence is not avoided, but I am envisaging here a kind of "critique" in which a wrong *spiritual violence* must be purged—from both philosophy and religion. The purification of the spirit from the temptation to violence, this is more than a merely intellectual task, even if the intellect without this purification risks its own spiritual corruption, no matter that it be used as the cleverest tool in the world. Religious finesse in the sense I intend directs us toward a critique not driven by hidden hatred, even when justified refusal is called forth in a situation of evil. I would say that the friendship of philosophy may need its purgatory on this point; and given that it is the human spirit that is tempted toward violence, perhaps our practice of being religious also needs its own purgatory.[25]

---

25. Think of Plato's *Republic* as critique in this sense: purgatorial of *eros turannos,* both in the individual soul, and in the relations of the groups in the community of the polis; seeking a catharsis impossible without the right metaphysical and ethical turn; turning the soul to discriminate the goods of finitude by the light of the good. The *Republic* is also a purgation of the religious: the image of the gods are potentially idolatrous, counterfeit doubles, images of superior being and perfection to which our ethical imperfections and crimes are not to be attributed. One sees "prophetic" dimensions to Socrates: in the *Apology* with respect to his

The suggestion now: perhaps it is the *prophetic mind* that is the proper name for the religious finesse that marries together something like the spiritual impulses of critique and metaphysics—purged of violence but not of the ethical energy to speak out the truth. The issue of finesse is intensified here to the extent that we sometimes have to discern the difference of the false and true prophet. No one determines himself or herself to be prophetic. There is an ultimate patience to it, even if the person's response to the patience pours forth in an energy of trying to do the true, trying to be true in doing the true. And yet the need of the prophetic mind appears more often in situations of extremity than in the moderate circumstances of domesticated life. We must decide where we stand, when the moment of truth comes upon us. Such a prophetic mind would incarnate something of the discriminating power that bears on the ultimate good of the "to be." By that good, properly understood, I mean a fidelity to the communication of the divine; by that power, the discernment of the difference of God and the counterfeit doubles of God.

There is a dimension of *witnessing* here, in the speaking out of the truth (*pro-phetes*: not quite to "foretell" but to "tell forth"), and the doing of the truth ("practice the truth with love"). The prophetic finesse may exhibit also a religious clairvoyance in the chiaroscuro of the equivocal time of life. I am not quite talking about the tension between Athens and Jerusalem. To be discerning in the difference, tension, and possible affiliation of these two is, of course, very important. But I am suggesting, in relation to Athens, a listening of reason, not always cultivated by reason, whether ancient or modern, because the listening is not of reason thinking it can determine everything through itself alone. This other listening of reason is rooted in a reverence and devotion, out of which reason's own confidence comes, confidence in its own power to know the truth, confidence in the truth as trustworthy and knowable, indeed lovable, confidence in the fundamental intelligibility and goodness of being.

Confidence is a *con-fides,* a *fides* "with"; it is already in fidelity with and to an other. The "con" is a "cum" or "with" that already announces a basic community or communication that *confides to reason,* unknown to it at the start, a grounding confidence, or trust, that there is truth and in-

---

posthumous vindication, in the *Phaedo* with respect to death and judgment, in the *Phaedrus* with respect to piety, eros, and divine inspiration. I wondered at the outset about a "right-wing" practice of critique? Is there not here a practice of critique that is neither "left" nor "right"?

telligibility to be attained, were it further to seek. This means, of course, that our reason is never simply self-determining; for this confiding, this *fides "with,"* this confidence, is what energizes all its processes of determining, including its own confidence in its own self-determining powers, and indeed its own powers of critique. This confiding is prior to critique and beyond it, and keeps critique from wandering from the just way. This confidence or confiding is first not known but *trusted*: trusted without knowing in the living participation in the good of the "to be"; trusted as enabling us, and already in some enigmatic way presupposed by every quest of knowing itself; trusted by the faithful enactment of being true in the ethical and religious good of life.

5 ✑ Metaphysics and the Intimate Strangeness of Being

Neither Deconstruction nor Reconstruction

Critique and deconstruction are family relatives. Mutations of the skeptical gene circulate in the bodies of both. If there is metaphysics after critique, where are we after deconstruction? Nowhere? Nowhere as metaphysicians? Or somewhere between deconstruction and reconstruction? Indeed the proposal has been made that what we need after the deconstruction of metaphysics is a reconstruction. I would propose a practice of metaphysical thinking other than either a deconstruction or a reconstruction. The intimate strangeness of being perplexes us as to whether these alternatives are entirely to the point. "Intimate strangeness" refers to the middle condition of our thought of being: being is strange because it has an otherness, indeed marvel, of which we are not the conceptual masters; it is intimate, in that this very strangeness allows no stance of thinking "outside" being—we are participants in what we think about. Being indeed gives us to be before we think about the meaning of what it is to be. The strangeness of being is as much about us, as we are within it.

It is true, then, that certain binary oppositions of inside-outside, reality-appearance, invisible-visible, and so on do not quite capture the task of metaphysical thinking. Deconstruction claims that such binary thinking is characteristic of (all) traditional metaphysics. I think this is only true at one level of consideration. There are other dimensions of consideration not to be deconstructed in metaphysics. Dialectical thinking already shows something of what is promised in the transcending of such binary oppositions. Even more so does what I call metaxological mindfulness. If this is true of deconstruction, then as a response to it, we do not necessarily need a reconstruction. At least not in this sense: reconstruction can imply that something has been destructured, perhaps even brought level to the ground, or lack thereof, and then we must rebuild. What if the destructuring does not itself address that intimate strangeness of being but a conceptual construction that functions more like a surrogate or a mimicry of it? Deconstruction might destructure the construction but not the intimate strangeness of being. Reconstruction as purportedly the positive opposite to deconstruction will not describe the affirmative task of a renewed metaphysical thinking.

"Deconstruction" is not plain "destruction," of course, though *Destruktion* is Heidegger's word, and the coarse commentator might be misled by an acoustical illusion to think something not quite tender is intended. Insinuated or not, the hint of terminological equivocation does no harm to the desire to be reputed as radical. I use the locution "neither/nor," a locution sometimes used by thinkers searching to be free from univocal binary opposition. I would say the issue turns on the nature of the freeing of thought that comes from thinking on the double, thinking beyond the doublets of "metaphysics." Our task is not reconstruction quite, but thinking anew the intimate strangeness of being, and with a way of thinking that seeks to do justice to both the intimacy and the strangeness. The intimate strangeness of being can be neither deconstructed nor reconstructed. Its immanence enables construction, deconstruction, reconstruction, but even as intimately strange it is also a sign of what resists being determined in entirely immanent terms. Mindfulness of this intimate strangeness is one of the things called for in a metaxological metaphysics.

Needless to say, deconstruction as an academic movement has passed like a wind over the already quite bare landscape of contemporary thought in the last thirty or more years. What was there to blow down, in that landscape, for that wind? The wind seems now hardly a gentle breeze. Is this a lull? Or is it the empty mellowness of exhaustion? Has a form of life grown grey? What would the Owl of Minerva discern in the dusk if it flew over that form? I would say that what is betrayed by the cultural phenomenon of deconstruction is not at all exhausted, if we include in its name the same old suspicion of all things old that has been a sign of modernity, or transgressive thinking touting itself as à la mode, for centuries now. One must wonder if "deconstruction" is exhausted in one sense: the word has passed the mutation barrier of public recognition, and so even a form of life as low as the journalist's can use the word without embarrassment—and without much understanding either. The word can mean almost everything, mean many things, and hence perhaps now means nothing much. There is no doubt that deconstruction went viral in certain quarters of academic studies some decades ago. That it went viral is symptomatic. As we know, there are kinds of viruses that may mutate, but they get into everything and one hardly notices. The strain may have been domesticated in its circulation. Or a more virulent strain may be in the incubation. One may be dealing with the surface symptoms of toxins and antitoxins that have a longer life than thirty plus years.

CONFESSING EQUIVOCITY

What more deeply interests me here is how the intimate strangeness of being might be seen in light of a certain family likeness of deconstructive thinking and forms of negative dialectic. My overall concern is less with, for instance, Adorno's negative dialectic as a cousin of Derrida's deconstructive thinking, but more with the negativity of dialectic and how perhaps its genes might still be turned on restlessly in such thinking. But perhaps it is proper briefly to confess a thing or two about my equivocal relation to deconstruction.[1] In all fairness I have made my efforts at sympathetic comprehension. I do confess to have written about deconstruction and dialectic years ago, at the time of its most virulent ascendency. In *Art and the Absolute* (1986) I dedicated a chapter (5) to "Dialectic, Deconstruction, and Art's Wholeness," making use of the triad univocity, equivocity, and dialectic. I granted the deconstructionist alertness to fixations of univocity and attentiveness to the dissembling of equivocity, but held that dialectic also opened a sense of mediated wholeness. I spoke of the artwork as communicating a kind of "open wholeness," but deconstructionists bucked at the temerity of any defense of art's wholeness. I was chastised for my "readings" or for my lack of "readings." (Ironically, *in illo tempore* the catch cry was: there are no "readings," only "misreadings.") But I was not back then, and am not now, primarily in the business of giving "readings." I am thinking about things. Let the philological police carry out their Scholastic surveillance of "readings"—or "misread-

1. A version of these reflections was originally presented at the 50th Meeting of the Metaphysical Society of America, Boston College, March 12–14, 1999, on the theme deconstruction and reconstruction in metaphysics. In this later version, among other revisions and rewritings, I have added my confession.

ings." Philosophy passes by as perplexed thinking about the astonishing strangeness of being.

I also saw then family likenesses between deconstructionist patterns of thinking and romantic irony, and indeed saw something in it that would draw us closer to the spirit of laughter. Laughing at philosophy, particularly in the mode of a certain mockery, can sometime seem to be an effective indictment of its rationalistic pretensions. In *Beyond Hegel and Dialectic* I dedicated to this theme a chapter (5) entitled "Comedy and the Failure of *Logos*: On Dialectic, Deconstruction, and the Mockery of Philosophy." There is also a chapter (6) entitled "Can Philosophy Laugh at Itself? On Hegel and Aristophanes—with a Bow to Plato." My own critiques of Hegelian dialectic are not entirely strange to some of the themes of deconstruction, though perhaps the ironies I find in dialectic are more of the sympathetic kind.

I tried to keep up—I am now talking about the time of deconstruction's heyday in the United States. I tried my patience in a good faith effort to get through the lush exfoliation of many of Derrida's texts. I was in communication with intimate admirers of Derrida who would try to counteract my diffidences by assuring me he was not the nihilist of journalistic caricature, indeed academic portrayal. Quite to the contrary, his inspiration was deeply ethical. Why this one admirer had only last night talked with Derrida on the phone about just this misperception! Alas, it was my misfortune to be a mere grammatologist. I only had the written word to go on. The admirer had his word on the phone, Derrida's "phonology," so to say.

Derrida's *logos* on the phone gave me pause certainly, but I must confess that the Paul de Man affair and its aftermath tested my hermeneutical patience. It was not just the overkill in deconstructive hermermeutics whereby De Man's alleged collaboration with the Nazis and taint of anti-Semitism was brought to a point of undecidability.[2] A simple confession or acknowledgment of mistakes made would have been enough. It was more the response immediately thereafter to the worries of critics. Of course, undecidability is a double-edged sword. It asks us to think on the double but also it can tempt us with double-think. It might be true that

2. Jacques Derrida, "Like the Sound of the Sea Deep within a Shell: Paul de Man's War," trans. Peggy Kamuf, *Critical Inquiry* 14, no. 3 (Spring 1988): 590–652.

deconstructive hermeneutics can help us weaken determinate certainties, but what if it were to help us prove the strong the weak and the weak the strong? We are in the space of dialectic, yes, but perhaps we need to worry about being too close to the spirit of a specious dialectic. Thinking on the double becomes double-think, double-speak. The doublings of *logos* pass too close to dubious equivocation.[3]

I am not making accusations. I am telling a tale, the tale of my own equivocal relation to Derrida's deconstruction. As I said, it was not the suggested undecidability of Paul de Man's wartime record that broke my own undecidability. It was more the tone of response to questions raised and the deployment of the offensive metaphor of "biodegradables" in response to critics raising fairly reasonable questions.[4] I was told by some excellencies in the academy that Derrida was the leading intellectual luminary at the end of the twentieth century. I found I had to give back my ticket to the show of light. There was then a turn to the ethical in deconstruction about which I heard from colleagues who continued to be admirers. This was for me more the phonology of friends than the grammatology of the master. Though not reading Derrida, it was impossible not to know of him, he was so much in the air.

I did note the mutation of tonality in concerns from a more Nietzschean to more Levinasian register. The virile phase of transgressive deconstruction seemed to give way to an almost hyperbolic concern for the other. (Transgression: Am I mistaken in the impression that this word now seemed less used, or used less virulently?) Deconstruction revealed itself as justice. The "thou" is older than the "I," Zarathustra intoned. Now it seems as if the older "thou" had made a big comeback. Many seemed to have become flagellants of the self in penitence before the excessive other, the "thou" they previously marginalized as the servile other. "Rome versus Judea," Nietzsche exclaimed, but Judea seemed to have stepped out of the

3. Relevantly to our larger purpose here, I am struck by something of the almost august ancestry of the strategy used by Derrida in his reflection on Paul De Man's war in pursuit of the point of undecidability, namely speaking "on the one hand . . . on the other hand." I am reminded of the ancient practice of *dissoi logoi*, or Aristotle's resembling way of speaking "on the one hand . . . on the other hand," or Abelard's *sic et non*, or for that matter Kant's approach to the antinomies of reason, and all of these as predecessors to Hegel's practice of dialectic, and as inherited by his successors, negative dialectic. The proximity to equivocity, dubious or not, is the pivotal point to be pondered.

4. Jacques Derrida, "Biodegradables: Seven Diary Fragments, " trans. Peggy Kamuf, *Critical Inquiry* 15, no. 4 (Summer 1989): 812–73.

desert and back onto center stage, even among erstwhile Nietzscheans. For the Levinasian penitents, the pagan Zarathustra has been dispatched back to his cave to languish for now in exile.

How does Rome become a convert to Judea or revert to it? That is never explained. One might speak, as Christopher Simpson does, of a "LeviNietschean" vision,[5] but how get these two together? They are not even married by a hyphen. One might invoke James Joyce with his "Jewgreek is Greekjew. Extremes meet." These two also are not married by a hyphen and it is not Joyce speaking. The phrase is often cited with great solemnity by the scholars (Derrida included)[6] but Joyce is having fun, having a laugh. It is *Lynch's Cap that speaks* in the Circe episode of *Ulysses* and its slightly crazed, hallucinatory atmosphere of the drunken brothel. The cap is a mocking voice ("Bah!" seems its watchword) and is answering a (slightly phrenological) question directed to it by Stephen Daedelus: "Which side is your knowledge bump?"[7] Joyce's laughter with his "two thinks at a time" points in the direction of a truer dialectical, postdialectical thinking, as well as echoing a thinking on the double. This thinking on the double can festively word the plurivocity of the metaxological, refresh astonishment about the strange intimacy of being at all. Even unto the drunken wonder of a talking cap!

5. Christopher Simpson, *Religion, Metaphysics, and the Postmodern: William Desmond and John D. Caputo* (Bloomington: Indiana University Press, 2009). I would add that John Caputo in his engaging and witty book *On Religion* (New York: Routledge, 2001) confesses at the end (chapter 5) to being torn between the two, between the ethical and the tragic visions.

6. Jacques Derrida, *Writing and Difference*, trans. Alan Bass (Chicago: University of Chicago Press, 1978), 153, also note 92, 320–21. Here at the end of his celebrated essay ("Violence and Metaphysics") he speaks of Joyce as "perhaps the most Hegelian of modern novelists" but if I am right Joyce is not at all Hegelian but a transdialectical, a metaxological writer. The Joycean end is not absolute knowing, or thought thinking itself. I would say it is in celebrating fidelity to the surplus overdeterminacy of being in its intimate strangeness, especially but not exclusively human being. The festive laughter of Joyce is metaxologically plurivocal. In Derrida's own footnote he suggests that "Jewgreek is greekjew" is "a *neutral* proposition, anonymous in the sense execrated by Levinas, inscribed in Lynch's *headpiece* (320)." Has finesse for the metaxological dramatics of the scene deserted these commentators? Neutral? No. It is inebriated comedy, mock serious, as often with Joyce, but making us laugh. Laughter, even at the "neutral," is always a release from the neutral. On Irish thinkers and writers as metaxological, see my *Being Between: Conditions of Irish Thought* (Galway, Ireland: Leabhar Breac/Center for Irish Studies, 2008).

7. James Joyce, *Ulysses* (New York: Random House, 1961), 504.

DISSOLVING THE SEDIMENTED

So much for confessing equivocity. I now turn to some philosophical matters at stake and take a step back in relation to more long-range considerations. I think it important to remember that very early in modernity metaphysics has been called upon to *justify itself.* This is so not only in Descartes vis-à-vis knowing (the ancients are "useless") and Hume (no reasoning and matter of fact?—commit the tomes of metaphysics and theology to the flames). It is especially so since Kant's onslaught against metaphysics as putatively dogmatic. The doublet of skepticism and dogmatism tilts strongly in the direction of the first. This tilt issues in a more and more virulent living of skepticism by philosophy, and not now against other knowledges, but most deeply *against itself.* An afterlife of this virulent skepticism is at the heart of what attracts many to deconstruction. As making claims about what is ultimate, *philosophical knowing turns against itself,* and especially against itself in the form of making ultimate claims that it purports to substantiate *through itself alone.* We find this latter ideal in early modernity. The unfolding of modernity turns the screw, and turns against just this claim of philosophy to be justified through itself alone. First skepticism turns against dogmatism for not being able to live up to the ideal of self-determining, self-justifying knowing (i.e., the ideal of modern philosophy). Then we find skepticism turning against even the very pretenses of self-justifying knowing, hence against the very ideal of modern philosophy.

Think here of Kant and Hegel and then of the post-Hegelians. Kant claimed to be woken from dogmatic slumbers, that is, from traditional metaphysics (supposedly). What of the post-Kantians? Does Kant call to heel the dogs of war given loose rein by skepticism? In fact, the hounds of negation pull savagely at the leashes of heteronomy, and the leash is loosed further: Kant is not yet self-justifying, self-grounding enough! The battle cry goes up: No givenness—autonomize knowing even more radically! So Hegel: his claims to completed skepticism—indeed his claim to self-completion, self-accomplishing skepticism. But where does that lead except to the claim to mediate completely any putative givenness, to the constitution of self-determining knowing in the *Phenomenology,* culminating with the posttranscendental reinvocation of the God of Aristotle at the end of the *Encyclopaedia*: *noēsis noēsis noēseōs.*

Is the battle cry followed by a sigh of peace, or sign? No. Now strut on stage the post-Hegelians, slightly sullen at the feeling that the dogs of negation have been kenneled again, or at least leashed too prematurely, too repressively, by Hegel's self-justifying *reason*. Perhaps reason is the leash. Perhaps we must unloose what is other to reason. And so the proposal: thought is not to think just itself; let it think what is *other to itself*. Post-Hegelian deconstruction might be seen as equivocally, very equivocally, trying to address this other to thought thinking itself, and so as standing opposed to the God of the philosophers, so far as the philosophers are Aristotelians. Inevitably they seem very impious to those whose God, secretly, or unknown, or confessed, is thought thinking itself, justifying itself as the absolute. What is that other? Sometimes it is named as will, will to power, Being, *Ereignis,* the coming democracy that will never come, the indeterminate other that has many names and no name, you name it.

There is a logic here and it might be endorsed—though I would hedge the endorsement with qualifications. Why? One has the impression of deconstruction (certainly more so before its ethical-political turn) as being dragged along by the hounds of negation, at the mercy of the momentum of an antimetaphysical unleashing, unable to bring the dogs of war to heel. One might command dogmatically the dogs to sit but no, they will not, now that all obedience is simply out of the question to whatever would thus impose itself. Nietzsche (more or less): never trust any thought that comes to one when one is sitting down. Fresh thought has no fixed seat, no *sedes,* it follows the flux. We meet again the nomads of skepticism of Kantian denomination. Thought on the move has no sedentary place. Nor is there settlement or ground or sediment to it. The nomads of skeptical thought go on walkabout. Do they know any songlines in the desert? *Queritur.* In Kant's metaphor we have departed from the small (and rather cramped) island of warranted truth,[8] and we are at sea, where all is flood or fog or gale or gush. Such are the turbulences of waking from dogmatic slumbers.

But how endorse? This way, anyway. Thinking has an inevitable tendency to sediment. We think—but determinately. We think this or that or the other. Determinate thinking is necessary but it is not *first*. What is before? An overdeterminate happening, and a more indeterminate open-

8. *Critique of Pure Reason,* B295

ing of mindfulness. It is also at this level, this before, that we come into the presentiment or intimation of the strangeness of being at all. The over-determinate happening and indeterminate opening are given in astonishment before the "that it is at all"—not what this is or that. This is *too much* for us, excessive. An original astonishment stuns us, rocks us back, impels an exodus of transcending toward beings. We *awake to ourselves* in this happening of the astonishing, already being in something more radically enigmatic and other, before thought thinks it, or itself, more definitely or determinately. This is agapeic astonishment: minding becoming porous to the giving of surplus givenness, a gift not a lack.[9]

There is more. Opened, we open beyond ourselves, *toward* what is given. This is not the loss of strangeness but perplexity about it. This is erotic perplexity: mindful we lack something, it seems too full, and we go beyond, toward it—to seek in its fullness what we seem to *lack*. Thus we wake to our ignorance. Perplexity: it is still strange, intimate. How now? As our perplexity becomes more focused into definite curiosity, thinking and the sense of being turn more toward the determinate: being as determinate beings, thinking as determinate thought. Here begins the temptation to turn from the intimate strangeness. Being becomes just strange –just "mere" being. Beings also seem as mere strangers over against us, without any intimacy, or intimation of something beyond the determinate thereness. Here surfaces knowing as a more aggressive curiosity: the otherness is a strange thereness to be taken hold of, to be gripped. It is to be fixed, placed, made subject as object to my cognitive project.

Thus we find the process of domestication, of sedimentation, of familiarization without wonder. Philosophy and science can share in this loss of strangeness and astonishment. There can also be an enfeeblement of perplexity with increasing technical mastery. We appear to be making the world anew: more and more intelligible, in accord with our measure, and with ourselves as measure. The stolidity of a dogmatic self-certainty comes to the fore. The happening of being, between strangeness and intimacy, has become sedimented: neither strange nor intimate just there; thus and thus; univocally thus and not otherwise; a spectacle of determinate beings and determinable process of which we are the determining measure. The porosity to original strangeness, impossible to anticipate,

---

9. See *Being and the Between*, chapter 1.

is hard at all now to acknowledge. Even the suggestion of it may arouse alarm in us. In a reversal into a new strangeness, by neutralizing being we end up making it alarming. We make beings more and more univocally intelligible but being as a whole seems more and more to sink into absurdity. Familiarity without wonder deprives being of its intimacy; strangeness without intimacy makes being a senseless surd.

DECONSTRUCTIVE UNSETTLING

And how now with deconstruction? See it as an interpretation of the tradition of metaphysics as settling into certain forms—becoming sedimented in certain sets of binary oppositions such as substance and accidents, real and appearance, determinacy and indeterminacy, and so on. We are said to fall under the bewitchment of these opposites. We privilege one over the other and so on. They become the taken-for-granted currency of our dominant ways of conceptualization.

There is, no doubt, some truth in these allegations. It is the destiny of thought to take on determinate forms; though it is not the destiny of thought to exhaust itself in such determinate forms, and especially so if the beginning is the excess of givenness communicated in agapeic astonishment. One can grant that these oppositions do have their truth. To think a determinate thought is to do so by relation to what it is not, and hence to think one thought you must think two thoughts, and hence binary forms are inherent in the process of thinking: no thinking without doubling, or thinking on the double. Thus binary doublets need not be entirely false to what is happening—though this truth is not entirely true. Because we have to think determinately, hence in terms of this form or that, there is no escape from the "metaphysics of presence" in this sense here, say, metaphysical thought of determinate forms such as we might find in a doctrine of categories. Deconstructive thought, like Nietzsche, tends to emphasize the danger of our falsification of flux by form. Its dissolving of fixed form tends to see the promise of more in formless flux.

See, then, deconstruction in the line of a skeptical waking up to the "falsity" of fixed form, informed by some sense of the loss of original forming. Very well. Take a further step and say: "Form is the outcome of forming; determination is the outcome of determining; this latter is process rather than product." Dogmatists fall asleep in determinate forms;

skeptics wake up to the forms as fixings of something impossible to fix finally. Thus clearly deconstruction is in tune with skeptic waking. Deconstructive skepticism is also on walkabout but does it want to help us listen to the songlines? Or exorcise them as specters of "metaphysics"? And yet we also find a new set of "forms," or at the least a panoply of quasi-doctrines: difference, supplement, trace, and so on. Why quasi? Is it because of fear of taking them as too ultimately fixed, too determinately there. On the whole, the temper of deconstruction withdraws from positing anything affirmatively in the univocal mode, even while it posits quasi-affirmatively in the equivocal mode. To match its battle cry of overcoming metaphysics, its quasi-positive catch-cry is neither a univocal "no," nor a univocal "yes," but perhaps might be: "perhaps."

This is a redoubled perhaps, but is it not redoubled in the mode of equivocity, if in the end we can say no ultimate "yes" or "no" to anything? "Anything" is necessarily determinate, but this raises the issue again, and we must again say "no," even as we surpass "anything." Does the ark of the "yes" then drown in the flood of "nos"? Nietzsche spoke of the perilous perhaps, but is this peril once again the double-edged sword that might either clear a path or kill a suspect?

Suppose we are willing to say: So far so good. Are we being woken up, in any way analogously to being woken from dogmatic slumbers—that is to say, from fixation on determinacy? But if we are being woken up, then woken up to what? Can one be just woken up to the fact that one was asleep, or perhaps always must be asleep or half-asleep? If we don't wake up to *something,* our being woken up is just another sleep—we wake from one "dream" to another, and hence the entire point of waking up has no point. Is it here that some rationale for "reconstruction" might be suggested? And this rationale: to give some articulate account of that to which we are waking up? Is it what I am calling the intimate strangeness of being? But if it were, is "reconstruction" the right word for such an awakening? Deconstructive thought would reject it—the word is too definite, too smacking of a new fixing. No fix is up to the fixing; there is something beyond fixing. Better then not to fix again, having unfixed?

And yet, yet: we cannot avoid talk of an *other* thinking? Consult Heidegger: an other beginning. We must think something other to thought thinking itself. Since Hegel every skeptic is tempted to dream of this other to thought thinking itself. The same can be said of those whom one would not pin down as skeptic, if a skeptic could be pinned down: Kierkegaard, Marx, Nietzsche, Heidegger, Derrida. Query: To what degree is this other thinking still too much shaped within a certain ethos of negativity, home to various offspring of Hegelian dialectic, not necessarily identified as such? Not thinking as determination; but thinking as negation; even though thought thinks against itself? For after all the point is to release us from the wrong kind of fixation on univocal determinacy, and negativity toward the determinate does seem to open up the space of something *not* determinate, something more indeterminate. But do we then revolve in a circle passing from negation to negation, all the while fearful of resting in any fixed determination? Fearful of determination, since this, we fear, freezes us; and this we fear is death?

If so, we negate again, or transgress, but now we seem caught up in the constant sustenance of negation, for the only constancy is perpetual negation, or transgression. Do we then end with nothing but the negative power of thought? Or the endlessly renewed gesture of transgression which, inevitably, becomes the tediously renewed gesture? Why? *Because we really cannot think of anything new.* Instead of thought thinking itself we see thought negating itself as determinate, but it is still thinking *itself,* though as negation, and so is only equivocally released from itself. More, if the other to thought must always remain other to thought, thought must come into the desert of its final futility. Instead of the triumphant closure of idealistic thought, the triumph of thought as negativity brings thought to *its own debility*—just in its self-surpassing as negativity. Every overcoming of negativity is pyrrhic, and there is no overcoming of negativity. No "reconstruction" at all seems possible on these terms.

In that respect, one has to wonder if deconstructive thinking shares something with the momentum of hypermodernism-postmodernism: the pathos of revolutionary newness. Granted, of course, that the arrival of the truly new is always deferred—hence too here the rationalized resistance to "reconstruction"—for this would imply that *something* had arrived, and this would be too determinate by far. Far better to continue to court the indeterminate. Let me note an odd thing here: there is a little word "*After*" that seems to have taken on a fashionable life of its own. We have books called *After Babel*; *After Virtue*; *After God*; *After Writing*; *Hegel and Marx after the Fall of Communism*; *Hegel after Derrida*; *After Christianity*; *After God* a second time; *After the Death of God*; *After God* a third time; *Anatheism: Returning to God after God.*[10] One might even write a book on the intimate strangeness of being whose subtitle is *Metaphysics after Dialectic.*

Of course, not all of the authors of these books align themselves with deconstructive postmodernism, but the recurrence of the word *after* does make one pause. After the ball is over there are trysts of lovers but also lots of let-downs. After this "after" are we ushered toward less postmodernism as toward a variety of neopostmodernisms? Well over a hundred and fifty years ago Schopenhauer had something to say about "after" philosophy (*Afterphilosophie*) in very impolite mockery of Hegelianism.[11] "After" and "post" suggest the arrival of the latecomer. Something is behind all this, but will it come out? Of course, this would be an odd arrival, since the deconstructive latecomer suggests we can never arrive. To arrive is to be fixed; and off such a determination wafts the perfume of death. Properly (if I can be licensed to use this word), there should be no "after," since we are always on the way, hence always "before" rather than "after." Perhaps we should even alter our watchword of metaphysics from "being between" to "being behind"!

One last sortie after Kant: Kant believed he was beyond skepticism, but in fact, his critique seems very much like a camouflaged mutant of skepticism. After Kant skepticism comes forth fortified with bolder and bolder claims of the subject to be *productive self-activating power. Sapere aude!* But this audacity of knowing can take serpentine turns. One of them is

10. In order: George Seiner, *After Babel: Aspects of Language and Translation* (Oxford: Oxford University Press, 1975); Alasdair McIntyre, *After Virtue: A Study in Moral Theory* (South Bend, Ind.: University of Notre Dame Press, 1984), 2nd ed.; Don Cupitt, *After God: The Future of Religion* (New York: Basic Books, 1997); Catherine Pickstock, *After Writing: On the Liturgical Consummation of Philosophy* (Oxford: Blackwell, 1998); David McGregor, *Hegel and Marx after the Fall of Communism* (Cardiff: University of Wales Press, 1998); Stuart Barnett, ed., *Hegel after Derrida* (New York: Routledge, 1998); Gianni Vattimo, *After Christianity* (New York: Columbia University Press, 2002); John Manoussakis, ed., *After God: Richard Kearney and the Religious Turn in Continental Philosophy* (New York: Fordham University Press, 2005); John D. Caputo, Gianni Vattimo, and Jeffrey W. Robbins, eds., *After the Death of God* (New York: Columbia University Press, 2007); Mark C. Taylor, *After God* (Chicago: Chicago University Press, 2007); Richard Kearney, *Anatheism: Returning to God after God* (New York: Columbia University Press, 2010).

11. On Schopenhauer and *Afterphilosophie*, see *The World as Will and Representation,* trans. E. F. J. Payne (New York: Dover Books, 1966), 2.442 (chapter 38). Payne's polite translation of the impoliteness has "pseudo-philosophy," rather than, say, "backside-philosophy" which would render at least a little of Schopenhauer's scatological insult. It would not be difficult to think of cruder versions.

the bold power derived from Kant's transcendental ego. For now this ego thinks of itself as constructing intelligibles. Why should it not also think of itself as deconstructing intelligibles? No reason at all. Then there is the fact that "destroying" seems much bolder than conserving, hence to make the more powerful point. This seems especially so when the dogmas of the "old" seem so moth-eaten (i.e., unjustified) and *worthy of destruction.* Think here of Nietzsche as both an heir of Kant (a black sheep inheriting his will, turning good will into will to power) and an early patron saint of postmodernism (inheritances should be "taken apart"). What is falling should be helped, that is, *pushed*—this is Zarathustra's naughty proposal.[12] The hypercritical impulse preens itself with its own assurance of justification, for it licenses itself in its hammering of all uncriticized positions (ideals—mere ideals—idols). Yet the earnest side, perhaps imbibed in the mother's milk of Kantian critique, cannot be entirely excised. One thinks of Derrida (*exaipnes!*) becoming earnest: deconstruction is justice. I could well imagine Nietzsche giving the meaning of this: Not I, Plato, am the truth, but I, Jacques Derrida, am the law. I confess again that I do not understand how the Nietzschean leopard changes its amoral spots, how they seem to fade into invisibility, turning Rome back into Judea, and becoming more like an uncomfortable Levinasian camel, moralizing till the cows come home which will be, agonizingly, never.

One recalls the discomfited Kant saying in relation to Fichte: God save us from our friends, our enemies we can take care of ourselves. Is Kant now squirming in the grave at what monsters his transcendental philosophy has spawned: not men of good will who do groundwork, but underground men who undermine all settled ground? Underground in the grave, of course, opposites meet, and above and below are melded in a common fate. What then seems the triumph of skepticism? A new dogmatism of negation? Underground I seem to see a spectral school of *new ascetics* who negate everything, and turn into preachers of the voluptuous anorexia of negativity. Preachers of a kind of blithe hatred, superior in their rigor, in their lack of rigor? As with Nietzsche, finally, "nay-saying" seems more all-consuming than "yea-saying." A "yea" has to justify itself, after all; we can say "nay" to (almost) everything. Every "yea" is a dogmatic dictation of affirmation, finally to be drowned in a sea of overwhelm-

---

12. "Oh my brothers, am I cruel? But I say: what is falling, we should push!" *Zarathustra,* III, "On Old and New Tablets."

ing negations. Still the bold sly self still gets its way: my "nay" to you is my "yea" to myself. All is false, everything is permitted; there is no truth, but I say that, ergo I am the truth. I, skepticus, dogmaticus, am the truth. A dictatorial dogmatism of negation reveals itself as the untrue truth of such skepticism. The critique of truth as correctness leads straight, or sideways, to political correctness—my correctness—or my incorrectness—it matters not a whit which—as long as it is mine.

DISSOLVING DUALISM, TRANSCENDENCE BEYOND AUTONOMY

Deconstructive thinking has an important point to make regarding excessively fixed dualistic ways of thinking. Does it do justice to what is more than such dualistic thought? There are forms of dialectical and postdialectical thought that try to do justice. Suppose we consider this point in relation to these three: first, with respect to Platonic dualism and transcendence; second, with reference to Cartesian dualism and the desire to secure knowing; third, in relation to the ideal of self-determining knowing. These three models are major determinants of the mode of metaphysical thought in the West. They reflect something of the ancient practice of metaphysics, the early modern practice, and its later idealistic acme. We have been philosophically bobbing in the wash of this acme since Hegel, not entirely sure if this *Titanic* has passed us by or just gone down. Many would like to believe the latter. Others again, in revolt against the idols of modern rationalism, have abandoned ship. But then we are at sea again.

Regarding Platonic dualism: We find a crude caricature in Nietzsche's cartoon of the Platonic otherworld. It is worth nothing that, structurally speaking, there is nothing new in the way Nietzsche rails against all "beyonds." It is almost a philosophical cliché, taken into the bloodstream of German thought since the heyday of idealism, even since grandfather Kant, that every heteronomy has to be "critiqued," even neutralized, lest it curb the self-assertion of autonomous freedom. Nietzsche gives us the rhapsody of Dionysus in his variation on the theme. In the anxiety to be free of transcendence as other there is a fixation about that transcendence. There is also a fixation in this sense: a diminution of finessed appreciation of the sources of our quest of transcendence as other, and the inversion of its noble eros into an ignoble, because dissembling, tyranny.

If we do understand our own transcending as oriented to transcendence as other to us, we will be less eager to caricature Plato. This orientation to transcendence as other is rooted in an original opening of agapeic astonishment, in the upsurge of our eros come to its passion in an intimate porosity of being. In Plato there is the surplus of the good as too much for us, blinding us if we look too directly at it, though we see all things by means of its light. Where here is the fixation on univocal presence? I see an interplay of insight and blindness, whether up above out in the sun, or down below in the chiaroscuro of the cave. What is our responsibility? Answer: not just to go up, but to live below, justly and mindfully, in the cave. What is philosophy? A lifelong adaption to the darkness. The sun is dark because lightsome; the cave is dark because in it we dwell in the chiaroscuro of the good, with the intimation of a light the cave does not produce itself. The cave is constitutively equivocal, and that is the happening of between-being we inhabit. Philosophy tries to interpret the equivocal signs of the good in the chiaroscuro of being. And yet in all this, we are beings in communication with the intimate strangeness of being at all. We are already beings with being, within given being; beings seeking to know that truth to which we are already in relation, otherwise there would be no seeking of anything as true. This double condition, clearly understood by Plato, always puts us in an intermediate place, between ignorance and wisdom. To be is to be unsettled in this equivocal chiaroscuro. This is more true of a richer understanding of Platonic philosophizing. It asks not simply for a deconstruction of false univocities, or for thoughtless consent to the equivocal, but for finesse in reading the signs of the chiaroscuro. Metaphysics asks *mindful finesse.*

Opponents of Plato often fix the fullness of Plato and then complain of the fixation. But one could say that dualism can *sometimes* be a strategy for safeguarding a sense of irreducible transcendence. It may not be the best way, but the intention merits deeper reflection than a too easy polemical rejection. There may be more at stake in dualism than either dualism or its rejection. "Plato, for example, becomes a caricature in my hands"—*also spraak* Nietzsche in *Will to Power.*[13] What tendentious tomes we would have been saved from, had Nietzsche's followers taken this statement to

13. *Der Wille zur Macht. Versuch einer Umwertung aller Werte,* 255 (§374); *The Will to Power,* 202.

heart. There is much beyond fixity in Plato already. Think of Plato, not Aristotle, as *the* philosopher. Whitehead: the safest possible generalization is that the history of philosophy is a series of footnotes to Plato. Even Nietzsche would agree, but with a different intent: All philosophy is "Plato," the great slanderer of life, lover of the "beyond," to be opposed by Homer, the instinctive deifier of life, the golden nature.[14] Once again what is at issue is the way Rome seems to have mutated into Judea. "After" Nietzschean aesthetics, and a certain turn to a kind of Levinasian ethics, we recall that in *Totality and Infinity* Levinas exempts Plato's good beyond being from the otherwise critical judgment called down on philosophy as ontology and as destined to totality.[15] "Metaphysics" escapes the tyranny of "ontology" and its allergy to heterogeneity, and in the name of the good. Clap your hands and sing: Our time is coming "Plato," if not already here!

Yes, we must clap our hands, but we must also remember that *two hands* are needed for clapping in appreciation. Two hands: the senses of metaphysics and ontology need not be an "either/or" between immanence and transcendence, if we recall the double sense of the *meta* as both "in the midst" yet also as "beyond." Recall that this is the double sense of metaxological metaphysics I outlined in my introduction. And perhaps we can applaud the truer intention of even Platonic dualism as contained or hidden in this double sense.

Regarding Cartesian dualism: I agree; there is here a greater exacerbation of philosophical fear of the equivocal. We find a greater insistence on univocity. Ancient *theōria* is denounced as "useless." Instead we must pursue a *mathēsis* of nature that will offer us precision, exactitude, clarity, and distinctness. Here we find a kind of metaphysics of presence. Leibniz: to be real is to be fully determinate. Modernity is caught in a certain bewitchment of exact and absolute determinacy. Whitehead, one of the great logicians of the twentieth century, rightly reminds us of the fallacy of simple location, showing how well he had escaped this bewitchment. Toward the end of his life in his lecture on "Immortality" he is blunt: "The exactness is a fake."[16]

---

14. Friedrich Nietzsche, *On the Genealogy of Morals and Ecce Homo*, trans. W. Kaufmann and R. J. Hollingdale (New York: Vintage Books, 1969), third essay, section 25, 154.

15. Emmanuel Levinas, *Totality and Infinity*, trans. A. Lingis (Pittsburgh: Duquesne University Press, 1969), e.g., 103: "The Place of the Good above every essence is the most profound teaching, the definitive teaching, not of theology, but of philosophy." See also 218 and 293 on creation and the good beyond being.

16. "Immortality," in *The Philosophy of Alfred North Whitehead*, The Library of Living

This bewitchment can be seen in connection with science, especially as interpreted scientistically; but also in politics with respect to the exacting determination of the absolute sovereign; in ethics in the exactions of absolute self-determination; in religion (certainly in early modernity) where God is absolute determination, whose ultimate determining will even predetermines innocents to hell. There is dualism here and a secret will to power. What is this God? Finally, a little too like the evil genius, marked by something uncomfortably close to an absolute will to power. Inevitably we will rebel, in the name of our desire to be self-determining, and our own will to power. But what are the sources of metaphysics here? Finally not in astonishment, but perhaps first in perplexity; and then in perplexity whose eros has transmuted into a voracious curiosity, an inquisitiveness finally relentlessly impatient with the chiaroscuro of being. True, sometimes when the univocal light does not soon come, a demand is made on our *faith to wait* for a better solution or method—not now, but later all will be clear. Even this patience is really *deferred impatience*. Its curiosity itself is one face of a will to power that is intent on *securing itself* in the fragility of being. It cannot stand the universal impermanence. It wants to recur to itself; wants to remake itself as the absolute constant for whose ceaseless curiosity there is no intimate strangeness of being at all.

The epistemic will to overcome strangeness also means the loss of ontological intimacy. It is hard to know which is first: loss of ontological intimacy or will to overcome strangeness. They seem mutually reinforcing. Perhaps it is the loss of the second, the intimacy, that produces the project of the first, the overcoming. Where, then, does the loss come from? The ontological impatience already witnesses a kind of slipping out of intimacy, for impatience cannot stay with what gives itself. Impatience reveals a mixture of powerlessness and power. Powerless before something given as other, we grow impatient and seek to assert our power in the face of impotency. We cease to be for it or with it, it must be for us or with us—on terms we now try to dictate. Being is then a strange other, but without the intimacy, it is stripped of what makes us *belong to it*. One thinks here in modernity of the stripping away of qualitative value in nature as other;

Philosophers, 2nd ed., ed. P. A. Schilpp (New York: Tudor Publishing, 1951), 700. The point, I take, is not the repudiation of exactness but its concrete contextualization. Relevantly, this lecture is preceded by another late lecture, echoing Plato, on "Mathematics and the Good" (666–81) which touches also on the theme of the exact (673–74).

or the excision of the traces of the divine in given externality; or the dehumanization of the human, by the human, thinking of itself as a machine—though no machine so strips itself, for no machine can be mindful of the intimate strangeness of being, or its own being. What we will to secure, with that we cannot be intimate. We can at most *play* at being intimate. But this play then is only the counterfeit of eros. The passion of transcending has mutated into a manipulation of the otherwise eros-less "object." We want to secure ourselves against the intimate strangeness of being through the neutered other. What, then, of ourselves as intimately strange? We must try to neuter ourselves too, or we invent the project, or ruse, of being absolutely self-determining. This too, while in flight toward itself, is in flight from itself and its own intimate strangeness—the immanent otherness that allows its own becoming of itself.

Regarding self-determining knowing: In one sense, this is an outcome of the above developments. I mean that the project of self-determining knowing is tied up with a certain devaluation of the ethos of being within which knowing is pursued: the intimacy of being becomes the valuelessness of being—mere thereness—contingency without any trace of anything other—this is being as the emptiest universal, not the fullest. Of course, there is also a peculiar *pathos in emptiness,* as there is in fullness, and hence even the absence of value is not itself valueless. Quite to the contrary, the "overagainstness" of the otherness of being produces a recoil in the human being toward itself as autonomous—as self-law. I, self, autonomous being, stake my claim to be recuperative of value in the emptiest of abstractions—that is, being. The more this immanent autonomy is absolutized, the more an other sense of transcendence is relativized, and indeed we are less in communication with the strangeness of being, and behind our backs a more estranged strangeness is in the making.

This has to do with what elsewhere I call the antinomy of autonomy and transcendence.[17] If we absolutize autonomy we must relativize tran-

---

17. I discuss this, for instance, in relation to art in *Art, Otherness, Origins,* chapter 8 ("Art and the Impossible Burden of Transcendence: On the End of Art and the Task of Metaphysics"); also in *God and the Between,* chapter 1. The point could be illustrated in terms of what I call *autonomia turannos* in "Autonomia Turannos: On Some Dialectical Equivocities in Self-Determination," *Ethical Perspectives* 5, no. 4 (1998): 233–52. The claim to escape from heteronomy ends up breeding new forms of *submission.* But some of these submissions are obediences to dark powers: we move from autonomy to fate; from Kant's good will to Schopenhauer's dark will to Nietzsche's Dionysian will to power; but what is this fate that Nietzsche preaches?

scendence; if transcendence is absolute, we must relativize autonomy. If transcendence as other cannot be relativized, autonomy must itself be relativized. In question here is not the denial of freedom, but the relativity between our freedom and transcendence as other. Freedom is not exhausted by autonomy. Being free in the between implicates freedom in its relativity to what is other to our selving. The realization that there is more to freedom than autonomy is dawning in postmodernism but the hesitation about transcendence as other is still widespread. In effect, we tend to have a lacerated, disillusioned, tormented autonomy: it can no longer take itself seriously and yet it cannot be quite released from itself. The relativization of transcendence with the absolutization of autonomy means just the evaporation of the otherness of transcendence. Insofar as deconstruction wants to think otherness, it must make more room for transcendence to come back more robustly into the picture. But how can this be done, if transcendence is identified too univocally with the supposedly dualistic metaphysics of the tradition, that is to say, "Plato" and "ontotheology"?

We seem caught in a bind. For to follow through on what is here intimated, we must be released from autonomous knowing—but toward what? Here there are diverse ways of balking. The otherness is not only in excess to determination but to self-determination. What is this excess? If we review the tale of self-determining knowing after Hegel, we find that something other to self-determining knowing makes self-determining knowing possible: there is an immanent otherness. In the inward otherness there is a resurgence of transcendence in immanence itself. A Nietzsche or a Heidegger would consent to an immanent transcendence, albeit differently; but transcendence as other is still broached equivocally. Transcendence as other is not the same as immanent transcendence. We are between the two, but if we fold transcendence as other back into immanent transcendence, we must always end up relating to metaphysics no more than *truculently.*

Suppose there is no need to "reconstruct" transcendence; suppose we need to be freed in our mindfulness to think transcendence. Is this freeing a "reconstruction"? One must have hesitations about this way of talking. Stronger still, it could be said that this is to put the cart before the horse. This more original freedom is not a matter of determination or self-determination. The release is a "being freed." Further still, and crucially: *the release has to happen before any reconstruction can be effective.* Any reconstruction is a determinate outcome built on a release that is not determinate in the same sense, because it rather serves as a source of determination. Deconstructive thinking suggests some understanding of the point. Nevertheless, we ought not to squander the opportunity offered because we suffer a paralysis before determination, fearing the falsifying power of determination.

For some reason I think of Mozart's Don Giovanni, who oscillates between this determinate woman and an indeterminate number of other women: *È tutto amore: chi a una sola è fedele verso l'altre è crudele* (It is all love: to be faithful to one is to be cruel to the others), the Don says— they see my good nature toward so many as deceit. For the best of intentions, we can endlessly remind ourselves that no determinate concretion can be it. It is endlessly other, a new "beyond" in a certain sense, almost an always elsewhere other. For how could it possibly be now here, for then once again it would be nothing? But what is the point in keeping our faith intact in an indeterminacy that, were it to incarnate itself determinately, would simply evaporate and leave us with nothing? We keep beating around the bush, but there is nothing in the bush.

This makes very difficult, if not impossible, any deep exploration of transcendence as other. Our hyperbolic skepticism keeps yanking us back, just at the point when the passion of thought might become porous to what comes to it from beyond its self-determination. Instead we find ourselves torn between determination and indeterminacy, variously moving back and forth between the two, and seeming in this to be transcending determinacy. But it is a quasi-transcending, an as-if surpassing that circles back to the finitude it fears to desert. The intimate strangeness of being, on this understanding, is not immanently rich enough with ontological hyperboles which make us porous to transcendence as other which is not a dualistic opposite but always in communication. Perhaps the paralysis of philosophy here is only local, not general. Nevertheless, the anaesthesia concerning transcendence as other has much to do with our still being captive to the taboos of Enlightenment and Kant, of anti-Enlightenment and Nietzsche: fear of God. This fear here is not the beginning of wisdom, but the *skandalon* over which autonomous knowing, believing itself already wise, will not leap over, cannot leap over. Deconstructive thinking rightly wants to undo the certainty of unwarranted self-belief, but when its skeptical diffidence goes in the opposite direction what then are we to believe? I am talking about the superiority of transcendence as other to human self-transcendence. Plato is less hung up about transcendence as other than the inheritors of modern Enlightenment, and its deconstructors. And yet there is immense subtlety and finesse in how he directs us to its excess. Is Derrida's turn to (quasi-)Levinasian ways here equivocal, a new triumph of "Plato" over "Nietzsche"—after Nietzsche? Had he at the outset of his career overtly presented himself as a seeker after "justice" or "messianicity without messianism," or "religion without religion," one feels sure the avant-garde crowd would have yawned, and looked elsewhere for the thrill of transgression.

If it is true that Derrida moves from Nietzschean aesthetics to Levinasian ethics, we are moving closer to family relations of Platonic metaphysics. This is "Jewish" ethics for Nietzsche—the slave preaching about the good. Of course, this "slave" is more nearly right than Nietzsche. If we follow Plato, we can speak of an intimate strangeness *beyond* being. But this "beyond" sheds its light on being. This means that being cannot at all be the neutralized thereness of modern objectivity; nor the objective correlative of our more absolute power of transcendental positing; nor the emptiest of abstraction of the idealists that proves indistinguishable from nothing; nor the Dionysian will to power which strangely presents itself as monstrously devoid of any inherent good. One of the richest ways of speaking of being would be to say: it is hospitable to the gift of the good. It is enveloped by a light of worth, illuminating its worthiness in itself and for itself.

The metaphysical milieu, the ontological ethos of our philosophizing, requires reflection in terms of this, reflection on this hospitality of being to the good. This is what so marked many forms of *premodern* metaphysics. One might say it is most lacking in metaphysics in modernity (except perhaps Leibniz: oddly, given his will to determinacy). It is absent in Kant, in Hegel, in Nietzsche. To what extent is deconstruction a victim of the same devaluation of being in modernity? Does not this same reconfigured ethos breed also the quasi-deconstruction of modern self-determination?

Quite clearly, if this hospitality of being for the good holds more true in premodern metaphysics, then we are differently in the milieu of being. How shockingly radical now might seem to us the old adage: *ens et bonum convertuntur.* But we do have to be porous to, willing to be exposed to, the intimate strangeness of being, a porosity and willingness beyond all will to power. To realize this, to be released to it, if I am not wrong, is to be on a different path to that of deconstruction. It is to be stirred into seeking by a different intimation of being and the good. Is there the danger that as we talk about being "beyond being," we fudge this issue here? Yes, if we treat all philosophy as if it were the ontology of neutral being or power—or will to power. This simply is false. It is a false projection of typical modern debilities onto the ethos of being and onto other precedent explorers of being.

BEING EMPTIED OUT

Suppose again our philosophical response is neither to be deconstruction nor reconstruction. To repeat: I do not deny the insights of deconstructive thinking about binary oppositions. Further, I think the facades of some univocal identities at times are to be appropriately exposed as falsifying exactitudes. I agree there are constitutive equivocities in the human condition, indeed in the ontological situation in which we participate, and these need honest recognition, need more finessed modes of mindfulness. Nor would I deny the significance of the movement between the determinate and what is more than all determination. The issue is what "more" there is. This "more" does not call for a balancing reconstruction, for this would be just another form of the not-quite-true binary thinking. The intimate strangeness of being is beyond construction, hence beyond both deconstruction and reconstruction. It is in the overdeterminate dimension of the given and the received. Not construction, not deconstruction, not reconstruction, we need metaxological thinking porous to the intimate strangeness of being as an overdeterminate happening. Metaxological metaphysics is mindful of this happening in its plurivocal voicing of the ontological promise of being. We need to return once more to thought as seeded in astonishment. If astonishment is original, being given offers itself as too much, as overfull, as more than determinate thought.

A great part of the difficulty in post-Cartesian metaphysics is the *evacuation* of being which, though it might be granted as universal, it is so as the emptiest universal. How could any reconstruction be an answer to the evacuation? The evacuation does not behold what is there, but fixes its counterfeit, a counterfeit its own thinking has produced. What then would reconstruction be, if what we need is to be able to behold what is there, and engage it on its terms, and not only our own? Perhaps we need deconstruction of the counterfeit(s) of being we have produced. But the deeper point would not be at all to reconstruct the original, for just the point is that it is not any product of our thought, not even a reconstructed product.

On the evacuation of being, we might turn to Hegel, believed by some to offer, in his *Science of Logic,* the high noon of speculative metaphysics: here being may be the first thought, but it is the emptiest, because the least determinate. Being is an empty indeterminacy. I see this as collusive with the loss of agapeic astonishment, and the will to make all knowledge completely determinate or self-determining in a categorial sense. All honor to Heidegger for trying to effect a countermeasure against this abstraction, or this initial determination of being as the least determinate. Hegel too proposed a countermeasure against the abstraction, but it was in initial acceptance that the beginning in being was impoverished thus. The too muchness of being as overdeterminate, its intimate strangeness as in rapport with us, out of its otherness that yet always remains other even while intimate, this is not to the fore in his philosophy. What is fulfilled and intensive being at the end of the *Logic*? It is the most determinate thought, indeed thought as self-determined and self-determining. But this is not the intimate strangeness of being that calls for thought.[18]

Does Heidegger vacillate here? His earlier work seems less accusatory against "metaphysics" as collusive in the oblivion of being, leading to the hegemony of cybernetic thinking. But if metaphysics leads to the emptiest, what then do we need? Heidegger will say a "destruction" *(Destruktion)* of tradition, and insist, not without some trace of equivocation, that destruction is really oriented toward a *renewal* of thinking of being (as not the emptiest). It is the crude commentator who thinks of casuists who say black, all the while meaning, with the help of mental reservations, white. The choice of words might seem equivocal, but, as I already suggested, no harm is done to one's avant-garde name: even if one is advancing, be-

18. Hegel's apotheosis of logic, his panlogism, is suggested by a coupling of his doctrine of the categories with being, understood as the emptiest category. There is an inevitable, *reasonable* reaction against this consummate emptiness, though it presents itself as categorial completeness and concreteness. The usual reactions are sometimes styled as irrational or nonrational; but the hyperbolic claims made by Hegelian reason make one wonder how reasonable *it* is. Schelling's positive philosophy expresses something of this wonder by contrast with Hegel's negative philosophy. Kierkegaard's efforts to make us mindful of existence recall us to the unreason of idealistic reason.

hind and out of metaphysics, to the origin, the revolutionary pathos of negation can be exploited. "Creation is destruction"—said Bakunin, the celebrity anarchist of the nineteenth century, and there were not too many mental reservations. Picasso said once that "a painting is the sum of destructions" but could we seriously say: reconstruction in metaphysics is the sum of deconstructions?

Metaxological thought turns us from being as the emptiest universal toward the intimate strangeness. In Heidegger, yes, we find something of this, but at least in the earlier work this is by way of *Dasein* and *Angst*. This last, in my view, is more modern than would suit Heidegger's truer ontological purposes of releasing us to being as other than subjectivity. It is too much within the reconfigured ethos of modernity which is the neutralization of being, its evacuation, and the compensatory apotheosis of human self-mediation. Hence it is the strangeness, without enough of the astonishing intimacy, that is communicated in *Angst*. *Angst* is a later-born unsettling of "subjectivity" that, more originally, is struck into openness by agapeic astonishment. It has all the negativity of estrangement as sourcing a perplexity of thought that cannot quite find its way home to its more original intimacy with being in its otherness. The otherness here with *Angst* is not agapeic. We are on the outskirts of the environs of ontological horror (such as we find in Nietzsche's *Birth of Tragedy*), certainly not in the milieu of the "to be" as "good."

We are much closer to this milieu with Heidegger's later stress on *Gelassenheit*. But how do we get from *Angst* to *Gelassenheit*? Or from *polemos* to *Gelassenheit*? It seems to me we need to grant a movement more the other way round in this regard: there is a more original porosity of being, and original porosity to being on our part, which releases us astonishingly into the between. This porosity is more primal, opening us before we wake to perplexity about what is there, and about ourselves. It is an opening before we fall from intimacy with the gift of being into anxiety before the strangeness of being.[19]

Polemos is not the father of all things. Porosity names a more archaic matrix of engendering. To come to metaphysical mindfulness is to find that porosity again unclogged, and to find the strangeness of being no

---

19. On Heidegger and the (unthought) between more fully, see my discussion in *Art, Origins, Otherness*, chapter 7.

stranger to the intimacy of the good. To be addressed by this intimacy of being and good is to be called to think against the modern neutralization or evacuation in which being becomes valueless. Facing this worthlessness of being, we have often turned to ourselves as determining the worth of being, for we find it impossible finally to settle for this valuelessness. The univocalization of being in all spheres is pernicious. Our turn to ourselves cannot be enough, for in the end, on this view, we also instantiate the overall valuelessness of being, and the values we create participate in the same valuelessness.

I cannot see deconstruction as a project up to the task of thinking the worth of being in the fullness of the ontological dimensions at stake. The matter certainly cannot be an ethics divorced from a metaphysics, for then we reduplicate the divorce of being and good from the other side, the side of the good. The impotency of Nietzschean genealogy to address the issue may be one reason why Levinas seemed so to overtake Derrida, in Derrida's own later thought. And if the ethical follows the aesthetic, can the religious be far behind? One thinks of Kierkegaard's stages on life's way as the practitioner of deconstruction grows old, and wiser age begins to put out tentative feelers toward that ultimate mystery—tentative, since the tender reign of the "perhaps" seems to ensure that every suggestion of determinate affirmation will be qualified, as if away, that is, qualified as if disqualified by a seemingly indefinite process of qualification. One should not complain at the gain in willingness to name the religious. A *nihil obstat* seems to have come into effect, the taboo against "religion" lifted, and freethinkers have rushed to take advantage of the permission granted.[20]

20. I have found John Caputo's work to be often more illuminating on religion than Derrida, the *patēr tou logou* (see Plato's *Sophist* 241d, also *Phaedrus* 257b). At times he performs the quasi-miracle of making more religious sense of Derrida than Derrida himself (see *On Religion*). This is a second quasi-miracle in addition to the first real miracle of revealing the surprising religious possibilities of deconstruction. One sees the point (it reminds me of a particular Pascalian use of skepticism). If the deconstruction of reason can make (univocal) reason founder on undecidability, might it not open a more hospitable space for the hazard of a certain faith? If so, we might move from the literalist univocities of creedal fundamentalism to ambiguous wanderings in the night of faith. Caputo is matched by a different wonder worker: Gianni Vattimo. In relation to Nietzsche's agon of Rome versus Judea, Vatimmo performs a quasi-miracle in the magic of turning Nietzschean nihilism into Christian *caritas*. His weak thought (*pensiero debole*) has a godlike power of transubstantiation, perhaps ordained to it by a kind of "weak catholicism." The weak God of Caputo (*The Weakness of God: A Theology of the Event* [Indianapolis: Indiana University Press, 2006]) is not unrelated to my own stress on the God of agapeic service, though I think the matter of divine power has to be seen in the light of

Returning to Heidegger, there seem to me something uneasy about the affiliation between him and deconstruction. Heidegger's efforts to rescue being from oblivion seems to have led to a second oblivion of being in many influenced by him. Who now speaks of being? His own quest seems to have led to the emeritus of "metaphysics" in the later Heidegger himself: metaphysics now portrayed as hell bent on consummating itself, consuming itself as cybernetics. In the upshot, all metaphysics is identified with "presence," perhaps identified with determinacy, and determinate being(s). The fate of extreme univocalization falls on all. But is that not just the fatality from which we are to be released? Released into finding our way to the porosity of being, with more ready philosophical patience to what communicates itself in and through the porosity?

If all metaphysics, indeed even being, is caught in determinate presence, it will not do if it is suggested that we must seek beyond being, if this "beyond" is too tied to the stylization of being as the empty universal. One might with Plato speak of the good as beyond being, but this need

---

surplus overdeterminacy rather than indeterminacy (see *God and the Between*, 314–21). In relation to some weak gods, we wonder if we are continuing the tradition of "as if" gods that Kant seemed to inaugurate. At a certain point, the lord of Lacanian misrule comes on the scene—Žižek the licensed postpostmodern jester, joking about "alcohol free alcohol," "caffeine free coffee," and so on. We could add "God without God" to "religion without religion." "Where's the beef?" the old advertisement once asked. You can't eat "as if" beef. You can "as if" eat it, but it nourishes no living body. Who could or would worship an "as if" God? You could "as if" worship, but this is "worship" without worship.

But if everything is qualified by a "without," do we not court a new "being without" whose destitution borders on nothing? "The rule is, jam tomorrow and jam yesterday—but never jam today," the White Queen said to Alice. The White Queen again: "It's jam every *other* day: to-day isn't any *other* day, you know." No wonder Alice says: "I don't understand you. . . . It's dreadfully confusing!" Have we set up a kind of "either/or" between determinacy and indeterminacy and then we oscillate between one and the other? Does there not persist a tornness, a laceration before determinacy as such? Whatever else, never jam today. (Some of Derrida's writings, for instance, his discussion of forgiveness, put me in mind of a kind of logical writhing. One recalls, by contrast, Aristotle's barely disguised irritation in the *Metaphysics* with the fluxgibberish of certain Heracliteans.) This oscillation eschews the self-determining of Hegelian reason, and yet for me it is not metaxologically porous to the surplus overdeterminacy and, as I would prefer, our seeking of direction to the divine via the indirections of the hyperboles of being. This oscillation does not quite fit into negative dialectic, though there are recessed traces of a mutant dialectic too proximate at times to a double speak. *Dia-logos* is also a kind of double speak, and naturally it is fair to ask if this is too neighboring to equivocal dialectic. This worry about the equivocal character of the oscillation cannot be avoided if one is committed to trying to think the overdeterminacies, the hyperboles of being, metaxologically. We can butter our bread, and even have jam—today. The surplus overdeterminacy means there is no today—without jam.

entail no violence to the intimate strangeness of being, or the light of the good being shed on finite beings and processes. But then we would inhabit the world differently than as a valueless thereness. Though we might try to speak of "being" as an X, itself empty of determination, because other than everything determinate, it is not entirely clear how different this is to the evacuation of being seen as the emptiest of indeterminate universals? I grant that this is not the intent. I also know that the deconstructionists themselves claim that Heidegger himself was too "metaphysical." The sons will correct the father and in terms of the father's correction of his fathers. But the evacuation of being seems to still spread its cloak of emptiness over all, even indeed over the putative flight into the beyond of being by means of postmetaphysical thinking.

INTIMATE STRANGENESS, METAPHYSICAL CONSTANCY

Why, then, do we say neither deconstruction nor reconstruction? We are given to be in the intimate strangeness of being—always. This is no construction, hence it cannot be deconstructed, cannot be reconstructed. Being thus given to be enables all construction, hence all deconstruction and reconstruction, but it is not any of them. Astonishment before the intimate strangeness of being given to be is at the beginning of our becoming mindful. Our perplexity can stay in communication with original astonishment, hence be in rapport with the intimate strangeness. It can also become definite curiosity. We make ourselves strange—"detach" ourselves, we think. We develop our difference, thinking it is outside the intimate strangeness, but it is not, cannot be outside. This happens all the time: we make ourselves "outside," though we continue to be within the more intimate strangeness. And so we always need the shaking up of what, *incognito,* sustains every effort of determinate and self-determinate knowing. At its best, desconstructive thinking allows a probe of this *incognito.*

Metaphysics may indeed offer us forms of late-born thinking, either relative to determinate intelligibilities (categories, ideas) or relative to processes of determination (being as becoming; or knowing as *relatively* self-directed). But these and metaphysics cannot be abstracted from the more original source: the ethos of intimate strangeness. Otherwise they become false in becoming true. A fuller mindfulness of itself returns it to, reopens us to, this intimate strangeness. So too it is at the ready for forms of otherness that are never self-produced, nor vouched for by the possibility of a categorial intelligibility. This ready alertness, patient yet acutely energized, is more in the nature of a release of agapeic mind. This release is needed for "reconstruction." In some way there is something here like revisiting a haunt, what haunts us (a theme recurrent in the later Derrida). What haunts us is old and new; neither old nor new, it is hyperbolic to epochal determination; it is something we are never done with, nor it with us.

Modern thought often suggests a kind of fall out of the ontological ethos of the intimate strangeness. *In that sense, what we need is metaphysics more than anything else—not postmetaphysical thought, but elemental mindfulness of the intimate strangeness.* True, given our knotted nature, we often have to suffer loss to lift up our eyes again in the mode of such elemental mindfulness. Metaxological metaphysics partakes also of posthumous mindfulness. Modernity is not always hospitable to the intimate strangeness of being. We see the loss in objectivism and in subjectivism; we see it reflected in the oscillation between foundationalism and relativism; and in it all, we sense lurking the sly instrumental reason, in which everything is a means, and nothing worthy simply for itself. When under the sway of a totalizing univocity, there is a kind of treason to contemplation in modern metaphysics. Of course, it becomes hard then to see that such a contemplation is not at all a disinterested neutrality. It has more of an affinity with religious meditation and artistic appreciation. This is *theōria* in an unmodern sense: nonpragmatic vigilance to the worthy. If our critique of instrumental reason is framed in a manner that frames the entire tradition of philosophy as "metaphysics of presence," we are still too modern, not postmodern enough, in not being deeply enough in rapport with what is communicated in this celebrating vigilance, itself neither old nor new.

What are some of the happenings where this intimate strangeness comes above the horizon of our mindfulness? In art: naming of the astonishing sensuous show of the worthy in the milieu of being, without objectifying it. In religion: the mystery of the divine; of the good too, and not just in a moral sense: ontological worth—the good of the "to be"; communication of the "That it is" and that "I am"—and these as enigmatically good—worthy of our deeming them worthy, because they are worthy. In philosophy: in noninstrumental thinking: in agapeic mindfulness especially,[21] in the thinking of the "to be," of the enigma of the "I am," of the mystery of God. In everyday life: walking down a sunlit street; or running a race; or sitting on a beach; or looking at a night sky; or scanning faces in a crowd. At their limits, the determinate sciences are also brushed by this sense of the intimate strangeness, though their drive will be to make it as cognitively determinate as possible.

What this suggests is that what we lack and need more than anything else is metaphysics. What kind of metaphysics? In my view metaxological metaphysics: thinking back down into the happening of the middle; becoming awake to our intermediate being, and to the intermediaries of the meaning of being. We always need to begin again. What if the truth of being's intimate strangeness were so elemental as to nonplus us? The point is not any rejection of determinate thought, but we need memory of the original intimation, even in all determinate thinking. This is a perennially recommended theme in the long history of philosophical thought: to begin again.

I offer a few points here, points more extensively treated, in one way or another, in *Being and the Between,* and reflecting something of the fourfold sense of being developed there. First, we need to think of being in terms of surplus overdeterminacy rather than as empty indeterminacy—the evacuated sense of being discussed above. There is neither deconstruction nor reconstruction of this surplus overdeterminacy, for it has to do with the ontological milieu within which all thinking, deconstructive or reconstructive, takes place. The intimate strangeness means rethinking being as (over)full. We are called to a kind of hyperbolic thought, in the sense of what exceeds all complete fixation in determinate categories.[22]

Second, this is not to shortchange the need of determinate forms of thought. There is an ineradicable need for univocal thinking, for we are oriented to making as much determinate sense as possible. This does not mean absolutizing the univocal sense of being, for there are recalcitrant ambiguities that are frequently not noticed or distorted by a wrong univo-

21. On agapeic mindfulness and agapeic being, see *Perplexity and Ultimacy,* chapters 4 and 6.

22. See my "Hyperbolic Thought: On Creation and Nothing," in *Framing a Vision of the World: Essays in Philosophy, Science and Religion,* ed. Santiago Sia and André Cloots (Leuven: Universitaire Pers Leuven, 1999), 23–43; here I try to make some intelligible sense of creation and nothing as hyperbolic thoughts. For a fuller development, see *God and the Between,* chapter 12; on transcendence and hyperbole, see also *Being and the Between,* 207ff.

calizing approach. One of the services of deconstruction is its effort to re-call us to the equivocities nested in the clarities of univocal thinking itself. A feel for equivocities is a sine qua non of genuine metaphysical thought about the intimate strangeness of being. But there is no method by which one could reconstruct the finesse of mind needed for this "feel." It is more intellectual art than technical geometry.

Third, the tradition of dialectical thinking has something to recom-mend itself as seeking to interpret what is at issue in the interplay of inde-terminacy and determinacy. If there is to be some recovery of the strength of dialectical thinking, the emphasis on self-determining processes must be guarded from the idealist search for the closure of self-mediating thinking. The intimate strangeness of being is not properly described in terms of such an idealistic totality. It intimates a sense of transcendence beyond totality. The intermediation of what I call metaxological thought is more released to this sense of transcendence. Again we need something like what I called an agapeic mindfulness that is not thought about itself but about the very otherness of being in its intimate strangeness. It sug-gests self-transcending toward transcendence as other. It suggests a sense of surplus being which also helps us turn to the ontological milieu as not evacuated of signs of the good of the "to be."

The intimate strangeness means being reveals a certain kind of onto-logical community: communication of difference and sameness, affinity and uniqueness, identity and otherness. We cannot accept the closure of the circle; or the illusion of the line, namely, that the later is better than the earlier—or higher. *Sed contra:* the highest, best, and its promise has always been with us; but we have not always kept the mindfulness of be-ing with it, or its promise. This loss, were it absolute, would be the death of metaphysics—loss of intimacy of the "to be" in which the strangeness is first made perplexing, then perhaps neutral, then hostile, and we end up hating it instead of loving it. Not philia, not eros, not agape but misousia, misology overtake us: hostile to the hostile otherness, we are tempted not only to say "better not to think" but "better not to be." This is not philia af-ter philosophy; it is *Afterphilosophie* and it is necrophilia.

Can the dogs of war, unleashed with thinking as negation, put a stop to this? Do we need different dogs: a different cynicism, if you like? After all, the same blood runs in the cynics as in the skeptics. Was this per-haps what was best in the cynical impulse: return to love of the elemental good of "to be"? Do we here need, as it were, a metaphysics of constance, not substance? The sun shines on us, even when Alexander stands in the way. Metaphysical constancy reveals what stands by us—in its intimate strangeness. And we, in knowing its fidelity, must stand by it constantly. The mysterious constancy of being does not require reconstruction, but solicits our renewed rapport with what is promising in the ethos of being, enabling all construction and reconstruction. Without such renewal, there is no rethinking: no agape of being, heralded for us, nor agapeic mindfulness, heralded by us: not the building, not the builder, not the energy—and not only of the builder and building, but of the blocks, those integrities of being that offer their humble reliability to the finite constancies of time.

Part 3

Metaphysics beyond Dialectic

6 ⚛ Metaxological Metaphysics and the Equivocity of the Everyday

Between Everydayness and the Edge of Eschatology

Philosophers have often looked with diffidence, if not disdain, on every-day life. We like to echo and reecho Socrates's controvertible claim: The unexamined life is not worth living. Everyday life is blithe in its careless first commitment to living rather than to thought; irritable with specula-tions not immediately perceived relevant to pressing practical concerns; untroubled about recessed obscurities in its own defining attitudes; un-disturbed by the ambiguities of its idiomatic ways of speaking. It gets by, and that is enough for the day, living carelessly with *logos,* living carelessly without *logos.* Philosophers have judged this to be the problem, not the solution. As if scalded by this happy stupidity, they have scolded common sense. The contentments of obtuseness are as a goad to them. Again and again they have dreamed of placing univocal precision where daily equiv-ocity otherwise remains in its reign, blithe with itself, uncontested by any-thing beyond itself. We philosophers must pass from original confusion to terminal exactness.

Is this the only way philosophers might *appropriately* respond to the equivocity of the everyday? Are there less hostile responses? Are meta-physicians fated to live on the flying island of Jonathan Swift's Laputa, while ordinary people down below keep their feet on the solid ground? Recall, however, that philosophy in the twentieth century has shown its own, more intimate concern with the everyday, whether in the continental engagement with the *Lebenswelt* or in the analytic engagement with the ordinary and its languages. Can we be philosophical friends of *doxa*?

I would describe the recent work of Stanley Rosen as very much concerned with the equivocity of the everyday and the appropriate philosophical response to it. Two recent books, *Metaphysics in Ordinary Language* and *The Elusiveness of the Ordinary,* contain essays of high quality that are written with an elegant clarity laced with refreshing wit, admirable in the sweep of their reference to the tradition of philosophy, yet sober in their respect for the moderations of common sense.[1] Rosen goes so far as to speak of himself as an "ordinary language metaphysician." Here is a representative citation:

The ordinary is that from which we make our approach to philosophy. It is not at all what Heidegger calls *durschnittliche Alltaglichkeit* (average everydayness), which is already a denatured residue of the richness of ordinary existence, the mode of life of the anonymous *das Man,* "one" or "they" in English. Ordinary experience is a question of "I" and "thou." It is therefore also not the Husserlian *Lebenswelt,* a kind of Kantian transcendental structure occupied by ghosts whose speeches and deeds are described in a vocabulary that abstracts from the psychic affects of emotion, value, and doctrinal conviction by which everyday life is in fact characterized. In short, ordinary life is not a kind of pallid or denatured existence, set off against more luxuriant and virile modes of experience. It is human existence in all its richness and complexity, and so it is not a *Gedankending* or artificial construction of a philosophical or scientific theory.[2]

I would say that everyday life too is a participation in the intimate strangeness of being, no less intimate or strange for the fact that ordinarily we do not make our participation in being a matter of more reflec-

---

1. *Metaphysics in Ordinary Language* (New Haven, Conn.: Yale University Press, 1999); *The Elusiveness of the Ordinary: Studies in the Possibility of Philosophy* (New Haven, Conn.: Yale University Press, 2002). Rosen is refreshingly free of the fashionable cant and intellectual idolatry attending some of the tin gods of contemporary culture. See the last chapter of *Metaphysics in Ordinary Language,* "Kojève's Paris: A Memoir." This is a little gem that offers us an engagingly opinionated view of encounters with the perhaps ordinary lives of some more than ordinary thinkers. It records Rosen's meetings with, and impressions of, many intellectual eminences of France in the early 1960s, including among others Koyré, Marcel, and Aron. It is witty and perceptive, conveying an atmosphere as well as a response. It gives us some sharply deflationary evaluations (I think of his remarks on Lacan), but there is also much praise and respect. The memoir offers us an honest assessment of Kojève. See *Hermeneutics as Politics* (Oxford: Oxford University Press, 1987).

2. *The Elusiveness of the Ordinary,* 296.

tive mindfulness. It is already saturated with ontological significances to which the philosopher must bring the respect of due mindfulness. It does not simply call out for reconstruction in a further technical or conceptual language. As participating in the intimate strangeness of being, there is something about it not asking for reconstruction or deconstruction. This too is of concern for a metaxological philosophizing.

I want to look at some of the issues here and the options. Let me first say something about Rosen's general concerns. Then I will offer a number of reflections on the theme of metaphysics and the equivocity of the everyday, in terms borrowed from my own understanding of metaxological metaphysics, not at odds with the spirit of Rosen's insights, though perhaps with a different stress on systematic considerations beyond self-mediating dialectic.

Rosen's conviction is that philosophy must begin with everyday life as the context where the questions of philosophy emerge. Moreover, we need to be aware of history, he says, not to subscribe to any historicism, but, at the minimum, to avoid "being hoodwinked by illusions of our originality."[3] The ordinary has a character that is not completely a historical construct; of this character the philosopher must become discerning. Rosen subscribes to the Socratic view that the human being is the philosophical animal, that everyday life itself is an expression of the love of wisdom of which philosophy is the fullest developed form.[4] While the history of philosophy reveals a diversity of views on fundamental philosophical questions, these questions are not only basically accessible to us, they continue to engage us, and indeed, where necessary, ask our reformulation. Least of all should they be avoided. "When we avert our gaze from history, it has a tendency to stab us in the back."[5]

In both the ancients and the moderns a recurrent concern about the nature of philosophy itself is just its relation to everyday life.[6] Rosen has always been concerned with the relation of theory and practice, not only in its ancient shapes but in its distinctive Hegelian and post-Hegelian forms. He has engaged with analytic philosophy in terms of its ability to give a satisfactory intelligible account of the context of analysis. He has taken issue with the work of the postmoderns as perhaps a late outgrowth

---

3. *Metaphysics in Ordinary Language*, xi.   4. *Metaphysics in Ordinary Language*, xii.
5. *Metaphysics in Ordinary Language*, xi.
6. *The Ancients and the Moderns: Rethinking Modernity* (New Haven, Conn.: Yale University Press, 1989).

of the modern separation of reason and the good. It would be a simplification to say that Rosen simply juxtaposes the ancients and the moderns. There turns out to be less antagonism between them than is sometimes suggested. For instance, there are "modern" aspects of Plato; while many moderns echo conditions that are old, less because they are old, but because they reflect something more constant in our condition, for instance, the recurring problem of relating theory and practice. This too bears on how metaphysics is related to everyday life. Our attitude to the second is not to be intellectually reductive or haughty. One might say it is to be attentive without being servile. We need more of a middle way: between sanctifying the everyday and taking flight into the rarified ether of technical, or transcendental, or systematic conceptualization.

What are some of the signposts guiding us in all this? First, the everyday is the matrix of intelligibility that also sources the intelligibility of philosophical discourse. Second, it is the matrix wherein arise all of our perplexities, scientific and philosophical, some of which are of deep moment. Third, these perplexities refer philosophy back to the matrix, even if philosophy, in a qualified sense, also frees itself from the everyday. If we simply claim to be unconditionally free from it, philosophers become comic figures like those thinkers in Swift's Laputa in constant need of *flappers*—servants who carry inflated bladders to strike the abstracted thinkers, on the ear to heed, on the mouth to speak, and all to bring them back from lostness in thought to everyday reality.

Against such Laputan thinkers, especially in post-Hegelian guise, Rosen takes issue. Good philosophy allows us to see something that is there in the matrix. In part this means that the philosopher must be a person of sound common sense. This is not all, since an eros is at work in the philosopher, and this may carry him or her to the limits of the more domesticated middle world. Rosen likes to repeat the claim from the *Symposium* that eros binds up the whole. But ultimately philosophical eros must also do justice to the perplexities that have their source in the everyday itself. This is no canonization of certain forms of common sense, for instance, the linguistic usage of Oxbridge dons. There is a fluidity to common sense. It shows a certain blend of the univocal and the equivocal. "In general, there are no univocal terms in natural language,"[7] nevertheless,

---

7. *The Elusiveness of the Ordinary*, 240.

"equivocity is grounded in the unity of being."[8] Philosophers need *l'esprit de finesse* to be attentive to such equivocity.[9]

The question of equivocity is also tied up with the issue of the esoteric and the exoteric. This sometimes gives philosophers, of a more callow rationalist bent, a dose of hermeneutical heartburn. But there may also be something quite commonsense about the whole thing, something quite exoteric about the esoteric. The heartburn has something to do with the suspicion that a dubious elitism is being recommended under cover of the distinction of esoteric/exoteric. Nevertheless, if saying, indeed being, has an unavoidable equivocity, the matter can never be that simple. Once again we need the mind of finesse. Our speaking is grounded "not in rules but rather in the innate mastery of equivocity," while "living intelligence . . . is the unity of our mastery of equivocity."[10]

While Rosen is concerned with issues bequeathed to modernity from the Enlightenment version of reason, he is by no means antipathetic to modernity. These concerns are evident in the fine essay "Sad Reason,"[11] but elsewhere also. The human being is fragile and nature is not always a friend to us. It can be a friend, but also can be unfriendly, not to say hostile. In a certain sense, we need to master it; this is natural. Hence Rosen's appreciation of the modern project (see, e.g., his discussion in *"Techne, and the Origins of Modernity"*).[12] What, then, do we say when the relation of the everyday and the theoretical takes the form in modernity of a reconfiguration of our relation to being, via science and technology? We absolutize *l'esprit de géométrie*, and even try to remake *l'esprit de finesse* in its terms. We risk a homogenization which ultimately generates a new perplexity about the destruction of the human as distinctive. We make a new reconfiguration of the everyday itself, mirroring the abstractions of

---

8. *The Elusiveness of the Ordinary*, 242.

9. The issue of equivocity, indeed perhaps the equivocity of being itself, certainly of genesis, is touched on in a number of essays. See, for instance, "Suspicion, Deception, and Concealment," in *Metaphysics in Ordinary Language*, chapter 1, as well as the essay "The Golden Apple," chapter 4. This last image comes from Maimonides's *Guide for the Perplexed*, an image used by Leo Strauss to illustrate the difference between surface and deeper meanings. The golden apple is covered by a silver filigree with very small interstices. The silver covering is valuable in itself, but those with keener sight can see through to the more valuable vision contained within. Rosen applies the image with respect to the interpretation of the *Phaedrus*.

10. *The Elusiveness of the Ordinary*, 241.

11. *Metaphysics in Ordinary Language*, chapter 8.

12. *Metaphysics in Ordinary Language*, chapter 7.

the sciences, technology, and mathematics. How, then, find our way to a more robust natural common sense as recommended by Rosen? The latter is made problematic, indeed denied, by many, and it is said, man has no nature, worlds are "made." Rosen is not totally opposed to this, though he demurs. If something more elemental has been covered over with the second nature of science and technology, everyday life itself seems more and more like a technical construct. Rosen wants to avoid this. How get a sense of the original, if the sources of *l'esprit de finesse* have been taken over by or reconstructed by the regnant *esprit de géométrie*?

The demurral that qualifies his appreciation of the modern project is outlined in "Sad Reason" in terms of the divorce of reason and the good in modernity. I would also speak of the divorce of *being* and the good, though this is not to the fore here. Reason and the good are divorced because modern reason is abstracted from the good of being, even in its equivocity. Or rather the equivocal face of being has been univocalized into a neutral thereness, or indifference, which finally is hard to avoiding turning into an opposing or hostile otherness. Rosen does not quite put it thus, and yet his discussion points to a certain ontological alienation of modern reason. Its alienation from the good is inseparable from its alienation from the good of the "to be." Again Rosen does not quite put it that way. He overtly states his "loyalty to the modern project": "My intention is not to repudiate the Enlightenment but to preserve and strengthen its best features."[13] Of course, one does wonder what follows if the ontological alienation from the good of the "to be" is perhaps more deep-going, if indeed the project of the Enlightenment not only entails this alienation but is built on it. One wonders then if finally also, on these terms, the notion of "the best" must be eviscerated. It becomes hard to see how we can come closer to something of the "best," without some more severe searching. The metaxological nature of our intimacy with the strangeness of being is at issue, for this also makes us rethink the worth or worthlessness of the "to be."

METAPHYSICS AS METAXOLOGICAL

I now want to offer some reflections on the equivocity of the everyday, in terms that go in slightly more systematic directions than Rosen would go.

13. *Metaphysics in Ordinary Language*, 126.

He has a certain diffidence about "system," and "theory building," and one can appreciate this diffidence. I connect this with the tendency present, especially in modern philosophy, to seek an "ontology" defined primarily by the self-determination of thinking, to the detriment of the interruptions of surprising otherness that break in on the speculative dreams of reason, musing out of itself. Hegel is perhaps the high point of this tendency to "system," offering us as metaphysics a speculative logic that is a categorial ontology. I think of metaphysics less as the system of categories defined by the self-circling of thought determining itself, as a fundamental reflection on the basic senses of being, or "to be," none of which we can speak about without mindful openness to what actuality as other to us communicates intelligibly to us. There is an openness to what is beyond self-determining thought in this understanding of metaphysics, an openness more consonant with the more original experience of wonder we find, for instance, in the Greek *thaumazein*. I refer to Hegel, but one might also refer, with suitable qualification, to Heidegger's fundamental ontology, which like the idealistic immanence of thought thinking itself, is still too univocally a philosophy of immanence. Even given talk about the everydayness of *Dasein,* there is at work what I call a "postulatory finitism" that has the effect of closing thought off from thinking the signs of transcendence as other to immanence. I mean metaphysics in a more "Platonic" sense, not in terms of the cartoon version bequeathed to us since Nietzsche, but as a practice of philosophy that, even in the immanences of everyday life, recalls us to a porosity to transcendence as other.

I come back again to these four basic senses of being: the univocal, the equivocal, the dialectical, and the metaxological. I will not say anything now about them other than this very general summary. While the univocal sense tends to emphasize determinate sameness and identity, the equivocal tends to emphasize difference that escapes univocal sameness, sometimes to the loss of any mediation between sameness and difference, identity and otherness. By contrast, the dialectic sense seeks to mediate differences, differences sometimes equivocal, but not by reduction to univocal sameness but by transition to a more inclusive unity or whole that seeks to reconcile the differences. Finally, the metaxological deals with the interplay of sameness and difference, identity and otherness, not by mediating a more inclusive whole, but by recurrence to the rich ambiguities of the middle, and with due respect for forms of otherness that are dubiously claimed to be included in the immanence of a dialectical whole. Rosen often uses the language of the whole, but I would put the primary accent on our being "in-between," on our thinking as also an intermediating that, once again, is not primarily directed to an inclusive whole of thought thinking itself but to a mindful porosity to the transcendence of being as both other and yet in intimate relation to us. I think that metaphysics, most fundamentally, is metaxological, and that mindful attention to the equivocity of the everyday is one of its important tasks. In what follows now, I will look at these four senses in turn, with reference to the equivocity of the everyday, and with contrasting remarks on how Rosen sees the matter, when this is appropriate.

UNIVOCALIZING THE EQUIVOCAL: COMMON SENSE, SCIENCE, AND PHILOSOPHY

A common attitude to equivocity is to want to get rid of it by means of a univocity that dissolves ambiguity. Common sense, science, and philosophy embody something of this response, but equivocity itself often seems like a hydra: no sooner is one head snipped than another head sprouts. Everyday life is defined by certain constant univocities upon which we rely, yet it is also permeated by equivocity. It is an interplay between the two, often with many shades of stress between these two. Living is not a theory or a formula, and as we say, a nod is as good as a wink. Inevitably one needs the ability to read the signs of what is communicated, for with this one is not sure how to respond. Sometimes the signs are unambiguous, for instance, when the green light clears one for crossing the street. Often the signals are mixed, and one is not sure if the stranger on the train smiled at one or snarled. Common sense as common is grounded in communication but this is a blend of the univocal and the equivocal.

Consider this example: The setting is Irish, and one in which "yes" and "no" are not quite univocal: I offer my guest a second cup of tea. When offered a second cup of tea, an ordinary Irish guest might often say "no." But "no" does not necessarily mean "no." It may be the ceremonial way of *not saying "yes" too quickly,* for this too-quickness would not be the fitting way to say "yes." Often, then, one finds taking place what one could call a kind of ritual of coaxing: Go on, have another cup, you will, won't you? One might even compare it to a kind of wooing. A ritual game is being played in which the ambiguities of the between and the interplay of guest and host are being negotiated. It may be good manners to say "yes" only after the third offer, and after one or two refusals. This is often understood, but there is no straightforward univocity to it. Visitors from another country who are more literalist and univocal, for whom "yes" is univocally "yes," and "no" "no," often do not quite know what to make of this. They think "no" means "no," and that "yes" means "yes," and are puzzled when they continue to be pressed, after they have said "no." Of course, the process can work the other way round too. A green Irish visitor to another country (as I was green once in America) may say "no" when offered a second helping of desert, and may be astonished to find he is not asked a second time! For he did indeed want that second slice of chocolate cake, but here his "no" was taken more univocally to mean just "no." Of course, a domain where "yes," and "no," and words like "perhaps," and "maybe," are fraught with ever more charged ambiguity is the *erotic*. If human life were just univocal, there would be no eros to it. A nod is indeed as good as a wink but one has to keep one's eyes open to discern the passing signs.

This is an example of what one might call the *saturated equivocity* of the everyday: an ambiguity not void of significance but one charged with more than can be reduced to this formula or that, this discourse or that. One might connect this saturated equivocity with what seems to be the plurivocity of the everyday. There is a plurality of voices at play, and this does not necessarily mean a cacophony, though this is not ruled out; indeed it often happens. This plurivocity can span a range between harmonious symphony and noisy dissonance. Yet something is being communicated. One wonders if any communication is possible without some such saturated equivocity or plurivocity. Without more than one voice, there is no redundancy, and without redundancy there is no communication, no speaking or hearing. Communication begins, in a way, with the second voice, not the first (this is somewhat analogous to the point Aristotle made in saying that the least number, properly speaking, is two).

This saturated equivocity offers to thought the milieu of intelligibility, and the medium within which intelligence moves. There is a *confusion* here, in the sense of a flow of things into one another, a passing, a mixing, a *fusio con*. There is also a passing of communication. One's growing up, and one's being educated into the common sense of a tradition is learning how to respond to communication, to participate in the communication in its passing. It does not just pass one by, and one participates also by communicating oneself. To grow into common sense is partly learning how to "go with the flow," as we say idiomatically. Being able to understand this *idiom* is itself a "going with the flow": we know what it means, even if we cannot give a discursive account. It is idiotic but it is not absurd: it is intimate to participation in a way of life. I use "idiotic" here with something of its Greek sense of what is not public, something intimate that is other to neutral homogeneity. And yet it is quite public, in the sense of qualifying the qualitative textures of the between-space of communication between selves and others. For all that, this idiotic qualification of the between-space of communication cannot be rendered exhaustively in the homogeneous categories of a discourse more neutrally public. It is from a someone to another someone or someones, not from no one to everyone and no one.

This idiocy has a recessed side, as well as an expressed side: something that is not expressly said in the said, though it is intimate to the saying; something present though not determinately presented; something implied rather than objectively asserted. There is "more" at play in the communication of the everyday than is overtly determined. What is this "more"? Is this something merely indefinite, as it is for some thinkers? I would prefer to call this "more" an "overdetermination"—not an indefiniteness less than determinacy, but something exceeding univocal determination and that yet communicates the possibility of determination. How speak of it then? I note three responses where this "more" is addressed, and where univocity comes to the fore differently.

A first response is *common sense itself.* This offers a way of living with the "more" of equivocity in terms of a way of life into which we are reared and educated. On the whole, the natural intelligence of humans takes shape practically, without the engineering of life or by the impositions of theories, though theory can intervene, and in our time very massively with science and technology. Common sense, and not only in the West, is more and more mediated through these forms—mediated but not exhausted by them—there is more. Here Rosen is a defender of common sense but not in the dogmatic form that is inimical to philosophy. There is more *recessed* in common sense than many theories fully express, and hence we need thinking that does not excessively fixate on theory. Nevertheless, common sense's idiocy can be idiotic and idiotic: madness and common nonsense can lurk there also. We know this from common sense itself. Common sense is itself a therapy of life against the kinds of merely mad idiocy. It is already a discerning response to the saturated equivocity—even if the response is itself saturated with equivocity.

A second response is *the philosophical.* Here we can find a rejoinder to this equivocity that is tempted to reduce it to reflective or conceptual univocity. There are many expressions of this, but in all the ideal of intelligibility seems to be determinate univocity, often influenced by the ideal of mathematical univocity. 1 = 1 and 1 only: not more, not less; there seems no ambiguity about 1. To be able to count to 2 implies the determination of what 1 is: 1 is 1 by being 1, and not by being 2, or anything more or less than 1. Determination and differentiation are inseparable. By contrast, with equivocity there is a doubleness, but it is not a determinate 2, but a potential duplicity. Properly counting to 2 is a way of conquering the saturated equivocity. We count 1 as determinately other than another 1. Thus the saturated equivocity is crystallized into this, that, and the other. With this principle of univocal determinacy, there is no reserve of ambiguity, it seems, at least in principle. In this light, many practices of philosophy are undoubtedly dominated by the will to reduce equivocity to univocity. Examples throughout the tradition might include the Socratic quest of a univocal definition of essence, Descartes's valorization of clarity and distinctness, Leibniz's investment in the calculative powers of a *mathēsis universalis,* the search of a higher transcendental univocity in Kant and his idealistic successors, more recent quests for an ideal logical language, and so on. But a dominant practice of philosophy is not exhaustive of philosophy, either its practice or its promise. There is "more" also to philosophy, as there is to common sense.

Once again Rosen is not against the search for determinate intelligibility, but also wants us to grant the "more" of philosophy itself, as well as of common sense. We find this particularly in his debates with contemporary philosophy, in the variants of its ordinary language versions.[14] Here we find a reaction against, and a therapy against, the temptations scientistically to reduce common sense, in the desire to overcome entirely its saturated equivocity. Were this successful, the plurivocity would be re-

---

14. See, e.g., his discussion of Moore and Austin in chapters 5 and 6, respectively, of *The Elusiveness of the Ordinary.*

duced to univocity. One thinks of the later Wittgenstein as gesturing toward this plurivocity against his own earlier infatuations with logical univocity.[15] Rosen helps us see that these therapies against the bewitchments of univocal theory are reminiscent of the Socratic turn to the *logoi* and the *doxa*. Of course too, many of these contemporary practices of philosophers are not without their own recesses of presupposition—often a variety of "Kantian" presuppositions, with their own various afterlives. Result: we tend to reproduce aspects of the difficulty at issue rather than address it adequately; we do not quite get a "return" to the ordinary, or quite the practice of a releasing philosophy. Rosen wants to restore respect for common sense, where it exists, but not at the expense of respect for philosophy. Something more to each is to be acknowledged.

Science and technology represent a third significant response to the saturated equivocity. Theoretical understanding calls forth practical application and we move beyond contemplation to intervention and to the reconfiguration of the given conditions of life. It is part of the human condition to interact with nature as other to us, and intelligently to order the given conditions of life by this interaction. As marking something constant in our condition, this is to be found in premodern epochs, but undoubtedly modernity is the epoch of its extraordinary expression. The power of practical univocity is mediated by the power of theoretical univocity and immensely increased with the development of more powerful mathematics. Mathematics itself is changed in its relation to the fuller context of life, in its ethical and religious dimensions. I often think of the geometry of the Demiurge of Plato's *Timaeus*: the milieu, the ethos of being, is defined by a material geometrics of the visible, aesthetic cosmos, but the making power that here brings the cosmos to be is not primarily moved by geometry but by finesse, aesthetic, ethical, and religious. The cosmos, as an aesthetic work of art, is for the Demiurge to be *the most beautiful and good possible*. One might venture: Geometry serves this divine finesse. In modernity the milieu of being is mathematicized, homogenized, approached problematically rather than theorematically. Geometry is made to serve a secularized finesse. This is a finesse that is not true finesse, since by being made such a servant its proper priority and superiority is disordered.

15. On Wittgenstein and Strauss, see *The Elusiveness of the Ordinary*, chapter 4.

But the main point holds good: again we find a dominant orientation to overcoming the equivocal, and not only in a formal sense. That we think of ourselves as problem solvers suggests that being itself is a problem, a problem to be definitively solved. There is, or will be, no problem without its solution. Which attitude comes first: there is no problem beyond us or being is a problem or set of problems? A question or "problem" perhaps not possible to answer univocally. It is true that there is a univocalizing orientation that sets no problem before itself that it does not think it can solve, on its own terms, through its own power alone. But we could well ask: What of the hyperproblematic? This again is the question of the "overdeterminacy," or the "more." One expression of this in Rosen's work is the already referred to separation of reason and the good in modernity.[16] It might be put this way: Reason separated from the good is not able to give a good reason, not only for why we should be good, but for why we should be reasonable.

I would say that the changed relation to the ethos of being in modernity has a momentum toward the totalistic, in the sense of an absolutely inclusive and immanent univocity, beyond which there is (to be) nothing. We find the stripping away of the signs of qualitative value. The objectification of nature as other in turn tends to both massively objectify the human being, as well as hugely to subjectify it. The subject produces the objectifying that will be the death of itself as subjectivity, death not least effected by its glut on itself as nothing but subjective.

I do not think we can underestimate the ambitions of modernity as a project for the reconfiguration of the everyday in its equivocity. There are those, like Charles Taylor, who stress modernity as the affirmation of everyday life. I see this as a kind of soft Hegelianism which is too silent about the most salient portents of the state of play. Modernity is rife with equivocity on this score: if there is an affirmation of "ordinary" life, more so is there a *project to reconstruct it*. But this means first negating it as it is, deconstructing it before reconstructing it (one thinks of Descartes's rules: break the complex into the simple, and then reconstruct it from them). There is the fact that more and more we refuse the given conditions of life. What is given is to be made over. Plastic surgery, genetic engineering, hybridizations of life, posthuman humanoids: we seem unable to be able to

---

16. Again see "Sad Reason" in *Metaphysics in Ordinary Language*, but also "The Attributes of Ordinary Experience," chapter 8 in *The Elusiveness of the Ordinary*.

tell the difference between true eros and pornography, a mind and a computer, a person and a machine.

This is the strange result of a project of univocity designed to do away with the strangeness of being as such. Strangely, its increasing attainment of homogeneity leads to the loss of qualitative differentiation, the loss of discernment, and with this loss the melding of everything as homogenously the same. With totalized univocity we end up with a promiscuous equivocity, itself oscillating with the univocity from which it only *apparently* departs. *L'esprit de géométrie* triumphs over *l'esprit de finesse*. But then we are unable to discern genuine differences; and we end up in a new promiscuous confusion in which high and low, better and worse, true and false, philosophy and sophistry, God and the counterfeit doubles of God are melded without boundary.

In sum: the conquest of equivocity generates its own equivocation, and so we drag along with us the condition we are trying to escape. Perhaps some postmodern responses have a good "nose" for this, but one wonders to what degree these responses are enmeshed in their own, sometimes debilitating, equivocities. It is not enough indiscriminately to exalt the equivocal. We need metaxological discernment of the plurivocity of being.

WORDING THE EQUIVOCAL: ART AND RELIGION

Let us look at the equivocal some more, and ask if it is possible to word something of the saturated equivocity at its deepest. Can we address without reduction and voice the saturated equivocity? I think religion and art try to do this. What of philosophy? The familial relation of art, religion, and philosophy will occupy us. Rosen is attentive to the nearness and distance of poetry and philosophy, less so to the relation of philosophy to the religious. There is a double attitude to poetry: it is something other than philosophy, and yet it is indispensable, perhaps even in philosophy itself. Some might propose a bacchantic celebration of the equivocal, and Nietzsche, in one of his masks, might be taken as a paradigm: a philosopher of the equivocal, but also an equivocal philosopher. Rosen is not to be aligned with any postmodern promiscuity of the poetic and philosophical, but his perception of something positive about the equivocity of the everyday opens him to the poetic. Poetic attention to the recalcitrances of the ordinary to univocal reduction offers a token of what the best of philosophy can also try to meet. The return of equivocity, despite all scientistic univocity, need not be a failure but can indicate something of our task as philosophers, indicate also something of what is to guide the task.

Rosen's double attitude to poetry reminds us of Plato's caution and respect, but there is also a sympathy to the Platonic practice of philosophy as a kind of *philosophical poetics*. One inevitably recalls the quarrel of poet and philosopher. If there is an *agon* here, it is a familial one—there is intimacy in the difference, even in the *polemos*. Perhaps the most intensive quarrels are between those who are most intimately related. There are moments when one wonders if the difference of poetry and philosophy is being collapsed, yet despite such moments Rosen's view is strong: there is to be no "mere" poetry, in the sense of the abdication of truth in favor of fancy.[17] We have to be truthful even when truth tells against us.

If the saturated equivocity is a significant ambiguity that requires finesse, art offers a form of finesse. Art, and poetry especially, tries to articulate the charged equivocity and divine its significance: it does not just express it, but seeks to shed light on it, to explore its intimate contours. This intimacy is connected with an attentiveness to singularities, which, however, are not neutrally expressed in terms of more univocal concepts. If art shows the equivocal, it also holds it for contemplation, and especially holds for beholding what is too recessed in it by our less discerning everyday perceptions. Think of a poem thus: what is articulated there is also reserved there. Sometimes the poem seems to say something, sometimes seems to say nothing, sometimes seems to say everything. Consider beholding of a great work of art: the sensuous communication of the work is not just of the explicit; it is a holding there for beholding of a significant reserve: by reserve it shows the recess of the "more." There is here something determinate yet exceeding all determination. This is connected to the inexhaustibility of the great work, a significance communicated but not to be finally fathomed.

Recall what Kant says about the aesthetic idea: a representation of the imagination which occasions much thought but to which no determinate thought is ever adequate. One might say: the aesthetic idea helps concretize the self-transcending of human mindfulness and moves it to

17. *The Quarrel between Philosophy and Poetry: Studies in Ancient Thought* (New York: Routledge, 1988).

what exceeds final determination, though, in fact, here in this representation something of that surplus is shown. There is also a release in us of a porosity to what is beyond us. This is very evident with music: there is a porosity to a beguiling and enigmatic communication, a porosity beyond our will to power. Thus the element of the involuntary that Kant disliked about music, when he compares it to the effect of a dandy taking out his perfumed handkerchief: the perfume spreads everywhere, is communicated, and no prior permission has been asked or granted by us for its effect on us. But, of course, Kant was irritated by the mischief to his own rational autonomy that music represented. It is our "being moved" by a porosity beyond rational will that got on his nerves.

Relative to univocity and equivocity, there may be mathematical form in music but the energy circling in the form, indeed circling as the forming, exceeds geometry: we need finesse for the energies of soul in the forming, and the communication of these energies. Leibniz does not quite foreground this energy when he says: "Music is the secret exercise of arithmetic which does not know that it is counting" *(Musica est exercitium arithmeticae occultum nescientis se numerare animi).* I would connect these energies and the porosity to what Plato suggests about eros and mania. We are overcome, we forget ourselves, sometimes to the point where we are unsure if we dream or wake, live or die. The beautiful story of the cicadas in the *Phaedrus* tells something of the rapture and of this saturated equivocity: the muses were born and song appeared, and music was such a boon for mortals, they were overcome with delight and forgot to eat and drink, and died, to be reborn as the endlessly singing cicadas.[18]

These remarks about art bring us to the border of the religious, and I would say analogous considerations arise here. Being religious reveals perhaps the most primal porosity of the human being: the nakedness of the soul before the divine. I will not treat of this more here, but I would stress that art and religion are not outside the milieu of the everyday. They are the ways of expressing the ordinary in its extraordinary promise. The milieu of the everyday is the between within which both take form. The extra-ordinary is "in" the ordinary, but this is only known and approached in and through the ordinary. Art and religion are each a dwelling with the ordinary, but what comes to manifestation there is more. The normal du-

18. See *Phaedrus* 258e7–59e.; also see *Art, Otherness, Origins,* chapter 1, for some reflections on mimesis, eros, and mania; chapter 2 on Kant and art (on music and the porosity, 78).

alistic antithesis of ordinary and extraordinary is not enough. Philosophy moves between one and the other: thinking their significance relative to the full dimensions of the milieu of being. In Rosen's own metaphysics of the ordinary something of being brought to, or coming to, such boundaries is stressed: something of the becoming porous of the ordinary to something more that shines in and through it.[19]

Poetry is one of the great human ways of keeping open the soul's porosity to the communication of the saturated equivocity. There are mere celebrators of the aesthetic—strands in postmodern Nietzscheanism seemed to be tempted to this—but then in the long run the spiritual seriousness of art is compromised, and we lose interest in art. Without a relation to truth and to philosophy, the aesthetic playing with possibility is no longer an "interesting" possibility for us. The seriousness of truth is needed—this is not to deny that play, and the playfulness of seeking truth, can also be very "serious."

Rosen spends more time on the relation of poetry and philosophy than on the relation of religion and philosophy. This is a complex issue. But there are reserves and recesses here too deep to fathom without intimate knowledge of the idiocy of the thinker. In the relation of Athens and Jerusalem, Athens seems very much to the fore, or favored. Is there something reserved or held back? I am guessing, but Rosen is not an atheist, but what kind of nonatheist he is is not easy to say. I do think this issue is more recessive in his thinking than I would prefer. But I grant: there are forms of otherness that, just as other, are masked: the reserve is in the honesty itself, not somehow hidden elsewhere. An elemental allegiance to being truthful can result in truth being astonishingly reserved: truth most open, truth most reserved.

Art and religion are ways of dealing affirmatively with the surplus equivocity; they are not defects from a univocity whose fastness allows us only to condemn equivocity. They offer forms of porosity, filled with finesse, to what is communicated in the saturated equivocity. Though they provide no "theory" of its meaning, in practice they can be superior to such theory, just by being in rapport with the communication. Again, one is hard put to give an "exact" account. There is no "exact" account. Giving an exact point: this is not to the point. Not giving the exact point, this is

---

19. See, for instance, chapter 9 of *The Elusiveness of the Ordinary*.

the exact point. "The exactness is a fake," Whitehead said, speaking toward the end of his life and—with a bow to the old Plato—while discussing mathematics and the good.

A way Rosen sometimes puts the issue here is in terms of the contrast of constructing and seeing, making and finding. This is perhaps a more post-Kantian way of putting the point. This post-Kantian way reaches a crescendo in Nietzsche: truth is a construction of will to power: my truth. Rosen has illuminated us on the incoherences emergent from the more coherent post-Kantianism of Nietzsche. But granting Nietzsche as a poet-philosopher, suppose poetry, and even more religion, direct us to something other than construction? Poetry is not just making. Eros and mania, intimates of the poet, are also always more than making. Think of *wooing* the muse. Wooing is not either making or finding: rather there is a porosity to wooing prior to any making; there is a "being found" before finding. In this we get some sense of the "more." Though this "more" might look like nothing, being no thing, there springs up in the "nothing" of porosity a certain energy, an inspiration, a movement, a being moved. And all this *before* we move ourselves. The "more" enabling the making is reserved in what we have made.

Perhaps Plato, in a guarded way, knew philosophy at its most intensively true as also inspired—neither constructing nor discovering but mindfully wooing something more primal and beyond that lets both discovering and constructing be possible. Might this seem to align him with Nietzsche? Yes and no. Yes, in regard to the primal source that cannot be completely rationalized in a univocal manner. For this source has to do with eros and mania. No, in regard to the utter irrationality of this source in Nietzsche. The fact is that, finally, the resources do not seem to be present in Nietzsche's thinking to distinguish between *eros turannos* and *eros ouranios*. Eros may be inherently equivocal, but much hangs on our awakening to the difference of these two forms. Philosophy is tested in its ability to discern the difference, even in the act of articulating this equivocity. Granting the *eros ouranios*, there is an other source of inspiration intimate to us that cannot be separated from ultimate being and from being good. Philosophy, as much as poetry and religion, can be participant in porosity to this source.[20]

---

20. Nietzsche calls this source *das Ureine* in the *Birth of Tragedy*. For fuller discussion, see *Art, Origins, Otherness*, chapter 6.

If Rosen is more involved in the conversation of the poet and philosopher than of religion and philosophy, yet religion is the more democratic art of the ultimate: for the many, and not only for them: the ultimate porosity. Job in his nakedness is beyond the distinction of the few and the many (whether conceived according to Plato or Nietzsche). The many and the few will all spend their moments on the ash-heap where the ultimate question cannot be evaded: What then the point of it all? One wonders about an influence on Rosen from Spinoza: religion has to do with obedience for the many, not truth for the few, that is, the philosophers. Piety as obedience to the sovereign may have salutary effects in terms of social order, but the intimate tie of religion with truth is weakened or even severed. But if we *are* this porosity to the divine—there is an intimate *metaxu*—then it is wrong to reduce religion to a more instrumental social role. Rather it lies closer to what is most ultimate for us. Of little help here is the relativization of religion by the rationalistic Enlightenment or by Kant, not to mention even more utilitarian instrumentalists, or post-Hegelian, or post-Nietzschean execrators. What is essential is being missed by this. Often what is at stake is covered over by more proximate social and cultural formations, and we have not philosophically, poetically, religiously come to some truer porosity to the source of transcendence in us. We are spellbound by the foreground and do not pay attention to the back-ground.

I would not propose something like Hegel's absolute spirit as the answer, for this privileges a speculative inclusiveness of philosophy that does not seem quite true to the saturated equivocities of the everyday, of art, of religion. I would rather more have a plurivocal interplay of art, religion, and philosophy: one that, while granting the saturated equivocity, helps mitigate the philosophical temptation to hubris, the religious danger of violent dogmatism, and the artistic intoxication with a lightheaded aestheticism. Even if there is a more open communication of the three rather than an Hegelian *Aufhebung,* still philosophy does have a singular responsibility to be mindful of what is going on in the others. This is its care, indeed its love of the others. It does not always live up to the responsibility. Its interest is in interesting itself in them as others; art and religion are more relatively free from the need to be thus reflectively interested in the others. But each is of interest to the others, insofar as this interest is in the true "being-between" (*inter-esse*) of porosity to communication with transcendence as other.

PHILOSOPHICAL RESPONSES TO EQUIVOCITY:
DIALECTICAL COMPLICATIONS

System is one philosophical response to the equivocity of the everyday, and the speculative dialectic of Hegel represents perhaps its most total expression. Nevertheless, one can be systematic without claiming to possess *the* system.[21] As I have stressed before, there are a number of ways of looking at dialectic or practicing it. These many ways are almost coincident with the essential configurations of the philosophical tradition, from Zeno, through Socrates, Plato and Aristotle, right through to Kant, Hegel, and now to those who overcome metaphysics or deconstruct the tradition, namely, the various antidialectical dialecticians of our own time. If postphilosophy is antidialectical, or even (less negatively put) postdialectical, it too cannot be understood without properly understanding dialectic. Given that I have said much about dialectic already, I will confine myself to one crucial difference which is central, and central for Rosen also: the difference of Plato and Hegel, and their respective practices of philosophical dialectic.

Dialectic can be seen as a way of mediating the equivocity of the everyday, and indeed the equivocities in other domains. The goal is not simply to reduce the equivocal to the univocal, but to win through to a sense of the whole more inclusive than equivocal differences that become dissolute, more internally differentiated than the rigid univocity whose determination yields oppositional dualism. Hegel's deployment of his speculative dialectic is often presented as the completion of the philosophical tradition, but those who deconstruct Hegel or claim to go beyond him often accede to just this interpretation. The difference is that this completion seems to them to reveal the defective nature of philosophy. If Hegel is this completion, the perfection then reveals a defection. What if he is not? Is there something equivocal in philosophy itself somewhere between the perfection and the defection?

Rosen does not accept the claim of Hegel, or the post-Hegelian deconstructor, because he reads Plato as not simply in a line of univocal continuity with what is effected in Kant, and its inheritance in Hegel's system.

---

21. See my "Between System and Poetics: On the Practices of Philosophy," in *Between System and Poetics: William Desmond and Philosophy after Dialectic*, ed. Thomas Kelly (Aldershot, U.K.: Ashgate Press, 2007), chapter 1.

Hegelian dialectic may be the most impressive of its modern speculative forms, but a speculative univocity returns at the end to close the system into the immanence of thought at one with itself. Hegel negotiates with the equivocal, and sees there opposites turning into opposites; but in this turning, he sees a return to unity in the sameness of the opposites. There is a different dialectic in Plato, if not in the theory, then in the practice of philosophy.

One way one might express this is to say that this practice of philosophy keeps the *"dia"* of dialectic open. Another way: *let philosophy allow, allow for the reserve of the everyday.* Thinking is not always a matter of making the reserve completely explicit. Explicitness is itself only possible on the basis of something reserved, as speech needs silence, and talking listening. There is something recessed in the saying, not fixed fully in the said. This is the "more" again, and we meet it in both the energy of mind, and the supple intelligibilities of everyday life. Something of this "more" is given articulation in the practice of philosophical dialogue itself.

By contrast, Hegel points to the self-determination of thought in which finally nothing is reserved. The logic this follows shows a movement from the indeterminate, to the determinate, and ending with the self-determining. What of the origin of all this? What if it were not the indeterminate, in the sense of the indefinite to be made determinate or self-determining? Suppose it were the overdeterminate? This would be the "more" that, though always communicated, is yet reserved in being communicated, recessed in being expressed. And then there is a certain inexhaustibility to what comes to manifestation. The overdeterminate thus would have to be seen as a kind of "too muchness": not less than determinacy but in excess of determinacy, and in a plenitudinous way. This might be said to point toward an indefectible sense of the surplus of the given, a given that is also given with reserve. And suppose this surplus reserve is what sources the determinate, even though qua resource it is more than every determinate form it sources? The everyday and its supple intelligibilities is (re)sourced in the promise of this reserved overdeterminacy. It is to be remembered that this sense of the origin also effects how we relate to the middle, as well as to the end. For the "too much" is not only in the beginning but in the middle and in any supposedly unsurpassable end. There is no unsurpassable end in Hegel's speculatively holistic sense.

See the Platonic dialogue as pointing us in the direction of keeping the "*dia*" of dialectic open to the givenness of this indefectible surplus. This "*dia*" can refer to a genuine two, in the sense of a dyad, and the need for two for a conversation. The "dia" might also be seen as a medium, or porous middle through which communication passes, as when we speak of a medium as diaphanous: the medium allows the light to pass though. The "*dia*" enables porosity to intelligent and intelligible communication. The Platonic dialogue presents us with the mediation of the equivocal, and, where appropriate, it also tries to offer univocal definition, but there is more than this offered, more than we can enclose in one round of conceptual self-determination. The "*dia*" of dialogue is itself the offer of a kind of saturated equivocity which is presented to us for reading and interpretation and for the education of thinking. It is not a mush of vagueness but a communication of signs, not only in words, but in the individual characters in conversations and in stories, and indeed in their significant silences. For what is said is not only carried by a communication in signs; but the "who" saying is also a sign that communicates; the saying itself is a sign of more than what the determinate said communicates. Platonic dialogue keeps the porosity of community open in the plurivocity of such signs.

There is both an immanent communication and sometimes a sign of what exceeds immanent communication. I am thinking of the sign given in the Seventh Letter: the *flash between* one and another that tells of something that is not of one or the other. There is living mind and its energy. But there is also the light of the good that is not directly noticed as it opens up the porous space between mind and intelligibility, the light that enables seeing but that is not itself directly seen because it is no thing. In a way, the porosity of communication is also like this no-thing, though in the case of human community this porosity is not constituted through itself alone, as if it were a *causa-sui,* or power of absolute self-determination. To the contrary, there is a givenness that is not self-produced, a givenness whose surplus Hegelian dialectic tries to ingest into an absolute process of self-determining thought.

Communication in dialogue gives shape to the human forms in which the energies of being and minding move and in and into which they flash. This is as much ordinary as extraordinary: it is happening all the time, in everyday life. An instance with reference to Rosen's long-fought defense of intuition: perhaps the astounding eureka moments testify to extraordinary breakthroughs of intelligence and intelligibility, but everyday life, as

Rosen insists, is sustained by acts of seeing, and seeing the point, without which speaking would not be, without which would not be any communication. We participate in what is happening, we live from it, we hardly notice it, we pay no attention. Philosophy is a reminder to pay attention: a reminder sometimes disciplined in a more systematic direction, sometimes more directly and poetically recalling the flash. Hence the matter is not always just a matter of trumping Hegel and other philosophers of immanence by means of the Good beyond being. That, of course, is extraordinarily important, but there is the more daily matter of finesse for this intimate flash of minding, and what the flash portends of what is beyond. Philosophy, as a reminder of the everyday, is also a minding that has finesse for these portents.

METAXOLOGICAL METAPHYSICS AND EQUIVOCITY: INTERMEDIATION WITHOUT REDUCTION

I conclude with two sets of remarks, one bearing on the systematic side of philosophy, the other bearing on what is at the limit of system. The metaxological concerns a *logos* of the *metaxu*. We have been addressing the everyday as itself a *metaxu* marked by a saturated equivocity, looking at different responses to this, from common sense to religion. Philosophy, as a certain mindfulness of the equivocity of the everyday, can take a metaxological form. Art and religion have much to offer in connection with the more affirmative, and not merely negative, sense of equivocity. Can philosophy also approach it in a nonreductive thinking?

The *metaxu* is at stake in all the discussion above because the fundamental relations between same and other, identity and difference are everywhere at work. There are communications between self and other and they are plurivocal, but this plurivocity does not always truly come to mindfulness in modern dialectic of the self-mediating kind. Dialogical intermediation is truer, and we find a philosophical exemplification of this in the Platonic dialogue. Such dialogue also makes manifest something of what we might expect of the practice of philosophy in the equivocity of the everyday.

The distinction of ontology and metaphysics is here relevant. If ontology deals with being as immanent, it can assume a form tending toward something like Hegel's system of self-determining thought, or perhaps fundamental ontology and its existential engagement with human immanence. Metaphysics is more metaxological in the sense of opening mindfulness to transcendence as other to our own self-transcendence, by means of an exploration of the signs of irreducible otherness, even in immanence. This is not a matter of the system but can be a matter of systematic thought. Hegel closes systematic thinking into the circle of the system, but there is no a priori necessity that thinking systematically has to take this modern form. There are rich networks of interconnections already at work in being. These networks do not constitute a closed or completed system to be discursively expressed by philosophy. The networks are concretized by open intermediations marked by sameness and otherness, identity and difference. Dynamic integrities of being take form as stable but open constancies. Our minding of these shows the living energy of thought which comes to mind out of a more original porosity before being, and opens beyond closure to what is other to thought.

Modern dialectic tends to interpret the passages between same and other, identity and difference, and so on in terms of self-determining thought. The intermediation tends toward self-mediation that circles around and back on itself, resulting in a closure of the immanence of thought. From a metaxological perspective, this is not a true intermediation; passing over the original porosity, it does not do justice to the passages between, where otherness as other, is just as basic, if not more, than self-determining thought. For even in self-determining thought, there is an inward otherness that reminds us of the opening porosity as well as intimating what exceeds every determinate and self-determining finality.

The between is the milieu of thought where philosophy arises and takes form. As itself a form of intermediated thinking, philosophy is not for itself alone. Its own self-determination is not the absolute point. It is a participant in this middle, does not overarch it from the outside; it is lifted up from within, but it too is always defined by passages in the between. In one sense, there is no return to the *metaxu,* since we never leave it; but there is a return in the sense of waking to what we are in; and realizing the porosity of the medium of finite life to what cannot be exhausted by the determinate forms of life in the between. Just as metaxological thinking opens to what is other in the immanence of the between, it is also open to something reserved that points beyond immanence. If there is a return to the recalcitrance of the everyday in its otherness to thought, there is also a searching of the "more" of the everyday as charged with signs of what exceeds immanence alone. Interpreting the signs of this "more" as communicated in the saturated equivocity of the everyday is intimate to the vocation of metaxological metaphysics.

The *metaxu* is explicitly a Platonic theme, at work in the dialogues, though not worked out explicitly in all its possibilities. Rosen himself exhibits in practice a mindfulness of the metaxological but it is not always foregrounded as a theme.[22] Putting an emphasis on the *metaxu* is helpful, I suggest, in softening the tendency to dualistic opposition in Plato between ideas and instances, visible and invisible, body and soul, time and eternity, and so on. A dualism of these pairs easily follows if their otherness is univocalized in terms of two fixed worlds. We might think rather of participation, *methexis*, as intermediation in this *metaxu*, rather than in terms of a determinate third that is a bridge between two fixed worlds, considered as dualistic opposites. We must remember the porosity of the *metaxu* to communication, and this whether the communication should traverse the middle from below up, or from above down.

I think here of what Plato suggests about eros as moving from below up, and divine mania as moving from above down. A metaphysics that only stresses mimetic relations can easily congeal into a fixed grid of proportional relations. An underscoring of eros indicates the self-surpassing energy of the soul as it passes through the *metaxu* and beyond itself toward the Good. Some attentiveness to mania can alert us to the ingression in the immanent *metaxu* of transcendent powers that inspire us, that lift us up in their gift of enthusiasm, powers we name as divine and which mark the interruption of the ordinary by the extraordinary. This can be in art, in religion, in philosophy itself. The resources for a plurivocal response to the between are thus indicated diversely through mimesis, eros, mania. The practice of philosophy, at its best, can also be the beneficiary of these resources. Platonic philosophy as *metaxu* can be daimonic between the human and the divine, though if we remember Pascal's reminder that we are a middle between nothing and infinity, the philosopher's tendency to *eros turannos* must be chastened.

22. In passing, the notion is important for thinkers like Buber, and even Heidegger, who in a number of places make some reference to *das Zwischen*. It is more confined to the human togetherness in Buber, while Heidegger does not give us the rounded development it requires; see my *Art, Otherness, Origins*, chapter 7, "Art and the Self-Concealing Origin: Heidegger's Equivocity and the Still Unthought Between."

The *metaxu* also defines a space between the systematic and what is beyond system. I would say that the Platonic dialogue itself gives important indications of the edges of the systematic. Rosen himself has long insisted on what has now become more widely acknowledged: the *dramatic nature* of these dialogues is indispensable in the showing and communication of truth. These dialogues offer us images of the practices of philosophy in terms of a living dialectic between singular human beings. These singulars give voice to their understanding of truth, none possesses it completely, yet each contributes in the play of voices to the furtherance of the search. Philosophical dialogue plurivocally mimics the possible pathways to truth in the middle, and indeed some of the possible departures from the path, also in the middle. Dialogue is a meeting in the middle of plurivocal *logoi,* each seeking to be true to, or departing from, what shows itself in the spaces of questioning and answering between thinking human beings.[23]

Interestingly, dialogue makes a call on us that we *pay attention to surfaces.* Surfaces, one might say, are where we find the *interfaces* of communication. Philosophy must be a mindfulness of surfaces as such places of showing. Plato gives us a philosophy of surfaces by offering us the drama of human interfacing. For words can be the richest showings in the interface: the surfacings of souls in the between and in communication with each other. Such articulating and articulated surfaces can be the communication of the deepest hiddenness. It is not accidental that we speak of eros surfacing: the incarnate human is aroused, inspired, beside itself. In surfacing, the singular soul faces the others, in the "inter" of interfacing. The surfacing promises an intimacy of communication to the one who loves or is loved. One might say that art is a happening where surface and depth coincide. The hypersensible shows itself as sensible. The intelligible shines. The Platonic dialogue is a deep drama of surfaces. It is a between of interfaces.

In a metaxological philosophy this calls for an attentiveness to *images,* and not just discursive concepts. Consider here the Platonic dialogue as an *iconic drama,* a mimesis of Socrates and others. We are given images of Socrates: stingray, gadfly, midwife, Silenus figure. But the saturated equiv-

---

23. See Dimitri Nikulin's fine book *Dialectic and Dialogue* (Stanford, Calif.: Stanford University Press, 2010).

ocity is here too. For there is something more and other to the original: Socrates is "in-between" and *atopos* (*Symposium* 215a2, 221c2–d6), and no one knows him (216c7–d1). A certain "silence," or reserve, about the original, generates the need for many images. Something similar might be said above the silent reserve of Plato himself in all his writing. "Plato before, Plato behind, in the middle a chimera"—so said Nietzsche, basing his jest on Homer.[24] But the chimera is also a monster. The excess in the middle is saturated with equivocal significance inseparable from the sacred.

One might make a similar point about the most powerful media of communication: words. Words are overdetermined; they mean more than they say explicitly, carry around within themselves unacknowledged origins. Words are excess: they express reserves of meaning but also reserve recesses. The aesthetics of Platonic thinking, and the art of the philosophical question, must pay attention to these intimations of what is recessed. For if words reserve recesses, there is always a *significant silence* in the very articulation itself. I say "significant silence" because if we are too bewitched by a Hegelian sense of articulation, silence quickly becomes *merely silence,* hence a testimony to the failure of the thought. Silence would then be an abortion of the concept that even a Socrates fails to midwife. What if there is a silence that is a sign not of our failure but a mark of respect for what is reserved, and asks to be reserved? We can encounter such a "successful" silence in the speaking of a great work of art: it reserves its mystery, perhaps it gives a sign, perhaps it says nothing yet intimates everything. Were one to call it a dialectical togetherness of silence and saying, neither the silence nor the saying can be *aufgehoben* into a Hegelian dialectic. That dialectic might strike one as verging on conceptual chatter, loquacious and prosaically blithe where reverent attendance is solicited. In a conversation with an other there are crucial moments when the true thing to do is to fall silent. Finesse for proper silence shows respect for the other in the unfolding of the communication itself.

Consider Plato's own silence: he says nothing in the dialogues, but it is *others,* especially Socrates, who speak. Even much of what Socrates speaks is attributed to others, Diotima, for instance, and hence there is not only an indirection but alas a certain silencing of the speaker in the speaking itself.

24. Friedrich Nietzsche, *Beyond Good and Evil,* part 5, §190, in *Basic Writings of Nietzsche,* 293.

There is a kind of "dialectical" togetherness of saying and silence in the art of the Platonic dialogue which points us in a metaxological direction. The dialectic of question and answer is impossible without *the pause* in speech of multiple silences. The interplay of saying and silence enacts a dramatics of the origination of thought as it becomes transformed in the metaxu between you and I. You address a question to me; your speaking asks my silence, as it breaks yours; when I respond, my speaking asks your silence, even as I break mine. Each of our addresses and replies is framed by silence. Silence frames the space of communication between us. Without multiple silences there would be no speaking and no communication. We both must be willing to fall silent to allow the middle space to be charged with the words that bind us, in both what they present and what they insinuate. Neither you nor I are exhausted by the communication that does eventuate, for there are silences beyond our speaking and silence, there are wordings beyond our words.

Moreover, even when in the Platonic dialogue there is an effort to speak a response that satisfies our questioning, another significant silence can come to be even in an approach to the consummation of understanding. The noetic intuition by which it is said the form is grasped brings us to a significant silence. There is also a repeated dramatization of our not being able now to "go further" with discursive articulations. Our logoi reach their limit in a bounding silence. This silence does not kill the struggle for articulation but allows it to be taken up into a new space of communication and furthered by a different saying. I mean the poetic saying of myth, itself the bearer of a silence that addresses a perplexity to philosophical thought, even while exceeding univocal conceptualization. A plurality of silences is intertwined with a plurivocity of sayings: the silence that encompasses our dialogue is yet intimate to it; the silences of the singular participants both separate them and allow them to be joined in communication; the space between the participants allows enabling silence and soliciting response; the silence bounding discursive concepts is hospitable to mythopoeic speech, itself the bearer of a silence that points beyond all discursive dialogue to the communication of the divine.

When one says that a metaxological metaphysics grants due acknowledgment to nonsystematic voices, it is not that the systematic voice is necessarily lacking its integrity. Being truthful asks an attendance of mindfulness that tries to stay as close as possible to the energy of emerging articulation.

Our attendance on the saturated equivocity of the everyday reveals that the energy of being and mind do not originally shape themselves as philosophical systems. Were one to wrestle with these energies and somehow form them more systematically, the same energies that nourish any system now would show themselves as exceeding that form. It is the necessary drift to excess in all serious thought that is communicated in the nonsystematic character of the thought. This can be a kind of saturated equivocity in philosophical thinking itself. This need not be put down to a defect of attainment relative to univocal theory or dialectical system. It may be a nonreductive intermediation of equivocity, allowed for by metaxological mindfulness. Nietzsche suggested that the will to system reveals a lack of integrity. One can heed his warning if by "system" he means that we can blind ourselves to the "too muchness" of being as happening, or blunt our awareness that the mind holds too much to be contained within a system. Excessive mindfulness has to find a different form, a forming beyond determinate form, to be true to the "too muchness" of the happening of being. Plurivocity invites the nonsystematic voice also needed by philosophy to speak of what is in excess of system.

Metaphysics is *struck* into astonishment at the overdeterminacy of being in the *metaxu*. This is like a wake-up call to the everyday, not our being asleep in it. It asks our endeavor to articulate the passages between: be these forms of intelligibility, or energies of erotic self-surpassing, or gifts (of mania) that come to us from sources beyond ourselves. Philosophy can be mindfulness of what is given overtly, as well as attentiveness to the reserved: the excess resourced in the saturated equivocity of the everyday. While there is a need to make explicit, so far as that lies within our power, this is never to exhaust the reserved. There is a kind of granting of what is reserved; a kind of memorial respect for what asks acknowledgment, even when it does not foreground itself. Metaxological mind passes between the expressed and the reserved. Given respect for common sense, there need be no dissolution of the saturated equivocity when we become mindful of it. It is illuminated. There is an access of light, in and through it. The light is not univocal; it is not self-determined; it is not merely equivocal in a negative sense. It is not absolutely immanent, since there is a play of light and darkness, and there is more to the light than to the dark.

There are some striking images in Plato of the soul trying to surface or reach surface. The surface sought is again an interface. I think of the image comparing humans to creatures who live in hollows but think they live on the surface. They are like creatures looking up through the waters of the deep ocean, seeing what is above, the sun and the sky through these waters, and mistaking the sea for the sky, though some do lift their heads like fish out of the waters and see the things in the air above (see *Phaedo* 109b–10b). One of the words in this passage is *ēschaton* which also has the meaning of "edge," or "verge": edge of the air, *ēschaton ton aēra* (109e2). Socrates here, of course, is in the process of telling an "eschatological" story, or *muthos*. We are the dull-faced fishes coming up from the dim murk of the bottom ponds with gulping mouths to taste the edge of air.

There is also the image of the cave: we are below the surface of earth; philosophical ascent strives to come to the surface; only properly on the surface can we look up and see. We stand on the ground by going up to the surface. Below surface in the deeps of the cave, there is one form of the play between light and dark. If we reach the surface of the earth, there is a different play of light and dark. Even were it perpetual day on the surface of the earth, we humans do not escape the equivocal. The "too muchness" of light would as much blind us as sight us—and perhaps we have to be blinded to be sighted—something must remain reserved or we die.

The everyday can become strange and mysterious again—like the face of a beloved familiar, long known and not known, granted to us but too often taken for granted. Reawakening to our dwelling on the surface means being faced with a mystery: at the extremity of our determinate knowing, and perhaps our mortal condition. One thinks of Orpheus and Eurydice: coming to the surface of the earth out of Hades, to turn back, the too direct look, even out of love, brings about vanishing and loss. The indirection is at the source of the song—as if in order to say something "straight," some crookedness was necessary. Indirection is a kind of living with the equivocal. Try too directly to confront and conquer it, the results are death.

There is no closure of the system, there is passage of mindfulness in the between. The philosopher shares this passing with the artist, the religious person, with the so-called ordinary person. Call philosophy then: being awakened mindfully to passages in the between; and the practice of a way of life: minding the passing—wording the between, mindful of passage, of what passes, and of what passes beyond.

7 ✑ Pluralism, Truthfulness, and the Patience of Being

Truth exists. Only lies are invented.

Georges Braque

TRUTH AND CONSTRUCTION

How we understand truth cannot be disconnected from how we understand ourselves, or from how we understand how we humans are to be. "How we are to be": this phrase indicates the human being as a creature with a certain *promise of being* that calls out to be realized in one way or another. Some ways will enable fulfillment of the promise, if we are true to what we are. Some ways may betray the promise, if we are false to what we are. The intimate connection of being human and being true is not a merely theoretical issue but has inescapably ethical and indeed religious significance.

In philosophy we are familiar with a plurality of significant theories of truth. I mention a few of them. There is the correspondence theory: truth is the adequation, more or less exact, of our intellect to things. There is the coherence theory: what is most important is not an external correspondence but the immanent self-consistency of our concepts or thoughts or propositions. There are idealistic theories in which the identity of being and thought is claimed, or in which, in Hegel's famous words, "the true is the whole." There are pragmatic theories of truth: truth is what works for us, in the long run. And there are more.

This plurality of theories might seem congenial to our own contemporary ethos which seems highly pluralistic. Yet none of these theories celebrate sheer plurality in an undiscriminating way. Our diverse answers to the question of truth call us back from any attitude that endorses "anything goes." Not everything goes. Rorty smirked that truth is what your colleagues let you get away with, but no discerning colleague would let him get away with this. We would smile at the joke and pass on. We would carry on thinking. For there are different senses of being true, some more appropriate to the more objective determinations of actuality, some more fitting for the elusive enigmas of the human heart. To be true to something is to enact a certain fidelity to that thing, hence depending on that thing, our "being true" will be different. There is a pluralism with regard to "being true" in that sense; but this does not preclude something more than diversity without relation. I will come to this later in terms of the spirit of truthfulness.[1]

Nevertheless, in the contemporary pluralistic ethos there is a fairly widespread attitude that is worth noting. I mean the view that connects *the true and the constructed.* Truth is our construction. Initially one might think this is a fine view. Not only do we the constructors of truth become the sources of truth, but we also begin to enjoy our proper destiny as its coming masters. What better augury for the betterment of the human condition, and the pathway toward the (true) self-empowerment of humankind, could there be? And, of course, the practices of science and medicine are one central area where this self-empowerment is in play. If we are such constructors, perhaps we can reconstruct the conditions of life that will overcome the given patiences that often drag down our energies, such as sickness, disease, death, everything bearing on our frail, finite bodies. Truth as a construction seems to offer a marvelous beacon of hope.

There is a widespread cultural attitude that endorses a pluralism of approaches to things, a pluralism possibly unlimited except perhaps by the powers of human invention and imagination. The call is to celebrate the many, let a thousand flowers bloom. This is not unconnected with a democratic ethos in which each different one is said to deserve the same respect as the next one. It is not unconnected with a view of tradition as a hegemonic univocalism that subordinates differences to a more or less tyrannical homogeneity. Truth, with a capital T, is judged guilty of such a tyranny. We must not seek Truth, but truths, or as Nietzsche claimed, my truth. Let a thousand truths bloom. But this is entirely too passive a proclamation: let us *make* a thousand truths. Again, on this view, all turns on

1. On different senses of truth and being true, see my *Being and the Between,* chapter 12.

the power of creativity or the force of free imagination. In Nietzsche, not surprisingly, the poets or the artists generally enjoy a preeminence: they are the creators par excellence, and hence in a sense they dictate the truth that is to be. There is no truth that is, truth is to be what we determine it to be, and in terms of certain values we consider the most important for life. I mention in passing that there is often a half-hidden metaphysical presupposition to this: reality "in itself" has a dark ugly side; the "lies" of art save us from *this* truth; art's *as if* "truth" gives us the constructed truth that allows us to live, protected from the Medusa stare of this truth.

The true is the made: so said Vico. *Verum et factum convertuntur.* The human being can only know what it makes: hence human truths are appropriate to us. God makes the world, and hence can know it; we can know what is proportionate to us.[2] Marx liked to quote Vico's maxim, but "making" for Marx becomes unanchored from the idea that there is a creator other than the human being. The human being is the only creator in a godless world. As the creators, the workers and makers of this world, we become the truth of this world, and indeed, through our own work, the creators of value also. The difference between Marx and Nietzsche is not so great on this score—it lies more in an accent than in a basic metaphysical difference: will to power as industrial production, will to power as poetic creativity.

While Marx is now in retreat, the attitudes he expresses are not quite so. We see this with Nietzsche, the patron saint of postmodern pluralism. And perhaps it is not surprising that the pluralism of the postmodern ethos throws us that strange mutant: the left-wing Nietzschean. Something of this has to do with the shared sense of transgressive thinking, as well as the familial bond with negativity as blooding our autonomies beyond old, established heteronomies. It is also connected with the view that truth is what we construct. For to construct we have to destroy; and, in this instance, this often means we have to transgress what is traditionally taken to be truth. Assault on the old truth is part of the intoxication of constructing the new truth. Once again, it seems that we must overcome the inhibition of the (moral) imagination to unleash hitherto untapped sources of creativity and construction in ourselves.

2. See *The New Science of Giambattista Vico,* abridged translation of the third edition (1744), by Thomas Goddard Bergin and Max Harold Fisch (Ithaca, N.Y.: Cornell University Press, 1970), §§331, 349.

BETWEEN ABSOLUTE TRUTH AND TRUTHFULNESS

I rehearse a widespread view, which I do not endorse. One need not deny a certain qualified creativity to the human being, but the meaning of the qualification is all important. The pluralism of truths often goes with, as I said, a perception of traditional theories of truth, especially the correspondence theory, as hegemonic and totalitarian. The truth, the absolute truth, is just there and given and to it we must submit; and then, the complaint goes forth, the putative possessors of the absolute truth—be they religious, political, ethical, or philosophical—are repressing us.

The interesting issue here is this: Perhaps we do not possess the absolute truth. Perhaps only God can and does. That we do not possess the absolute truth is not a postmodern view—it is as old, for instance, as Plato. Human beings are not God, hence we do not—and in a sense cannot—possess the absolute truth. But the consequence does not follow that we are simply to construct what truths we consider relevant or interesting for ourselves. We do not possess absolute truth, yet we seek the truth or the true. And we could not seek at all were there not some relation between us, our desire, and the truth sought. To seek is always to be related to the truth sought. Hence to know we have not the absolute truth is already to be in relation to truth. Otherwise we could not know our ignorance, nor seek what we lack and obscurely anticipate. In short, we are intermediate beings, neither in absolute possession of truth, nor in absolute destitution: somewhere between.

The important point is that this condition is not something we construct; this "somewhere between" is the space, indeed the ethos of being, within which we might seek to construct, but it is presupposed by all our constructing power. This being in the between, the *metaxu,* defines our participation in the milieu of being within which our own middle being intermediates with the truth, truth that might well be beyond us, though not out of relation to us. In other words, there is a relation to the truth that is prior to, and more ultimate than, any claim made that the truth is something we construct. We are in the space of truth, or truthfulness, which itself contributes to our own endowment with capacities to discern the difference between the true and the false, and more mediately, this truth and that. To have that endowment is to be marked by something given, not something we construct through ourselves alone. Gift is prior to construction.

You might still wonder why this is significant. I think it immediately calls forth a different relation to the whole question of truth. It makes us understand ourselves differently, including the fragility of our finite being, and not least how we relate to our incarnate condition. It asks about a respect, indeed a reverence, for something that we do not ourselves create or construct, but that is intimately necessary for the truthfulness and worthiness of all our own efforts at constructive or creative life. There is a call of truth on us that is coeval with our being: it is constitutive of the kinds of beings we are. It releases us into a certain freedom of seeking, but this freedom and release are not themselves self-produced. There is something more at work in our searches for truth than simply our own searching and the results of that searching.

TRUTH AND TRUTHFULNESS: OUR INTERMEDIATE BEING

If we take seriously this intermediate nature of the human being, what becomes evident is quite other to an "anything goes" attitude to truth. Rather there emerges in our very searching a call to fidelity to truth we do not possess, and yet that endows us with something eminently distinctive. It is a somewhat paradoxical fact that the constructivist view (as we might call it) emerges from a deep *skepticism* about truth: the traditional view that we can know the truth in itself is questioned, and indeed despaired of. And there is a switch from such a sense of truth as other to us and to our own powers, to a sense of ourselves as capable of making what truths we need in the circumstances we find ourselves. The paradox: We veer from a skepticism that is stymied by the difficulty of such an ideal of truth to an orientation in which "truth" seems far more easily to hand, in what we construct ourselves. And since this last seems to be within our power, instead of skepticism about the otherness of truth, we can be given over to intoxication with our own truth-making capacities. We reject the god of absolute truth, but there is a new god in the wings, and mirabile dictu, this god is we ourselves. When this god comes we are finally now liberated as self-liberating, autonomous creators.

I would see our intermediate being differently. Let us grant we do not possess absolute truth. Then this very granting is itself witness to our participation in truth *not constructed*. To say "granted" is to give oneself over to something we do not construct ourselves: we grant that something has to be accepted as granted. It is true we do not possess the absolute truth, and so we are in intimate relation to truth, no matter that we do not know the absolute truth. We are constrained by a necessity that limits all our pretensions to absoluteness, as well as all our claims to unconstrained constructivism.

The point could be put less negatively, and perhaps it is better put that way. It is not a matter just of showing certain deep instabilities in denying a sense of truth that is not our own construction—although this is important. It is rather a matter of attending to the fact that in the search for all truth, even in the denial that we possess the truth, we are called upon to "be truthful." One can be truthful, even in searching for the truth, and even in knowing that one does not possess the truth. Our being truthful is a testament to that intermediate condition, the human seeker as between the fullness of truth of the divine and the ignorance of the beast: beyond the second, though the first be beyond us, and yet in intimate relation to what is so beyond us, by virtue of the call to be truthful.

Being truthful is an exigency that makes a call on us before we endeavor to construct any system of science or philosophy that might claim to be true. It may call us actively to construct; but the call itself shows us to be open to something other than our own self-determination, something that endows us with a destiny to be truthful to the utmost extent of our human powers. In that regard, there is no way of separating the theoretical and the practical, the metaphysical and the ethical. For this being truthful is also called to a fidelity that solicits a way of life appropriate to it, a fidelity that issues in a way of being mindful in which we are to live truthfully, and to live truly.

This being truthful is not an objective truth that lies "out there, somewhere," univocally fixed in advance. It has more to do with the immanent porosity of the human being to being as it is, and to what is good and worthy in itself to be affirmed. It may be the case that there are forms of truth that take on a more objective and univocal character such as we find in the so-called hard sciences. I think this is true. But the search for such truths itself testifies to this other sense of being truthful, which is as much an ethical as a theoretical demand. For instance, the scientist seeking objective truth must be faithful to the call of being truthful—or else the whole edifice of objective science is itself corrupted. Once again it is a sense of truthfulness having to do with *what we are:* not what we seek simply, not what we are simply, but what we are to be, as beings that seek truth and that seek to be truthful.

And yet if it is not simply objective, it is not simply subjective either. We know the call to be truthful intimately in our own selves, yes, but there is something transsubjective about it. Something here comes to us, something here endows us, something here gifts us with a power we could not produce through ourselves alone. The spirit of truthfulness in us points to something transsubjective in our own selves or subjectivity. As transsubjective, it is "objective" in the sense that it is other to us, even while it is in intimate relation to us. But it is not objective in terms of this object or that. In that regard, the spirit of truthfulness witnesses in what is objective to something that is transobjective. Without it we would have no participation in objective truth, but it is not this or that objective truth, but our participation in something more fundamental.

I might put it in terms of Pascal's very helpful distinction between *l'esprit de géométrie* and *l'esprit de finesse.* The former is appropriate to objective truths such as we pursue in the hard sciences and mathematics. But the latter is required when we deal with the human being, in the deep ambiguity of its being, somewhere between nothing and infinity, marked alike by wretchedness and glory, and called into relation to God, beyond all our knowing had not God already mysteriously made himself known to us. The spirit of truthfulness, our being truthful, is first more related to *l'esprit de finesse* than *l'esprit de géométrie,* which is not to say the latter does not participate in it. In a sense, this spirit of truthfulness transcends the difference of the two, if we are tempted to see them as dualistically opposed. But it is itself intimate to the finesse of the human being.

Finesse is very important in a time such as ours in which *l'esprit de géométrie* is often in the ascendant. Finesse recalls us to modes of mindfulness in attunement with the fuller subtleties at play in human existence. Geometry is greatly helpful when univocal exactness is required, but this is not always most appropriate in addressing the equivocities of the human heart. Pascal is a great exemplar of the tremendous advances in the modern scientific univocalizing wrought by empirical and mathematical science. Unlike Descartes and Spinoza, Pascal was not bewitched by its power, or seduced into making it the one and only way to truth. Spinoza is not lacking his own finesse, but in his ethics *more geometrico* I can find no appropriate name for the generous acknowledgment of finesse as such. "Geometry" seems entirely to take over the role of finesse. Spinoza amazingly claims that the human race would have lain forever in darkness were it not for the development of mathematics. "Truth would be eternally hidden [*in aeternam lateret*] from the human race had not mathematics, which does not deal with ends but with the nature and properties of figures, shown to humankind another norm of truth."[3] Is a kind of soteriological power being claimed for mathematics, without which humanity would be lost forever in the caves of night? If this means that mathematics rescues us from, or advances us beyond, ends *(fines)*, would not its saving knowledge then be a purposeless knowing in a purposeless universe? Such an advance beyond darkness would be an advance into a different darkness. In that new darkness, which is the ultimate darkness for us of a purposeless world, a new finesse beyond geometry would be needed to illuminate us.

Finesse reveals a readiness for a more intimate knowing, bearing on what is prior to and beyond geometry. It bears on a mindfulness that can read the signs of the equivocity of human existence, and not simply by the conversion of these signs into a univocal science or a philosophical system. In a way, here the power of the poetic come into its own, as well as its sister, religious reverence. Finesse is by its nature an excellence of mindfulness that is singularly embodied. It cannot be rendered without remainder in terms of neutral and general characteristics. It cannot be geometricized. We come first to know of it, know it, by witnessing its exemplary incarnation in living human beings of evident finesse. There is no geometrical "theory" that could render it in an absolutely precise univocal definition.

Finesse refers us to the concrete suppleness of living intelligence that is open, attentive, mindful, attuned to the occasion in all its elusiveness and subtlety. We take our first steps in finesse by a kind of creative mimesis, by trying to liken ourselves to those who exemplify it, or show something of it. This creative likening renews the promise of finesse, but it also is itself new, since it is openness to the subtlety of the occasion in its unrepeatable singularity. Singularity here does not betoken a kind of autism of being, nor does it mean that any communication of its significance to others is impossible. Rather this singularity is rich with a promise, perhaps

---

3. *Ethics*, part 1, appendix, in *Spinoza Opera*, ed. Carl Gebhart (Heidelberg: Heidelberger Akademie der Wissenschaften, 1924), 79; see *The Chief Works of Benedict de Spinoza*, trans. R. H. M. Elwes (New York: Dover Books, 1955), 77.

initially not fully communicated, and yet available for, making itself available for, communicability. Communicability itself cannot be confined to articulation in neutral generality, or homogeneous universality. Finesse is in attendance on what is elusive in the intimacy of being, but that intimacy is at the heart of living communicability.

Witness the dominance of the often scientistic and cybernetic forms of thinking in our time—though again these are often complemented by a kind of self-serving subjectivity in which the gratification of private desires is the point of it all. Think of this paradox: how the Internet—an extraordinary result of cybernetic thinking and *l'esprit de géométrie*—is infested with pornographic sites: on the one hand, hard geometrical heads and, on the other, the mush of erotic exploitation, without the heart of reverence and modesty.

Pascalian finesse should be given a place of honor in the context of postmodern pluralism in view of the latter's claim to celebrate ambiguity, equivocity, and so on. For finesse has to do with a discernment of what is worthy to be affirmed in the ambiguity. It is not the indiscriminate glorification of ambiguity. It is the excellence of mindfulness that does not deny the ambiguity, is not false to it, but seeks to be true to what is worthy to be affirmed in it—and not everything is worthy to be affirmed. If nothing else, finesse is not a matter of construction. Quite the opposite, the gifts that it fosters are receptivity and attentive mindfulness of singular occasions, happenings, persons, openness to the singularity of things, a readiness for the surprising and the genuinely other. It nourishes a feeling for the intimacy of being itself, and the secret spirit of truthfulness in our own intimate selves. Religion and art have often been the great fathers and mothers of finesse about finitude. Without finesse there is no discerning ethical judgment. Without finesse there is no spiritual seriousness in philosophy. Without finesse the political huckster, even the well-dressed criminal, succeed to the place of the wise statesman.

TRUTHFULNESS AND THE PATIENCE OF BEING

Finesse, and not just geometry alone, is needful in the practice of medicine. But we live in a time of ascendant geometry and it is not always clear if we have the finesse to match what geometry constructs. I now want to connect more explicitly these remarks on truthfulness with anthropological consequences that have an ethical and theological bearing. I connect this with the patience of being.

I mean that the constructivist generally thinks that our being is to do, to act: in the beginning and in the end, and in the middle is the act, the constructive act. Goethe wrote *Im Anfang war die Tat!* Not quite—not quite for us human beings, certainly. My point is not a denial of construction but a relativization of any tendency to absolutize its claims. Our constructive act is not the first or the last, or the middle either. This follows from the sense of being truthful outlined earlier. The spirit of being truthful indicates first on our part a certain patience to the truth before we ourselves are called to be truthful in a more active sense. We find ourselves in the middle space between absolute ignorance and absolute truth; we do not create this middle space; this is the middle space wherein the spirit of being truthful makes its solicitation to us. We need finesse to be attentive about this, since it is not merely an objective truth, nor merely a subjective opinion or preference, though it is intimate to us, hence subjective, and yet other to subjectivity, and hence objective in the sense of being other than our construction—it is not "made up."

I would say that there is a patience of being before there is an endeavor to be, a receiving of being before an acting of being, in accord with our singular characters as humans. The patience and receiving make the endeavor and the acting possible; and when acknowledged with finesse, they are understood differently than they are within a philosophy that seeks the self-absolutizing of our activist character or our endeavor to be.

There is a *passio essendi* more primal than the *conatus essendi*. This last is the phrase Spinoza uses to describe the essence of a being: the essence of a being is its *conatus*—and this is defined by its power to affirm itself and its range. This range for Spinoza is potentially unlimited, in the absence of external countervailing beings who express their power of being in opposition to us, or in limitation. Note that for Spinoza *conatus* is the being of a being: it is the being of the human being. Without an external limitation, the endeavor to be is potentially infinite, like a motion that will continue indefinitely without a check from the outside. One might infer from this, in the sphere of human relations, that an external other always presents itself as potentially hostile to my self-affirming. The other, so seen, while needful for my flourishing, is potentially alien or opposed to my self-affirmation, and hence one strategy of continuing the *conatus* will be for one to disarm that other in advance. Big fish, eating little fish, grow bigger.

Such a relation of implicit hostility can come to define our embodied relation to the rest of nature. The latter as other can be as much the source of our sustenance as a threat to the integrity of our healthy self-affirming being. It is equivocal, but the equivocal face is most known in the threat to us that we meet in disease, infection, and finally death. Against this equivocity, we must protect ourselves, by overcoming the threat. By contrast, on this view, a passivity is something to be avoided or overcome. Being patient to something places us in a position of subordination: to receive from the other is a sign of weakness. To receive is to be servile, whereas to act and to endeavor is to be sovereign. The emotions, for instance, are servile, the dominating reason is sovereign. One sees how this fits in with the ethos of modernity in which the autonomous subject as self-law is implicitly in ambiguous, potentially hostile relation to what is other, or *heteros*.

Some of these concerns seem to me to be in the background of the constructivist theory of truth. We are not gifted with truth, or even the power to discern truth as other to us, but we make it for ourselves. For ourselves: for we ourselves are the truth of the construction. We self-construct—even to the point of constructing, or reconstructing, the bodies originally given to us. Or of which we are originally the victims, since we did not first choose our bodies.

What of the *passio essendi*? We are first given to be, before anything else. At a theological level this bears on our being creations: creatures of an absolute source that gives us to be and gives us to be as good. This is the good of the "to be" in which we participate but that we do not construct but rather that allows us to construct. This view goes at a different angle to the modern constructivist view, but it is dependent on the recognition of an otherness more original than our own self-definition. We are only self-defining because we have originally given to be as selves, and as selving; only creative because created; only courageous because encouraged; only loving because already loved and shown to be worthy of love; only become good to the degree that we are grateful for a good we do not ourselves produce; only become truthful because there is a truth more original than ourselves that endows us with the power to seek truth and the confidence that should we search truly we will find that truth (insofar as this can be understood by the finite human being).

Being patient, or being in the patience of being, is not here a defect. It is only a defect from the point of view of a *conatus* given over to the temptation to affirm itself alone, and hence closed off from the acknowledgment that it is at all because it is first affirmed to be: created. The patience of being might be theologically connected with *the givenness of creation*. Very frequently we take this givenness for granted. Creation as a being given is as a being granted, but this being granted we take for granted. This is the primal *passio essendi*. It is an ontological patience in that here is named the original receiving of being at all. That beings are at all, something and not nothing, signals a deeper ontological givenness than, say, the indigent being of immediacy in Hegel's conception. There is an idiocy of being, a given happening of the intimate strangeness of being, that is more primordial than any spontaneous happening of this event or that, or our determinate participations in this or that form of life. Without this ultimate and ontologically intimate givenness, nothing finite is constructed or can construct itself. The self-affirmation of the finite follows on the received affirmation of the finite that is its being given to be and received in being as thus and thus. In an ontological patience before this surplus happening there is for us the offer of an agapeic astonishment, or wonder, before there is determinate or self-determining cognition. Wonder, marvel, reverence all reveal something of what is *good and worthy of affirmation* in the patience of being, even apart from any construction or further mediations by our own endeavor to be.

What I am saying is that there is no denial of the *conatus* but rather a changed vision of it that sees it as deriving from something other to itself. If we think of *the healthy body* we immediately see something of the *conatus* in the will to self-perpetuation and self-affirmation that marks it. This is our being—to affirm itself and indeed to affirm itself as good—it is good to be. I do not deny this at all. The question is its meaning and whether there is something more that relativizes self-affirmation, gives it to be at all, and makes it porous relative to something other than itself, and not just as a servile passivity. In fact, we find ourselves in this self-affirmation; we do not first construct it. Spontaneously we live this affirmation of the "to be" as good—we do not first have a choice—it is what we are. And since we find ourselves as thus self-affirming, there is a patience to this primal self-affirmation. There is something received in our being given to be, something not constructed through our own powers alone.

Of course, we have to say "yes" to this original "yes" to being, and we can develop our powers diversely. The endeavor to be in a more self-chosen way here emerges, and necessarily so. If we decide to live in a healthy way, it is following on the first "yes," but it is the living of a second "yes" that tries to respect, for instance, the integrity of the body, to live with finesse for its subtle rhythms, to embody a kind of reverence, even for a sort of sanctity that is intimate to the human body. But none of this tells against the more primal patience.

Modern constructivism forgets or wants to forget this patience. There is even a hatred of that patience that can come to be expressed, for all patience is a reminder of our status as finite creatures, and hence is a constitutive sign of the fact that we are not the masters of being, not even of our own being. The weaknesses of the latter are often rejected, refused. And there is a qualified sense in which that refusal has some right. But when it loses any porosity to the more primal patience, its seeming self-affirmation is really a kind of self-hatred, for this endeavor to be is in flight from itself, from what it is, from the patience of being that gives it to be at all in the first instance. The conditions that make possible its being at all are refused. Hence we find ourselves in the impossible situation of the flower trying to ingest its own ground—impossible, yet were it even conceivable, it would show the inner self-hatred of the flower that must only destroy itself in this way of absolutizing itself.

One wonders how much of modern constructivism is in flight from this patience, and hence from itself, even when it seems to flee only to itself. The patience of being shows what is not our own, even in what is most intimately our own. Just so the spirit of being truthful shows some sense of truth more primally other than our self-determination, in the deepest intimacy of our own self-determination.

BEING TRUTHFUL AND PATIENCE

Being truthful is impossible without this patience. It calls for the practice of finesse: this is a matter of giving the time for this patience, in order to attend to what is both within us and before us. True, given the energies that carry our endeavor to be, it tends to happen again and again that there is an *overriding* of this patience by the *conatus*. Being alive is to find oneself always tempted to this impatient overriding. The fulfillment of life is impossible if this happens. We have not taken the proper time, and respected the rhythms of time, to attend to what is within us and before us, and hence to be truthful concerning our proper response to the promise of our being, and indeed to its sickness, when we have deserted what is good in promising. This is also to say that the healthy perpetuation of life is itself conditional on a perpetual recurrence of the patience, and a perpetual receiving of the promise of life. This recurrence and this receiving come to their term when we meet the limit of mortality: when death reveals the finitude that calls time on the endeavor to be.

This recurrence of patience, however, is not only a matter of when the endeavor to be meets an external or hostile limit and is brought low. It is always happening, and its gift of promise always being offered, even though we do not notice or acknowledge it. It concerns the gift of life as received, granted to us in the first instance, but, in the rush forward of the endeavor to be, taken for granted rather than as granted. In the sweep of a life, the external limits of encroaching others, or the limit of mortal time, both internal and external, can serve as reminders of this more primal patience of being, in which we may again consent to the goodness of the gift of life. Alternatively, at the other extreme, we may continue to turn against its givenness in rejection, just because it is given and not produced by us: not made by us, hence beyond our full self-determination. We can so insist that everything be subject to our self-determination that we betray the joy of this gift, in the overriding of our own self-affirmation. Consent to death, in gratitude for the gift of life, is our final opportunity to make our peace with this patience.

BEING PATIENT AND BEING INCARNATE

This patience of being is intimately related to our incarnate being. Being incarnate is first something given before we "construct" it as other than given. We do the latter, for instance, in adornment, or in interventions that strengthen the body, such as athletic training, or in medical interventions that normally are for purposes of allowing the body as it is to regain itself and its native energies. Initially we are patient to these energies of the body, though these energies are themselves active and dynamic—and most especially when we are young. They live us, instead of us always directing them. It is entirely fitting that we come to direct them as best we can, and in the light of what we discern to be the best for ourselves. But we are not always wise in our directions, and again more likely unwise than wise if we forget this patience of being, and override its more finessed insinuations with a too self-insistent endeavor to be. Even when the energies of the body are brought toward their maximal expression, there is needed a kind of fidelity to this patience—it is not a matter of just exerting oneself, though it is obviously this too. There is more than self-exertion when this maximum is approached.

Thus, athletes will speak of remaining relaxed, even while still striving, or of finding oneself "in the zone," or being "in the flow" and then one is flowing—as if asleep in one sense, but awakened in an intense awareness that takes no notice of itself. I think of the Buddhist: form is emptiness, emptiness is form. I take this here to mean that more often than not we get in the way of ourselves, as it were; we let the *conatus essendi* unfittingly override the *passio essendi.* And to let the flow pass, or begin to pass again, we must get out of our own way; and then we are more truly on the way, and on the way as more truly ourselves. Form is the harmony of energies working in intense accord, but the harmony must be empty of the clogging self-insistences that hinder rather than release the energies of selving. They hinder just by insisting on themselves, without patience for selving, and the other secret sources of enabling that hiddenly contribute to every act of accomplished excellence.

This asks of us also an orientation of respect and reverence for the body. Respect and reverence are family relations to patience. Each requires a mindfulness other than one that is objectifying of the body, and its practical correlate, the utilitarian exploitation of the flesh—whether in pornographic sex, or the sale of body parts, or whatever. One might say that the patient body, understood in the terms discussed earlier, is already an incarnate sign of a love beyond instrumentalizing.

One might see the great artist as serving the celebration of this passion of being. One might also see those involved in the care of the sick as called to behold the bodies of the patients as incarnate signs of this love beyond instrumentalizing. The least of these are incarnate signs of the divine, calling those still in robust health to the practice of a love that also signals something beyond the instrumentalizing of the others. The service of the medical healer has always been a sign of this care beyond instrumentalizing.

In the case of human beings, this care is noteworthy in the manner it takes on certain unconditional characteristics: those who from a biological point of view seem worthless are deemed worthy of a sacred respect.

I know there are those who will bridle at a phrase like "sacred respect." And it is only too true that there are massive trends in our time geared to the project of, so to say, *deconsecrating the human body.* The space between deconsecration and desecration is often, alas, infinitesimal. Here I think that the loss of the patience of being in modern Western culture is potentially disastrous: loss of the finesse needed to discern the rightness of this deeming of sacred worth. The profit and the loss of human lives are reckoned on a utilitarian calculus, to the profitless loss of being truthful to what we more intimately are.

THE PATIENCE OF BEING, HEALTH, AND SICKNESS

To be human is to be patient but to be patient is not necessarily to be sick. It turns out also that the doctor, or nurse, or healer, or caregiver is also a patient, and not only the sick person. There is a health in patience that makes possible the healing of the sick. Thus in the relation of doctor and patient, there is the call of this patience that extends to both sides. Being truthful to the relation asks patience as much from the healthy as from the sick. Needless to say, this is often difficult, if differently difficult, on both sides: on the side of the weak, because the *conatus* is laid low or enfeebled; and on the side of the still healthy, because of the zest of the *conatus,* and because the weak are hindrances to the blithe continuation of life. Being truthful to the more original patience can be deeply salutary in reminding us that every human being is on *both sides of this relation;* now more on this side perhaps, but in turn the reverse will be the case, and the strong will sere.

Yet, whether on one side or the other, or on both, there is again a deeper sense of patience that is not a matter of sickness but of mindful porosity to what transcends us. In any case, we are never just dealing with a problem to be solved by a neutral geometry, the brilliant interventions of amazing technologies, for instance. Porosity to what transcends us makes us potentially liable to attack from hostile others, human or nonhuman; but it also constitutes the promise of our community beyond hostility with others. The being truthful of finesse is always needed. And again, whether on one side or the other, or on both, this is not just a matter of judging how things stand with our own endeavor to be; it is a matter of a fidelity to the patience of our own being, and that of the suffering others. One might perhaps here speak of a kind of *compassio essendi,* a compassion of being, in which both strong and weak can participate. And perhaps this *compassio essendi* communicates a sign of what a more divine love might be for mortal creatures.

THE PATIENCE OF BEING AND RELIGIOUS POROSITY

One might say that perhaps the most ultimate and elusive form of finesse deals with how the patience of being brings us to the boundary of the religious. It places us in a space of porosity between the human and the divine. There we are sometimes involuntarily placed, when in sickness our helplessness is brought home to us. We might ask "Why me?," but to whom is our defiance or appeal addressed, if there is nothing, no divine other porous to our outcry? The outcry is not just addressed to ourselves, or to human others. Either to nothing, or to God.

Those who are healthy and who wish to heal are themselves often placed in this porous space of helplessness—when they can do nothing further for the person slipping away. They too can be visited by a despair that may be a portal to religious consent—or defiance that closes down the porosity to the divine. Nevertheless, one must say that we can come to know intimately that there is a patience that is graced.

There is the harder consent of those who must say "yes" to their finitude. None of us is exempt, and we will all come to the fearsome challenge of this harder consent. In a certain regard, we are always coming to this consent, or fleeing it, in every moment of our life. There is also a graced patience in that attendance on others which is a service of their good, even if it does little or nothing to serve the advancement of some agenda of the servant. We become witnesses to the *compassio essendi* in the care we take of the other for the sake of the other. In this care, we may be released beyond ourselves in a minding of the other potentially agapeic. One sees a certain confluence here between truthfulness and the patience of being, in love of the pluralism of creation, most known in our love of singular human beings who have been our companions on a way of mystery. Being truthful is a patient service— service of the truthful self that is service of the truth of the other, service of the good that solicits our attention to the good of the others. This patience is graced, since it receives in readiness, at a boundary at the limits of our self-determination. Patience lays us open to secret sources of strengthening that make us porous to the religious intermediation with the divine.

8 ❧ The Confidence of Thought
Between Belief and Metaphysics

The term "metaphysics" has diverse meanings for different thinkers, but in the popular mind it deals with matters beyond the realm of ordinary experience. In minds schooled with some smattering of philosophy, metaphysics might now mean something like a caricatured version of Platonism: there is an other world, up there beyond, and metaphysics gets us there, into outer space, not through experience, but by pure thinking. A caricature is not something untrue, but it exaggerates a true feature, and it does make something evident, but in the exaggeration it distorts, hence in being true it is also false. We have been dealing in caricatures of metaphysics, in perhaps a minor key since Kant, in perhaps a major key since Nietzsche. There is something both intimate and transcending about metaphysical thinking. We can so stress the transcending that we forget the intimacy, thus lending credence to the caricature of the unworldly, aboveworldly, otherworldly thinking. We can so stress the intimacy that we stop the self-surpassing of transcending thought, and perhaps with the well-intentioned desire to secure what we can know within the boundaries of immanence itself. But there is more. Metaphysics does have something intimate to do with what is above, what is other, what is beyond, but not in such a wise that it tramples on what is intimate to the world as given to us and as we come to know it. Metaphysics is metaxological: between the strangeness of being, and the intimacy, between the robustness of immanent givenness and the elusive mystery of what is more than just the given immanence (see chapter five).

What of believing? Metaphysical thinking asks such questions as: "What does it mean to be?" "What is the meaning of the 'to be'?" Such questions necessarily are bound up with such questions as: "What does it mean to be good?" "Is there something about the 'to be' that might be called good in a fundamental sense?" The issues of nihilism are here at stake. If the "to be" comes to nothing, "nothing" then has the primordial place and the last word. Such questions are both metaphysical and ethical, in that for human beings the good of the "to be" is in question in a radically intimate way. To what does it all come? Every human being lives a response to this question, even let nothing be said about it, or nothing be said in response to it. The questions "What is the meaning of the 'to be'?" "Is there a good about the 'to be'?" inevitably bring us to the question of origin: origin of the "to be" itself, and its worthiness to be mindfully affirmed and not only lived. Religious traditions have called that origin God. Thus the above questions dovetail with the question: "What is God, what is it to be God?"[1]

In the longer tradition of thought we find a companionship of the religious and metaphysics. This companionship is disturbed, if not broken, in modern thought, with repercussions for the nature of metaphysics, as well as the hospitality of thought to religious belief. Modern thought, after all, claims to begin anew with doubting, not with believing. I will argue that this companionship is crucial for both the confidence of thought and the faithfulness asked of religious belief. An entire rethinking of metaphysics is needed in the light of the promise of a postmodern renewal of this companionship. The breach of companionship in modernity is an interim: between a premodernity where the companionship was perhaps so taken for granted that its enabling power was not always appreciated, and sometimes abused; and a postmodernity when the idea of philosophy enabling itself through its own immanent resources alone has run into the ground. In the night of nihilism philosophy can rediscover that without acknowledgment of its relation to what is other to itself, so-called autonomous self-determining thinking revolves around itself as its own void, avoiding or even voiding the ontological robustness of its intermediation with the full givenness of worthy being.

But is it not just the *lack of confidence* in reason that is most notable in postmodern thought? I would say that modern doubting seems to express a confidence in autonomous reason, but a kind of overconfidence can swell and prepare a fall. There is an overconfidence that produces a

---

1. These three questions are intimately bound together, and addressed respectively in *Being and the Between*, *Ethics and the Between*, and *God and the Between*.

bubble of inflation, but the bubble bursts, and long thereafter we must pay for the afflatus that, after all, was not so divine. The situation is perhaps still more equivocal. For the confidence of modern reason is also coupled with a belief in the powers of critique. But these powers, handled in a certain way, produce a lack of confidence in reason, and not least in metaphysical thinking. I think of Kant. True, there were idealistic reactions that again stressed even more the confidence of autonomous reason, for even the negating powers of critical reason seem amenable to redirection in terms of this confidence. I think of Hegel's confidence, overconfidence: every negative can and will be harnessed to the triumphant benefit of self-determining reason.

This peculiar combination of the lack of confidence in reason and the overconfidence falls away from the in-between character of human thinking. The eros of thinking might be said, pace Plato, to mingle *poros* and *penia*. Stress the *penia* only and there is no movement of transcending. Stress only the *poros* and the plenty overflows perhaps into the power of thought's exultation in itself as if it were a God, and not a finite participation in something divine. Too little, and there is no thought. Too much, and there is a kind of thought that is also no thought, for it deserts our in-between condition. Too little confidence and overconfidence are both to the detriment of the middle way of metaxological metaphysics. Too little and too much confidence are also bound up with the projects of critique and self-determining thought. I will raise questions about both from the standpoint of a considered confidence in the metaxological character of metaphysics.

There is also the question of the recessed roots of metaphysical thinking—again understood in this metaxological way. These recesses are not necessarily in this or that belief but in *a more primal trust in the intelligibility of what is*. The confidence of thought asks a willingness to hearken to what is worthy in the beliefs of religion. Once again an old companionship calls for a renewal, after the great divorce of modernity. Like many divorces, there is often something equivocal here too. For the virtues of the abandoned companion are often called on, or sneaked back in, though under names not sanctioned in terms of the old companionship. Philosophy will try to do what properly only religion can do—as we see with Hegel. Or philosophy might ask art to do what properly only religion can do—as we see with Nietzsche. In my view we need a new postmodern porosity between the religious and the metaphysical. Of old in modernity we

knew the self-understanding of the philosopher as a scientist or techni-
cian or revolutionary and latterly as perhaps even a poet after his or her
own fashion.[2] But the more archaic companionship of the philosopher
with the religious and its vocation is worth new thinking and renewal.[3]

BELIEVING: WHAT TO CREDIT

There are different senses of belief. The most immediately striking has
perhaps to do with what one holds to be reliable in terms of this or that
state of affairs. When one is asked: "What do you believe?" one might answer: "I believe in one God, Father Almighty, maker of heaven and earth,"
and so on. Of course, there are everyday beliefs: I believe I have compe-
tent colleagues; I believe my fellow card players will play straight; I believe
fruits and vegetables are good for my health; and so on. Belief seems to
be bound to a determinate this and that. Religious belief also seems to
be so directed to such a determinate state of affairs. It is perhaps here we
encounter beliefs in the sense of doctrines, articulated in terms of insti-
tutionally sanctioned formulations or propositions. Needless to say, doctrines in that sense are very important. They articulate with some determinacy what a believing community holds to be centrally significant in
defining how it understands itself, and not only in terms of itself but in
relation to God as above and more than it.

Of course, we can become so fixated on the letter of the doctrines that
the spirit is forgotten. The question is important here, for the issue arises
as to whether more determinate doctrines are to be seen as coming to
articulation out of (sometimes) recessed communications, or community, marked by what I will call a *reserve of overdeterminate trust:* not just
trust in this or that, but a more primal trust which enables the investment of determinate trust in this and that. This reserve is not the possession of any individual, but rather enables the individual to be trusting.
Likewise the written determinacy of doctrines is, so to say, underwritten
by that reserve and its communication with the more original source of
credit-worthiness. Against fundamentalist literalism, the determinacy of
religious articulations is not simply univocal. Often redolent of sugges-

2. See *Philosophy and Its Others*, chapter 1.
3. See "Consecrated Thought: Between the Priest and the Philosopher," *Louvain Studies* 30
(2005): 92–106.

tion and evocative ambiguity, these articulations call for finessed interpretation. If the reserve of faith is not intimately available, one might play
cleverly with propositions, but there is a foolish cleverness. Something
analogous might be found with philosophical thinking. We go round and
round in the technical manipulation of precisely fixed propositions. It is
especially important for metaphysics to remain mindful of these reserves
that enable thought to think at all.

What we believe shows itself as what we can credit or do credit. Belief
seeks a bond with the credit-worthy. We often invest the word *credit* with
an economic meaning, but the economic meaning itself emerges out of a
more basic meaning. There is economic credit because there is more than
the economic, in the sense of utilitarian exchange. What we credit is what
is worthy of trust. We credit a person who is worthy of trust. What constitutes trustworthiness? A credit-worthy person is not one with a big bank
account but one we can rely on, someone of constant integrity who answers for himself or herself. The trustworthy person is one on whose word
we can count, one whose promises will be kept.

We are not far off from religious connotations. The word *credit* comes
from *credere,* to believe. We say "*credo*"—"I believe"—and we announce
what we consider to be worthy of trust. Being worthy of trust is not just
our *projection* of anticipation onto some receiving other. It comes out of
something already enigmatically received from the other, some witness of
reliability already intimated. Trust ventures something about the integral
reliability of the one or the source trusted. The venture is an adventure,
in the sense of a venture toward *(ad)*, but also an advent, in the sense of
something coming toward us in the venturing of expectation. This has an
ontological intonation. Something about the *being* of the trustworthy is at
issue: what they *are* is thought trustworthy. This is especially the case with
the human person. Ultimately it is not this or that characteristic that we
consider trustworthy: it is the integral person as embodying a promise of
true constancy who is deemed worthy of credit. An integral person is a
witness to trustworthiness.

Of course, we also come across the language of economics when we
speak of the investment of credit. It seems we are dragged back to a cal-
culated venture of exchange where, in the end, nothing is an end in itself,
and everything a means. Once again I think this is not the primary meaning of the investment of credit. Rather one might say that investment re-

flects an investiture. What is an investiture? It is a granting of enabling power—a granting by a source that is capable of properly re-sourcing the one invested. The reserve of enabling power is passed over, communicated from a source to a recipient, and the credit-worthiness of the recipient is so, not first in virtue of itself, but in terms of the communicating source, and derivatively in terms of the re-source vested immanently in it. Thus for us the first issue is not a matter of that wherein we invest our credit—this comes later. More primally, it is a matter of what is it that we find about ourselves as already invested with certain powers. We are the recipients of investitures. We are endowed. We are endowments. Our very being, our "to be" is an endowment. There are enabling powers, re-sources, first given before they can be invested in something further.

One thinks of the parable of the talents: the gift of the talents is first; the investiture of talent is a promise of fruit; credit is given to beings considered credit-worthy; we are ourselves invested in, we are the investment. What is the return? It is not quite the economic profit of God as a speculative creditor. It is the generosity of the endowing God who calls to agapeic return. This is not a surplus profit in the sense of adding this or that to a determinate store. It is simply generosity and thankfulness lived as both self-enabling and more than self-enabling. It is participation in the overdeterminacy of a surplus good which in being given away is not depleted but augmented. The return is to give away the gift, in the sense of passing on the endowment with the generosity fitting to the gift. We own nothing, and we are most profitable when we make no profits for ourselves, but pass on the increase in generosity that cannot be increased, and that is itself nothing but increase of participation in the good of the "to be."

BELIEVING AND DETERMINATE KNOWING: FROM EPISTEMIC DEFICIENCY TO REVOLUTIONARY ARDOR

This way of thinking about believing stands in contrast with the notion of belief as bound to a set of determinate propositions. To speak properly of the credit-worthy, of the sources of the trustworthy, I believe we need to speak of more than the indeterminate, the determinate, and the self-determining. We need to speak of the *overdeterminacy* of the endowing source. Let me first remark on how we might look on indeterminacy, determinacy, and self-determination.

To know, it will be said, is to know something—something determinate. If we hold belief to be bound to a set of determinate propositions, the philosopher is immediately tempted to ask about their warrant, rational and evidentiary. What we believe is defined as a set of potentially epistemic determinations to be judged on the grounds of rational argument and empirical evidences. There is nothing wrong with asking the warrant of determinate positions or propositions, of course, but this is not the end of the matter. What constitutes the epistemic ground of the credit-worthy is not simply epistemic, in the sense of something entirely separable from metaphysical and ethical considerations, nor indeed from religious ones. Calling on Pascal's distinction between *l'esprit de finesse* and *l'esprit de géométrie*, I would say the credit-worthy is more a matter of "finesse" than of "geometry." "Geometry" is not at all to be looked at askance; nevertheless, the appropriate philosophical relevance of geometry is not itself determined by geometry itself. It is finesse that determines the fitting intervention of geometry. And it may not be fitting to intervene geometrically, as if this were the one and only way, or the finally determinative orientation, when the matter at issue is the investment of ultimate metaphysical and ethical credit.

The danger with an overweening intrusion of geometry is that the matter of belief now seems to be defined in terms of deficiencies rather than resources. The deficiencies are epistemic: I believe when I do not know, when perhaps I cannot know. To believe and to know become disjoined. In believing, the evidences are not fully forthcoming. Were they fully forthcoming I would know and not believe. When one believes, one does not yet know. When one does know, one no longer believes.

The stress on determinacy plays here an important role. Belief may entail a determinacy that is more or less successful with respect to this or that state of affairs, but by its nature cannot be fully successful with respect to full determinate evidences. Further, if belief is a determinacy, it is one now seen in the light of an indeterminacy. Our ignorance shows the indeterminacy: we know not, and the indefinition of our not-knowing should properly be overcome with more and more univocal determinacies; otherwise we remain epistemically deficient. There would seem to be no such thing as indeterminate knowing. To know is to know a determinate somewhat. By contrast, it is out of indeterminacy that belief is said to sprout. It is a supplement to ignorance that claims to substitute for knowing. It turns out to be an indeterminacy when subjected to closer scrutiny. I believe this or that to be the case, but when I inspect the determinacy of belief, it dissolves because it cannot be fully warranted by the determinate evidences.

The resulting tendency to separate knowing and believing in this way of looking at the matter is fateful for the relation of belief and metaphysics. Thus in modern philosophy, belief tends to be seen as extraneous to knowing. To believe is to project beyond ignorance, and to claim unwarranted knowing beyond the evidences. To know is to submit to immanent justifying warrant. Knowing comes to its truth through itself, not through anything other that remains beyond its scope. For knowing, there is nothing beyond its scope. To extend the scope of knowing is to contract the space into which we can project belief.

There is a certain univocity to the claim here: belief and knowing are homogenous. I will indicate more fully that this kind of homogeneity of determinacy is not appropriate either to the sources of religious believing, or to the sources of metaphysical thinking, sources bound up with the nature of the ontological, religious, and ethical confidence that is intimate to what we are. With this homogeneity, however, metaphysics becomes defined in terms not of the indeterminate but in terms of the quest for determinate knowing first, and then for self-determining knowing. Metaphysics ought to be determinate knowing via the methods of immanent knowing. It must determine the field of the knowable through itself alone (rationalism), or via perhaps the acknowledgment that another determinacy is needed from sensory evidences (empiricism). If the latter is the paradigm of knowledge, we seem to end up with skepticism about metaphysics—the evidences of sensory experience cannot deliver rational necessity (as we see with Hume). Kant clearly sought a togetherness of these two: rational necessity and experiential evidences. But with Kant, no less than with Hume, metaphysics clearly dies a death as transcendent metaphysics, even if it is resurrected, in a very qualified way, as bearing on transcendental knowing, or the immanences of practical reason in the form of moral autonomy.

Here the stress on determinate knowing passes over into self-determining. For the transcendent entails a reference to the "beyond," and self-determining reason issues its negation to this reference. This negation is also reason's prohibition *to itself* as tempted to claim to know the beyond.

By contrast, transcendental knowing, in Kant's sense, is concerned with the conditions *immanent* in knowing itself. Once again claims to know the transcendent must be abjured. For Kant this is entirely compatible with the ideal of knowledge as overcoming the overclaimed determinacies of belief, as well as the indeterminacy of faith. Of course, Kant famously spoke of sacrificing knowing to make room for faith. But this is equivocal relative to the issue here at stake. It is moral faith to which Kant refers, and so we remain within the immanence of self-determining reason, even if it is now practical reason rather than theoretical reason. Faith in what is beyond reason: this is not what Kant offers. There is perhaps something beyond the employment of reason in natural science but this is not faith beyond reason. Kantian faith credits the trustworthiness of the rational self-determining powers of practical reason. This alone is what Kant considers credit-worthy in an ultimate sense. If there is something like an equivocal opening to God in Kant, this has not to do with religious faith as such. Every faith, religious or otherwise, must be judged credit-worthy by practical reason. Moral faith, in the light of the idea of autonomous reason, be it theoretical or practical, is the faith that reason has in itself. We come back to the moral self-confidence of practical reason in itself.

Kant's metaphysics of morals might seem to be the resurrection of metaphysics in light of moral faith, but the issue here too is very equivocal. The end of metaphysics in a more traditional sense is bound up with a certain understanding of determinate knowing and experience. For Kant, we can invest qualified trust in determinate knowing, but not in the traditional metaphysics. Similarly with respect to religious belief, this too offers only a slender warrant; any credit-worthy warrant must come from the reconfiguration of religious belief in moral terms. Religious belief offers nothing trustworthy at all if it claims to go beyond empirical experience and moral reason. The faith Kant allows may have the same name as religious faith, but what carries the identifying name is a changeling—or, if you agree with Kant, it is the legitimate child and true heir. To the end of traditional metaphysics seems to be added the end of traditional religious faith. In fact, Kant's line of thinking leads to permanent *suspicion* of belief in terms of critique. Kant is the rationalistic fussy grandfather of critique in this sense, but he will generate children and grandchildren who are not fussy in his sense. Brimming with rational (over)confidence, some will colonize all reality with system; others, full of suspicion about things traditional, will turn with revolutionary vehemence from speculative theory to the "terrorism of theory" (Bruno Bauer). From moral action honoring old decencies and duties, practical reason, alternatively (over)suspicious and (over)confident, will set to work in overturning it all, in favor of its belief in itself as the womb of a new world or epoch.

CRITIQUE, SELF-DETERMINING THINKING, BELIEVING

Is there metaphysics after critique? I have addressed this question in chapter 4, but it is worth dwelling on the fact that the project of philosophical thinking as critique emerges with respect to a certain rational dissatisfaction with epistemic fixation on determinacies. If thought is to be self-determining, everything that appears other to thought must be subject to the determination of thought. But this means the displacement of this "other" from any position of being in the original place and its reformulation in terms that compel it to come before the tribunal of self-determining reason—on the terms of the latter. These terms first and foremost determine the truth of the matter. The project of critique emerges from a sense of distrust about determinate propositions, seen in the light of a skepticism concerning putatively dogmatic determinacies. If religious beliefs are made up of such dogmatic determinacies, they must be put to the test of the tribunal of critique. Need I say that Kant especially comes again to mind here? I confine myself now to the general point.

Though critique presents itself as somehow more than skepticism, it is the skeptical impulse that is energetic at its core. What is given is not self-justifying. It must justify itself before critical thought, thought as reflective not immediate, thought as questioning and not assenting without further ado. Thus religious beliefs or political allegiances must be justified, not through themselves but through critical reason. Since they possess elements that are other to reason, a negative judgment seems always a real possibility, if not predetermined from the start. Recall here the critique of faith by the Enlightenment, a critique not separable, in the end, from certain political commitments. This example is not merely of antiquarian interest, since some of current characteristic attitudes often mimic this earlier critique. Of course, we find here faith protecting itself by jettisoning doctrinal claims. For just such claims as *determinate* invite the skepticism of critique. Seeking to escape this by such jettisoning, faith risks becoming a vague belief in a something "other" that "somehow" is beyond critique. It is as if the alternatives were either strong determinacy or weak indeterminacy. Strong determinacy of faith brings forth the oppugnancy of skeptical critique. Reactive to this, a weak indeterminacy of faith seems so fluid that determinate thought cannot step twice, in a definite way, into its fluid waters. As Hegel saw, faith and enlightenment are here in a kind of collusion.[4] In a sense, they are one and the same, since all determinate content becomes vaporized, whether in the negativity of critique or in the weak indeterminacy of undefined faith.

Hegel did not like this outcome. He has a point, even if, as we shall see, one need not embrace his response, which is an intensification of the claims of self-determining reason. It is the abstraction of reason that is to blame, he claims, not reason as such. True reason entails a negativity of thought that produces a positive outcome. In his singular way, Hegel is a more thorough rationalizer of faith: more truly self-determining reason can take the entire measure of full religious belief. From determinacy and indeterminacy and the oscillation between the two, the dialectic of reason will prove self-determining. I think this is not the end, or the beginning of the matter. As already suggested, there is an overdeterminacy more than indeterminacy, determinacy, and self-determination. Hegel offers a reconfiguration of indeterminacy and determinacy in terms of self-determining thought. He passes over the overdeterminacy—something revealed in both faith and thought, and shown not in weak indeterminacy but in true confidence. I will come to this.

The main point now is that critique as negating thinking cannot produce any content on its own. Every determinacy may be deconstructed, but the end result is not something credit-worthy as determinate. For all determinacy lacks credit—lacks credit that is ultimately justified. We are left with indeterminacy. If this might seem to allow us to be open to "something other," nevertheless we find ourselves here forbidden from determining this "other." For then we are back with the determinate, which then must be critiqued—and so on and on. We might say it is a "something," an X. Even this is too determinate, and can set off another bout of hand wringing about the fixation of determinacy as such. We found (in chapter 5) something of this anxiety of determinacy at work in decon-

---

4. G. W. F. Hegel, *Phänomenologie des Geistes*, 376ff.; *Phenomenology of Spirit*, 321ff.

structive critique. We pass back and forth between fixed univocity and unfixed equivocity. The affirmative cannot simply come from thought as negativity, whether understood in Hegelian, in post-Hegelian, or indeed post-Nietzschean, post-Heideggerian deconstructive form. Thought must open itself to something other to thought thinking itself. I have also argued that it cannot do this truly without its companionship with the religious—though great art can also be a worthy, enabling companion.

Critique may demand that the determinate others justify any confidence in them, and critique may have confidence in its own deconstructing powers but this self-confidence will eviscerate itself in the long run, when critique is turned back on itself and it finds no reason why it should not devour itself in self-negation, where before it devoured the fixity of the determinate others. Such self-devouring critique is not really remedied by what Hegel in his *Phenomenology of Spirit* calls "self-completing scepticism" *(sich vollbringende Skeptizismus).*[5] For this too presupposes something more than thinking as negativity, and this "more" is not something that Hegel explores well enough, if at all. This "more" bears on the overdeterminate. For Hegel, thinking is a matter of the negation of both the indeterminacy and the determinacy: of the indeterminacy, because it is too empty; of the determinacy because it is too fixated. One is a poverty that generates nothing as such; the other is a fixation that prevents the fluid unfolding of the process of thinking qua process. Thinking as negating must deconstruct the fixations but in this, Hegel holds, thinking *comes to itself* as thinking; *comes to itself* as self-determining; *comes to itself* as overcoming the indeterminacy of its starting point; and ends up *beholden to nothing but itself alone,* and its own immanent resources. Hegel has no mind for, does not keep in mind, the overdeterminacy as such.

In some such manner, we move from extreme critique to what presents itself as the robust self-confidence of reason in itself. We move from Kantian timidity to Hegelian hubris. The timidity and the hubris are defined along a homogeneous line of consideration. Indeed the Hegelian hubris is quite intelligible if this line of consideration exhausts the matter. I think it does not. As already suggested, the gift of the overdeterminacy is overlooked in all this. There is a confidence of thought prior to and beyond critique and it is not adequately described by Hegel's self-

5. *Phänomenologie des Geistes,* 67; *Phenomenology of Spirit,* §78

determining thought. It is worth noting that the latter is defined by a dialectic with religious belief, presented as a set of representational determinations which must be conceptually overcome, *aufgehoben*. This overcoming is determined entirely through a reason oriented to the telos of being absolutely self-determining. My point is not that religious representation is immune from critique—not at all—clearly it calls forth critique. My focus is on an issue that does not even get acknowledged, much less explored, if indeterminacy, determinacy, and self-determination are held to exhaust the matter.

The matter is not one of defining faith over against Enlightenment reason. It is not a matter of sublating faith into speculative reason. For faith in both these instances is either a set of determinations or a bare indeterminacy. There is a more basic sense of confidence, and this must be explored—and not to be either critiqued or sublated but to open a porous dialogue between it and the adventure of thought. This adventure of thought is as much endowed by this other confidence, as it finds itself perplexed by it, as it finds that it peters out in nothing if it does not constantly return to this reserve of confidence. It is an overdeterminate reserve that invests reason with the power to be true to what is: to be true, to be faithful, not only to itself but to what is beyond itself. This issue transcends the difference of inner and outer, the immanent and the transcendent. It bears on a transcendence that is as much intimate to immanence as beyond its full resources when immanence makes claim to a self-determining self-sufficiency.

THINKING AND TRUSTING

We are right to believe what is trustworthy. Moreover, what is trustworthy is beyond critique. It offers itself from a source that is not captured by critique. The connection of the trustworthy and the true is important. The true is what shows itself trustworthy. Here we need to acknowledge the intimate inseparability of being true with our own being truthful. There is no truth for us without our being truthful, which does not mean that being true is exhausted by our being truthful. What is true holds true even when we are untruthful or untrue to it. Of course, we can be truthful not only to ourselves but to what as other is shown to us, to what is communicated to us. Being truthful opens to what is beyond itself in its own most intimate integrity of honesty. The trustworthy, the credit-worthy, alerts us to what is worthy to be believed in this intimate sense.[6]

In this connection thought and belief cannot but be regarded as companions. Thinking truthfully about something is crediting it, or being credited by it, in such a wise that the relation between us and it is rendered trustworthy. The relation itself embodies a kind of ontological trust. It will hold, we think. We hold to it, because we trust it will hold. We trust it because it holds true.

What is at issue is not only a trust in this or that determination which we might express in this or that univocal proposition. We are pointed to a trust that is more basic than trust in this or that. Our being truthful itself testifies to something of this more basic trust. Why should we be truthful? There is no answer to this question in terms other than truthfulness itself. There is something basic about being truthful. And this holds, even though in truthfulness a porosity opens in us to being true, to being as true. In its radical intimacy it is an opening to what as true transcends us. The metaxological nature of this is evident: in the midst yet beyond, immanent yet called to what transcends us.

We are called to be truthful even when we do *not know* the truth, and even when we have to confess we do not know it. A confession of ignorance or being wrong testifies to the spirit of being truthful. For to pose the question of truth is to find oneself in a relation that holds one to being truthful. This is even true if our purpose is to mock truth, as Pilate (in) famously did. This call to be truthful is something immanent in thinking itself, and is not exhausted by a relation between thinking and some fixed state of affairs external to it. This does not mean there is not an otherness at work, but it is not one that can be simply objectified in terms of any such fixed externality. Being truthful testifies to a trust that to be true will bring us into the company of the true or truth.

In this light, suppose we look again at critique, in the mode of posing questions. No matter the severity of the posing of a question, the very posing is not just a position or the positing of this or that truth. It is an ontological-epistemic orientation to what perplexes or baffles us. Nevertheless, it is one in which there is an anticipation that an answer will respond one way or the other to the question posed. The matter is not one

6. See *Being and the Between,* chapter 12, on different senses of being true, as well as the discussion of being truthful in the previous chapter.

of the "what" about the posing of the question, and the definite propositions or positions that would answer the posing. It is the very posing itself as the embodiment of an orientation to what is true. This orientation
to the true is the living enactment of trustfulness that there is a true to be
known. And this is true, even when the question is posed in the spirit of
suspicion.

Even to be confronted finally with the absurd is still to go toward it
with the anticipation of trustworthy truth. True, when we meet the absurd
our expectation is defeated or disappointed, but the expectation is more
primal than the defeat, and since we know the defeat, expectation already
resurrects itself in the disappointment. We cannot but be beings that live
in a trust in the true. It makes us the kinds of being we are. We live between the question and the true and the question itself reveals a prior relation to the true—not only with respect to its own truthfulness but with
respect to the possibility of truth as other to our expectations. Living this
primal trust, we are the expectation of the unexpected.

It is worth remarking that the search for the true is never a matter
of *self-confirmation* simply. Something is confirmed for us, but there is
also an ingression of something other that, so to say, takes us out of ourselves. This exceeding of ourselves is not just with respect to this truth or
that truth as other, but with respect to a more primal relation between
us and the true. This relation is intimate but not merely immanent; it is
transcending and relates us to what transcends us; this other beyond or
above us is not a fixed objectivity over against which we stand in a relation
of something like dualistic opposition. The intimacy and otherness mean
also that it is not a matter of us either sublating this truth or of our being
sublated by it. We always move in the between of communication where
otherness and intimacy are both inseparable and irreducible.

This prior sense of being truthful cannot be articulated fully in the
language of the autonomy of thought. Quite the opposite: it shows all
thought to be already implicated with something other to itself. And it
shows this, whether we approach the matter from the intimacy of thought
seeming to communicate with itself, or of thought in relation to something beyond itself that communicates with it. The posing of a question is
a between, is an intermedium, of communication, already underway before the posing wakes up to itself, either in self-enjoyment, self-critique,
other-enjoyment or other-critique. This between-being of the question

makes it impossible to claim that the posing of the question is to be ruled by the *nomos* of *to auto,* the law of itself. There is a heteronomy at work here but it is no squashing otherness. It is releasing and enabling of the very search for truth. We are enabled to seek the truth before we possess the truth, and this prior enabling is not determinate thought, nor determined through ourselves alone, hence it cannot be defined in the logic of autonomy. This prior enabling is just what allows us to be relatively autonomous at all. We would not be autonomous were not autonomy enabled by something prior to and other to autonomy. Self-determining thinking is released into its own freedom to think for itself by an enabling resource that is not itself, a source not to be captured in terms of this or that determinate thought, or by thought's own determination by and for itself. There is more that allows thinking to be itself more than itself.

THE CONFIDENCE OF THINKING

This prior sense of being truthful in relation to the true throws light on the confidence of thinking. What does confidence mean? We notice the reference to *fides* in confidence—there is a *con-fides,* a faith with. One might say there is a companionship of faith, companionship marked by a fidelity. Confidence thus enfolds within itself relationality to something beyond self. It is like trust: even when one trusts in one's own power, there is more than what one can empower, or own, completely through self-trust alone. I trust because I am trusted, because I am entrusted.

In practice, I trust I can do this or that, but I must hazard my talent to confirm my trust in myself, hence I must always open myself to what is beyond me. But even before the confirming hazard that redounds to the adventurer, there is already a confidence in the adventuring, and hence an opening to what is other to me before there is an opening of me to what is other. My trust in myself is impossible to determine purely through myself alone. The confidence that is invested in my trust is enigmatically related to what is not of itself alone. Trust in oneself would seem to come down to oneself alone, but in trying to come down to itself alone it draws from a reserve that cannot come down to itself alone.

That said, this entails no reason at all to eradicate this intimate reference to oneself. The most intimate reference to oneself shades into a porosity to what exceeds oneself alone. This may not always be acknowledged. Nonacknowledgment can be paradoxically greater *consequent* to the confirmation of the trust in oneself through the venturing that hazards itself on the other. Self-pleased ingratitude too often follows enjoyment of something given to one. For the nine lepers among the ten healed, restoration overwhelmed thanks, and we must count ourselves mostly among these nine. There seems an inevitable tendency to elide thanks to the source that gives courage to the trust in self. Ingratitude is not a helpful companion of mindful granting.

I would say there is no confidence in self without this other to self confiding in one. Confiding in one: again there is the note of intimacy. When a companion confides in me, I am invested with a trust. I am answerable to the trust of the other because I am endowed with the promise of being trustworthy. I do not constitute this trustworthy promise or character through myself alone. This is impossible in the nature of the case. It is not only this or that secret, or item of information, that is confided in me. Being confided in by the companion extends to the totality of what I am, and seems nothing, in a way, for it is not quite this or that. Being confided in enters into, permeates, the integrity of what I am and its reliable promise. Being taken into confidence reveals a trust in my constancy. We are integrities of being not totally self-constitutive but constituted in virtue of a relation of reception to what is other and beyond us—a beyond that, nevertheless, communicates intimately to the very being of what we are.

I am worthy of confidence in being thus confided in. This is a kind of ontological confiding that makes possible my confidence. It comes to me from an other who releases me as the recipient of communication into my own being for itself, capable of itself, and confident in its power, its own powers, but not just power that is its own. On the basis of this confidence I can set out to determine myself this way or that, or indeed to determine if such and such is or is not the case. In other words, this prior confidence, this prior communication of confidence, is not a determinate confidence that tells me this or that, it is not a self-determining confidence, but something more than both. And it is not merely indeterminate, thenceforth to be made either determinate or self-determining. In language I introduced earlier, I would say it is over determinate, over self-determining also, in the sense that it is more than determinate and self-determining confidence. "Over" here means: not overpowering, but power that, though over one, releases; "over" in the sense in which (in an immemorial image) a guardian angel might watch over its mortal charge, let it to seek the fullness of its own promise. In being let go, we are kept in mind. We are mindfulness, and capable of minding because we are kept in mind: already minded before we mind this or that, or determine our minds thus and thus.

The case is analogous to courage, and I have discussed this elsewhere.[7] There is no courage without being encouraged; just as there is no love without first being loved, or speaking without being addressed. There is no communication from us without our being in communication. We are in what enables us to be ourselves as wording our being, but what we are in is not just our own being, and the wording of it is more than words we can simply call our own. The first word comes to us in the woo of the mother who coaxes us into our own words. We arrive in a communication long under way without us, and we come into it as recipients of its resources and reserves, though also in time we come to complaint, and alas, like Caliban, being taught to speak, we also learn quickly to curse. Words, of course, are the most intimately personal but no word is owned by us exclusively. Words, intimately personal, enable the universal, enable the intimate universal. This is how I have described the community of being religious.[8]

This prior confidence has implications for the practice of thinking, in a general sense, and in its current forms. As briefly suggested at the beginning, one aspect of postmodern times is a lack of confidence in the affirmative powers of thought, coupled with a hypertrophy of suspicious critique. One might see this as a reaction to the confidence of modern reason which, in Enlightenment form, assumed the face of a certain self-confidence. Since this self-confidence was formed in rejection of religious belief, it tended toward an *assertive* self-confidence. We do not submit ourselves to heteronomous religious sources; we insist on thinking for ourselves; there is to be no self-incurred tutelage; and so on. Call this the assertiveness training of modern reason, building up its postreligious confidence in itself.

There is something not entirely happy about this. There is a self-confidence which, when self-assertive and under the aegis of a certain au-

7. "The Secret Sources of Strengthening: On Courage," *Is There a Sabbath for Thought?* chapter 7.

8. For example, in *Is There a Sabbath for Thought?* 1–32.

tonomous self-determination, is simply untrue to what it itself is, as already the beneficiary, indeed beneficence, of a confiding. We have already received such beneficences before we think for ourselves. They are confided to us. This is true of a people, of a religious tradition, and it is no less true of an individual. One might ask, for instance: Who was the mother of the *cogito*? The *cogito* has no mother. How then was it wooed into words? It is as if the *cogito*, masking Descartes, would be self-born. Consider the later Nietzsche, not always masking himself: he would be mother and father and offspring of himself, all in one. Far from being serenely confident, this strikes one as a compensatory assertiveness that feels it has to create a space for itself by negation or subsumption of another. Its self-assertiveness has to continue to assert itself, lest it collapse back into the other(s) from which it wants to distance itself or against which it wants to revolt. The determinate other has to be overcome, the indeterminate formlessness has to be overtaken. Self-determination becomes self-wording self-assertion in the case of overconfidence; it becomes indeterminate self-negating in the case of reactive underconfidence. Overprojection produces its boomerang in the twin that is its *incognito* understudy, namely, abjection. Are there strains of postmodern thinking that fear collapse in this sense: the confidence of reason cannot truly be restored by self-assertion, once that confidence has turned against itself? And what trustworthy truth is confided, can be confided in reactive abjectness?

I return again to Hegel as representing the acme of a certain Enlightenment self-confidence of reason. His hyperinflation of our reason's claims produced a speculative bubble and a long antiphilosophical deflation from which we have not yet fully recovered. Recovery asks something like a fuller résumé of the prior reserve of confiding. This entails a self-confidence that knows its power to be always, in the primal place, second; self-confidence grateful to have received what it has been granted; confidence not rancorous against external limitation, nor against itself for being finite; confidence that yet, as being confided in, is released into an adventure of seeking what is intimately of itself and more than itself; confidence purged of rancor against God.

For there are different forms of self-confidence, and the wrong self-confidence overtakes the "con" of *con-fidence*. It lets the self override the relation to the other hidden in the con-fidence. It overtakes any *passio essendi*, as it wills itself to become a *conatus essendi* that takes over. I mean a *con-natus* that in its endeavour to be itself occludes the "con" of its own being "born with," for it would be self-born. No longer would there be anything over it; it would overtake whatever it receives, claiming it for itself. Taking all over, it would come to be, in a self-birthing, its own absolute self-confidence. This certainly is a temptation of reason understood in the modern sense of self-determining. Consider Hegel's overtaking of religion, though it might be dressed up in the language of a certain companionship of the *Begriff* and the *Vorstellung*. This is a companionship of a provisional sort, since the religious friend must cede to philosophy the ultimate place of ultimacy, just because it fails to be absolutely self-determining. Religion does not have the requisite absolute confidence in reason's own power of self-determination. The kern of the matter remains an overtaking, for all the pious Hegelian talk about preserving the religious. There is a conceptual reconfiguration of the *passio* of religion, and the community of the intimate universal, in favor of a self-absolutizing *conatus* of thought that claims to be the concrete universal. The intimate universal is not this concrete universal.

I recall Hegel's very confident remarks about the courage of truth *(der Muth der Wahrheit)* in his inaugural lecture in Heidelberg, repeated at Berlin: "The human being . . . should and must deem himself worthy of the highest. . . . The initially hidden and concealed essence of the world has no power to withstand the courage of knowledge."[9] This is very definitely a rousing call against any abjectness of the human spirit. Initially we may be perplexed, but if we hold fast and call upon courage, we can be confident that the initially hidden essence of the world will be unable to hold out against our knowing. We must not be discouraged; knowing will triumph! This is self-confidence with bells and whistles and without apology.

9. "Der Muth der Wahrheit; der Glaube an die Macht des Geistes ist die erste Bedingung der Philosophie; der Mensch, da er Geist ist, darf und soll sich selbst des Höchsten würdig achten, von dem Grosse und Macht seines Geistes kann er nicht gross genug denken; und mit diesem Glauben wird nichts so spröde und hart seyn, das sich ihm nicht eröffnete; das zuerst verborgene und verschlosse Wesen des Universums hat keine Krafft, die dem Muthe des Erkennens Widerstand leisten konnte; es muss sich vor ihm aufthun, und seinen Reichthum und seine Tieffen ihm vor Augem legen und zum Genusse geben." This is the Heidelberg version, *Gesammelte Werke* (Hamburg: Felix Meiner, 1968), 18.6; the Berlin version, 18.18, is slightly more clipped and direct. One thinks of Hegel here paying his philosophical respects to the Enlightenment motto of Kant: *sapere aude!* Of course, Hegel thought that Kant was not courageous enough, since his "knowing" stops with appearances. Hegel holds that philosophical courage must dare more, enact itself more audaciously.

What of the courage itself? We call upon courage, but how *call* upon courage? Can we call upon courage, entirely confident that it is a resource within our command? Is there not something to courage that exceeds determinate command? Courage surges forth from sources hard to pin down to determinacy or to encapsulate in self-determination. We do not so much call upon courage as that something is called forth in us and from us in courage. Courage suggests a resource, a source, at once deeply intimate to our being, and yet not within the total possession of our confident self-command, even when we are commanding persons and self-possessed. We call on courage and an enigmatic power of confidence can come to be held out to us, and only then do we find that the recalcitrance of what holds out against us may no longer hold. This means that our courage can never just be ours alone; it comes out of secret reserves that involve our *"being encouraged."* There is a "being en-couraged" before "being courageous."

Perhaps Hegel's confidence is not entirely misplaced. It can be so: the courage of truth being given, the knowing will come. But the crucial issue is the enigma of our "being given" that courage, and the nature of the coming. Because we have courage, knowledge comes, but whence comes the courage itself? To have the knowledge we must first have the courage. The courage does not come from the knowledge but the knowledge from the courage. Courage offers an enabling of mindfulness and its seeking of the true. This suggests a courage of knowing *before* knowledge, a courage beyond determination and self-determination. Such courage seems to be encouraged by sources we cannot know in advance, maybe can never know in a fully determinate manner, given that these sources make determinate knowledge itself possible. Such courage brings to mind the secret con-fidence of truth.

This means that knowing presupposes a courage that knowledge itself cannot make fully determinate, and whose secret source it cannot completely comprehend. Knowing is successful on the basis of a courage whose secret source lies recessed in the always presupposed enabling powers that knowing can never claim for its own. Our coming to know reveals something more in the nature of *our being given to understand.* We are given to understand on the basis of unknown sources of knowing that release us into understanding. We do not know freely, we are freed into knowing. This freeing is more original and ultimate than our own self-determination. Knowing is possibilized by an empowering that is an *en-couraging of mindfulness*. We might say: the courage to know has been con-fided to us, and because of this confiding we have confidence. Such a confidence is different to the courage of Hegelian knowing that, as self-determining, is primarily self-encouraging.

I do not believe abjectness of thought is the true response to the Hegelian self-confidence of reason. This self-confidence becomes overconfidence, in occluding the more original, confiding source of courage. When such overconfidence becomes confidence over all, we are corrupted by a spiritual hubris. One would not even attribute that kind of confidence to a God, and especially not if that God is agapeic, which Hegel's is not. The agapeic God is a God of releasing the other into its own being for itself.[10] The agapeic God is the God of the most ultimate confidence—confiding freedom to the mortal creature, to the finite human. This is a venture on the mortal creature, full of the hazard of an extraordinary confidence, the confiding that is the investiture of freedom to be at all, and to be oneself. This confiding is an endowing: a giving that gives resources that can be put to work and enjoyment—with a promise that is to be redeemed, but that is not exhausted in self-satisfied self-determination.

In this light, the truer sense of our confidence is not the self-confidence, not the overconfidence, but the confidence that is a between-endowment. The *con, cum*, "with," of *con-fidence* opens the between space of communicating difference which it also crosses. The confidence of our endowment can grant its (re)sources in itself and its source in more than itself. This confidence can grant a superior other, a God over it. It does not have to overtake everything to be itself. It knows the mutilation involved when such a kind of self-confidence takes over. There is tyranny of faith in oneself which is lack of faith in anything else. This becomes in turn a suspicion, a distrust that can turn into destruction of the other. For every other is a reminder of the lie that this self-affirmation is: a lie that is not truthful with itself, much less with the other.

In such a world the sources of a more original trust are blocked up, and the soul cannot look up. The ontological porosity that goes with confidence as a between-endowment is clogged. Confidence as a between condition is both confident and the recipient of confidences. I see this in

---

10. On this more fully, see *God and the Between*; on Hegel's God as erotic rather than agapeic, see *Hegel's God: A Counterfeit Double?* passim, but especially chapter 4.

the light of the intimate universal. In our hearts we know something of being the recipient of confidences, even if the confiding power is often enigmatic and nameless. Our confident heart, having being confided in, participates in the intimate universal. Often we have to silence the clamor in and around us to hear such confidences. We live in a world full of shouting. Wording the between becomes harder in this pandemonium of shouts.

IN CONFIDENCE: METAPHYSICS AND THE INTIMATE UNIVERSAL

Wording the between, that is to say, giving a *logos* of the *metaxu*: such is the task of a metaxological philosophy. This, one can now say, endorses a fitting affirmation of the confidence of thinking. True, this fitting affirmation has to be in the right register and with the right note. Much hangs on the "how" of the affirmation. The extremes of overconfidence and abjectness are to be avoided. We can be confident in thought because we are recipients of confidence(s). There is an intimacy and patience here beyond critique. In this intimate patience a communication of metaphysical astonishment may also come. One cannot project astonishment; one cannot project surprise; one must be opened, or become open to, its happening. Astonishment comes to us before we go from it toward what is beyond us.

There is a confidence both prior to and beyond nihilism that can never be entirely exhausted, as long as we remain the beings we are. This means that there is a future for metaphysical thinking. This is not first a question of particular doctrines to be renewed or taken over from the tradition— though respect for modes of thinking showing reliable constancy over time is very important. Even less is it a matter of thinking that all thought hitherto is something to be deconstructed. It may well be true that there are fixations that have to be made fluid and porous again. But if the undoing of the fixity does not lay itself open to the deeper source of confidence, it risks being merely an updated version of thinking as negation. This too ends up with almost nothing, in the end. It does not come again into confidence but vacillates between saying something and saying nothing, with a tilt toward saying nothing, even while seeming to say something. The primal confidence can indeed cause us to look with diffidence on some fixations but there are different ways of looking, and it is all-important that the looking be informed by love of the true. The determinacies of thought may hide their own recession of the deeper confidings of thinking. Wording the between asks of us finesse for discernment concerning these recessions. The ontological love that is present in being truthful is not to be betrayed. There can be a knowing that glories in supposedly telling the truth, but if this telling is informed with secret traces of hatred, the spirit of truth is itself corrupted.

Consider how we might correct the conduct of another that is amiss: the correction can be communicated in a spirit of less than love. Two persons might say in correction of the fault *the exact same things,* but the "how" of the saying, reflecting the "who" of the sayer, in one case might fulfill the truth of the situation, and its promise, and in the other case might betray it, turning truth-telling into an ontological violence. Such truth-telling tells the truth, in one sense, but since the "how" of the telling, and the "who" of the one who tells, are lacking in the love of truth revered by truthfulness, the telling warps the spirit of truthfulness. Of course, traditional metaphysics has been charged with an ontological violence, but one has to be very qualified about this. There is an indictment of metaphysics that tells us as much about the indictor as the indictee—the indictor who cannot see the tradition in any other light except that of an erring. Such a teller cannot invest any trust in it. In the name of what is this refusal of trust? In the name of truth, or truthfulness, one might say. Of its own truthfulness? But the deeper we know this, the more we know that we must be finessed in diffidence about judgment on the other as putatively not in the truth. The truth of something "other"? Well then, hewing to the path of truthfulness must continue. And on this path perhaps the best of metaphysical thinking has always passed.

I am not saying this in merely reactive exoneration of traditional metaphysics. The true confidence of thinking is beyond self-assertive indictment and reactive exoneration. There is one great circumstance that calls again for mention: the companionship of religion and metaphysics in the past. To my mind this provides a source of affirmation that gives a confidence, as much expressed in religious faith as in the trust in reason itself, as much admonitory of the overreaching ambitions of human power as in solidarity with human poverty, as much rejoicing in the excellence of human nobility as compassionate in sight of the tragedies of failure, as much tender to human limitations as laughing with its folly. Of course, the distrust of traditional metaphysics is often coupled with a distrust of, disdain for, even violence to religion. But this reveals the extremity of the situation. What is most needed is what is least acknowledged as so needed. To confess this need would be to seek release from the scientistic bewitchments of fixated determinacy, as well as to de-idolize the idea of self-determining thinking. It would be to move beyond the deconstruction of both the determinacy and the self-determinacy, not so much in the direction of a new construction as toward a renewed patient mindfulness of the intimate strangeness of being.

The confidence of thought entails an ontological trust and epistemic fidelity without which the very enterprise of thinking, and all our seeking for knowledge, can only come to nothing. We know the seeking can turn against the search itself. Yet this turn against itself of searching thought reveals the same deep-down companionship of the confiding. Patient mindfulness must open itself again to this passion of thinking—passion as an undergoing and a receiving—passion, one might also say, as an inspiration that already carries us in an arc of transcending, unchosen at first by us and rather choosing us before we, always late(r), choose for it. This patience is *ecstasis* into a darkness that is not grim but lightening. In this we see the family resemblance to religious faith. This is no univocal light but a trust that comes to hold steady, to be held steady in the play of light and darkness, in the equivocal twilight, or dawn, that marks our metaxological condition. There is a going into the cave of our own ignorance, but we must be vigilant that our own hugging of ourselves against the darkness does not become also our self-retraction against the communicating light.

The confidence of which I speak is not a matter of fideism, just as the trust of faith is not simply a sacred "say so"—as can happen with fideistic interpretations. Reason and faith are in a darkness that is not dark. It is the darkness of a mystery that is not alone enveloping but intimate to our undergoing of metaphysical astonishment and perplexity at our middle condition. When all things are considered, this mystery is what, in our heart of hearts, we love as ultimate. Love is in confiding. We are loved when another takes us into his or her confidence. We love another when we are taken into confidence. We are by our very being taken into confidence. The call on our being is to take what is given into our own confidence.

This is reflected in the task of metaphysics as a mindful love of being, as a knowing fidelity to what being reveals itself to be. This is reflected in the consolation of being religious: in the dark night of the seemingly absent God, trust is confided, dark trust that grows lighter with love as it dwells more and more with its own darkness. There is nothing of escapism in this. There is a mysticism of deeper communication, and it is in love with the good of mortal things because secretly the divine love of mortal things has been confided to them.

This issues in a service which I think can only be called agapeic, generous giving, surplus to determinacy, and self-determinacy, and no mere indeterminacy but an overdeterminacy of availability. What is confided to us is the confidence to lay ourselves open, even in the attack of the hostile other, for even there, there is the promise of good, more always than the face of oppugnancy turned against us. The face turned toward us, the face opposing us, has buried deep in itself, as in a grave, the intimate ontological love that is itself and more than itself. The ontological confidence can be resurrected from that reserve only by witnessing it as already still alive in the neighbor who smiles its gift toward the retracted one, unasked. This is an ethical-religious service—enacting an idiotic smile of the love of God that has set us on the way and that does not go away even when we are away, even astray.

Deprived of the worthy, we cannot still but desire the worthy. We desire what is worthy for itself, what is worthy of ourselves, what is worthy of the promise of truth that has been confided to us. We love the trust that has been confided in us. Metaphysics can be a form of this thinking love. The love of the trust is not just our own love, or our own trust. When we are loved we are trusted. When we love we trust. When we think, we trust that there is truth to be heard and communicated. When we truly think, we are in love. Trust in thought is our participation (sometimes even thoughtlessly) in the agapeics of being.

What do we trust? This question has to be asked about the confiding and its ultimate source: Could a neutral causality or valueless process or mechanism truly confide? If such neutered being or valueless process were the final answer, could there be any confidence at all in thought, such as we have discovered it to be? If being were a neutral mechanism or valueless process, of which we too were instantiations, would not the confidence of thought become ultimately unintelligible, indeed a meaningless swindle? The confidence, being called on, and put to work fruitfully, would finally come to the truth which would show us that there is no ground for confidence at all.

We would be theorizing on the same branch that we are confidently sawing off with our own thoughts. Having sawn through confidently, confidence itself would simply fall to the ground and evaporate. Its basis for trust in itself would come to nothing. Its confidence in itself would destroy itself.

Suppose one were to reply: This power of the process of being is in one, is one, and is over against one—and this process as a whole is power and nothing but power. But what kind of power? Will to power? But devoid of reference to what is worthy to be trusted, to the trustworthy, how relate to this power? How affirm it, in the sense at issue, if it too is nothing but valueless happening? How can one have confidence in, how can one trust, valueless happening? Would not our own affirmation of it, or of ourselves, be then too a valueless happening? And would not then the self-confidence of this power be also strangely out of place? Out of place, since if the whole of happening is said to manifest this neuter process, it is hard to make sense of the stress of singularity, singularity of a personal character, that is expressed in self-confidence. The same holds for the stress of intimate communication that attends all acts of confiding, or being confided in.

"Being out of place" is itself hard to make intelligible if there is not something to the confidence that can shed light on the possibility of the *betrayal* of promise, as well as the redemption. For confidence communicates the promise of some good. To speak of the betrayal or redemption of promise ultimately can have no meaning in a world of worthless process or valueless being. Similarly, the courage of knowing makes no sense in any such neutralized world. Would not the extremity of such a way of thinking point toward a totally deconsecrated world? From where would come such confidence in an entirely deconsecrated world? Such confidence could not be endowed in such a world. Yet we continue to enjoy its benefit—though, properly speaking, on this view the confidence should not be at all. For neutralization is not neutral. In due course, we come to despise the neutered world; perhaps it is ontological contempt that already would neuter the world. We turn against, have already turned against its saturated equivocity. It is warped confidence that deconsecrates the world.

Warped confidence lives on in every act of desecration, and that is why it is warped: it continues to be indebted to what it has come to hate. Think here of the example of the *torturer* and trust. The torturer lives in a world that seems quite different to that of the neutered world of valueless being. Torture is an activity saturated with value—though it is hatred, whether hot or cold, that drives it. Yet there is a connection between the torturer and valueless being. The torturer takes the next step to deconsecration: he desecrates the other. The torturer tries to gain access to the mortal intimacy of the idiotic soul. He seeks access, by force or guile, utterly to destroy trust in the victim. He desecrates the soul's place of intimate confiding. He tries to destroy trust in God. His violation says: Your God is dead; you too will die, and deeper than the death of your body will be the destruction of your spirit—and its confidence. Without trust life is impossible for us. When nothing confides in us, nothing communicates with us, we are as nothing. When confidence dies or is killed, we are condemned to be nothing. That we *are at all* means that the intimate confiding is communicated into the secret chambers of the soul. The torturer wants to ransack these secret chambers, perhaps kill God in the soul. All too often we are our own torturer. We kill God in ourselves.

Even in prison, we come to the edge of the air (*ēschaton ton aēra*; *Phaedo* 109e2). This time the air is a song. *Bist du bei mir* (If you are with me): the haunting music sings of the love that is confided, even in the meeting with death. It seems to me reasonable to suggest that the source of a confiding must in some measure be proportionate to the character of the confidence. Perhaps more than proportionate. A liar does not confide the truth. A source of truth does not confide a lie. A liar may betray the truth in telling a lie. Even the lie is told with the confidence of truth. If we are confided trust in truth, in our being truthful, what does this say of the source of the confiding, the confidence? The source of our confidence must reflect something of the nature of that confidence: it is confided both as trust that the world can be truly known, and as self-confidence that we can trust the powers entrusted to us. At its deepest, confidence is personal, both as singular and as communal. If our confidence reveals something both intimate and universal, in a personally stressed singularity that opens to all that is beyond itself, we might expect that the source of the confiding too will reflect something of the nature of the intimate universal.

Between ourselves, and speaking now in confidence, there is something entirely fitting if we think of God as the endowing source of the confiding. You object that this is a leap. But must philosophy slouch? And as it slouches, oddly strut with self-confidence? Slouching toward what? You say: walking is enough. But walking lifts us up. In confidence we leap. Even though we are tested in our confidence in the divine, the confidence is endowed by the divine. God confides the promise of the intimate universal. Trust is invested in what is worthy to be trusted—but what most is worthy to be trusted is what loves us in the proper measure. This measure for us is an infinite measure. We would be infinitely loved. In our most idiotic intimacy, we live ourselves never as a neutral replaceable something but as intimately singular. God is the endowing source of the intimate universal. Only the personal, transpersonal God could endow the trusted singular with the universal as the intimate universal. *Bist du bei mir*: the air quickens our confidence, heartens it, but it is love that the air consecrates.

9 ∽ Analogy, Dialectic, and Divine Transcendence

Between St. Thomas and Hegel

Especially since around the time of Hegel, affirmations of divine transcendence have often been attacked in terms of a variety of philosophies of immanence. For such philosophies, immanence constitutes the ultimate horizon, not only for all life, but for philosophy itself, and beyond which nothing further is to be thought. Often the idea of transcendence they attack is defined in very dualistic terms: immanence is pitted *versus* transcendence, time *versus* eternity, the "here-and-now" *versus* the "hereafter," and so on. One might question whether such dualistic conceptions, sometimes imputed to the entire Western tradition of metaphysics ("Platonism") and theology (Christianity as "Platonism for the people"), are true to more nuanced understandings of immanence and transcendence. One might also ask if the notion of analogy has the promise of resources not genuinely granted by such philosophies of immanence in general. One might ask the same question of dialectic. It is true that Hegel's dialectic is a foe of dualistic thought, but one can wonder about his philosophy of speculative dialectic lying on the same plane as these philosophies of immanence. I take Hegel to be exemplary of a form of modern dialectic, claiming to meet the challenge of every form of dualism, and indeed to culminate in an entirely immanent mode of thought. Though many post-Hegelians might attack Hegel's philosophy of rational totality, they often share the same commitment to immanence and nothing but immanence. A consideration of speculative dialectic vis-à-vis divine transcendence will have significance beyond Hegel for our contemporary philosophical options, as well as our theological or atheological predilections.

The notions of analogy and dialectic are almost coextensive with the entire tradition of philosophy from its inception in Greek thought.

Among other things, both have to do with the nature of intelligible discourse and indeed the intelligibility of being itself and our mindfulness of it. Dialectic is associated with the diverse practices of philosophy, be they Socratic-Platonic or Hegelian, to just cite only these two instances. Analogy is often associated with the senses of being in classical metaphysics, as well as how we might intelligibly speak about the divine. I want to look at how each might guide us in thinking of difference, particularly with respect to the otherness of the divine. I will look at analogy in St. Thomas as entailing a balance of identity and difference, continuity and discontinuity, with a tilt toward hyperbolic difference in the case of the divine, a difference that always borders on a kind of equivocity that we cannot entirely mediate, though this does not preclude that the divine might mediate it or be mediated in it. By contrast, I will look at Hegel's speculative dialectic as trying to mediate that equivocity, and in a manner that relativizes the divine difference in terms of a more encompassing immanent whole.

My exploration will be thematic rather than historical: looking at the univocal, equivocal, and dialectical senses of being and being divine, I will offer, at least toward the end, a suggestion or two about what I call a metaxological rendition of analogy that keeps open the space of transcendence, even while it does not close off the promise of communication between immanence and transcendence. The (metaxological) reconsideration of analogy need not be only a retrospective glance at a supposedly exhausted tradition, but may harbor promise for a renewed thinking of the thought of divine difference, after Hegel himself and after the deconstruction of Hegelian totality.

I acknowledge I am not an "expert" on Aquinas, but he is one of those thinkers for me whom I would call *companioning*. Such a thinker one does not necessarily make into an object of scholarly research, but yet he forms a presence as a companion. As with some companions, sometimes one does not pay attention for ages, and then one is engaged again. Yet some relation can abide even in the gaps of silence. This is the way with companions on the way.[1] Reading Aquinas, one can have the feeling of

---

1. A version of these reflections was given as the Aquinas Lecture at the University of Dallas, January 28, 2010. One can be called back, sometimes in surprise, to this companioning relation by invitations to give such a lecture! That call or invitation completes a triad, the other two invitations yielding: "Is There a Sabbath for Thought: Reflections of Philosophy and Peace," delivered at John Carroll University and St. Charles Seminary, Cleveland, Ohio, March 21, 2002,

standing in a cathedral and of not being able to make out the sense of the strange sensuous languages of signs and symbols. There is something enigmatic to the many different figures and yet also a kind of intimacy. In the strangeness there is the suggestion of immense significance, though what this is exactly is hard to say. It can happen that sometimes a surprising light shines in the strangeness. Light breaks through and one is illuminated—by mystery. I note that even Hegel felt something of this in the gothic cathedral. In his philosophy there is no real systematic place, conceptually or sympathetically, for the soaring transcendence we experience in such cathedrals. Nevertheless he was touched by it. Soaring transcendence got behind the conceptual defenses of his systematization and transported him, as if in an involuntary way. So I believe—not least given that in his discussion of architecture in his *Lectures on Aesthetics* this is the only time Hegel, so to say, takes fire.[2]

BEING AS PLURIVOCAL

Let me first say something of the importance of the different senses of being. Being is said in many ways: *to on legetai pollachōs*. Aquinas echoes Aristotle: *ens dicitur multipliciter*. We must take this multiplicity or plurivocity seriously, not only in light of the prodigious diversity in immanence, but of the relation of immanence and transcendence. Thus classically this plurivocity situates analogy with reference to Aristotle's distinction between it and the univocal and equivocal senses. This is taken up by Aquinas and put to work, whether by Aquinas himself or his admirers and commentators, in relation to what we might say about God and how we might say it. Here is how he puts it in his commentary on Aristotle's *Metaphysics:*

It must be noted that a term is predicated of different things in various senses. Sometimes it is predicated of them according to a meaning which is entirely the same, and then it is said to be predicated of them univocally, as animal is predicated of a horse or of an ox. Sometimes it is predicated of them according

revised and published in *Is There a Sabbath for Thought?* chapter 10; and "Exceeding Virtue: Aquinas and the Beatitudes," delivered as the Aquinas Lecture, National University of Ireland, Maynooth, March 4, 2003, to appear in *Thomas Aquinas: Scholar and Thinker,* ed. Michael Dunne and James McEvoy (Dublin: Four Courts Press, 2011).

2. See my discussion, "Gothic Hegel," in *Art, Origins, Otherness,* chapter 4.

to meanings which are entirely different, and then it is said to be predicated of them equivocally, as dog is predicated of a star and of an animal. And sometimes it is predicated of them according to meanings which are partly different and partly not (different inasmuch as they imply different relationships, and the same inasmuch these different relationships are referred to one and the same thing), and then it is said to be predicated analogously, that is, proportionally, according to the way in which each one is referred by its own relationship to that one same thing.[3]

Very generally, the univocal sense puts the stress on sameness; the equivocal puts the stress on difference, a difference sometimes dissimulated by our ways of speaking; the analogical somehow mixes the same and the different, being partly one and partly the other, and with reference to the relation of the sameness and difference to something shared by both.

As has often been pointed out Aquinas's own formulations are not extraordinary extensive, and do not dwell more directly with the immense significance they have, as many of his admirers have done after him.[4] Something is at work that is woven into the texture of his thought. Some have wanted to underplay the metaphysical dimensions said to be at issue; others have taken these metaphysical implications in directions more explicit and explicated than in Aquinas himself. I am myself more drawn to the metaphysical side of considerations, believing the plurivocity is of being itself, and not simply our ways of talking about it. Our ways of speaking it are to be true to being's way(s) of bespeaking itself—plurivocally. We need not subscribe to a kind of linguistic Cartesianism where our voice and being's voicing are set apart in a dualism. The event of voicing, whether ours or of being, is itself sufficient testimony to communication and communicability beyond dualism. But what is this "beyond"—this beyond of dualism? It cannot be such as to abrogate the distinct realities

3. *In IV Metaph.*, lect.1, 535; see *Summa Theologiae*, ques. 13, art. 5; see Rudi te Velde, *Aquinas on God: The "Divine Science" of the Summa Theologiae* (Aldershot, U.K.: Ashgate Books, 2006), 109–10. I have learned much from this thoughtful book.

4. There is no need to enter the thorny debates concerning different sorts of analogy. The analogy of proportion concerns a comparison of two relations; the analogy of attribution concerns a relation between two terms, one of which is marked by a certain priority (in the often cited example, we speak of an animal or medicine as healthy, but the health of the first is primary). Here we have analogy with regard to *pros hen* equivocation, or analogy *per prius et posterius*. Another type of analogy, of special interest to us in terms of the likeness of the divine and the created, and the transcendence of the divine, concerns the participation of the creature in God as the origin or as creator. I speak of this below in terms of the analogy of origination.

of the partners in communication, and yet it must testify to a space of be-tweenness, of relationality between the two in which both are in commu-nication. Analogy says something important not only about a middle way between univocity and equivocity, but about this very between. Analogy is itself a between, and communicates a between—and to cite the most important case, in the *likeness/unlikeness between* the creation and God.

In my own work, I have hewed to something of this scheme, though diverging in the way I formulate the fourfold sense of being: the univo-cal, the equivocal, the dialectical, and the metaxological. I will offer only this very general summary. While the univocal sense tends to emphasize determinate sameness and identity, the equivocal tends to emphasize dif-ference that escapes univocal sameness, sometimes even to the point of indeterminacy, and the loss of any mediation between sameness and dif-ference, identity and otherness. The dialectical sense seeks to mediate dif-ferences, differences sometimes equivocal, but not by reduction to univo-cal sameness but by transition to a more inclusive unity or whole which, it is claimed by some, contains and even reconciles the differences. Fi-nally, the metaxological, stressing the between, deals with the interplay of sameness and difference, identity and otherness, not by mediating a more inclusive whole but by recurrence to the rich ambiguities of the middle, and with due respect for forms of otherness that are dubiously claimed to be included in the immanence of a dialectical whole. Where dialec-tic, especially in Hegelian form, tends to move from the indeterminate to the determinate to the self-determining, the metaxological is shaped by a fourfold, namely, the overdeterminate, the indeterminate, the deter-minate, and the self-determining. The overdeterminate, as not less than determinate, and exceeding all determinates and self-determining, is cen-trally important for addressing the transcendence of the divine.

But where is analogy in all this? In the traditional account we have the univocal and the equivocal, without explicit mention of the dialectical, and no mention at all of the metaxological. I would align the metaxologi-cal with the analogous in this regard: an analogy is always *between* some-thing and an other. The nature of that between is at issue. It is susceptible to different articulations. I see the univocal as reducing the differences of the between to sameness. I see the equivocal as opening up ambiguous passage between differents, but sometimes exploiting the indeterminacy of this passing to dissimulate on the basis of likenesses. For likeness can also be used to deceive—for instance, a *counterfeit* can be so extraordinarily good as a likeness that it is (mis)taken for the original. That we can be so deceived by the equivocal has caused philosophers to be particularly worried about it. Yet this must also be said: the ambiguity of differencing and passage can also be related to the matrix of creativity, of coming to be, of transcending beyond determinacy, of pointing to something more primal than determination and self-determination. Pure univocal determinacy would yield something like a static Parmenidean whole. With equivocity we have a world closer to Heraclitean becoming where the tension of opposites is also a sign of a more ultimate togetherness. (The postmodern emphasis on flux as such tends toward the absolutization of equivocal difference.) The fact is that analogy is very close to equivocation in this more positive sense. The matter is even more challenging for thought, if any sameness in the likeness has to be balanced, or overseen, by an ever greater dissimilarity. This is evident in Aquinas's way of talking about God. The difference is one greater than which none can be thought. And yet analogy struggles to think it, in some way.

One might say that the dialectical, like the analogical, is a mediation of the equivocal. Yet there are different practices of dialectic, and hence the mediation is also understood differently. Some practices of dialectic safeguard the openness of differents. I think of Socratic-Platonic dialogue in which the plurality of speakers, and the doubleness of questioner and interlocutor, are essential to the conversation. Other practices of dialectic, and especially modern dialectic, tend to change the mediation into a holistic self-mediation. Hence there ceases to be any excessive dissimilarity of the partners in conversation which always is more than the similarity. For this reason a kind of higher univocity often comes back.

Granted, one might have some sympathy for such a tendency to holistic mediation, especially when there is a reciprocal symmetry between the partners in dialogue. But when the other is the divine other, there is an asymmetry that cannot be reduced to reciprocal mutual determination. Vis-à-vis this asymmetry, the metaxological recurs to the equivocal in an affirmative sense. There is irreducibility to the doubleness of the partners in communication. The likeness between them is as a (dynamic) likening that must entail unlikeness. Indeed, it especially grants asymmetrical relations that do not preclude intermediations, especially when the communicating other is the divine. A kind of metaxological analogy would stress the between space, marked by this holding together of sameness and difference, yet open to an asymmetrical dissimilitude, a space more than a deceiving dissimulating equivocation, since it has more to do with the matrix of rich and strange signs of the overdeterminacy of the divine. Metaxology would be a kind of dynamized analogy where the energy of transcending passes from the divine to the creature, and the creature to the divine, in a porous between, itself originally given to be by the divine, the divine as both always more than this between and yet most deeply intimate to it, as its mysterious endowing source and conserver.

HEGELIAN DIALECTIC AND THE PLURIVOCITY OF BEING

I will come back to this, but let me venture a first sortie with respect to Hegel. Hegel does not use this vocabulary of univocal, equivocal, and analogical, but his philosophical concerns are not unconnected. We might connect the univocal with the principle of identity: a thing is what it is and not anything other. A distinction is fixed by *Verstand,* and without such distinctions we lack determinate intelligibility. Hence univocity in this sense stands at the heart of intelligibility.

By contrast, we might connect Hegel and the equivocal by saying that this has to do with *the more than one,* in the sense that difference and otherness are evident in attention to the development of the determinate and identical thing. Pure identity without difference is unintelligible. Hegel will say that identity gives rise to difference in the immanent sense of showing itself to be self-differentiating. The question of equivocal otherness comes up as to whether it is a doubling which falls away from intelligibility, understood as determinate. Pure equivocity might seem to dissolve itself into something like flux without form, differentiation without any stabilization of identity, and hence show itself resistant to articulate intelligibility. But if it is purely unintelligible, then how speak of it at all? There must be something more, something other than the purely equivocal.

Rather than resort to an analogical sense at this juncture, Hegel brings in the dialectical. The dialectical is related to the double, the *dia* of *dialegein.* Things are more than univocal, more than equivocal, but there is a mediation of these two. In this mediation, the fixity of univocal identity gives way to more fluid differences, while these, in turn, are not merely dissolving moments of flux but mediating moments of a process of be-coming. In due course, this becoming, for Hegel, shows itself to be the self-becoming of a more inclusive self-constituting whole. There is here a kind of mediated return to identity—not the first univocal identity but speculative identity. This is very complicated in Hegel and we must guard against too reductive presentations and criticisms (some postmoderns are prone to this). Could one venture that this is not unreminiscent of anal-ogy with relation to *pros hen* equivocation, in that the equivocal differ-ences, the many senses, are ultimately referred to one focal sense, in this case, Hegel's absolute. The nature of the one is not a matter of a determi-nate proposition, or linguistic unit. It is the speculative whole in the end, to the self-mediation of which both the fixations of univocity and the dis-solutions of equivocity contribute.[5]

Hegelian dialectic is very much concerned with the issue of the me-diation of differences, and not least the putative difference of finite and in-finite. If we formulate the matter in terms of Hegel's view of the *Verstand* (e.g., something marking Enlightenment deism), we find a strong tenden-cy to conceive of these two as each a fixed univocal domain for itself: the finite is finite, the infinite infinite, each being what the other is not. Thus the *Verstand* defines them by negative relation to each other. Each is what it is by not being what the other is. This is a manner of proceeding by way of univocal identity, by way of a sameness that fixes into an "overagainst-ness" vis-à-vis what is other to it. The result is the paradox: the dualis-tic way produces the opposite of what it intends. It makes of the infinite something finite—for it is bounded by the fixed finitude. In producing

5. It would be too large an issue here to go into what Hegel says about the *speculative Satz* in his *Phenomenology of Spirit*, §§59ff., and his chosen example "God is Being" (§62). Worthy of thought are his suggestions about the rhythmical fluidity of speculative thinking, as well as his view that the focus of such thought cannot be fixed to this or that univocal subject or predicate. Nevertheless, the sense of both being and God that informs both Aquinas's analogical understanding and my own metaxological metaphysics comes from a very different space of thought. A warning sign of this difference I find in the way Hegel thinks we should avoid the name "God" as a word that "is not immediately a Notion [*Begriff*], but rather the proper name, the fixed point of rest of the underlying Subject; whereas, on the other hand, e.g. 'Being' or 'the One,' 'Singularity,' 'the Subject,' etc. at once suggest concepts. Even if speculative truths are affirmed of this subject, their content lacks the immanent Notion, because it is pre-sented merely in the form of a passive subject, with the result that such truths readily assume the form of mere edification" (§66). God: "the fixed point of rest of the underlying Subject"? Rarely has the bud of speculative truth in "God" been made to wither so quickly, in this wintry *nunc dimittis* of "mere edification."

the contradiction of the finite infinite it actually upends the dualism of the two. Thus arises again the issue of the mediation of the two. What is at stake is the *transition* from finite to infinite, from infinite to finite. This will seem hopelessly equivocal to someone who rigidly insists on the principle of univocal identity. One can think of Hegel as proposing that we have to pass through this equivocity to think the passage from one to the other, and to mediate the togetherness of the two.

Transitions have to do with between spaces, with dynamic passage in a between. All this might seem very congenial to thinking the divine transcendence: we pass from finite to infinite; the infinite passes into finitude. The first passage seems to reflect our seeking, moving from the world to God; the second seems to grant God's revelation from Himself to the world. We have what looks like a two-way mediation in the between, giving form to the togetherness of transcendence and immanence. Many have been attracted to this picture, but there are troubling shadows in it. It may be helpful in response to dualistically fixed transcendence, but it raises its own problems, especially for those who hold to something like the irreducibility of divine transcendence, even granting a relation, be it revelation or not, of the divine to all being.

"Transcendence" is not a word favored by Hegel, and if he stood for anything, it was a philosophy of immanence. He does have a feel for the human being as marked by self-transcendence, as striving beyond itself, and many-sidedly so in being religious. Nevertheless, he offers a criticism and rejection of a God who is "beyond." This, for him, is a problem rather than any answer. His answer is a speculative philosophy of holistic immanence. Does this not only risk, but enact, a deformation of divine transcendence as other? Do we so attenuate transcendence as other to us that we produce a "God" that is not God—a counterfeit double of God? As understood in the great monotheistic traditions, God is not finite creation or nature, not humanity or history. This "not" signals a qualitative difference. This difference does not obviate the happening of communication *between* God and these created others, natural and human. The communication entails transition in a between, but it is not a matter of "overcoming" the difference in a dialectical-speculative whole.

In a more general respect, this divine transcendence has come to be seen as problematic in modernity, due to the rampant univocalizing and objectification of nature, and to developments of human self-transcendence, especially when it defines itself in terms of its own exclusive autonomy. A logic of *self-determination* insinuates itself into all our thinking, and divine transcendence becomes viewed in an equivocal light. There seems to be not only a tension but a certain antinomy between our autonomy and divine transcendence. How think autonomy and transcendence together, when something about each seems to strain against the other? The ideal of autonomy emphasizes our determining power. Transcendence must stress the importance of some otherness. The *trans* is a going beyond or across toward what is *not* now oneself; there is an otherness not reducible to our self-determining. This transcendence cannot coexist with an absolutized autonomy that is absolutely for itself. The antinomy is this: if autonomy is absolute, divine transcendence has to be relativized; if that transcendence is absolute, autonomy must be relativized. Western modernity generally has been drawn toward the first alternative. Hegel proposed a dialectical-speculative solution to this antinomy. Finally, there is no absolute transcendence as other. The absolute as self-determination relativizes all relations to transcendence as other, by including them within its own self-completing absoluteness. In this light, Hegel is the epitome of the privilege given to self-determination in modernity, representing its dialectical-speculative consummation. The absolute is self-determining being, identified with the free self-realization of reason itself.

I have more fully argued the case elsewhere,[6] but I think Hegel's speculative-dialectic of God is marked by a dialectical equivocity: a dialectic that claims to answer equivocities in the relation between God and humans, or religion and philosophy, only to hide *new equivocation* in its purported answer. We find not a simple evasion of divine transcendence, but rather a dialectical reconfiguration of its meaning such that its ultimacy is relativized. Hegel enacts a *project* in reconstructing God, in constructing his "God," a project deriving from religious sources, but diverging from them in a decisive reconfiguration of divine transcendence.

If one were to talk of analogy here, one might say that the *pros hen* gets transformed into entirely immanent self-determination. Divine transcendence is a mere *Jenseits* to be overcome by that immanent self-determination. There is equivocity in religious representations: they fix the divine "beyond" in an imaginative figure; and while the spirit is at work in the

6. See my *Hegel's God—A Counterfeit Double?*

representation, the representational form keeps the divine away in transcendence. Hegel wants to overcome that "away": the equivocity of the religious representation of the "beyond" is to be conceptually overcome in a new speculative-dialectical univocity. This is not a univocity that reduces differences to a simple sameness, but an inclusive unity that contains differences within itself, including the purported difference of divine transcendence, so representationally fixed by religious ways of thinking.

This philosophical knowing of God has its own equivocal sting to its tail. One recalls the manner in which it seems to reverse itself into the atheism so prevalent in intellectual and cultural circles themselves influenced by Hegel (I think obviously of people like Feuerbach and Marx). I think Hegel himself envisaged something more like a postreligious humanism, but in more extreme hands his absolute knowing seems to pass back into a virulent negative dialectic, and thence over into atheistic critique and deconstruction of all religion. It is not now that we do not know God, but there is no transcendent God to know. Absolute knowing generates its humanistic double of God and inverts into atheistic critique in search of pure immanence without God. Kant's overcautious quasi-theism or moral deism, having yielded to Hegel's pantheistic overconfidence, is replaced by a humanistic atheism, hubristically overconfident. The speculative access to God leads to the atheistic overcoming of God, and thus to no God. This post-Hegelian outcome, taken as a sign of an equivocity in Hegelian dialectic, is one reason why one might want to reconsider again the way of analogy as preserving the divine transcendence, while not closing the possible relation of immanence and transcendence.

PROTOCOLS, PLURIVOCITY, AND DIVINE MYSTERY

I would like to ask this question: Is it a limitation of Hegel that he does not have a plurivocal sense of being? Such an articulated sense, or lack of it, would surely affect the meaning of philosophy's own systematic side. We would have to ask if indeed philosophy must be directed to the one totality, or rather toward a plurality of *logoi* about *to on*. This question also affects how we think of the plurivocity between religion and philosophy, and indeed art. If there is no sense of the plurivocity of being, is there not the danger, as I think we find with Hegel, of a recurrence to a higher speculative univocity? The ghost of Spinoza comes back to haunt him thus.

The question of plurivocity is also connected with the question of the ways we do and might (legitimately) speak of God. There are many ways, obviously, but the matter here is especially important with regard to the *proper protocols* for approaching this issue of God. If I am not mistaken finesse for these protocols diminishes notably in the modern epoch, and I take this to be inseparable from the will to univocity we find in so many areas, and not only in mathematics, science, and technology. Think again how Spinozist univocity has its afterlife in much of German idealism, and indeed in contemporary philosophies of immanence (see, e.g., Deleuze). The plurivocally articulated space between immanence and transcendence is collapsed into the plane of immanence, beyond which nothing greater is to be thought, nothing greater can be thought.

How we are in the between, how we think in the between, is not given enough mindfulness. This is true also of the between marking the space of difference between us and the divine. The proper protocols concern how we articulate, or find articulated, this between-space, and how from it we venture thought about the divine as such. With the notion of analogy, Aquinas is in a healthier place on this issue of proper protocols. Analogy demands a finesse which is itself a kind of reverence for the proper protocols. To know that there is a proper question of protocols is already to display a certain philosophical-theological finesse. Is Thomistic analogy more finessed than speculative dialectic?

If we come back from this to Aquinas, in between the temerity of a Hegel or a Spinoza and the timidity of a Kant, we find that the sense of divine mystery looms large; the sense of the incomprehensibility of God is huge. *Deus semper major.* We know that God is not what God is.[7] We find the reticence of a wisdom of limits, of finitude, that would not claim to be on a par with the divine knowing. There is a kind of wiser not-knowing that does not lead to the atheistic reduction above mentioned. This not-knowing is not an epistemic defect simply at the beginning and to be overcome by the fuller development of knowing along the immanent continuum of its own self-becoming. One does not argue to this wise nescience simply at the end—it constitutes something of the ethos of another way of thought.[8] Within this ethos there are indeterminate igno-

---

7. *ST*, I, q. 3, a. 4, ad. 2: we cannot know the being of [*esse Dei*] but only that God is [*Deus esse*].

8. Josef Pieper's, *The Silence of St. Thomas: Three Essays*, 3rd ed., trans. John Murray and

rances and determinate cognitions, but the sense of astonishing mystery is in another dimension to such ignorances and cognitions, and companions all efforts at determinate knowing, and overcoming ignorance.

Hegel putatively argues through, along the continuum from ignorance to knowing, from indeterminacy to self-determination, and to the end of absolute knowing. Percolating into the whole development is the ethos of his thought as marked more by rationalistic recoil to mystery, if not secret hostility to it. There is a porosity of religion and philosophy in Aquinas which is different. Religion is the great companioning sister, the older sister of philosophy that cares for the primal reverences.[9] There is also a different dialectic, to be sure. The medieval dialectic is not the same as the modern idealistic one, though one finds a scholarly variation on dialogue. I mean we find in Aquinas a finely calibrated dialogue of authorities, Scripture, reasonable argument in question and answer. The *summa* is architectonic and systematic but differently so than the idealistic version of system. The latter mingles the Spinozist sense of the One with the Kantian call (amplified, adapted, and modified, to be sure) for completeness of the categories derived from one principle.

There is a finesse for divine mystery percolating through the *summa,* rising up from a religious ethos where, at best, the practices of prayer keep unclogged the soul's porosity to the divine. The sap of the mystery of God flows in the body of the work, though this is not always immediately evident on the surface, where sometimes a kind of forensic univocity marks Aquinas's way of proceeding. More rationalistic philosophers tend not to be attuned to that sap and turn Aquinas's thought into a Scholasticism closer to the prototype of modern rationalism. (I suppose the manualistic way of packaging Aquinas evidences this very much.) There is a kind of reversal of this in Hegel, in that religion is more a prelude to philosophy on the hierarchy of absoluteness. Philosophy finally is the more ultimate arbiter, not the inspired receiver to thought of what comes from beyond our thought.

Daniel O Connor (South Bend, Ind.: St. Augustine's Press, 1999) is marvelous in capturing something of this ethos and its reverence for mystery.

9. We know that philosophy was described as an *ancilla* and while this can sound like a form of servility, especially to modern ears used to the (now) louder language of autonomy, there can be a service that is not servile. Such service can witness a reverent attendance on the mysteries of the divine. One thinks of Mary as handmaid: to deem this a mere servility would be to be deaf to the "yes" in her "let it be done unto me."

The sense of mystery is not unconnected with analogy. The whole issue of figurative expression of the divine is, of course, central here, and there are many kinds of figures, metaphorical, symbolical, analogical, hyperbolic, to name four I consider especially important.[10] The matter of analogy does raise the issue of whether *for us* there is an ultimate transcendence of figures. Those captive to univocity tend to believe we can supplant figures with proper meanings. But can the proper meanings themselves be determined with full univocity? This is impossible with God. If there is an analogy with regard to *pros hen* equivocation, does this too supplant the figure with the proper? This too is doubtful even if there is a proper one, and that proper One is God. This is a proper One that exceeds all figures and always and ever is beyond our determination.[11] The will to make God absolutely univocal ends up with no God. In fixation of a one it fixes on an idol.

In some regard or other, all religious and theological thought is in figures. We are trying to figure out what the divine might be like. The likeness does not preclude an affirmation of what God is, but given the transfinite being of God, no finite figure can be entirely true to God. The question of the figure is also something with implication for the practise of philosophy. Philosophers are also figuring things out. I think especially of questions at the limit. Recall, for instance, the iconic story told in Plato's *Timaeus*: it is a tale of ultimate origins, and indeed purposes, but it is presented as a likely story. This is true to the nature of the issue in question, for here there is an entirely right truthfulness in travelling the iconic road of the likely.

Our need of figures in dealing with God also often reflects our figuration and reconfiguration of the ethos of being. The premodern configuring of that ethos was more porous to communications between faith and reason, theology and philosophy. It is worth noting that the iconic has a more universal ontological significance in Plato's sense of the cosmos: in the *Timaeus* (29b) it is said that it is entirely necessary that the cosmos be a certain icon *(pâsa anánke tónde ton kósmon eikóna tinos eînai)*—and this in tandem with the huge importance of geometry. The modern reconfiguration puts the stress on a more thoroughgoing (mathematical)

---

10. See *God and the Between* on this topic, especially chapter 6.
11. God: "existing above all things, the principle of all things, and removed from all things" *(supra omnia existens, quod est principium omnium, et remotum ab omnibus)* (*ST*, I, q. 2, a. 2; q. 13, a. 8, ad 2).

univocity, to the depreciation of the figurative to a questionable equivocity, perhaps permissible in aesthetic play but unworthy of precise truth. It also tends to close off the porosity of religion and philosophy by insisting that the latter is to become entirely autonomous and self-determining. And yet, religiously speaking, there is more truth in the finesse for figures. Such finesse entails a figuring of how the divine is figured or indeed figures itself forth. Different thinkers will be inclined to name the divine in terms of different figures said to be exemplary. I think for Aquinas, Christ; for Nietzsche, Dionysus. One thinks also of G. M. Hopkins's poem "As Kingfishers Catch Fire": "for Christ plays in ten thousand places, / Lovely in limbs, and lovely in eyes not his / To the Father through the features of men's faces."[12]

The Hegelian sublation of figures into concepts is not quite what is most important. One could claim that the figures can be more intimately true to the mystery of transcendence than rational concepts claiming in full self-determining power to pluck out the heart of the mystery. Figures, of course, can be turned into idols. But it is no less true that we can also manufacture idols in concepts. The idols do not have to be in wood or stone or paint. By comparison with how Hegel conceives the relation of *Vorstellung* and *Begriff,* the doctrine of analogy requires a different approach to the figures. In Hegel the mediation of figure and thought yields to philosophical comprehension and the representation is taken up into a more complete self-comprehension. This is not the way in Aquinas: both philosophy and theology come to limits where neither can make such self-determining claims. This is true at the beginning, it is true at the end. What we receive, what we are given, precludes any such a closure of self-determining thought. There is an open between, and the figure can often be more true to this openness. It gives articulation to the porosity of the between space—not only between philosophy and theology—but also between all thought in immanence and divinity. Divinity is both transcendent and immanent, gleaned in the figure through a more reverent finesse, closer to the receiving porosity of prayer than to any active self-determination of rationalization.

Finesse for mystery is not at all devoid of deep and testing perplexi-

12. Gerard Manley Hopkins, *Gerard Manley Hopkins: The Major Works,* ed. Catherine Philips (Oxford: Oxford University Press, 2002), 129.

ties. In analogy we find a relation of sameness and difference. In analogies of proportion, it is a relation of relations: a is to b, as c is to d. If we think of analogy with regard to *pros hen* equivocation, where do we find the proper One? If we are concerned with a common finite term, this will be something determinate, and hence available for more definite articulation. But if it is God, this One reserves its mystery, even as it shows it, so there is no determinate term we can fix on absolutely. The way of this "proportion" exceeds univocal determination and dialectical self-determination. It is a sign of the disproportionate. How then articulate this? Is it merely indeterminate, then, in an equivocal way? This must always be a perplexity about any naming of God, whether figurative or (quasi-)conceptual. Hegel's response is to insist that indeterminacy gives way to determination, and finally to self-determining thought. But this is untrue to the God who astonishes and perplexes.

I would say we are not to think of the divine as less than determination but as in excess of all determination and self-determination: divine mystery is in the (hyperbolic) dimension of the overdeterminate. If God is the "missing" One, we are missing, for God is missing because the least missing, God being everywhere and nowhere. True figures figure forth what is not there and yet intimately there in all that is there. No determinate univocity, no indeterminate equivocity, no self-determining dialectic would be possible if each was not possibilized by this self-reserving over-determinacy that yet communicates its giving of what is. From it comes the enabling power of all articulations, though it is not to be identified with determinate and self-determination articulation. Sometimes we seem to look on what looks like an empty space: there seems to be nothing there. But it is there as the enabling and reserved companioning power that endows all that is there with its being there at all. It enables, it is not an enabled. There is nothing it wants from the enabled, for it gives enabled being for the good of itself. The holy of holies is not there where we place or impose the fixed figure. At the end of thought Aquinas might invoke a figure of lowness to speak of his thought's relation to the highest: *videtur mihi ut palea*.

THE "IS" AND THE "AS"

It might be illuminating here to consider the nature of the "like as" we find in analogy. There is no simple univocal "is" when we say analogously (as Plato does) that the Sun is like as the Good: as the Sun is to the visible, the Good is to the invisible. Related to this Aquinas speaks of an *agens analogicum,* and I will return to this. Here I look at the analogical "as" which so qualifies the "is" as to obviate the reduction of differences to a univocal identity. But what of the "is"? As a philosopher of being, Aquinas is committed to the ultimacy of the "is"—whether in the domain of finite creation, or with regard to God as *ipsum esse per se subsistens,*[13] and beyond all finite determination.

Consider here how we find in Kant a kind of "as" but it is in the form of an "as if." Kantian thinking is often informed by dualistic difference but he does say that we have to think *as if* God existed. The grounds of this "as if" are in what is in a qualified sense, namely, our moral being. Nevertheless, a kind of equivocation hovers over the Kantian "as if." Kant's "as if" is finally a *projected* transcendence. God is as a regulative ideal whom we must postulate, but whom we cannot quite affirm to be, though we must think of as being, in order to render certain immanent circumstances intelligible, crucially our moral nature. Much more could be said about this, but Kant seems to keep too close to a certain cautious equivocal approach. Now it is "yes," now "no"; now we must dare to know, now we can know nothing; if we dare to know, we know only appearances, nothing of the thing itself; now we are restrained within limits, now it seems we go beyond them, even in plotting them.

Hegel jumps on what we can take to be equivocity in Kant's postulating "as if," claiming we cannot make it intelligible outside of some true "is." We cannot deny the thing in itself intelligibly without in some other sense affirming it to be. A projected ideal is no help if it is not more than regulative; in some sense, it must be constitutive. Even to be regulative, it must be constitutive, in some sense. Hegel responds by dialectically retracting the projected "beyond" back into immanence. He completes the "subreption" into transcendence by reversing it, and bringing the "beyond" back to its true source, namely, immanence.

13. See *ST,* I, qq. 3ff.

There is a kind of analogical thinking in the Kantian "as if": we must think the world on the likeness of it being in the hands of the just God to make sense of our moral experience. If Kant could have made autonomous morality absolutely secure through itself, he would have gotten rid of God as risking heteronomy. It is to his credit that he (reluctantly) did not. Many of his successors thought it a blot on his record. Thereby they reveal that they were not, like Kant, so much haunted by the heteronomous God as wanting to exorcise the spirit of that God entirely —in a new project, not the postulated projection of God, but the human project of entirely immanent self-determination, in effect projecting *itself* as God.

In Aquinas, there is a different thinking of the irreducible transcendence of God. There is an "is" in analogical likeness that does not mean the same thing as Kant's "as if" or Hegel's "is." It is not an "as if" as a regulative ideal that we postulate or project into the "beyond." There is an affirmation of the "is" but the meaning of the "is" differs between the created and the creator. The "is" is not being as the most indigent of categories. In a sense, there is something indeterminate about it, but not because it passes into nothing, but because it is overdeterminate, even in finitude itself: more than every determination, though every determinate being participates in the gift of being. There is something more to God, as more even than the overdeterminacy of given being in the finite creation. This sense of exceeding difference means that Aquinas is at home with an "as" that is not a univocal or speculative "is," nor yet an equivocal "as if." Just as his "is" is not the Hegelian "is," so his "as" is not the Kantian "as if."

We might say there is an overconfidence in human reason in the Hegelian "is," there is an overcautiousness in the Kantian "as if." Aquinas is somewhere between the overconfidence of the first, and the underconfidence of the second. Once again, his meditations take place somewhere between metaphysical temerity and timidity. He does have confidence in reason but as qualified by what one might call the aesthetics of our finitude. We are embodied beings, hence our mindfulness is rooted in the senses and the sensuous. Analogical thinking reflects this aesthetic figure/figuration of the human being. The analogy of being reflects the aesthetics of finitude; but these are aesthetics which show the art of the divine in giving creation to be. The world is not a work of art creating itself, a work of art giving birth to itself, to cite Nietzsche. There is a divine art but its working is more than the work wrought, though without the working the world would be nothing.

Think of how the argument from design, considered as an argument from analogy, is touched with equivocity. The likeness can work in different ways, and cannot get away from unlikeness, hence allowing an openness in the inference. If the pot seems bad, perhaps the potter is an apprentice or incompetent, as Hume suggests. But one might look less negatively on the openness in the play between likeness and unlikeness. Granting something unavoidably equivocal about that openness, we may be called on to muster a metaphysical finesse to read the signs of the divine communicated in that openness. The openness is itself a between space in which immanence and transcendence can never be reduced to one, though it may be diversely intermediated. The plurivocity of signs is here significant. Thus the likeness of the watch of Paley's version of the argument draws very much on *mechanism* as a sign of the machine maker. There are richer signs. One might think of design as mathematical (beloved of more "Platonically" oriented thinkers), taken as an analogical sign; one might, as more pantheistic thinkers do, look on the *organism* (in its purposive, nonpurposed design) as a sign of the immanent divinity; or we might consider the *human being* as an analogical sign whose freedom and striving to be good (singularly and in common) are hyperbolic signs in finitude of what cannot be finitized—signs that as self-transcending are promising pointers to more ultimate transcendence.[14]

Granted that there are difficulties with the analogical "as." Retaining a proximity to equivocity that cannot be entirely dispelled, the question is to what extent this proximity is an enabling or a disabling one. It is not an easy place to be between immanence and transcendence. I take Aquinas as a thinker willing to live with that difficult between, in fidelity to the God beyond the finite creation, the immanent whole. It seems easier to live with a univocal one than to live in an equivocal doubleness, and live between one and the other. There are ways of being at ease which are not the ways of being true.

Once again it is not that there is no One, but there is a singular transcendence to God as the One, which indeed gives the between to be as other to itself. We can say that this singular transcendence of the divine would put Aquinas at odds with the Spinozist immanence that was to influence many after him, Hegel included. This is, in some ways, evident

14. These are some of the themes I deal with in *God and the Between* in connection with God and the hyperboles of being.

already in Aquinas's diffidence about the ontological argument, reformulated by Spinoza and defended again by Hegel after Kant's critique. The argument might be true for God who has a true knowledge of God and for whom there is no disjunction of being and thought. With human beings this is not so. Disjunction counts. Hence we have to work mediately in and through the world of immanence to its "beyond." This again is to think in a sometimes tensed between space. There is a difference of a true monotheism and any monism. Paradoxically, true monotheism, in affirming the singularity of God, is an affirmation of difference, not its reduction to unity. And the difference is not a fall from the One but a creation of divine generosity invested with its own power to be. The endowed creation is originated with the promise of its own original self-becoming. God does not have to become in order to be Godself. The logic of self-becoming is not appropriate to God, though this is not to deny a dynamic activity to God. This *actus essendi* is beyond coming to be, endowing finite coming to be and becoming.

Interestingly, here Platonic dualism can be looked at more sympathetically if we think of it as trying to keep open the space of this other transcendence. One could credit the equivocal Kant with something similar. Aquinas might have been drawn to Aristotle and the immanent idea. Hegel very definitely was. And yet the Aristotelianism of Aquinas does not lead to the holistic immanence of Hegel. It is transformed into a vision of creation as itself an ordered totality, with hierarchical relativity holding a multiplicity of beings and processes together in the universal impermanence, indeed in endowed creation as a universal togetherness upheld by the continuing creation of God. But the network of relativities that constitute the given creation points beyond itself as a likeness, points to an other original, communicated in but not exhausted by the analogical likeness.

Analogical indirection is not without another difficulty, almost the opposite of the one mentioned above, namely, its proximity to equivocity. As I have put it elsewhere, this is connected with the danger that a quasi-mathematical form will be preponderant.[15] Analogy with regard to *pros hen* equivocation is recurrently tempted with the consolation of a more fixed univocity as a stable reference point. After all, analogy has its root in mathematical proportion, and in that respect one is also inclined to a kind of univocity. The temptation is then that the difference of the cre-

15. See *Being and the Between*, 215–16.

ated between and ultimate transcendence is mapped as a ratio on a quasi-univocal grid of relations. Such a grid easily freezes into a two-tiered system of otherwise unrelated terms, and hence risks the dualistic opposition between "here" and "beyond," between immanence and transcendence as other, an opposition that it is the great power of analogy to circumvent. The transcending that is testament to the togetherness of the terms is a dynamic connecting, not a static connection.

This dynamic is the passing of one toward and into an other, as well as the receiving of the communication of the other that passes toward and into one. This dynamic expresses our wayfaring to transcendence; in a deep sense, it is our wayfare. We must follow its signs, for they are not just our signs, since the way is shown in the faring. The togetherness of the divine and the human, the connecting, is not an analogical structure, but an analogical likening, where likening carries this faring between the divine and the human, a faring both receptive and energetic. This is not a static likeness but a creative likening. For instance, when I liken myself to you, my imitation is not at all "passive," even when I am nothing but faithful to the original I am imitating. It is receptive in an originative fidelity to the original. Porosity becomes creative love in this fidelity.

METAXOLOGY, ANALOGY, AND HYPERBOLIC TRANSCENDENCE

Our self-surpassing calls on us to be related to the *disproportionate* in what is proportioned to us. There is a sense here in which the movements governing the thought of Aquinas and Hegel are the reverse of each other. Hegel's speculative dialectic would bring all transcendence home to immanence, and if there is a vertical movement, it is, so to say, downward. Aquinas's analogical thinking would open immanence to transcendence, bring it home to the God above all things, and if there is a vertical movement, it is thus upward. A sense for divine disproportion is more at home with the latter, I would say.

I would speak of the disproportion of God in terms of hyperbolic transcendence.[16] When Aquinas says that God is beyond every genus,[17] there is a kind of nescience with respect to the proper One, and the question

---

16. See *God and the Between* for the relation of God and what I call the hyperboles of being.
17. *Deus non est in aliquo genere. Deus non est in genere substantiae.* See *ST,* 1a, 3, 5.

arises, as we saw: If the One removes itself into unsurpassable transcendence are we left with nothing? If the dissimilitude is so excessive, then the side of unlikeness is so disproportionate to all likeness that we seem not to escape entirely an equivocal result. Can we live with this equivocity, and how can we? I would like here to invoke how Aquinas, as many commentators have pointed out, makes use of the threefold way, the *triplex via* of causality, remotion (negation), and eminence.[18] I would like to comment on all three but it is especially the third, the *via eminentiae,* that relates to hyperbolic transcendence and its excess to us.

With respect to the notion of *causality:* After Hume and Kant the legitimacy of using causality to argue for God has been questioned. Clearly this modern sense of cause is more restricted and restrictive than in Aquinas. Generally, one might say that a cause determines a be-cause—a cause of being, a cause of being this or that, or being a kind of this or that, a cause of being what the kind is, or what this or that is. But a be-cause refers also to the *cause of the "to be."* This be-cause is presupposed by every other be-causing, because were it not, they would not be anything, and there would be no be-cause at all. Be-cause refers us to the ultimate original cause of the "to be." Clearly this line of argumentation is congenial to Aquinas's way of thinking.

Nevertheless, it is true that "cause" has come to assume a more equivocal face in modernity, even in the very process in which we have tried to make cause entirely univocal. I mean first the withdrawal from the plurivocity of the four causes in Aristotle's way of thinking, and the way efficient causality has too often been tied to something closer to mechanical efficiency and determination. This sense of cause, if predominant, does not let us appreciate the sense of be-cause as the cause of the "to be." If we think of Aquinas in its terms we will see his use of causality in terms of intramundane determination, and God will be the highest being among all other finite beings. This is clearly a univocalizing reduction of divine difference.

There is also Kant's claim that cause is to be confined to determinate finitude, not to be used beyond immanent experience. Whether Kant is right or consistent is not now the issue. Given this contraction of cause,

---

18. Derived from Dionysius's *De Divinis Nominibus.* See Fran O'Rourke's fine book, *Pseudo-Dionysius and the Metaphysics of Aquinas* (South Bend, Ind.: University of Notre Dame Press, 2005), chapter 2, especially 31–41.

either to effective determination, or a priori transcendental form (and this too does not have the ontological richness of the be-cause in the sense I just explained), I think we perhaps should speak of origin and origination, and refuse the confinement of this to a determinate origin, since what is at issue is really the ultimate origin of the determinate. I will return to this in regard to what Aquinas calls the analogical cause. For at issue with God is not a determinate becoming, not a self-determining self-becoming, but a more *original coming to be* that gives determinate and self-determining being. This is be-cause as giving cause to be. This is a point relevant to the transformation of the first mover argument from a physical to a metaphysical plane.[19] The ultimate ontological movement is not finite motion within the infinite succession of time, but a more original bringing to be. This is not a moving of what already is in being. It is a be-cause, a cause of the "to be," a causing to be of the "to be." The primal motion of origination would be creation.

With regard to *remotion*: this has to do with a different motion, namely, that of the *via negativa* where we remove ourselves from finitude, or remove the finite predicates or realities, none of which can be identified with the divine. Negation is central to Hegel's dialectical thinking and bound up with determination and self-determination. But the *via negativa* is not just determination through negation. It is a purgatory of finitude that opens a space of emptying out in which what is more than finitude can be approached. It is a poverty of thought but the poverty is a ready indigence to receive what is not to be described in the language of negativity. This sense of the "more" means that the *via negativa* is always balanced by the *via eminentiae*. I would say that the *via negativa* makes the dissimilitude inherent in analogy into a purgation of our fixation on finite determination, but in the endowed poverty of dissimilitude it opens analogy to the hyperbolic: the more, the *huper*, the above—beyond the determinate and self-determining.

This opening to the hyperbolic is made way for by the *via eminentiae*. One might say that the hyperbolic frees the *via negativa* from reduction to, or bewitchment by, the logic of determinate negation. There is a sense of the nothing in excess of determinate negation, just as there is a

---

19. On this subject, see John Wippel, *The Metaphysical Thought of Thomas Aquinas* (Washington, D.C.: The Catholic University of America Press, 2000), 457; and Rudi te Velde, *Aquinas on God*, 51ff.

sense of the indeterminate in excess of the indefinite. The hyperbole offers a *via eminentiae*, in a metaxologically reformulated sense, as a way of excess that *throws beyond* finitude. But the *via* does not simply proceed from lack to perfection, but from perfection and plenitude, indeed from perfection in the between to pluperfection in transcendence. The divine pluperfection is always already more, always is and will be more, eternally more. The hyperbolic way will pile up perfection on perfection, knowing it will always not be enough to do justice to divine transcendence. This *via eminentiae* would be the hyperbole of praise. It is a singing rejoinder to the ambiguities of the *via negativa* which might otherwise fall into an empty nothing, or an idolatrous totality.

This might itself seem too hyperbolic, but if so, there is august precedent for it, precedent laced with its own ironical humor. In Plato's *Republic* we find a striking togetherness of the analogy (of origination) and the hyperbolic. Socrates, as we know, does not offer an account of the nature of the good in itself. He suggests that his surmise of the good in itself is above and beyond the impetus on which his flight takes wing. Rather we are presented with the indirection of the offspring of the good *(ekgonos te tou agathou)*, one which is most nearly made in the likeness of the good (506e). It is interesting that he refers also to the story of the father *(patēr)*. However, he is reserved: this is a story that we must postpone to another occasion (506e). Again the notion of analogy is brought in. The offspring of the good stands in analogy *(analogon;* 508c) with the good itself. In thus invoking analogy, it is also to be noted that the nonidentity in likeness is stressed (508a–b, 509a). Of course, the most famous expression concerning the excess of this difference of the good is to be found in its enigmatic being "beyond being," the *epekeina tēs ousias* (509b9). Here is where eros and the hyperbolic make their appearance together. After Socrates has said this, Glaucon responds, but the response is the bemused exclamation (509c1–2): "By Apollo, a daimonic hyperbole [*daimonias huperbolēs*]!" What I see here is reference to the fact that eros is a daimon, a spirit between *(metaxu)* mortals and divinity. Its great temptation is to allow itself to be warped into an *eros turannos*. Nevertheless, eros as daimonic reveals an energy of self-surpassing in the soul that elevates the soul to the highest reality. It is the heights of the divine that are at stake. But our counterfeit pretension to be the highest must be deflated. In Glaucon's response we have something of this deflation, but it is one that speaks truly (perhaps unknowingly) of what is at play in the highest eros: a daimonic hyperbole. Overall we can see Plato as leading upward and into the *metaxu* between mortals and divinities. There he ventures boldly an iconic saying about the ultimate. This iconic saying relativizes the ultimacy of our saying but does not relativize the ultimate.

Returning to the theme of divine disproportion: The likeness of the *sunousia* ("with being," "being with") of God and creation makes no sense apart from the unlikeness of the *huperousia* ("above being," "being above," even "beyond being") of the God beyond the finite whole. The hyperbole of *huperousia* names the divine measure beyond all finite measure. The hyperbolic measure beyond our measure instead measures us. We are not going from perfection here to ultimacy there; but there is perfection here, because there is ultimacy there. Perfection here is an image of an ultimacy there whose pluperfection always exceeds immanence. There is a reversal into an asymmetry; finite perfection is a created image of ultimacy. In the hyperbolic way of the *via eminentiae* hubris becomes humility in the face of the superior. The latter it really a *being thrown beyond itself,* since the movement into the *huper* could not be effected by our self-determination. The *huper* exceeds self-determination: even if we are thrown back on ourselves, it is such that at the same time we are differently thrown beyond ourselves. Humility before divine transcendence becomes a movement of exaltation into the superior.

Given the humors of the hyperbolic, perhaps it is wise to attend to movements within the same family of metaphysical transcending, evidenced in the fact that Aquinas speaks of an analogical cause or agent *(agens analogicum).* This is a deeply suggestive idea, and at least helps some way to thinking the togetherness of transcendence and immanence. I take analogical cause in a more ontological sense. It is not that God is a cause on analogy with some finite cause. Something about the be-causing of God is analogical, issuing in analogical likeness and unlikeness. The creation of the different is here named, but with a difference that is not a dualistic opposition, but in some community between itself and the endowing origin.

If we contrast this with a *univocal cause,* this latter would give rise to an effect the same as itself—it would be the same again. Applied to God it would be a kind of cloning: the be-cause causes the cause to be—*causa sui.* (It is not incidental that *causa sui* is so important for Spinoza, for

Hegel.) God in creating would give rise to God again, and creation would be God's self-creation. Hegel's God is not far off such a self-cloning divinity. Cloning is autism writ large: the auto autographing itself, signer, signature, and sign, just one: signing signing signing. If creation were such, it would be metaphysical cloning as autism writ large, written not into the cosmos but written as the cosmos. Analogical causation is entirely other, since it creates the other and for the other, and this creating is not a self-othering, but through unlikeness, it gives the release of the created other into its own being for itself, a being which, as upheld in the network of relativities, is yet also in relation to the ultimate source of all between-relations, namely, God.

By contrast with analogical causation, *equivocal causation* would be the production of the different as effect which had *no relation* to the effecting cause. In effect, the effect would be no effect. Such sheerly equivocal causation seems unintelligible, since causation as an enacted be-causing is a relation in which an outcome arises, an effect. An equivocal cause would be no be-cause, since instead of bringing to be out of nothing, or bringing to be out of something, it would connect nothing with nothing, that is, not bring to be and not connect. Since nothing would connect, there would be nothing. Strangely enough, the ultimate outcome of such equivocal causation would not be the world of flux but a paradoxical reversion to absolute univocity, namely, a frozen motionless sameness indistinguishable from nothing.

Analogical causation would be the effecting of what is both same and other. How balance the same and other, if there is an otherness, transcendence to the origin as God? "Creation" is a name for this analogical causation, perhaps better called "origination," since causation in modern philosophy, as I said, has been so univocalized as to be robbed of such resonances. Creation is a giving to be, a bringing to be in which what is brought to be is other to the giving source. And yet as related to the giving source, it shows some likeness, some sameness to it, insofar as it is at all. The analogy is the being of the given in its being like the giving of the being of the source. The likeness has something to do with the "why" of the creating, namely, to communicate the good of "to be." Because? What is the be-cause of bringing to be? Nothing more than the good of the be-cause, nothing more than that it is good to be. This good of the "to be" is what both the origin and the created share, because the origin shares it by giving. The created is given a share in, participates in, this ultimate good of the "to be."

The God of Aquinas, in the language I use, is not an erotic absolute (as Hegel's is) but an agapeic origin, in giving being to be out of the surplus plenitude of self-exceeding generosity. Nevertheless, one might suggest that there is a sense of erotics that participates in the agapeic to the extent that a surplus generosity is at work, something not always evident when we think of eros in terms of a lacking seeking its fulfillment. There is a fullness already real that gives from its surplus, capable of creatively endowing beings other than itself. This is close to the meaning of divine creativity.

It is interesting to see something of this *incognito* generosity, as imaged in finite becoming, in the spread in time of finite generations. I am thinking of how *generational likeness* between ancestors and descendents is neither univocal nor equivocal. A familial resemblance is analogical. Recall how sometimes we search the faces of children to see resemblances to their parents. There is no univocal geometry that will guarantee an identification of the relation of the present to the past generations. One needs a kind of finesse to see the subtle play of likeness and unlikeness, and sometimes, as of a sudden, to see the likeness in the unlikeness. Sometimes too when, say, we peruse photos of long gone generations, we are startled to see appear there before us, in the image of the dead, the face of someone living, whom we now see before us. Between the generations there is an enigmatic heritage of likeness and unlikeness. Each new generation is absolutely new in one sense, and in another sense, is already old, since its present identity carries the inheritances of relations, of generations, most of them completely unknown to the now living. It is here hard to fix a *pros hen,* and yet there is something at work in the commonality of the succeeding generations that binds them together. We find a variable mingling of like and unlike, across many generations, but the likeness and unlikeness are defined by reference to common, though often hidden or unknown, origins. One might say that family likenesses are sourced in the transcending energy of erotic generation, but they are embodied relations that transcend generations, relations also not just erotically defined. The energy of generation becomes incarnated in resemblances between originators and offspring, some more expected, some more surprising. Such analogical likeness of origination is defined by *the communication of a community with all its promise.* The generational power in the universal impermanence is both erotic and beyond eros, holding generations together in their resembling differences, through networks of family relations that extend the power of being over time.

Aquinas does not put his points in these terms, to be sure. And yet the ultimate enigma of the absolute analogous cause does put us in mind of the ultimate common source that remains reserved and yet is there intimately at work in the passing of being from one generation to the next, being immanent in all such passing and yet always more than what is in passage. Consider how we call God "Father." Interesting is that when Aquinas speaks of the world to come he calls it *patria,* the land of the Father.[20] This need entail no rancor against time, but rather the acknowledgment of a bond of love between what has passed, what is passing and what is to come. Familial relations transcend the divide between time and eternity. Of course, when we call God "Father" the analogy of origination is not just a matter of biological engendering; nevertheless, a kind of generational likening is suggested, as well as this promise of enduring community. Ultimately that community is one of agapeic generosity. If one could venture something about divine erotics here, these are more to the fore when God's love for humans is less likened to a family as to a lover and beloved, or bridegroom and bride, as in the Song of Songs. The love broadcast by familial likening shows a communal extensiveness, while erotic likening can stress the intimately, passionately intense. But it is *love* that is broadcast in the network of generational relations: the love of the "to be" as good.

Given to be be-cause of (agapeic) love of the "to be" as good—this is a view hard to grasp for many influenced by the modern divorce of being and good. For many, this elemental sense of ontological value will be a blank, given the contraction of be-cause into valueless efficiency, given that being then has no value until we impose value on it. It is not surprising in this latter world that we usurp God's creativity by making the world in our image and likeness. We remake it as analogous to ourselves. We are then the analogous cause. We are the *pros hen.* We are recalled to the equivocation of Hegel's dialectic I mentioned above (at the end of the third section). We here become the hyperbolic in being, but it is in the

---

20. See, for instance, *ST,* 1a2ae, q. 69, a. 2, where Aquinas is discussing the beatitudes.

mode of hubris. We are full of ourselves, too full of ourselves, but it is not the surplus plenitude of generosity, but the usurped superiority of a will to power that will have nothing higher above itself. We then make ourselves into the One, but it is tyrannical eros that rules all, both others and ourselves. Being number one thus is the collapse of the difference of analogy into a univocity of human will to power, and with this collapse we show ourselves to be the counterfeit double of God. The sense of the hyperbolic in Aquinas as properly of God and God alone, obviously, is at the opposite extreme to this warping of analogy into counterfeit identity. An analogical sense for the hyperbolic brings a catharsis to hubris, and a promising humility to human beings in the between. Instead of the counterfeit heights in immanence of absolute knowing, analogy is made porous to the superior, in a poverty of thought that knows it is as straw.

10 ∽ Ways of Wondering

Beyond the Barbarism of Reflection

Near to the beginnings of modernity Giambattista Vico famously speaks of what he calls the barbarism of reflection *(barbarie della riflessione)*. While the connection with wonder is not explicitly made by him, this barbarism is intimately related to the loss of wonder that recurrently befalls humanity. The barbarism of reflection comes at the end of a cycle of unfolding: human beings originate as humans from more feral conditions when struck by the lightning bolt of Jove, develop their powers from the barbarism of the senses, arriving eventually at what seems like the consummate self-conscious, reflective form of life. But this consummation brings an unanticipated end in the form of the barbarism of reflection. I connect this barbarism with a fall from wonder, and the malformation of its endowing gift. The barbarism of reflection arises when *our very powers of knowing* have seemingly perfected themselves, but in so doing they have managed to clog the deeper ontological and epistemic springs out of which original wonder flows. The light coming at this end reverts to a darkness, deeper than the darkness at the beginning, for this darkness thinks that now at last it is enlightened.

The barbarism of reflection might be called a counterfeit double of true enlightenment, and like all counterfeits offers itself or takes itself to be the true original. Why is it this counterfeit double? Because it has malformed the endowment of original wonder, while claiming for itself the crown of wonder's true fulfillment. Vico suggests that the barbarism of reflection is a condition casting its light, or shadow, over an entire epoch. If that epoch is ours, naturally we must ask if our enlightenment is under its shadow. This barbarism entails a condition of knowing that knows nothing of the truly worthy, for it is an enlightenment devoid of religious reverence and wisdom.

The striking passage in the *New Science* where Vico famously describes this barbarism is powerful in its eloquence, and worth quoting at length:

> But if the peoples are rotting in that ultimate civil disease . . . providence for their extreme ill has its extreme remedy at hand. For such peoples, like so many beasts, have fallen into the custom of each man thinking only of his own private interests and have reached the extreme of delicacy, or better of pride, in which like wild animals they bristle and lash out at the slightest displeasure. Thus no matter how great the throng and press of their bodies, they live like wild beasts in a deep solitude of spirit and will, scarcely any two being able to agree since each follows his own pleasure or caprice. By reason of all this, providence decrees that, through obstinate factions and desperate civil wars, they shall turn their cities into forests and the forests into dens and lairs of men. In this way, through long centuries of barbarism, rust will consume the misbegotten subtleties of malicious wits that have turned them into beasts made more inhuman by the barbarism of reflection than the first men had been made by the barbarism of sense. For the latter displayed a generous savagery, against which one could defend oneself or take flight or be on one's guard; but the former, with a base savagery, under soft words and embraces, plots against the life and fortunes of friends and intimates. Hence peoples who have reached this point of premeditated malice, when they receive this last remedy of providence and are thereby stunned and brutalized, are sensible no longer of comforts, delicacies, pleasures, and pomp, but only of the sheer necessities of life. And the few survivors in the midst of an abundance of the things necessary for life naturally become sociable and, returning to the primitive simplicity of the first world of peoples, are again religious, truthful, and faithful. Thus providence brings back among them the piety, faith, and truth which are the natural foundations of justice as well as the graces and beauties of the eternal order of God.[1]

This passage strikes one as saying something very true, in a number of senses: true to the way human knowing sometimes develops; true to the counterfeits of wisdom that some forms of knowing create; true to the corruption of the soul that follows when its secret reserves of wonder are ex-

---

1. *The New Science of Giambattista Vico*, abridged translation of the third edition (1744), by Thomas Goddard Bergin and Max Harold Fisch (Ithaca, N.Y.: Cornell University Press, 1970), 381–82 (§1106).

hausted; true to a fulfillment that is really a dissolution of this wonder. I take Vico's remarks as emblematic of the loss of wonder that often shadows the perfection of the project of determinate cognition. I am thinking of the instrumentalizing approach to being such as we find in the project of science-technology, or the administrative-bureaucratic mind that holds it can regulate human affairs with abstract universals but that lacks the finesse of concrete practical wisdom. The collusion of scientistic and aesthetic will to power drives persons into themselves as monadic caves, making them over as machines of self-serving desire. The outcome is loss of wonder, loss of piety, and the clogging of the porosity that places us beyond our selves in ethical community with our fellows and in reverence before the divine.

Worth noting is that the barbarism of reflection is the outcome of a certain kind of *knowing*. Vico says: "Men first feel necessity, then look for utility, next attend to comfort, still later amuse themselves with pleasure, then grow dissolute in luxury, and finally go mad and waste their substance."[2] This axiom comes back to haunt us as the project of science-technology gains more and more power and seeks more and more to perfect itself. The madness to which Vico refers, the substance we waste, relates to our being as wondering creatures, the meaning of how we live our wonder. I will say that it is not primarily wonder that drives on to the barbarism but rather a hyperbolic curiosity, subserved by and serving a sometimes secret, sometimes open, will to power. If there is wonder in the beginning, what comes with such hyperbolic curiosity after is not more wonder but the dispelling of wonder. And with this dispelling, the subjection of what is other to our measure, not our subjection to the wonder that exceeds our measure.

There is a wonder before the barbarism of reflection, there is barbarism in the middle when wonder is reconfigured as voracious curiosity that spends itself in ceaseless accumulation of determinate cognition. Is there the hope of wonder renewed after the barbarism of reflection runs its course? So long as life continues, one has to say yes to wonder. This is not a matter of reviving our capacity for wonder. In a way, we do not have a capacity for wonder; rather we are capacitated by wonder—and capacitated through it to wise mindfulness. Since this capacitation is not determined through ourselves alone, *we alone* cannot revive it. Wondering is

2. *New Science*, axiom 66.

not a power over which we exercise self-determination; it witnesses to a given porosity of being that endows us with the promise of mindfulness. If there is to be a revival of the capacity, it is in coming home again to this porosity—and its capacitating of our powers. Ingredient in this home-coming is our capacity to know incapacitation.

Bear in mind that wonder is not a univocal concept. It is not first a concept at all, but a happening, and as a happening it is plurivocal. For reasons that will become clear, it is important to distinguish three differ-ent modalities: astonishment, perplexity, and curiosity. These are internal-ly related to each other, but they reveal a different stress in the unfolding of our wondering. If we do not properly understand these different stress-es, we can mistakenly think all wonder is subsumable into the curiosity that makes of all being an object of determinate cognition. This subsump-tion might consume curiosity, but it is the death of wonder. This death seeds the arising of the barbarism of reflection.

WONDER AS ASTONISHMENT

Turning to the first modality, it is important to stress the primal charac-ter of wonder as astonishment. There is a wonder preceding reflection that takes the form of a certain ontological astonishment. Wonder before the being there of being and beings is precipitated in this astonishment. In a certain sense, all human mindfulness is seeded in this astonishment. This has to do not with a process of becoming this or that but with porosity to the "that it is at all" of being. That being is, that beings have come to be at all, this is prior to their becoming this or that, prior to their self-becoming.

A caution: the word "wonder" strikes one today as a bit too subjectiv-ized: it is seen as the "gosh" feeling, the "wow" experience to which we give vent before the surprising and the strange. I do not deny the gosh and wow of wonder but there is an ontological bite to original wonder, perhaps captured better in English with the word *astonishment*. Consider some ordinary ways of thinking about wonder: what precipitates aston-ishment, often implying admiration, we call a wonder, a marvel, a prod-igy, something marvellous. The wonder may be even seen as a miracle, something extraordinary or even supernatural. Likewise, a wonder can be taken as a communication or a sign, such as an omen or portent. Those who perform wonders are wonderworkers, *thaumaturges*. We do not have to be with Alice in Wonderland to be struck into wonder. If there is something ordinary about wonder as astonishment, there is also in the ordinary something communicating the extraordinary.

We say, for instance "no wonder" and thus we acknowledge that what happened was no surprise, was as one would have expected. If "no wonder" is a sign of continuity, wonder marks the happening of a discontinuity. Thus too if the wonder can be a sign communicating discontinuity, the sign can also strike one dumb—one is dumbfounded, for something spectacular and stupefying is intimated about the wonder. In astonishment there is *the stress of the emphatic:* the unexpected is not anticipated to happen and yet it happens. When we say "The wonder of it is . . . " and refer to a happening, we are suggesting something beyond expectation: the surprising has communicated the emphatic.

Being struck by astonishment has something of the blow of unpremeditated otherness in it. Extreme astonishment can seem even to deprive one of sensation. The blow of otherness stuns us, seems to stupefy us, as if inducing a kind of blackout. Many of the characteristics of astonishment—bewilderment, shock, consternation, deprivation of self-possession, benumbing, being "stricken" by amazement—astound one even unto a kind of ontological stupor. The happening is idiotic, with a singularity prior to all reflective thinking and deliberate action.

This idiocy of astonishment sounds negative, not our negation but our being negated. And yet it is more the affirmative "too-muchness" of the happening that is outlined in the event of astonishment. There is an intrusion of ontological frailty in the unpremeditated event of coming to be: it might not have come to be, it might not have been at all. And yet it is—surprising eventuation that hovers before us, floating above its own possible not being. It is hard for us to think on this boundary between being at all and possibly not being. Our porosity to the eventuation has the double character of itself happening as an opening, and being also a kind of "no-thing." This is not thinking as negativity but rather enables its possibility. This is evident in the fact that, in the opening of porosity, the rupture of surprise, while striking into us, takes us beyond ourselves: the self-transcending of thinking is possibilized. Astonishment is not just a subjective feeling. It is more like the seeding and first fertilization of the promise of "subjectivity" by an enigmatic communication to sleeping mindfulness from out of the intimate strangeness of being.

We are moved into a between space where, in a sense, we go from our minds to the things; and yet there is no fixation of the difference of minding and things; our mindfulness wakes to itself by being woken up by the communication of being in its emphatic otherness. Already before we more reflectively come to ourselves, there is the more primal opening in astonishment, an opening of which I speak in terms of a certain porosity of being. There is no fixed boundary between there and here, between outside and inside, there is a passage from what is into the awakening of mindfulness as, before its own self-determination, opened to what communicates to it from beyond itself. We do not open ourselves; being opened, we are as an opening. Astonishment awakens the porosity of mindfulness to being, in the communication of being to mindfulness, before mind comes to itself in more determinate form(s). In that respect also, it correlates with a more original "coming to be" prior to the formation of different processes of determinate becoming, and the more settled arrival of relatively determinate beings and processes. This is an important point in relation to the difference between wonder in the modalities of astonishment and curiosity.

It is hard to think this more original porosity of astonishment, for all thinking already presupposes it as having happened. All determinate knowing proceeds from it, but it is not yet determinate knowing; nevertheless some sense of it can be communicated. I behold the majestic tree and murmur: "This is astonishing!" I am not projecting my feeling; I am being awakened by the tree, and am awakening to myself, in a more primal porosity, where the striking otherness of this blossoming presence has found its way into the intimate recesses of my now roused and receiving attendance. This astonishment is not a vector of intentionality that goes from subject to object; it is a porosity prior to intentionality, and hence refers us back to a patience of being more primal than any cognitive endeavor to be. It is a mindful *passio essendi* prior to and presupposed by every *conatus essendi* of the mind desiring to understand this or that. First we do not desire to understand. Rather we are awoken or become awake in a not yet determinate minding that is not full with itself but filled with an openness to what is beyond itself—filled with openness, if that is permissible to say, for such a porosity looks like nothing determinate and hence seems almost nothing, even entirely empty. Being filled with openness and yet being empty: yet this is what makes possible all our determinate relations to determinate beings and processes, whether these relations be knowing ones or unknowing.

A certain reversal is signaled here in terms of how we often think: the communication is from what is other to us first, and then from ourselves toward that otherness as other. The first initiative does not lie with us, and yet something is initiated. As initiating, we are always seconds. Consider the notion of "beholding." We tend to think of beholding as a movement from us to something other to us. Beholding something seems to put the perceiver in a position of active superiority to the being beheld as other. My beholding seems to confer on me the preeminence: the other beheld may be marvelous but my beholding seems to be the privileged glory. This kind of beholding, I would say, is too full of itself, and hence lacks the fertile emptiness that is filled with openness. Not being properly nothing, it beholds nothing. I would say that the first astonishment makes us ask if there is rather a *"beholding from"* being-other.

There are lines from William Wordsworth's "Lines Written above Tintern Abbey" that suggest the point:

> . . . Therefore am I still
> A lover of the meadows and the woods,
> And mountains; and of all that we behold,
> From this green earth; of all the mighty world
> Of eye and ear. . .[3]

Note the wording: "behold from." First astonishment is not unlike such a "beholding from." "Beholding from": what is there as other communicates to us, and we are called beyond ourselves. There is *a reversal* of directionality relative to the more normal reflective understanding of being "conscious of. . . ." "Beholding from" seems to be first a "consciousness from. . . ." Perhaps this is already indicated in the word *consciousness* with its "with" *(cum)*: con-*scientia* as a "knowing with." Such a "knowing with" originates in a relating, coming as much from the other known, as from the knowing itself. "*Cum*": there is the coming toward us of what is other, there is the giving of the other, and astonishment is overtaken by the gift of an original porosity. The porosity is not the knowing of this or that but is the awakened opening that enables further the knowing of this or

3. William Wordsworth, *William Wordsworth*, ed. Stephen Gill (Oxford: Oxford University Press, 1984), 134, lines 102–6.

that, the "knowing with" that is communicated from the otherness of being as given. This is not at all to deny the possibility of a two-way mediation in beholding: both a "beholding of" and a "beholding from." But this two-way mediation, this intermediation, is possibilized by the opening of a more original porosity between what is other and ourselves. In "beholding from" the otherness of being opens itself from itself in its otherness, offers itself for minding, minding which therefore is only a "beholding of" because it is first a "beholding from."

Another sign of what is at issue with first astonishment: consider how when hearing the word *beholding* we are tempted to think of a *taking hold* of something. One thinks of the German word for concept, *Begriff*: *begriefen* (verb), as "conceiving," seems to suggest a taking hold of, a gripping, a grasping, a seizing. I would say that in "beholding from" there is something more like a *being taken hold of*. In first astonishment what is other seizes us, and we then go toward it out of our seizure. Being gripped puts us in the hold of the other-being, in the sense that it enthralls us, puts us in its thrall. Our receptivity to it is both ruptured and enrapt. One is captivated, as if the sight of the other descends on us, showers itself upon us, and we fall in love with it. First astonishment thus implies a kind of love. Wordsworth speaks very aptly when he describes himself as still a "lover . . . of all that we behold from this green earth." Beholding is a kind of "being beholden" to the green earth for the marvel of its givenness. We feel the call of a certain fidelity to the earth in "being beholden," but this is not imprisoning but *releasing*—releasing of mindfulness toward what is offered to us in given being as other to us. We answer for our "being beholden" in seeking to be truthful and to be true to being.

It is a well rehearsed theme that philosophy begins in wonder and Aristotle is often cited: "All men desire to know" (*Metaphysics* 982b11ff.). Aristotle sees the connection of marveling and astonishment when he reminds us of the affiliation of myth and metaphysics, and also the delight in the senses. Nevertheless, our desire to know is understood essentially as a *drive to determinate intelligibility,* which on being attained dissolves the initial wonder launching the quest. The end of Aristotle's wonder is a determinate *logos* of a determinate somewhat, a *tode ti*. This end is the dissolution of wonder, not its deepening or refreshing. Significantly, as I mentioned on a previous occasion, Aristotle invokes geometry to illustrate the teleological thrust of our desire to know (*Metaphysics* 983a13ff.). I take geometry here as representative of determinate cognition whose *eureka* solves the problem but also surpasses the wonder.

Admittedly there is a tension here when Aristotle grants that the *divine knowing* (in which in *theōria* we sometimes participate) is wonderful *(thaumaston)*; indeed it is even more wonderful still *(thaumasiōteron)* if divine knowing exceeds ours, as it does (*Metaphysics* 1072b24–27). Such a divine knowledge is not the determinate cognition of geometry but of the thought that thinks itself. Recall that this is the famous passage to which Hegel refers at the end of his *Encylopaedia* and which I have mentioned on previous occasions. One might note that the living and eternal enjoyment of such self-knowing is the possession of this self-thinking God. One sees why Hegel would consider this appropriate. With Hegel we are beyond the determinate cognition of a determinate somewhat; we are in the freer space of *self-determining knowing*. The question is whether there is also *more* in *our* access to wonder than can be exhausted by self-determining knowing. Indeed the question extends to the knowing of God, whether there is even more also to the God of agapeic mindfulness.

Apart from God, I think the issue of our wonder is better put in Plato's *Theaetetus* (155d3–4) where *thaumazein* is named as the *pathos* of the philosopher. *Pathos:* there is a patience, a primal receptivity. This is not the self-activating knowing such as we have come to expect from Kant and his successors in German idealism, as well as in varieties of the constructivist epistemology we find in different contemporary inheritors of this Kantian stress. There is a pathos more primal than activity, a patience of the soul before any self-activity. One could say: there is no going beyond ourselves, no activation of our self-surpassing powers of transcending, without this more primal patience. I stress this since in modernity patience has often been relegated to a servile passivity supposedly beneath the high dignity of human power as self-activating, as self-determining. The truth is that no one can self-activate themselves into wonder. It comes or it does not come. We are *struck* into wonder. "Being struck" is beyond our self-determination. We cannot "project" ourselves into "being struck." It comes to us from beyond ourselves. It does not come in the spiky oppugnancy of a hostile estrangement, though the hateful can strike one. It comes in the communication of an intimate strangeness that makes us porous to what before us is enigmatic and mysterious.

Helpful here might be a brief comparison between first astonishment and curiosity (to be more fully treated later). Curiosity is more to be correlated with a determinate cognition of a determinate somewhat *(tode ti)* or "object." By contrast, in astonishment it is not that an "object" as other simply seizes us, making us passive while it is actively dominating. What is received, as we undergo it in "beholding from," cannot be thus objectified. What seizes us is the offer of being beyond all objectification, and the call of truthfulness to being. This is not first either subjective or objective, but transsubjective and transobjective. "Trans": we witness a *crossing between* "subject" and "object" and an intermedium of their interplay which is more primordial than any determinable intermediation between the two. The happening of this "being-between," in the occurrence of "beholding from," reveals a porosity beyond subjectification and objectification and we are beholden to what eventuates in this between, making us answerable to its truth in our own being truthful. In the intimate strangeness of the porosity an excess of being flows, and overflows toward one. This is astonishing, not because initially we make no sense of it, but simply because the surprise of being's being there at all is there at all.

Ontological surprise is there at what is there at all and as "too much" for us. We could not anticipate it, so surprising is the pure gift of what is granted in the porosity. The surprise is not only before the being there of being, as transobjective, as more than any determinate being. It is also the surprise qua surprise at surprise itself. And this, so to say, double surprise, redoubled surprise is transubjective—the being-awakened of minding at all, to being as other to it and to its own very self as minding. The first astonishment is a mindful joy in this redoubled surprise of being.

One might say there is a primal *"being pleased"* with being, prior to all cognitive thematizations and objective determinations. We come to ourselves more mindfully as concrete singularizations of this ontological surprise. There is an ontological pleasure in our being at all. We love the "to be" in our own singular "to be." There is nothing "egoistic" in this self-love. Our pleasure with simply being greets, and is greeted by, the elemental agape of being itself, and in this astonishment draws its breath, so to say, or has its breath taken away in an unpremeditated love.

If there is something *childlike* about such a beginning, a point worth reiterating is that this does not mean it is merely *childish*. The childlike opening is our finding ourselves astonished already in the porosity of being. We do not produce astonishment; astonishment *opens us* in the first instance, and there is joy in the light. The child *lives* this primal and elemental opening; hence wonder is often noted as more characteristic of earlier stages of life. Thus too, as has been also noted, children sometimes astonish us with their spontaneous tendency to ask the "big questions." First astonishment is more intimate with the primal porosity that constitutes the human being as metaphysically opened from the outset. The later developments of curiosity and sophisticated scientific knowing are seeded in the primal porosity but what its grant enables we too quickly take for granted. Then, alas, this maternal porosity can be long forgotten when the project of science comes more fully on the scene. The child points to the night sky and murmurs "Look, the moon!" The astonishing has won its way into its heart. Later, the astonished child is recessed, even driven underground, in the curious project of (say) space exploration which lifts off the earth on the technical constructs of determinate cognition. The child is not only father to the man, but the man is the shield of time that shelters, or denies, the idiotic child it was originally born as. If the child dies, the shield shelters nothing, and the man dies too —a self-guarding hollowness, and not the elemental porosity. The callous of a self-circling *conatus essendi* covers over the idiotic pathos of the exposed child. The barbarism of reflection is the mania of reason that erupts when the ontological tenderness of the reverent child has been calloused.

This more primal porosity of first given minding is at the origin of all modalities of mind, but as intimate with the giving of the first opening, it can be passed over, covered over. It enables the passage of mindfulness but the endowed passing can be passed over, since we come to ourselves in this passing. First a happening, it is only subsequently gathered to itself in an express self-relation. In this being gathered to itself, there is the risk of a contraction of what the first opening communicates. The gathering concretizes us as determinate, and as thus ontologically concentrated, we can contract the opening of the porosity to just what *we* will grant as given. I will come back to this when dealing with perplexity and curiosity, and with modes of minding that are determinate and self-determining. Nevertheless, as coming to mind in astonishment the porosity happens, we do not produce it, we do not determine it, it communicates from beyond our self-determination. Prior to the more determinate and determining selving of mindfulness the porosity that is neither of self or other happens as the between space in which, and out of which, a variety of determinate and self-determining forms of minding come to be. These latter are derived, not original. What is more original is the between of porosity.

Some ways of indicating how this happens might be correlated with what I call the hyperboles of being: the idiocy of being, the aesthetics of happening, the erotics of selving, and the agapeics of communication.[4] As already indicated, first astonishment opens up the marvel of being at all: the "that it is." I call this the idiocy of being. Idiocy seems to have the implication of the unintelligible, but the question here is rather: While some surds might be absurd, is there a surd that is not absurd? Is the givenness of being such a surd? Idiocy also has a certain implication of intimacy. Does not idiotic astonishment open us to a feel for the *intimate strangeness* of being, an intimacy that yet intimates something beyond estrangement? We often undergo this intimation in astonishment. It is true that after the first astonishment the impulse comes to search for the intelligibility of the idiotic. But the intelligibility sought is not exhaustive of the idiotic, as the surplus givenness of the "that it is." Beyond even a complete summation of determinate characteristics, this "that it is" always abides in the mystery of its surd givenness. The mystery is not dispelled, no matter how extensive our determinate cognition. There is a wonder that comes to this mystery again and again, as hyperbolic to all determination.

We see something of this also in what I call the aesthetics of happening. In opening his *Metaphysics* Aristotle interestingly says: A sign [*sēmeion*] of our desire to know is our love of the senses. His words are significant: *hē tōn aisthēseōn agapēsis* (*Metaphysics* 890a23). There is an agape of the aesthetic. We are not talking about sensing as the intake of the empiricist's sense impression. The aesthetics of happening is a feast (*agape*) for the senses. It is shot through with marvelous beauty and communicates the excess of something sublime. But both beauty and the sublime are not proportionately regarded by determinate cognition such as the finite sciences give us: they are hyperbolic to determinative science. Not that they are merely subjective—again a characteristic response of modern thought—they are both transobjective and transsubjective. There is an overdeterminacy about them, again in mirror of the agapeic surplus communicated in the happening of original astonishment.

Not only the idiocy of being, and the aesthetics of happening, but

---

4. See, for instance, *God and the Between,* chapter 6.

the "too-muchness" can be communicated in the erotics of selving also. First astonishment might rock us back on ourselves but it also releases us toward what is there in a great energy of going out, of self-surpassing toward being in its otherness. The "too-muchness" of the energy of self-surpassing—this is first something that overtakes us. We are already beyond ourselves before we come to ourselves, surprised by the energy of self-surpassing that surprises even the selving. If I can refer to the account of the double parentage of eros given by Diotima-Socrates in Plato's *Symposium* (203a–204b), I would say we often think of eros too much in terms of the *penia,* and not enough in terms of the *poros.* In the tale told there of origins, beside *penia* the other parent of eros is *poros: poros* who at the feast of the gods is drunk, and with whom, sleeping, somehow *penia* couples, and out of their union eros is born. There is a divine porosity, drunk with divine festivity, at the secret origin of eros. I see in the sleeping festivity of the drunken divinity the promise of something more agapeic, in any case something not reducible to the *penia* of the other parent. There is a secret surplus at work, too much for any account that would privilege only the lack of our desire. There is more. I will return to the erotics of selving with perplexity as the second modality of wonder.

Finally, I would say that this surplus of the "too-muchness" is most signaled in the agapeics of communication: in community there is a paradoxical conjunction of surplus and poverty—something may be lacking but it is not that lack alone is communicated—communication communicates beyond lack. This is why I would say there is something of the promise of the agapeic in the first astonishment. There is a communication beyond lack, an intimate community beyond estrangement, in first astonishment. This is not initially known as such, nevertheless, the first wondering is rather akin to a kind of love, to a kind of falling in love. This is a happening that enters intimately into us before our autonomy can preempt exposure or impose closure. Likewise, it exceeds fixation on this determinate thing or that. Even more: if we are astonished at this quite singular thing, the porosity seeps beyond fixation on any finitized locus of wonder. It is the intimate communication of the "more" in the this, here and now that seeps beyond finite boundaries, that calls us further in an enigmatic permeability of one thing to another, and of ourselves into the promise of a love with all things other.

WONDER AS PERPLEXITY

I now turn to perplexity as a second modality of wondering. We pass from original overdetermination to a mingling of indeterminacy and determination. We are apt to think of perplexity as signifying our being troubled with doubt or uncertainty, our being puzzled. The word *plexus* in *perplexity* suggests a plaiting, a twining, an entanglement. We find the sense of something involved, com-plex, interwoven, something intricate and difficult to unravel, perhaps so knotted we wonder where to start with trying to untangle it. Plagued by perplexity, as we sometimes put it, our thoughts seem to be tormented with some vexing matter we cannot comprehend. Not only is it difficult to understand, but we may find ourselves thinking: we do not know what to think. There is nothing of calm serenity in this modality of wonder; instead, there is often anxiety, bewilderment, distress, trouble, and perturbation.

Perplexity arises out of first astonishment. How so? An important element of the agapeics of first astonishment is the way original wonder does not so overtake us as to squash us as selving but comes to release us into our more evident being for ourselves, into mindful selving as promising of itself, and perhaps of more than itself. We are granted to come to be ourselves, freed also into our own self-becoming in the between. This is part of what I call the erotics of selving. The original "too-muchness" is not indeterminate, not determinate, but exceeds all determination. In the first instance it is overdeterminate, but as such endows the promise of self-determining. If astonishment holds the promise of the agapeic, there is awakened in it the erotics of self-surpassing. In being thus awakened, we are as selving, and come to ourselves as enabled more fully to become ourselves. Out of this more primal awakening both perplexity and determinate curiosity are born as further modalities of wondering.

Being awakened in the primal astonishment, the "too-muchness" of given being can seem to *oppress* us.[5] Given to be as ourselves, the inti-

---

5. Burke connects astonishment with horror: "astonishment is that state of the soul, in which all its motions are suspended, with some degree of horror"; see *A Philosophical Enquiry into the Origin of Our Ideas of the Sublime and Beautiful*, ed. Adam Phillips (Oxford: Oxford University Press, 1990), part 2, section 1. He is not wrong but he is not entirely right either, since in terms of the analysis I offer here there is, in what he says of astonishment, a kind of mingling of wonder as agapeic astonishment and as erotic perplexity. The sense of horror becomes more overt, I think, *on the turn* of wonder from first astonishment to perplexity. Some of these nuances will be

mation intrudes that we cannot be its full measure. Though we are not the measure of the "too-muchness," we yet want to know it in full measure. In this disjunction troubled perplexity arises: we do not know, we would know, we know we do not know. We are stressed in the baffling difference between what we know is too much for us, and our intimately known desire to know just that "too-muchness." Perplexity is born in the baffling difference wherein our mindfulness is torn between its desire to know and its intimate knowing that it does not know what is too much for it. To live with this baffling difference is not easy, and there is the inevitable urge to diminish its stress in seeking a knowing which reduces the "too-muchness" to proportions that allow us to appropriate its difference. We are then faced with the urge to develop the desire to know as our way of subjecting the given "too-muchness" to our measure, that is, to the proportionate measure of ourselves as knowers. Often perplexity takes off in this direction, but not always, and the entire situation is always more equivocal, since wonder as perplexity is recurrently haunted by faces of otherness that are just so as *disproportionate* to the determinate measure of our determinative cognition.

Perplexity comes to live the porosity of mindfulness differently to first astonishment. Coming to ourselves as ourselves, we also come to more explicit mindfulness of the *otherness* of the rest of being, just as other to us. Being is not over against us, but it is not identical with what we ourselves are. This otherness can be intimated even in the intimacy of our own being; it is not only an issue of an external otherness. The "too-muchness" can come over us or surge up in us, even unto the threat of drowning us by its excess. Instead of the green earth, the element of the porosity of perplexity is here more like that of water. As we say, we are "put at sea" and ask: What is this otherness of the "too-muchness"? The porosity seems to have no boundaries in its open space of communication. For this reason, if we are only overwhelmed, we risk not being able to relate to it, risk not to know at all what is sent or flows toward us. Inevitably in perplexity we stake ourselves as questioning what it is. We come to ourselves as questioning, and finally too as questions to ourselves. Perplexity is still wrapped around with the overdeterminacy of being, and it can sometimes be unbearable to be caught in the cloud of unknowing. Inside not see-

---

evident from my analysis, itself less psychological and more ontological-metaphysical than Burke's.

ing, we seek to see, cloaked in too much of light or too much of darkness. Wordsworth speaks of "the burden of the mystery"—it is with perplexity that this burden troubles us, almost without cease.

What we call "everyday life" is the intermedium of this mystery, though often what we deem ordinary is a dimmed-down version of this mystery. We make the mysterious intermedium of being into something familiar in this sense: no longer taken *as* granted but taken *for* granted. The intimate strangeness of being becomes too familiar and diminishes in strangeness—and perhaps in ontological intimacy also. But the mystery of the intermedium is not made the less perplexing because it is made the more familiar. The "too-muchness" becomes the too familiar. The strangeness of the "too-muchness" keeps coming back, keeps resurrecting itself beyond familiarization. There is much of this overdeterminate perplexity at work in philosophy, in great creations of art,[6] indeed in the struggling religious soul that finds itself on a dark way along which it seems destined to be the bearer of the cross of the mystery.

Perplexity is a modality of wondering that brings us more into the *equivocity of being:* the play of light and darkness, the chiaroscuro of things and ourselves; the dark light of unformed things and things forming; of ourselves formless and seeking form and being returned to formlessness; of all things enigmatic and intimating; of ourselves the most baffling of beings, at once shouting absurdly and absurdly singing. Perplexity is not the reverse of astonishment but our waking to the troubling equivocity of the "too-muchness," given in the astonishment. The equivocity is shown on both the sides of self-being and other-being. One might say the equivocity of the perplexing "too-muchness" is both transobjective and transsubjective. There is too much to the thereness of what is there; there is too much to the intimacy of being waking up to itself as our selving. Other-beings and selvings come from formlessness beyond form, are themselves as form-

6. One thinks of John Keats's "negative capability" "which Shakespeare possessed so enormously"—"Negative Capability, that is, when a man is capable of being in uncertainties, mysteries, doubts without any irritable reaching after fact and reason"; see *John Keats,* ed. Elizabeth Cook (Oxford: Oxford University Press, 1990), 370 ("Letter to George and Tom Keats," December 21? December 27, 1817. "Negative capability" is somewhere *between* first astonishment and perplexity, suspended in first wonder and touched with the troubled perplexity of doubts and uncertainties; and not yet overtaken by determinating curiosity which brings obsession with univocal fact and reason. I would say that the perplexity of the poet calls secretly on a wonder before art and more primal, a *prior* porosity opening a metaxological mindfulness that is not hostile to reason or fact but is not univocalizing of them.

ing and coming to form, and finally point beyond themselves and all finite form. The troubling equivocity can fill us with great foreboding in face of the mystery of life, and every human being knows something of its discon-certment and dismay. It can drive us to distraction, it can drive us mad. It is never too much to say that it is always and ever too much for us to say.

Perplexity awakens a *seeking* for what is true in all significant art, in all intellectually honest philosophy, in all spiritually serious religion. Mostly, however, the seeking has no fancy names, as ordinary persons in accus-tomed community, mostly out of the limelight, seek to thread the way of truth (with a bow to Parmenides). I see the wondering of perplexity to be more erotic than agapeic in the following respect. We are aware that we lack the measure of what faces us—we wake to our nonknowing in know-ing something of our participation in the "too-muchness." There is porosity, there is always porosity, but there is also the *penia* (poverty) told of in the myth of eros's parentage. *Penia:* the sense of something we need, the sense we do not now have it. It is as if we have fallen out of the astonishing rapture of porous participation in the intermedium of being, and instead of finding ourselves as knowing in that outside, we find we are ignorant—but ignorant in a manner that oppressively knows it does not know. The oppression of perplexity now is, so to say, felt in the bones, not yet made the theme of a more explicit philosophical reflection or religious practice. Perplexity is the living of a lack of knowing—a lacking living itself as knowing it is lacking.

The equivocity of this perplexity is in the *doubleness* of being *both* the dismaying destitution of not-knowing *and* the ignorance of a voracious desire to know. Perplexity is first-born from original astonishment, but we wake up to ourselves even before and beyond the second-born desire to know. As a modality of wondering, something about perplexity is more primitive than what we normally call the desire to know. For we have al-ready passed through treasures and dispossessions to get to the quotid-ian awakening of what we more ordinarily call the desire to know. This more primitive perplexity takes shape in the archaeology of the selving that comes to be out of the original ontological porosity. Of course, as transobjective and transsubjective, this perplexity is not just a matter of selving alone with itself. As coming to awakening out of the porosity, it is already an equivocal way of "being with" what is other than selving—a "being with" that is ingredient in waking selving both to itself and what is other to itself. Perplexity as wondering, like the primal astonishment, is a way of being between the "too-muchness" of other-being and selving coming to wakefulness of both itself and what is other.

In wondering as perplexity, given the equivocal play of light and darkness, we are closer to something like Plato's condition of the cave. In perplexity, however, we are not in the cave as prisoners who do not know they are prisoners. These latter do not know perplexity as an awakening. Perhaps these prisoners, that is, we ourselves in this condition, do have a dull presentiment that not all is as it seems. There is presentiment in perplexity but the dullness has already been tenderized into the pain of not being able to take for granted what now more and more enigmatically presents itself as being opened for questioning. To be perplexed is to realize that one is held in check by something too much for one's own power. The chiaroscuro of being shows the troubling face of the equivocal "too-muchness" which holds us in a kind of thrall. To be enthralled is to be under a spell, but some thralls stop us, stupefy us. The "too-muchness" bewilders, befuddles, bemuses, bewitches us. Perplexity can be nonplussed by the equivocity. Nonplussed, we may appear to be stupid, but there is a salutary stupefaction in the wondering of perplexity. In moments of more ontological porous mindfulness that break into perplexity, we know that there is light, and that there is an access of light in perplexity truthfully undergone. That light might be the Siamese twin of the darkness, and yet the twinned darkness does not make it any the less the light. It is *we ourselves* who are twinned: participants in the perplexity which both burdens and enlightens, double-headed between the burden of the mystery and the godsend of light that gives ontological uplift.

There is also the following deep equivocity. This we can see with an extremity of perplexity when it takes on the shape of *horror:* ontological horror before the being there of being in its excess to our rational measure. In the cave we can turn *downward* as well as upward. Perplexity can come over us in the feeling of *being blocked from ascending into the light.* We would find light, but we find ourselves darkened, darkened in the very seeking for light itself. Not the measure of the light, we are also not the measure of this darkness. We cannot go up; perplexed, we find ourselves falling. We may not want to fall, but we still find ourselves falling.[7]

7. Think of the *aporiai* of thought as showing a lack of *poros:* we are unable to find a way across, are at an impasse. In the *Theaetetus* Plato again and again stresses the philosopher's suffering of the aporetic. The question is related to perplexity. In the end perplexity is not

Different responses to this are possible. One might respond in still seeking to hold true to the presentiment that there is the true above us. Or we might respond in the manner of a Schopenhauer or a Nietzsche or a Dostoevsky: we dig *down* instead of ascending on high. Notice that in this going down there must still be some *fidelity* to the sense of something true, if we are to affirm such a descent as worthy of pursuit. Perplexity can be *redoubled* in such a descent, and the redoubling has to do with our worry about the absence of the true, in our seeking for the true. Paradoxically and perplexingly, the worry about the lack of the true is in the light of the seeking of the true. Up or down, the perplexing light keeps coming back to haunt us—even as a ghost there of what, it seems, should not be there at all.

I want to suggest that perplexity tinged by horror at the possibility that there is nothing true is very widespread in the ethos of post-Enlightenment modernity. *Below* Plato's cave, we can come to wonder if there is any ground *under* the underground. Perhaps there is a second underground. Perhaps there is an abyss below rather than the sun above. We come to be perplexed between the abyss and the sun. When perplexity is turned back downward, into the sunless (under)ground under the underground, we can find the kind of mixture of eros and horror that we encounter in a thinker like Schopenhauer; or the mixture of horror and erotic ecstasy that we find in Nietzsche: perplexity tinged by horror paradoxically mutates into wonderful affirmation of even the horror. Schopenhauer: because the dark primal origin is prior to reason—a voracious Will, an *eros turannos*; art may put this into abeyance, and so alleviate us; ascetic religion may uproot it and so seek to save us from it. Nietzsche: be-

---

dissolved but it can be the anticipation of a new occasion of trying to understand. It can also be addressed by myth or likely stories. Univocal theories are not enough. The way of philosophical perplexity is wayless. There is a noplace that is the place of thought (Socrates is described as *atopos*; see *Symposium* 215a2, 221c2–d6). This noplace witnesses to the porosity of the soul. Concerning perplexity one also thinks of Kant and metaphysics: there are questions we cannot avoid raising but cannot also answer; we must raise them but we cannot put them to rest in a univocal science or theory. Perplexity here is not like pure reason. It reminds one of trying to rest but being unable to find a comfortable position; one keeps casting around for a better position but finally the perplexity does not get dispelled. With some thinkers, it can be the opposite: they try to get away from perplexity by a strategy: "on the one hand, this," "on the other hand, that." Indeed, is there not much of zigzag in Kant? Perplexity can remind one of a fever where one restlessly turns this way, that way. Of course, this can generate the idea that thinking is itself a kind of sickness, reflection a curse, as happens with the underground man of Dostoevsky, and here and there with Nietzsche. The barbarism of reflection makes reflection itself the barbarism of the mind. This is perplexity sickened with itself, not the first astonishment, nor the posthumous wonder, I will discuss at the end.

cause horror before the dark origin is very like facing Medusa—the Gorgon's head will turn all flesh to stone if looked on too directly—the horror can be deflected from this petrification, Nietzsche hopes, into erotic ecstasies in the Dionysian rapture that also comes up from the dark depths. But as Heraclitus says: "Dionysus is also Hades" (fragment 15). Nietzsche, we know, wanted to stand at the meridian under the sun and sing his fidelity to the earth, but how ultimate can such standing in the sun be, if under the ground under us the Dionysian origin is a Hades that turns every tongue to stone? I do not ask the question in criticism of Nietzsche. It is the horrifying question all true perplexity must face: Is death the petrifying truth of life, or is there to life something good in excess of all death, and to be affirmed as such? Is death the true, or is the true beyond death? This is the perplexing question about which tragic art makes us wonder. It is an ultimate perplexity deeply intimate to all the great religions. The wonder of true philosophizing brings us to it too.

I note a connection with Vico's barbarism of reflection. I mean that the danger of madness from such extreme horrors of perplexity might well *drive more moderate rational men away* from all such perplexities. Moderating rationality must protect us from horror, protect us from Hades. Sanity will seem to reside in keeping one's distance from the horror. This is very understandable and rational philosophers have often been banner carriers for this salutary sanity. But in pursuit of this sanity there can come to be an unperplexed apotheosis of univocal knowing, such as we find, for instance, in the ideology of more scientistic worldviews. The rallying cry then is: Tame perplexity with manageable curiosity and methodical rationalization of all epistemic and metaphysical excess. But for those souls touched by the extremer perplexity, this salutary sanity can hide its own shadow and indeed drive more thoughtful humans to madness. I do not mean now the madness of the barbarism of reflection, but the madness of knowing that any such scientistic apotheosis of univocal knowing is truly mad. Scientistic madness secretes its own counterfeit double as that rational enlightenment that absolutizes itself.

I think of Dostoevsky's underground man and his bitterness against the regnant "geometricization" of the world. This latter is the barbarism of reflection in the form of modern rationalism. Against the certainty of 2 plus 2 equals 4, the underground man rages. His rage is madness to *l'esprit de géométrie* but perhaps *l'esprit de géométrie* has already generated the form of enlightened madness that keeps an epoch in thrall. The underground man rages in a fallen world but it is a world fallen partly because of the absolutization of univocal knowing, one that evacuates every space of the extremes of perplexity, or any secret hiding place where wonder at the mystery of being might fructify. It is unfortunately also true that the perplexity of the underground man has itself become so embittered and spiteful that it seems to have evacuated its own intimacy with the primal astonishment. Without this intimacy perplexity itself easily becomes just horror and hate, just as *eros uranios* becomes *eros turranos*, an eros that is no longer love at all but secretly inspired by the spirit of hatred. The underground man is himself so fallen in this fallen world he seems only able to dig down further into dark Hades, neither seeking to climb up out of the cave, nor awaiting any resurrection that might release him from hell. He curses the darkness, but his curse is itself darkness and only darkens darkness. It desecrates the world of fallen univocity but in that desecration what restoration of the world is there, what saving knowing?

Perplexity comes back again and again, and again as double-faced: we can be opened, and open ourselves, and opened either to moving up or moving down, and sometimes both to moving up and moving down. Often we are enabled to move up only because we have moved down. We sometimes have to spend our season in hell before the light of heaven breaks on a new dawn. Even despite the scientistic will to absolutize *l'esprit de géométrie,* the power of perplexity to outlive geometry, as *posthumous perplexity,* so to say, is evident in that religion and art continue to grow on the soil of the dark equivocity. The darkness of the earth communicates the burden of the mystery. This side of death, the perplexity is ineradicable finally, and the soil of art, religion, and philosophy will always put forth new sprouts.

We can, of course, treat that soil as a problem, sterilize it of threats, and try to turn its fertility for art, religion, and philosophy into a disposable resource for more and more determinate cognition of this, that, or the other. Encounter with enigma happens in a between space, alternatively enchanting and tormenting. Because it is tormenting, we are inclined not to let it be; we want to univocalize and neuter its fertile equivocity. Once again then begins the process that culminates in the barbarism of reflection. Rather than dwell with the perplexity, we become curious about this thing and that, and thus we seek to surpass, indeed even to do away with, both astonishment and perplexity.

WONDER AS CURIOSITY

I turn now to curiosity as a third modality of wondering. Here the over-determinacy of astonishment can be too easily forgotten, just as also the troubled indeterminacy of perplexity can be dulled. If to be is to be determinate, here to be is nothing if it is not determinate. Being is nothing but determinacy and to be exhausted in the totality of all determinations. The danger: hostility to ontological astonishment is twinned with the annihilation of the wonder of being itself.

Of course, we cannot but be curious, given our inextirpable desire to know the world around us and ourselves. The adventures of the human spirit are carried by the energy and honesty of its magnificent curiosity. The devil is in the details, or God is, we say; and often we think of the curious person, in his or her desire to know, as giving careful attention just to the details of things. Such attention, we think, can sometimes be carried to excess; it can be addressed to unworthy objects; we inquire into things, but too minutely. There is healthy curiosity; there seems also to be an undue or too intrusive inquisitiveness in which we are curious about what does not properly concern us. Curiosity, in a good sense, finds things interesting and surprising; its desire to know is open to the novel and strange; in turning to what is curious in things, inquiry fastens on their *interesting determinacy,* often with the twist of the odd.

Curiosity as an interest is marked by a between-character: it too is metaxological, it is an *inter-esse.* There is something binding mind and what interests it, though when the curiosity tries to bind the interesting to itself, it begins to tilt toward the intrusive. Novelty is important for the curious mind: the queer, the peculiar, whatever arouses closer attention. We also talk of a curious argument, one marked by ingeniousness or excessive nicety or subtlety. Those who are collectors of curiosities search in out-of-the-way places for things or people out of the ordinary. Interestingly, inquisitiveness, whether in approved or unapproved senses, can lead to *inquisitions,* in which novelty itself is suspect. The inquisitor is particular about details because the details revealed are unapproved. There is a desire to know what one has no right to know; *prying curiosity* intrudes on what properly does not concern it.

The *inter-esse* of curiosity is an openness to what is, a participation in the porosity of being. It too is a form of love of the intimate strangeness of being. But the above double-edged character means that, qua wonder, curiosity is not a pure porosity to what is true. What we are in the idiotic recesses of our being infiltrates our manners of being curious. There can be something closer to the purer porosity in the reception of astonishment, the awakening of perplexity. There can also surge up a will to know marked by a *conatus essendi* that wills to overtake, subordinate, if not extirpate the porosity and patience that are more intimate to the idiotic, ontological heart of our being. I stress this doubleness again, since one might claim that in our time this second possibility has taken on such an all-pervasive life that it seems to have an irresistible power of its own, and not really to come to be out of the more original porosity at the origins of wonder as astonishment and perplexity. The fuller plurivocity of wonder can only be recovered if we keep these differences in mind, within curiosity itself and between curiosity, astonishment, and perplexity.

Curiosity can be said to emerge from perplexity, both continuing what is at work in it, and also redirecting it in significantly differently ways. Out of astonishment perplexity sees the light, as the indeterminate seeking is born out of the gift of overdeterminate wonder; while out of perplexity can descend curiosity, as the determinate questioning that tries to overcome and put to rest the discomfort of indeterminate seeking. Curiosity is mediately related to astonishment, in that it is shaped by the fact that we are not the measure of what perplexes us. What disturbs perplexity irritates curiosity—not to be the measure of what exceeds our grasp. There is an undergoing about being perplexed, just as there is about astonishment, a patience. In perplexity we are overtaken by troubled thought about what faces us—we are lacking in the knowing of it and know our lacking. But we also know our lacking desire to be more than lack, and so we can turn differently to all that is before us. We can forget our "being between" because we stand on one side facing the "too-muchness" and wonder if we can make ourselves the measure of the other side. Though not finally the measure, now we come to move into the ordinary light of day where we think of ourselves as subjects over against objects. If originally we are not the measure of what perplexes us, now we think we are or might be that measure. Thinking we can determine it in our measure of thought, curiosity arises as minding that carries the seed of wanting to be the measure. This wanting lays the foundation stone of the world as the crystal palace—with a bow to Dostoevsky again.

I recall here how Vico talks also about a *barbarism of the senses (la barbarie del senso)* as well as a barbarism of reflection. See this as Vico's naming something of the "too-muchness" at the beginning, experienced as our being overwhelmed by the aesthetics of happening. Lost in this "too-muchness," we are barbarians in our own participation in the aesthetics of happening because asleep in the saturated immediacy of what is sensuously given. The artist often helps us articulate this "too-muchness" of the aesthetics of happening, without the reduction of its equivocity to some set of univocal propositions. Vico reminded us, against the conceit of scholars, that the first humans were poets. The philosopher who remains faithful to *thaumazein,* wonder as astonishment, also seeks to articulate it, and indeed lay out as best as possible the contours of its intelligibility. The pathos does not vanish in the effort to understand, but rather finds itself inhabiting the "too-muchness" with a light-accessed mindfulness, and this, even granting the extremities of perplexity. There can also be, however, a will to univocity that becomes impatient with this first wonder in its overfull brimming, as well as the troubled thought of perplexity. It wills to reduce the equivocity to theoretical and pragmatic univocity. Wonder as curiosity is crucial to this process.

If perplexity is a firstborn child of primal astonishment, curiosity is a secondborn. If astonishment is overdetermined, if perplexed mixes the overdeterminate and the indeterminate, curiosity dominantly stresses the determinate. Often we think of wonder in this third modality as confronting problems. This is understandable: the "It is!" of first astonishment turns into the "What is?" (indeed "What the hell is it?") of perplexity, turning now into the sober "What is it?" of curiosity. With this last form of the question we ask about the determinate being there of beings, or the determinate forms or structures or processes. We move from ontological astonishment before being toward ontic regard concerning beings, their properties, patterns of developments, determinate formations, and so on. It is essential to the becoming of our mindfulness that we move into curiosity. The overdeterminate is saturated with determinations, not an indefiniteness empty of determinacy. The question "What is it?" turns toward the given intricacy of this, that, and the other, and there can be something even reverent in this turning, for it too shares in our porosity to the astonishing givenness. We can marvel as these given intricacies, coming to admire, and even be in awe of such immanent richness. Curiosity releases the self-surpassing energy of our questing to know in the mode of determinate questions bearing on this richness.

Our curiosity can be engrossed in this richness, and this can be a kind of loving fascination. In it can also lurk a will to possession. Curiosity is not in essence a will to determination that masks a will to power. But there can be an engrossment that shows, as we say, an "unhealthy" curiosity. The phrase suggests that there are forms of inappropriate curiosity. It is not curiosity itself that always determines what is appropriate. For there can be a desire to know whose quest is questionably intrusive. Intrusiveness shows the lack of reverence before the intimate. Intrusiveness shows no respect for the properly secret. Intrusiveness knows no measure that would recall it to the ontological humility of our patience of being. Intrusiveness refuses all distance between us and the mystery of being. Intrusiveness collapses being's granted otherness into the self-determining measure of intrusiveness itself, into itself as the measure that determines what is other.

Where curiosity about determinacy is more than will to power, it retains a certain fidelity to the basic ontological porosity of our being that is communicated in the primal astonishment. This does not always happen. Quite to the contrary, our determinate questioning is tempted to think of itself as the measure of the "too-muchness," now seen as capable of being defined in terms commensurate with our own power to determine. If now there is determination, it is determination proportionate to our power to determine. The porosity is overtaken, overridden by a will to determinacy that loses touch with the *passio essendi,* while the endeavor to be and to know hides a will to power: a will to overtake emergent form, a refusal to be overtaken. In this refusal the seed of the death of wonder is sown— even in the seeming full flowering of the bloom of wonder itself.

On this point discriminations are necessary. Curiosity is, in the main, expressed in our power to pose determinate questions to determinate problems, each in principle soluble. A problem is not a problem if it is insoluble. The possibility of a solution is built into the definition of problem as such.[8] I illustrate by returning to previously cited remarks of Aris-

---

8. Gabriel Marcel has important things to say on problem and mystery in, for instance, *The Mystery of Being*, 2 vols. (London: Harvill Press, 1951). On the issue of solubility Kant shows his usual cautious equivocity when he writes: "Astonishment [*Verwunderung*] is the obstruction of progress in our thought, on account of a hindrance—a kind of fear—that it hits

totle in his *Metaphysics* (982b11ff.): in announcing our desire to know, he acknowledges its likeness to myth and the marveling going with myth. This is closer to the first sense of wonder as astonishment. That the myth or religious story is invoked is much to the point, since primal astonishment and religious piety are close relatives in the family of ontological reverence. What of when Aristotle returns to the issue and illustrates the matter with geometry (*Metaphysics* 983a13ff.)? Here we begin with a question, and this is a wonder and a curiosity, but the problem is determinate, and we proceed by intelligent means to solve the problem. We take determinate intelligible steps (in geometry, say, we construct, or extend a line here), and the solution becomes perspicuous to our univocal intelligence. When we solve the problem the wonder dissolves. This is ingredient in the logic of a certain kind of curiosity. But if we think the first and third modalities of wondering are the same, we seriously err, and cover over what is most challenging in the first modality, that it cannot be dispelled, though it can be deepened. Deepened here means: the porosity comes to be more unclogged, mindfulness verges more on the purer porosity.

I might add that this recourse to geometry is recurrent through the philosophical tradition, especially in modernity with thinkers like Descartes, Spinoza, Kant, Husserl. Even Vico is not free of the attitude that connects wonder with determining curiosity: "Wonder is the daughter of ignorance; and the greater the object of wonder, the more the wonder grows."[9] Then: "Curiosity—that inborn property of man, daughter of

upon something for which it finds no rule." This obstruction does not entirely meet Kant's approval, yet he is not entirely dismayed, and his epistemological housekeeping allows him to balance the books of cognition. He finds a silver lining in the cloud of astonishment. For astonishment might lead to "a hope of finding one [a rule] in the future, if it is an actual event [e.g., a nebula]." Were this to happen, Kant is willing to extend some approval, and "therefore, astonishment is actually quite pleasant." Admiration is given Kant's scientific imprimatur, but the miraculous earns no *nihil obstat*. Thus: "Admiration is an always continuing astonishment which remains even when we know the cause [rule] for it. Actual miracles which allow us no hope—strike down the mind. My cognition is *eo ipso* forbidden to me, all pondering comes to an end. But objects of admiration elevate the mind." See Kant's *Lectures on Metaphysics* in *The Cambridge Edition of the Works of Immanuel Kant*, trans. Karl Ameriks and Steve Naragon (Cambridge: Cambridge University Press, 2001), 371. Though touched by wonder at the starry skies above and the moral law within, Kant does not impress one as gifted with much of the primal ontological astonishment in his philosophizing; though as I indicated in note 5 above, there is a kind of irritated perplexity that will not fit into the mold of scientific solubility. I thank Garth Green for bringing the above passage in Kant to my attention.

9. *New Science*, §184.

ignorance and mother of knowledge—when wonder wakens our minds, has the habit, wherever it sees some extraordinary phenomenon of nature, a comet for example, a sundog, or a midday star, of asking straightaway what it means."[10] Answering the question of curiosity, one takes it, amounts to an overcoming of the ignorance of the wonderful, which now, converted into knowledge, is no longer wonderful. Vico's remarks here are not discerning enough about the differences between astonishment, perplexity, and curiosity.

A certain *will to univocity* is at work in all this, and one might trace a line of continuity from ancient Aristotle to more contemporary positivisms on this score. The underlying view is something like this: to be is to be intelligible, and to be intelligible is to be determinate; what cannot be made determinate cannot be said to be intelligible, and indeed cannot properly be said to be. This creates huge questions, not only about the indeterminate and the overdeterminate, but also the self-determining. Early in modernity Pascal was a genius of *l'esprit de géométrie,* but he saw the absolute necessity for another modality of mindfulness for what cannot be determined in that univocal modality, *l'esprit de finesse.* Without *l'esprit de finesse,* Pascal might well have been a geometrical positivist instead of a tortured soul, racked by often unremitting perplexity, relieved by intermittent, unpredictable gleams of the astonishing. Finesse is a mindfulness porous to ontological nuance—dealing with everything of the overdeterminate, the indeterminate, and the self-determining—and yet not merely self-determining, nor merely indeterminate. Finesse is a mode of mindful participation in the overdeterminate. Finessed mindfulness comes out of surplus attention, secretly mothered by astonishment, fostered by perplexity in excess of the problematic, for it finds the finitely problematic itself problematic—a problem it cannot solve through itself alone. Something in excess of finite determinability keeps coming back to haunt it.

L'esprit de géométrie might want in principle to univocalize all concepts, and perhaps every matter in question; but to affirm *l'esprit de finesse* is not to deny the space of intelligibility. Finesse, like first astonishment, does not negate that space; rather there would be no space of determinate intelligibility without them. Yet they communicate of what, as intelligible, is transdeterminate: hyperintelligible, if you like. This might look like a

10. *New Science,* §189.

surd if you think intelligibility is exhausted by what is subject to univocal-ization; but this surd is not at all absurd, if approached from the direction of the opening up of, our being opened up to, the hyperintelligible. Finesse, like first astonishment, is not unintelligible but, as hyperintelligible, has more to do with what I call the *intimate universal.* You cannot univocalize it, but this does not mean it is absurd. To be is not exhausted by being determinate (or self-determining either); being intelligible is also not exhausted by determinate intelligibility. With finesse as companion, there is no need for philosophy to either celebrate the irrational or become hostile to reason. Reasonableness in the mode of finessed mindfulness can be the safeguard of astonishment and perplexity, keeping itself open in porosity to religion and art. Indeed it draws attention to the opening in *scientific thinking itself* to the marvellous intelligibility of finite processes, a marvel putting us in mind of what exceeds finitization. Wonder beyond the barbarism of reflection makes a call on a renewal of *l'esprit de finesse.*

Since solubility is built into the notion of the problematic, if we lack a sense of wonder beyond and before curiosity, we risk deeming any question that does not admit of solubility as beyond all consideration. If it is not a problem in this soluble sense, no longer need it engage our curiosity—until it is turned into the proper form of a soluble problem. Without finesse, this attitude can lead to a tyrannical determination of the questionable—a questionable determination of the questionable, since it means we will only accept as a problem what we deem capable of solubility on the terms we determine or dictate. All the great mysteries of life will be banished as not properly problems. The extremes of positivism and scientism give doleful witness to this form of stupidity. All the great questions are redefined as pseudoproblems. Though banished, they do not vanish: they keep coming back again and again in the first two modalities of wonder, the astonishing and the perplexity. We can, of course, try to white them out by means of a certain curious construction of the image of the world as washed free of mystery. The elephant is in the room but no one is allowed to say there is an elephant in the room. The elephant is the monster of the transproblematic mystery of being. It is also the transproblematic mystery of our own being. For we can live the existential pretense that we are not questions to ourselves, running from the porosity and patience, the very endowments that allow our very running on all false ways taken for the direction of truth. This is the counterfeiting of the true in the name of univocal truth. There is a defect of basic truthfulness about all this.

The univocalizing of being that this determinative curiosity tries to effect, I should say, is not untrue to things. There are forms of univocal truth, there are precisely formulated questions which are to be answered in clear and distinct answers. They answer to what is fixed as determinate in the unfolding of happening. The happening of becoming takes on more or less fixed forms and our determinate curiosity can be slaked by knowing what these are. There are many forms of univocity here, answering different kinds of curiosity, for instance, mathematical, scientific, and common sense. Nevertheless, the determination of curiosity comes out of something preceding and exceeding determination. What we determine as univocal is itself emergent from a milieu of being that is more than any and every univocal fixation. In this emergence what precedes determinate univocity and what exceeds it is not a mere indeterminacy. Rather the determinate gives evidence of being sourced in the overdeterminate. If we are only curious about the more or less fixed forms that come to form, we lose sight of the more than determinate forming and source of forming. Attention to this is not outside of wonder, but it is not wonder in the modality of determinative curiosity.

My point, then, is not to deny a kind of truth to the univocal determinacy settled by curiosity and settling it; it is to argue against the kind of scientism that follows when we claim this is wonder and that this exhausts the processes of being and knowing. With this scientism the outlook takes hold that the univocalizing approach is the one and only approach. This is a contraction of the plurivocity promised in the other modalities of wonder. Determinate curiosity has its place within the embrace of the more original sense of wonder, and while it occludes it, it cannot itself even function, much less prosper, if it does not dip back again and again into the primal modality of the originating astonishment. Scientism is itself a kind of sclerosis of this astonishment, even as it seems to be a hypertrophy of determinative curiosity. Science is also born from it, though its form takes shape in terms of the secondborn wonder of curiosity. The mother of mindfulness in astonishment has to be honored, and the original porosity seeded again and again with determinate figures of intelligibility—though none of the latter exhaust the fecundity of the former.

When we ride on the surge of curiosity and forget that these figures have been shaped by our univocalization, curiosity colludes in the loss of the sense of ontological mystery at its most deep. There is a contraction of wonder relative to all the hyperboles of being. There is a loss of marvel before the idiocy of being—this is now a mere surd, taken for granted as an otherwise absurd thereness, not an intimate otherness given as a marvel granted, rousing ontological delight and appreciation. There is the dimming of the marvel of aesthetic happening: the world is stripped of the qualitative textures of sensuous communication and becomes a bare neutral thereness, less than the glorious, saturated creation it is. There is a mutation in the erotics of selving and the urges of an *eros turranos* induce a turn of the desire to know and its love of the true in the direction of will to power. Finally, there is an occlusion of the agapeics of community where the overdeterminacy of ethical and religious love has an absolute intimacy and into which the intrusiveness of determinative curiosity can only be a desecration. Knowing becomes raping.

Consider how the eros of knowing can mutate into an *eros turannos,* generating shapes of curiosity that are carriers of a restless will to power. Why do I want to know? Because I want to enter into the secret of what is other. Why enter? Not because I love the secret but because possessing it, I advance myself, I overtake its intimacy, I take over. There is a love of the secret that is truly a love; there is a curiosity that wants to know the secret for its own purposes and not for love of the secret. Reverence for the other is not among those purposes. Likewise, thinking, qualified by such curiosity, is in the mode of a grasping. Reaching out to grip what is there, it seeks to get a handle on it to turn it this way or that, as I so determine it to turn. This move from the indeterminacy (really overdeterminacy) of the secret to determinative cognition is governed by the rule of self-determination. I am not really curious about the other—in my desire to grasp it, grip it, handle it, it is my own power that is at issue and that is pursued. Grasping is a grabbing. It is not a caressing or being caressed. It is not a conceiving wherein I must await impregnation,[11] wherein I must become porous to what is sent to me, wherein the embrace of love in con-

---

11. It is true that conceiving as *concipere* coming from *con-capere,* implies "to take in," "to hold," "to take to oneself." But while the hold, the taking in, is there in conceiving, as something generative, there is more of the pathos in conceiving, more of the receiving in being impregnated, and becoming fruitful. There is something of the *poros;* and the *co-natus* is not just self-active but entails a being "born with."

ception is not grasping. Conceiving, in this fecundating sense, is a truer metaphor for knowing in allowing openness to the porosity, to the *passio essendi,* and the seed of knowing sown and gestating in the soul. Curiosity in the determinative modality does not await the arrival of love but hurries things along according to its own more itchy desire. This is the loveless love that, as the medievals deemed it so, masks concupiscence.[12]

Such a univocalizing curiosity alters our feel for the ethos of given being, and indeed a deformation of our sense for all the hyperboles of being, namely, the idiotic, the aesthetic, the erotic, and the agapeic. Thus loss of ontological mystery is coupled with loss of aesthetic marveling, and if there is an ontological mood here it tends in the long run in the direction of disgust. Paradoxically we strip the world of its aesthetic marvel, but disgust is itself a living repudiation of such stripped-down thereness. An ontological karma comes home to us: the valuelessness of being we sought to crystallize does not, in the end, strike us as valueless but as repulsive. Disgust at the blank surd comes home to us, as our curiosity is more and more inclined to be a revolted and revolting interference with the intimacy of being. Secretly we might want to bring the world alive again but now this is expressed just exactly in the mode of the repulsive and the disgust-

---

12. *Concupiscentia oculis* is not quite a quaint monkish concern. Think only of "the look" of Sartre. It is connected with beholding and "beholding from." There is no "beholding from" in Sartre, for the killing look that objectifies me, and deprives me of my freedom is not "beholding from." One might venture that where there is no "beholding from" there is also no true "beholding of" as the admiring look of love. "Beholding from" undergoes a *release* of freedom in the companionship of what is other. Consider here these different ways of looking and beholding. First Spinoza: his earliest biographer Colerus tells us that for recreation, for fun, Spinoza would throw flies into the web of a spider and when the fly met its fate, its death, Spinoza would laugh with glee. Schopenhauer saw something dishonorable in this. Schopenhauer was an atheist but he borders on the apopleptic at Spinoza's attribution of divinity to devouring nature. Spinoza and Schopenhauer would agree that big fish eat little fish in cannabilizing nature, but Schopenhauer could not stomach Spinoza's glee in this (see Arthur Schopenhauer, *Parerga and Paralipomena,* trans. E. F. J. Payne (Oxford: Oxford University Press, 1974), 1.73). In Spinoza's looking the *conatus* as self-assertive is in the ascendant. Second Augustine: there is a touching remembrance in his *Confessions* when perchance he finds himself watching as a lizard or a spider catches flies (*Confessions,* 10, 35). He is caught up in looking but his response is quite different to Spinoza's: it is not the glee of ascendant *conatus;* there is patience deeper than concupiscence, and this too can be present in transforming *how one beholds.* In Augustine's recounting, a praise of God's mysterious work displaces, indeed replaces, the concupiscence of curiosity and of the eyes. One might say that first astonishment comes again to mind with this praise. See also *Of True Religion (De Vera Religione),* intro. L. O. Mink, trans. J. H. S Burleigh (Chicago: Regnery Press, 1964), 38 (67–68), on *curiositas* in connection with "lust of the eyes" (1 John, 2:16).

ing.[13] Repulsion seems to bring us alive once again, and the barbarism of reflection becomes coupled with the now voyeuristic carelessness to, now sadistic interference with, the intimacy of being.

This intimacy is to be guarded with reverent finesse but we now revolt against this. We see this with the disordering of the erotics of selving. A kind of aesthetic sadism, devoid of wonder, may seem fascinated by the flesh but erotic hatred has usurped the place of love. For the flesh of the world is here first neutered only to make it all the easier to quell all compunction in advance of the assault now unleashed on its worthless and revolting thereness. The barbarism of reflection is not only our going mad and wasting our substance, it is our ransacking the substance of the flesh of all things.

When this happens in our metaphysical attunement to being, the wonder given in astonishment becomes little more than confrontation with the world as a worthless whole. The surplus good of its being there, of its otherness, that is communicated to us in the agapeics of being, is not granted by us as more original. The world is there but it has no value in itself, for itself. It arouses no marvelling or admiration or celebration. It is there and that is all—valueless process, ongoing from nothing to nothing, and between nothing and nothing. What then could be there in the worthless whole that could call forth our festive affirmation of its "to be" as glorious or good. These latter seem merely subjective appraisals or projections. And given our diminished porosity to first astonishment, ultimately there seems no reason why we should project thus and not otherwise. It is more likely to be otherwise, since human beings cannot help but value or deem

13. Consider the distance charted by this change: Kant said that *disgust* was the one feeling art should not represent; now some parts of the fashionable avant-garde seem to find nothing more thrilling than the disgusting. It used to be *de gustibus non est disputandum,* now it seems *de disgustibus non est disputandum.* The disgusting is to be tasted with gusto. A sign of this: Umberto Eco edited a book entitled *History of Beauty* (New York: Rizzoli, 2004) and it received demure attention, while by contrast his *On Ugliness* (New York: Rizzoli, 2007) was a loud success. Would Kant have been disgusted at the ironical gesture of Piero Manzoni who a few years before his death in 1963 canned ninety samples of his own excrement and called these works "Merda d'Artista"? Cans, I mean works, have been bought for large prices by the Museum of Modern Art in New York, the Pompidou in Paris, and the Tate Gallery in London. Since their first creation, about half of the works, I mean cans, have exploded, due, it seems, to a fault in the design. Schopenhauer derided Hegelianism as *Afterphilosophie,* but should we now talk of *Afterkunst*? Not the art of the between but the "art" of the behind? What a fall of finesse there would be behind that afterart. The issue of "excrement" comes up when, down below, I discuss posthumous wonder and the world being restored.

worthy. What is not worthy to be deemed worthy cannot be maintained as merely neutral, for as unworthy to be deemed worthy it is already unworthy and hence its purported neutrality must tilt us over to the side calling forth our antagonism or negation. Otherness as such then becomes estranged thereness set over against one, and we set out to be always over it. We know ourselves as voracious strangers in this vacuous strangeness.

Strangely enough, the experience of strangeness, at an extreme, can be the prelude to some return to wonder in the modalities of perplexity and astonishment. What we find lacking wonder brings forth in us another wonder. A world lacking wonder perplexes us; but perplexing us, we might begin to wonder at it again. For its emptiness, or hostility, or repulsiveness, or even its mere thereness seem to us *uncanny,* and so we are brought to the border of *looking again,* and beholding the strangeness of being as intruding again into mindfulness. It intrudes—beyond our intrusiveness—and not violently either, but simply by the silent constancy of its continuing to be there. If we let ourselves be stilled by that silent constancy, we are opened again either to perplexity or astonishment. We see the neutered in a light that is not neutral and that cannot be neutral. In fact, there is a light there that should not be there at all, if being itself does not light itself. Even as supposedly neutral, this light is there, and so there is more than the neutral, turn we or not toward granting it to be so. It is so. Even the darkness of the world when understood as darkness is understood as darkness, and so is illuminated by a light that should not be there at all, if darkness is the ultimate.

I stress that the particular understanding of curiosity now under review turns the teleology of wonder into a movement from the indeterminate to the determinate, and thence from determination to determination, all the way to the totality of determinations that are held to exhaust the whole. This kind of curiosity turns against the indeterminate, for this purportedly cannot be grasped, for only the determinate is thus graspable. Behind this grasping can operate a metaphysical *ressentiment* against anything in the ontological situation that exceeds curiosity's measure. Really this grasping puts a disguise on a secret hatred of the overdeterminate. Equally all perplexity troubled by the "too-muchness" tends to be deemed an oppressive equivocity and as such no longer to be abided. There is no abiding with the mystery of given being. There is to be nothing abiding about the mystery of given being.

If we conceive the teleology of knowing thus, and claim that this is the one and only path to the end of true knowing, the end result must be the evacuation of spiritual seriousness not only in art, and religion but also in philosophy. For there is no room now for *thaumazein* in the modality of agapeic astonishment or in the modality of erotic perplexity. Great artworks, like religious reverence or awe, may offer us striking occasions of originating wonder—ontological admiration, appreciation of being. If such wonder is entirely impelled out of its initial hiddenness by determinative curiosity, the porosity is no longer kept open in philosophical mindfulness. Philosophy, lacking the initiative of originating wonder, must itself atrophy, its ontological astonishment or perplexity substituted for by the virtuosity of technical cleverness or the secondhand Scholasticism of commentary on commentary. It becomes treasonous to the wiser patience of the first astonishment.

POSTHUMOUS WONDER: RESTORING THE WORLD

Where does curiosity end? It has no end. Wonder ends if determinative curiosity is taken to exhaust all the ways of wondering. Nevertheless, curiosity does not have the last word, as it does not have the first. Now to end, I want to consider the resurrection of astonishment and perplexity in the "too-muchness" of being as given, as communicated, and in whose mystery we always participate. We cannot make this mystery an object of curiosity simply just because the power to objectify lives from a participation in it which is nonobjective. This participation calls on the promise of a new porosity, equally transobjective as transsubjective, in a mindfulness exorcized of the bewitchments of the barbarism of reflection. I want to suggest a second wonder, both as perplexity and astonishment, in the hyperbolic dimension of the overdeterminate, posthumous to every form of determinate curiosity.

We will not cease from extending our curiosity; the accumulation of more and more determinate cognition—this will continue. That accumulation certainly can serve our technical determination of things, and a more self-regarding humanist self-determination. But if there is something before and beyond determination and self-determination, namely, the overdeterminacy of given being, there is the ever fresh source of the originating and the outliving wonder. It gives birth, it will be reborn. It never died, for it was always being reborn, though we do our worst to abort it, while claiming our choice to be for life.

Let determinative science continue to perfect itself, there is still something recessed, taken for granted, reserved. My point now is not hostility to determinate science and its progress but memory of this overdeterminacy making determination possible, and recessed in the self-determination that regards itself alone. When we canonize the primacy of self-determination we sign the death warrant of surprise, and so also of wonder as astonishment; but this death warrant can never be fully executed, since it would be the death of self-determination also. Between life and death wonder always lives on. If this might seem like an enfeebled condition, it can be seen otherwise. It can be seen as what I will call a *posthumous wonder.*

What I mean is related to the idea of posthumous mindfulness, an idea I have proposed in a kind of metaphysical thought experiment.[14] It goes something like this: Suppose, having died, one were to awaken anew to life, thinking as if one had outlived one's given interim of life, beholding given life from beyond the normal division of life and death. Suppose we were to think from out of the future when we will be dead, about what is worthy of affirmation here and now. How would one behold now the interim of life, as if from beyond death, looking on life as if posthumously, wondering what in life is worthy of ultimate love—affirmed as worthy in the good of its "to be"? Such a posthumous mindfulness could not be defined in terms of instrumental reason. One is to behold now what is worthy to be affirmed for itself, not what is useful for this or that utilitarian project. Beyond the instrumental relation of means and end, posthumous honesty would serve nothing but praise of the worth of being, of truly worthy being. Suppose one were restored to the world in the following sense. Imagine what it would be like if, having died, one were restored to life a hundred years hence? What would one love to behold again, behold with a kind of love? What would one mourn to see utterly destroyed? What are the nameless things we now love which we would delight to greet again? What are the intimates of being we would love to greet us? Would not our wonder about such intimates be much more than curiosity? Would it not be love? The thought of posthumous mind jolts us *back*

14. See, for instance, *Philosophy and Its Others,* 278–81.

into life now, and makes us wonder about such intimates that *now* bless being, without which life would be metaphysically bankrupt. Posthumous mindfulness makes us wonder about what we so love now that its loss or desecration would grieve us to the roots on our restoration to life.

Curiosity killed the cat, information made him fat, the old rhyme says, but as the old saw does not say, one of the curious things about curiosity is that it keeps on being *reborn,* even when it is a killer. There is in all curiosity the eros of transcending which is more than *penia* or lack, and it always finds itself, unbidden, the beneficiary of unpremeditated *poros.* This is the porosity of being fluid to the infusion of divine festivity beyond death. "Dionysus is Hades," Heraclitus says; but Hades is also Dionysus. Life passes into death, death passes into life. In the porosity of being, passing into being and passing out of being themselves pass into each other, and passing out is passage now that also passes on the gift of being. This is not reflection; this is happening; and reflection can become mindful of what is happening—beyond the barbarism of reflection.

Reflection per se is not barbaric. Reflection is an indirect relation to the things themselves, indirection inevitable with the mediating powers of minding. What is barbaric is reflection that has become the prisoner of its own mediating abstractions: the abstractions do not serve the true things themselves but themselves alone. Thought just thinks itself, not what is other to thought thinking itself. It revolves in an autistic circle of its own self-reflection, not truly reflecting the "too-muchness" of given being in its otherness. Reflective thought thus at home with itself produces an alienation from what is other to thought. The barbarism is the hall of mirrors of thoughts that reflect only themselves. The human being is sunk in its own self-reflecting subjectivity—not porous to the given world in its wonder, not out in the between. Retracting the milieu of the between, the intermedium of being, into its own self-mediation, it finds nothing but itself. Thinking circles around itself and while it seems most at home with itself, its self-circling is a kind of self-imprisonment. The barbarism of reflection is a mirror of this, a mirror that escapes the determination of self-mediating thought in enacting the karma of its estrangement. This enactment is a loss of porosity, loss of the *passio essendi,* a malformation of the *conatus essendi,* now no longer a *co-natus,* a coming to birth with, but an energy of self-being that circles around itself and betrays the ecstasis that natively puts minding outside of itself in the between. The opening of mindfulness beyond reflection does not deny reflection. It entails a fresh ontological-metaphysical patience and a piety posthumous to consummated curiosity.

If there is wonder after and beyond the barbarism of reflection, as there is wonder before, it cannot be defined just in terms of determinate cognition and its indeterminate extension. The latter might follow, if the vector of endless curiosity was all, curiosity that is in the business of putting wonder in its place, killing it in the act of overcoming it. Posthumous wonder outlives curiosity in the hyperbolic dimensions of the overdeterminate. None of the hyperboles of being is treated truthfully in the barbarism of reflection; indeed they hardly arise as troubling perplexities. But none ever ceases to be astonishing and perplexing: not the idiocy of being, the "that it is at all"; not the aesthetics of happening, the glory of creation in its beauty and sublimity; not the erotics of selving, source of human greatness and wretchedness; not finally the agapeics of communication, promising the ennoblement and sanctification of human life, and the blessing with good of all of the "to be." All these hyperboles again and again call us to the wakefulness of astonishment and perplexity beyond the curiosity otherwise so well served by determinate cognition. Posthumous wonder is not the enemy of determinate curiosity, but conducive to a kind of unknowing knowing of something metaphysically ultimate in the idiotics of being, the aesthetics of happening, the erotics of selving and the agapeics of community.

It is important to grant that there can be a *second hyperbolic perplexity* as well as astonishment. Posthumous wonder might have to pass through a kind of purgatory. I illustrate by recalling a curious claim of the poet Yeats: "Descartes, Locke, and Newton took away the world and gave us its excrement instead. Berkeley restored the world."[15] The claim about Descartes, Locke, and Newton seems outrageous: What is this excrement? Part of the point is the implication that they evacuated the world of the richness of its qualitative textures, given before the work of modern science and its abstractions, and consigned thereafter to secondary status at best. Such abstractions would be constructions of the curiosity that kills. (Wordsworth: "We murder to dissect.")

But how could Berkeley restore the world? Berkeley, in his own cu-

---

15. W. B. Yeats, *Explorations,* selected by Mrs. W. B. Yeats (London: Macmillan, 1962), 325.

rious way, claims that to be is to perceive or be perceived. Does not this dissolve rather than restore the world? Nevertheless, Berkeley is insistent that he merely affirms, by contrast with the concepts of scientific "reflection" and "metaphysical" constructions, this given world as it is. My interest is not the further interpretation of Berkeley but this question: What would it mean to restore the world? It would mean granting that we have lost the world—I would say, lost the sense of the wonder of it. Restoring the world would ask restoring the sense of this wonder. It is not that what is there is lost, for it is still there. The matter concerns *how it is between us and it*. (This "between" is relevant to the interpretation of Berkeley's curious claim about being and perceiving or being perceived.) We have lost the relation between us, or substituted one that lacks wonder for love of the world. This is what it would mean to give excrement. The last word would be given to the offal, the surd as the mess. There would be nothing of the good of the "to be" in this mess, this cess. Instance: *ecological excrement,* the foul, fetid dump rampant technical hubris has often, alas, made of nature.

Restoration of the world would have to pass through the purgatory of this second hyperbolic perplexity. The excrement is within us as well as without. I mean here also to recall our modern, postmodern pride in not "naively" reaching above the cave to the sun of light, but in digging the hole deeper, under the underground, all with bravado for the dirty truth. We reduce even the ambiguous chiaroscuro of daily life to excrement down under. We move in the shadow of Schopenhauer: down below, there is something other to the principle of sufficient reason; there is the dark origin; there is nothing of intrinsic worth in being as given. This takes us away from the *thaumazein* of minding we find in ancient *theōria*. Without this sense of celebrating contemplation, all reason becomes easily instrumental, servant of a secret tyrannical other: will to power, *eros turannos, thanatos*. I do not say that first wonder or posthumous wonder asks us to deny a sense of the surd in the idiocy of being—a surd in being other to our determinative and self-determining reason. The issue with the second perplexity is whether this surd is absurd, or mysterious with a meaning hard to decipher. Is the mysterious surd just excrement? Do we go under the underground into the shit—as if that were at bottom the "truth."

Heraclitus again: "Dionysus is also Hades." The second perplexity rather must wonder: "What the hell is this?" Are we staring at Medusa, the

Gorgon's head that gave Nietzsche terror? But if this is the "truth," we pet-rify. Nietzsche wanted to protect us from that petrification, to console us with art—we have art to save us from "truth," he says. But the truths art gives us are "as if" truths, while *the* truth remains, as ever, reserved with the petrifying look of Medusa. By contrast, as an artist Yeats sought res-toration not protection. He admired Nietzsche but held Vico in high es-teem. "O rocky voice / shall we in that great night rejoice?"[16] Facing the horror the second perplexity puts the question: What would restore, who could restore the world in its wonder? What would we behold from the green earth, to what would we be beholden? Who will offer the posthu-mous wonder, beyond the barbarism of reflection? Would one not need a god to bring life out of hell, and beyond Hades bring us to life again?

Because the posthumous wonder cannot be the product of our self-determination, we cannot determine its *advent,* its coming again and again, its *corso e ricorso,* to speak with Vico. This coming again is not a matter of reviving our capacity for wonder, as if it were some power we could turn on at will. Rather we are capacitated by wonder, and its coming anew is in-separable from us knowing a certain incapacitation vis-à-vis both determi-nate and self-determining power. Being stricken anew by wonder is more a grace than our work. We can do nothing to earn it, though we can di-vest ourselves of our false fixations of determinate finitude, and the untrue self-inflating forms of self-determination. Mostly we are clogged on our-selves—we are full of ourselves, too full. We have to let the emptying of this clogging—get ourselves out of the way of the flow, the overflow. We cannot just will this, but we have to be willing. We can make ourselves ready, but the ripening does not come through ourselves alone.

Unclogging the primal porosity is not unlike becoming as a child again. Of course, many acknowledge something of the child in astonish-ment, but this can be double-edged. The childlike might be seen as *only childish.* One thinks again of Auguste Comte's law of the three stages. First, religion for the childhood of the human race: here we are closer to wonder, and hence childish credulity. Then, metaphysics and its abstrac-tions for the adolescence of humanity: abstractions distance us from the first immediacy of astonishment, but they are not yet true thought. Final-ly, positive science for the maturity of the human race: now disciplined,

---

16. See "Man and the Echo," in W. B. Yeats, *The Poems,* 393.

regulated curiosity knows positively of reality in all its detail. The teleology of knowing is mapped onto an inexorable move from the indeterminate to the determinative. My question again returns: What then of the overdeterminate? This (Comtean) teleology consecrates the latecomer's amnesia of the reverent child and henceforth there can be no true ground for any reverence, or source of originating wonder. Human astonishment goes off into a fugue state. It ceases to know itself any more, except as a lack or deficiency to be overcome by more determinate, positive cognition. Paradoxically, it then courts a new childishness, an infantilization of the human spirit, at the apex of its "positive" knowledge, because of this its fugue state.

By contrast with Comte's three stages, one might recourse to Vico's *corso e recorso* of the three ages of gods, heroes, and men. Between the triads of Vico and Comte we find surface similarity but the animating spiritual impulse is quite other. The age of the gods is an age of original wonder, the age of heroes is intermediary between gods and mortals, the age of men brings the age of reflection. While at the extremity of the last, the barbarism of reflection takes holds, nevertheless, in the *corso e recorso* of time the gyre turns again and again. There is always a once more.

I am not quite subscribing to Vico's cyclical view of history; rather I am suggesting that in every "once more" it is the overdeterminacy of the mystery of being that abides, and we too must abide it, and abide with it, for we abide in it. It never is overcome, for it is over and beyond all our overcoming. It surpasses all our surpassings, and indeed communicates the endowing source that enables our own self-surpassing. The abiding of the overdeterminacy is not to be described in the becoming of any cycle, or in any linear development from an indefinite beginning to a determinate or self-determining end. It possibilizes the promise of every becoming or cycle but is more than every determination or self-determination in each becoming or cycle. Vico's ideal eternal history suggests the mystery of providence, and this is perhaps for some too determinate a way of putting it, and yet it is a fitting way to name the mystery in the course of things that we cannot subject to our determination and self-determination. The persistence of piety in Vico is a sign suggesting this abiding mystery: for him in the end there is to be no vanishing of piety, though the barbarism of reflection ends without piety. The barbarism of reflection ends in disaster just because of the squandering of piety and the originating wonder that seeds all our seeking and surpassing, though never exhausted by any. If the barbarism of reflection were the absolute end, Vico's clear message would be that this would be the destruction of the human being.

After Hades: resurrected astonishment in the modality of posthumous wonder; wonder that has died to the instrumentalizing of all being following from the absolutizing of determinative curiosity; wonder promising release beyond the self-determining that circles around itself alone; wonder reborn to the hyperbolic overdeterminacy of being, in its idiotic, aesthetic, erotic, and agapeic communications. *Corso e ricorso,* coursing and recoursing: this is the constant rhythm in life's inconstancy. Recourse: it will come again, for it has never left. I think of this instance: Vico coursing again in James Joyce: it comes again, the origin in the end—and now with comic wonder—ringing the true with laughter—beyond horror the hurrah of a divine guffaw—this is the festive laughter of posthumous mind.

There is sabbatical thought that rejoices in the intimate strangeness of being. The artist can cooperate in the restoring wonder: the glory of the sensuous, the sounding that resonates in our porosity of soul, the word that utters intimate secrets. The religious person can participate in restored wonder: sacred amazement at the unbelievable goodness of God. The philosopher can think in the services of this restoration: wonder at the mystery of thinking, at the thereness of the "to be" at all, and the splendid enigma of the good of the "to be." True restoration serves the redemption of the intimate strangeness of being. The artist will have to spend a season in hell, to be readied for looking beyond horror. The religious person will have to be released from the heaviness of moralizing earnestness and accept the holy lightness of good beyond moral good and evil. The philosopher will have to descend into the noplace of the porosity, from which minding, in its endowed poverty, can begin again its ascent to thought, in the dark night of the sacred.

We are not feral. We are not gravediggers in the cave. We can stand on the surface of the earth. The difference between earth and heaven still stands. The space between them is still open. The earth is porous to what heaven pours forth. Piety comes to wording in the porosity of this between—wording the wiser patience of posthumous wonder, wording wonder as the reverent yes.

Bibliography

Adorno, Theodor. *Negative Dialectics*. Translated by E. B. Ashton. New York: Continuum, 1983.

Aquinas, St. Thomas. *Summa Theologiae: A Concise Translation*. Edited by Timothy McDermott. South Bend, Ind.: Christian Classics, 1989.

―――. *Commentary on Aristotle's Metaphysics*. Rev. ed. Introduced and translated by John P. Rowan. Preface by Ralph McInerny. South Bend, Ind.: Dumb Ox Press, 1995.

Aristotle. *Metaphysics, Books I–IX*. Loeb Classical Library, No. 271. Translated by Hugh Tredennick. Cambridge, Mass.: Harvard University Press, 1933.

―――. *Metaphysics, Books 10–14. Oeconomica. Magna Moralia*. Loeb Classical Library, No. 287. Translated by Hugh Tredennick and G. Cyril Armstrong. Cambridge, Mass.: Harvard University Press, 1935.

―――. *On Sophistical Refutations. On Coming-to-be and Passing Away. On the Cosmos*. Loeb Classical Library, No. 400. Translated by E. S. Forster and D. J. Furley. Cambridge, Mass.: Harvard University Press, 1955.

―――. *Posterior Analytics. Topica*. Loeb Classical Library, No. 391. Translated by Hugh Tredennick and E. S. Forster. Cambridge, Mass.: Harvard University Press, 1960.

Augustine, St. *Confessions*. Translated by R. S. Pine-Coffin. Harmondsworth, U.K.: Penguin Classics, 1961.

―――. *Of True Religion (De Vera Religione)*. Introduction by L. O. Mink. Translated by J. H. S. Burleigh. Chicago: Regnery Press, 1964.

Barnett, Stuart, ed. *Hegel after Derrida*. New York: Routledge, 1998.

Bonaventure, St. *The Journey of the Mind to God*. Translated by P. Boehner, O.F.M. Edited with an introduction and notes by Stephen F. Brown. Indianapolis, Ind.: Hackett, 1993.

Burke, Edmund. *A Philosophical Enquiry into the Origin of Our Ideas of the Sublime and Beautiful*. Edited by Adam Phillips. Oxford: Oxford University Press, 1990.

Caputo, John D. *On Religion*. New York: Routledge, 2001.

―――. *The Weakness of God: A Theology of the Event*. Indianapolis: Indiana University Press, 2006.

Caputo, John D., and Gianni Vattimo. *After the Death of God*. Edited by Jeffrey W. Robbins. New York: Columbia University Press, 2007.

Comte, Auguste. *Introduction to Positive Philosophy*. Edited with introduction and revised translation by Frederick Ferré. Indianapolis, Ind.: Hackett, 1988.

Cupitt, Don. *After God: The Future of Religion*. New York: Basic Books, 1997.

Derrida, Jacques. *Of Grammatology*. Translated by G. Spivak. Baltimore: Johns Hopkins University Press, 1974.

————. *Writing and Difference*. Translated by Alan Bass. Chicago: University of Chicago Press, 1978.

————. "Like the Sound of the Sea Deep within a Shell: Paul de Man's War." Translated by Peggy Kamuf. *Critical Inquiry* 14, no. 3 (Spring 1988): 590–652.

————. "Biodegradables: Seven Diary Fragments." Translated by Peggy Kamuf. *Critical Inquiry* 15, no. 4 (Summer 1989): 812–73.

Descartes, René. *The Philosophical Writings of Descartes*. 2 vols. Edited by J. Cottingham et al. Cambridge: Cambridge University Press, 1985.

Desmond, William. *Art and the Absolute: A Study of Hegel's Aesthetics*. Albany: State University of New York Press, 1986.

————. *Desire, Dialectic, and Otherness: An Essay on Origins*. New Haven, Conn.: Yale University Press, 1987.

————. *Hegel and His Critics: Philosophy in the Aftermath of Hegel*. Albany: State University of New York Press, 1989.

————. *Philosophy and Its Others: Ways of Mind and Being*. Albany: State University of New York Press, 1990.

————. *Beyond Hegel and Dialectic: Speculation, Cult, and Comedy*. Albany: State University of New York Press, 1992.

————. *Being and the Between*. Albany: State University of New York Press, 1995.

————. *Perplexity and Ultimacy: Metaphysical Thoughts from the Middle*. Albany: State University of New York Press, 1995.

————. "Autonomia Turannos: On Some Dialectical Equivocities in Self-Determination." *Ethical Perspectives* 5, no. 4 (1998): 233–52.

————. "Hyperbolic Thoughts: On Creation and Nothing." In *Framing a Vision of the World: Essays in Philosophy, Science, and Religion*. Edited by Santiago Sia and André Cloots. Leuven: Universitaire Pers Leuven, 1999.

————. *Ethics and the Between*. Albany: State University of New York Press, 2001.

————. "Sticky Evil: *Macbeth* and the Karma of the Equivocal." In *God, Literature and Process Thought*, edited by Darren Middleton, 133–55. Aldershot, U.K.: Ashgate Press, 2002.

————. *Art, Origins, Otherness: Between Art and Philosophy*. Albany: State University of New York Press, 2003.

————. *Hegel's God: A Counterfeit Double?* Aldershot, U.K.: Ashgate Press, 2003.

————. *Is There a Sabbath for Thought? Between Religion and Philosophy*. New York: Fordham University Press, 2005.

————. "Consecrated Thought: Between the Priest and the Philosopher." *Louvain Studies* 30 (2005): 92–106.

————. "Neither Servility nor Sovereignty: Between Metaphysics and Politics." In *Theology and the Political*, edited by C. Davis, J. Milbank, and S. Žižek, 153–82. Durham, N.C.: Duke University Press, 2005.

————. "Between System and Poetics: On the Practices of Philosophy." In *Between System and Poetics: William Desmond and Philosophy after Dialectic*, edited by Thomas Kelly, chapter 1. Aldershot, U.K.: Ashgate, 2007.

————. *God and the Between*. Oxford: Blackwell, 2008.

————. *Being Between: Conditions of Irish Thought*. Galway, Ireland: Leabhar Breac/Center for Irish Studies, 2008.

Eco, Umberto, ed. *History of Beauty*. Translated by Alastair McEwen. New York: Rizzoli, 2004.

————. *On Ugliness*. Translated by Alastair McEwen. New York: Rizzoli, 2007.

Hegel, G. W. F. *Phänomenologie des Geistes*. Hamburg: Felix Meiner, 1952.

————. *Phenomenology of Spirit*. Translated by A. V. Miller. Oxford: Clarendon Press, 1977.

————. *Wissenschaft der Logik*. Hamburg: Felix Meiner, 1963.

————. *Science of Logic*. Translated by A. V. Miller. New York: Humanities Press, 1969.

————. *Enzyklopädie der Philosophischen Wissenschaften im Grundrisse (1830)*. Edited by Friedhelm Nicolin and Otto Pöggeler. Hamburg: Felix Meiner, 1991.

————. *The Encyclopaedia Logic (with the Zusätze): Part 1 of the Encyclopaedia of Philosophical Science with the Zusätze*. Translated by T. F. Geraets, W. A. Suchting, and H. S. Harris. Indianapolis, Ind.: Hackett, 1991.

————. *Hegel's Philosophy of Mind: Being Part Three of the Encyclopaedia of the Philosophical Sciences*. Translated by W. Wallace. Oxford: Oxford University Press, 1971.

————. *Lectures on the Philosophy of Religion: One Volume Edition, The Lectures of 1827*. Edited by Peter Hodgson. Berkeley and Los Angeles: University of California Press, 1988.

Heidegger, Martin. *Einführung in die Metaphysik*. Tübingen, Germany: Niemeyer Verlag, 1957.

————. *Introduction to Metaphysics*. Translated by R. Manheim. New Haven, Conn.: Yale University Press, 1987.

————. "Das Ende der Philosophie und die Aufgabe des Denkens." In *Zur Sache des Denkens*, 61–80. Tübingen, Germany: Max Niemeyer Verlag, 1969. English translation by Joan Stambaugh. "The End of Philosophy and the Task of Thinking," in *On Time and Being* (New York: Harper & Row, 1972), 55–73.

————. "What Is Metaphysics?" In *Pathmarks*, edited by William McNeill, 82–96. Cambridge: Cambridge University Press, 1998.

Joyce, James. *Ulysses*. New York: Random House, 1961.

Kant, Immanuel. *Sämmtliche Werke*. Edited by Karl Vorlander. Hamburg: Felix Meiner Verlag, 1990.

————. *Critique of Pure Reason*. Translated and edited by Paul Guyer et al. Cambridge: Cambridge University Press, 1989.

————. *Critique of Practical Reason*. Translated and edited by Mary Gregor. Introduction by Andrews Reath. Cambridge: Cambridge University Press, 1997.

————. *Critique of the Power of Judgment.* Edited by Paul Guyer. Translated by Eric Matthews. Cambridge: Cambridge University Press, 2000.

Keats, John. *John Keats.* Edited by Elizabeth Cook. Oxford: Oxford University Press, 1990.

Kearney, Richard. *Anatheism: Returning to God after God.* New York: Columbia University Press, 2010.

Kelly, Thomas, ed. *Between System and Poetics: William Desmond and Philosophy after Dialectic.* Aldershot, U.K.: Ashgate Press, 2007.

Levinas, Emmanuel. *Totality and Infinity.* Translated by A. Lingis. Pittsburgh: Duquesne University Press, 1969.

Marx, Karl. *Frühe Schriften, Werke,* Vol. 1. Edited by Hans-Joachim Lieber and Peter Furth. Darmstadt, Germany: Wissenschaftliche Buchgesellschaft, 1971.

————. *Early Writings.* Translated and edited by T. B. Bottomore. New York: McGraw-Hill, 1963.

Maimonides, Moses. *Guide for the Perplexed: Silence and Salvation.* London: Routledge, 2007.

Marcel, Gabriel, *The Mystery of Being.* 2 vols. London: Harvill Press, 1951.

Marcuse, Herbert. *Eros and Civilization: A Philosophical Inquiry into Freud.* New York: Vintage Books, 1962.

————. *One Dimensional Man.* Boston: Beacon Press, 1964.

McGregor, David. *Hegel and Marx after the Fall of Communism.* Cardiff: University of Wales Press, 1998.

McIntyre, Alasdair. *After Virtue: A Study in Moral Theory.* 2nd ed. South Bend, Ind.: University of Notre Dame Press, 1984.

Manoussakis, John, ed. *After God: Richard Kearney and the Religious Turn in Continental Philosophy.* Bronx, N.Y.: Fordham University Press, 2005.

Nikulin, Dimitri. *Dialectic and Dialogue.* Stanford, Calif.: Stanford University Press, 2010.

Nietzsche, Friedrich. *Werke: Kritische Gesamtausgabe.* Edited by G. Colli and M. Montinari. Berlin: De Gruyter, 1967–1984.-

————. *Der Wille zur Macht. Versuch einer Umwertung aller Werte.* Leipzig: Kröner, 1930.

————. *The Will to Power.* Translated by W. Kaufmann and R. J. Hollingdale. New York: Random House, 1967.

————. *Thus Spoke Zarathustra.* Translated by R. J. Hollingdale. Harmondsworth, U.K.: Penguin Books, 1961.

————. *On the Genealogy of Morals and Ecce Homo.* Translated by W. Kaufmann and R. J. Hollingdale. New York: Vintage Books, 1969.

————. *The Gay Science: With a Prelude in Rhymes and an Appendix of Songs.* Translated with commentary by W. Kaufmann. New York: Vintage Books, 1974.

————. *The Birth of Tragedy.* In *Basic Writings of Nietzsche.* Translated by W. Kaufmann. New York: Modern Library, 1992.

O'Rourke, Fran. *Pseudo-Dionysius and the Metaphysics of Aquinas.* South Bend, Ind.: University of Notre Dame Press, 2005.

Pascal, Blaise. *Pensées.* Translated by A. J. Krailsheimer. Harmondsworth, U.K.: Penguin Classics, 1995.

Pieper, Josef. *The Silence of St. Thomas: Three Essays.* 3rd ed. Translated by John Murray and Daniel O Connor. South Bend, Ind.: St. Augustine's Press, 1999.

Pickstock, Catherine. *After Writing: On the Liturgical Consummation of Philosophy.* Oxford: Blackwell, 1998.

Plato. *Platonis Opera Omnia.* Edited by Gottfried Stallbaum. New York: Garland, 1980.

Pseudo Dionysius. *De Divinis Nominibus.* In *Pseudo Dionysius: The Complete Works.* Translated by Colm Luibhéid. New York: Paulist Press, 1987.

Rilke. R.M. *The Poet's Guide to Life: The Wisdom of Rilke.* Edited and translated by Ulrich Baer. New York: Modern Library, 2005.

Rosen, Stanley. *Hermeneutics as Politics.* Oxford: Oxford University Press, 1987.

———. *The Quarrel between Philosophy and Poetry: Studies in Ancient Thought.* New York: Routledge, 1988.

———. *The Ancients and the Moderns: Rethinking Modernity.* New Haven, Conn.: Yale University Press, 1989.

———. *Metaphysics in Ordinary Language.* New Haven, Conn.: Yale University Press, 1999.

———. *The Elusiveness of the Ordinary: Studies in the Possibility of Philosophy.* New Haven, Conn.: Yale University Press, 2002.

Schilpp, P. A. *The Philosophy of Alfred North Whitehead.* The Library of Living Philosophers. New York: Tudor Publishing, 1951.

Schopenhauer, Arthur. *Sämtliche Werke.* Edited by Wolfgang Frhr. von Lohneysen. Stuttgart, Germany: Cotta/Insel, 1960–1965; Darmstadt, Germany: Wissenschaftliche Buchgesellschaft, 1968.

———. *The World as Will and Representation.* 2 vols. Translated by E. F. J. Payne. New York: Dover Books, 1966.

———. *Parerga and Paralipomena.* 2 vols. Translated by E. F. J. Payne. Oxford: Oxford University Press, 1974.

Short, Philip. *Mao: A Life.* London: Hodder & Stoughton, 1999.

Simpson, Christopher. *Religion, Metaphysics, and the Postmodern: William Desmond and John D. Caputo.* Bloomington: Indiana University Press, 2009.

Steiner, George. *After Babel: Aspects of Language and Translation.* Oxford: Oxford University Press, 1975.

Spinoza, Benedict. *Spinoza Opera.* Edited by Carl Gebhart. Heidelberg, Germany: Heidelberger Akademie der Wissenschaften, 1924.

———. *The Chief Works of Benedict de Spinoza.* Translated by R. H. M. Elwes. New York: Dover Books, 1955.

Stepelevich, Lawrence, ed. *The Young Hegelians: An Anthology.* New York: Cambridge University Press, 1983.

Taylor, Mark C. *After God.* Chicago: University of Chicago Press, 2007.

Vattimo, Gianni. *After Christianity.* New York: Columbia University Press, 2002.

Velde, Rudi te. *Aquinas on God: The "Divine Science" of the Summa Theologiae.* Aldershot, U.K.: Ashgate Press, 2006.

Verene, Donald. *Hegel's Recollection: A Study of Images in the "Phenomenology of Spirit."* Albany: State University of New York Press, 1985.

———. *Hegel's Absolute: An Introduction to Reading the "Phenomenology of Spirit."* Albany: State University of New York Press, 2007.

Vico, Giambattista. *The New Science of Giambattista Vico.* Abridged translation of the third edition (1744), by Thomas Goddard Bergin and Max Harold Fisch. Ithaca, N.Y.: Cornell University Press, 1970.

Wordsworth, William. *William Wordsworth.* Edited by Stephen Gill. Oxford: Oxford University Press, 1984.

Wippel, John F. *The Metaphysical Thought of Thomas Aquinas: From Finite Being to Uncreated Being.* Washington, D.C.: The Catholic University of America Press, 2000.

Yeats, W. B. *Explorations.* Selected by Mrs. W. B. Yeats. London: Macmillan, 1962.

———. *The Poems.* Edited by Daniel Albright. London: Everyman, 1990.

Index

⚮

The Intimate Strangeness of Being: Metaphysics after Dialectic was designed and typeset in Minion by Kachergis Book Design of Pittsboro, North Carolina. It was printed on 60-pound Natures Book Natural and bound by Thomson-Shore of Dexter, Michigan.